POLITICAL STATISTICS

By
HAROLD T. DAVIS
Northwestern University

With an Introduction
By
KENNETH W. COLEGROVE
Northwestern University

THE PRINCIPIA PRESS OF ILLINOIS, Inc.

Evanston, Illinois

Copyright, 1954

By

The Principia Press of Illinois, Inc.

TABLE OF CONTENTS

CHAPTER 1. POLITICAL SCIENCE AS A STATISTICAL SCIENCE

1. Historical Introduction 1
2. Politics as a Science 7
3. The Role of Postulates in Scientific Inquiry 9
4. The Role of Mathematics in Science. 11
5. Political Science and Economics 14
6. Political Science and Sociology 16
7. The Problem of Political Statics 20
8. The Problems of Political Dynamics 23
9. Concluding Remarks 26

CHAPTER 2. ENUMERATION AND FREQUENCY DISTRIBUTIONS

1. Measurement. 29
2. Graphical Representation of Data. 31
3. Frequency Distributions. 38
4. Binomial Frequencies. 42
5. Ogives or Cumulative Frequency Curves. 45

CHAPTER 3. THE CENTRAL TENDENCIES OF DATA

1. Averages 50
2. The Arithmetic Mean 51
3. Simplifications in the Computation of the Arithmetic Mean . . 54
4. The Root-Mean-Square or Quadratic Mean — The Standard Deviation 57
5. The Coefficient of Variability 61
6. The Median 64
7. The Mode 66
8. Minor Averages — Concluding Remarks 68

CHAPTER 4. ELEMENTS OF THE THEORY OF PROBABILITY

1. Definition of Probability. 70
2. The Multiplication and Addition of Probabilities 74
3. Binomial Frequency Distributions and the Theory of Probability 78
4. The Normal Frequency Distribution 80

5. Areas Under the Normal Curve. 83
6. Probable and Standard Errors. 87
7. Sampling and the Use of Probable and Standard Errors. . . . 89
8. Distributions Which are not Normal 92
9. Polls of Public Opinion 96
10. Forecasting the Election of 1944 99
11. Forecasting the Election of 1948 105
12. Concluding Remarks 106

CHAPTER 5. THE THEORY OF CORRELATION

1. Functional Relationships 108
2. The Graphical Representation of Functions 109
3. The Linear Function 110
4. Fitting a Straight Line to Data 111
5. General Formulas for Fitting a Straight Line to Data 115
6. Correlations 117
7. The Correlation Coefficient 118
8. Properties of the Correlation Coefficient. 121
9. Lines of Regression 123
10. The Size of State Legislatures 126
11. The Traffic Problem. 132
12. Applications to the Problem of Voting Behavior. 135

CHAPTER 6. SOME PROBLEMS IN POLITICAL SCIENCE

1. Introduction 138
2. The Problem of Representation. 138
3. Measure of Inequality of Representation 139
4. The Problem of the Philosopher King 144
5. The Problem of Legislative Tenure 148
6. The Judgment of Tribunals. 154

CHAPTER 7. THE STATISTICS OF TIME SERIES

1. Origin of the Problem 158
2. Index Numbers 158
3. Types of Index Numbers. 160
4. Index Number Tests. 162
5. The Problem of Trends 167
6. The Problem of Cycles 172

TABLE OF CONTENTS

7. Population and Production Trends. 177
8. Concluding Remarks. 183

CHAPTER 8. POLITICAL SCIENCE AND THE DISTRIBUTION OF INCOME

1. Historical Summary 185
2. The Distribution of Income. 188
3. The Concentration Ratio. 194
4. The Curve of Income Distribution 196
5. The Concentration Ratio and Production 201
6. The Concentration Ratio and Political Disturbances. . . . 209
7. The American Civil War 212
8. Conclusion. 217

CHAPTER 9. POLITICAL SCIENCE AND ECONOMICS

1. The Mechanistic Theory of History 219
2. The Growth of Population 224
3. The Relationship of Prices to Political Events 231
4. The Diocletian Inflation and Its Political Significance 237
5. The Price Inflation of the Sixteenth Century. 241
6. How England Became Mistress of the Seas 247
7. The Relationship of Wages to Change in Price 253
8. Economic Variation and Politics 258
9. Concluding Summary. 264

CHAPTER 10. THE PROBLEM OF CONFLICT

1. The Problem 266
2. War and Price Inflation. 267
3. Patterns of Prices in Modern Wars. 269
4. The Frequency of War. 273
5. The Size of Wars 277
6. The Cost of Ancient Wars 284
7. The Cost of Modern Wars. 287
8. How Wars are Financed 289
9. The Theory of War Tensions 298
10. The Problem of International Trade 302
11. Other Theories of Conflict 305

12. History of Attempts to Solve the Problem of War. 309
13. Cohesion and its Significance in the Theory of Tensions . . . 313
14. Conclusion. 316

APPENDIX

1. The Laws of Exponents 321
2. Logarithms. 323
3. Determination of Logarithms 326
4. Calculation by Logarithms 329
5. Exponential Equations. 331
6. Semi-logarithmic and Double-logarithmic Scales. 332
7. The Use of Tables 334
8. The Validity and Analysis of Data 338
9. Sources of Data Used in the Body of the Text 341

MATHEMATICAL TABLES

Table 1. Powers and Roots 349
Table 2. Four Place Logarithms. 350
Table 3. Values of $I(t)$, Area Under Normal Probability Curve . . 352

INDEXES

Index of Names 355
Index of Subjects 359

FOREWORD

Political science in the past has been reluctant to apply the methods of statistics to its problems. In spite of the stimulus given as early as 1928 by the pioneer work of Stuart A. Rice on *Quantitative Methods in Politics* and by the application of the theory of correlation to the interpretation of voting behavior by Harold F. Gosnell and by a few other studies of this nature, there has been no concerted effort among students of political science to advance this trend of thought.

But it has been a belief, long cherished by the writer, that progress in political science could be hastened by a systematic application of the methods of statistics to its problems. Since instruction in these methods has not been a traditional part of the training afforded students of politics, it seemed highly desirable that a course in "political statistics" be initiated. The present book is the result of an attempt made several years ago to present the elements of statistics, together with examples illustrating the application of statistical methods, to majors in political science at Northwestern University.

In attempting to formulate a proper setting for the course, it became clear that some mathematical prerequisites were necessary. Such prerequisites have seldom been imposed upon students of the social sciences except in the case of economics, where great progress has been made in recent years in applying both mathematical and statistical modes of thought to its problems. It appeared that political statistics, in its present status, could be presented to students with a basic training in the elements of algebra. The present book shows how far the material can be covered by means of this elementary discipline. It is clear, however, from some of the later chapters, that a knowledge of the higher methods of the calculus is ultimately required if a student is to make progress into the deeper problems of the subject.

In a memorandum describing the nature and purposes of the new course to the members of the Department of Political Science at Northwestern University, the following comments were made:

It is assumed that the new course is offered, not for the purpose of training political science students to become statisticians, but rather for the purpose of introducing students to the application of the statistical method to political data.

Fields of Political Data. Theoretically, every field of political data should be capable of statistical investigation. In the present status of political science, however, various fields more readily lend themselves to the application of the statistical method. Among such fields are: (1) relation to climate, geography, and population to forms of government; (2) voting behavior of citizens; (3) economic, educational, and occupational qualifications of legislative, executive, and judicial bodies; (4) political consequences of income distribution; (5) relation of the business cycle to political reactions; (6) measurement of public opinion; (7) progress of revolution and counter-revolution; (8) relation of disease and public health to political behavior; (9) relation of form of government to war and peace; and (10) measurement of trends in war and peace.

Statistical Methods. It may not be too ambitious to hope that the course might successfully apply the following statistical methods: (1) graphical representation; (2) frequency distributions; (3) index numbers; (4) measurement of trends; (5) analysis of time series involving the measurement of seasonal and cyclical fluctuations; (6) the problem of sampling; and (7) elementary probabilities and the normal curve of error.

Limitations of Scope. Timidity has always been a handicap to scholarship. The great contributions to research which have widened the frontiers of knowledge have without exception been made by scholars of outstanding courage like Aristotle, Newton, and Descartes. Brilliant imagination and daring intrepidity in the construction of hypotheses are the very essence of great research. Obviously, the failure of political scientists in general to employ the statistical method in the past means that many years will elapse before political statistics attains the development that has been reached in the discipline of economics. Equal attainment within the discipline of political science can only be accomplished by bold endeavor. Courageous scholarship, however, does not mean the abandonment of scientific caution. Every assumption should be clearly formulated and patiently examined. The accuracy and comprehensiveness of data must be constantly and scrupulously challenged. The most rigid examination of predictions must ever be maintained. Conclusions drawn from the

FOREWORD

projection of a line of trend are always subject to error. In particular, lines of trend which are supported by insufficient data must be firmly rejected as unreliable scientific conclusions. One of the purposes of the new course should be to train the student in the application of rigid criticism to every step in the analysis of data. The development of the study of political statistics will be retarded by any laxity in this self-discipline.

I am confident that there will be political scientists in all parts of the world who will welcome the invasion of our discipline by a mathematical scholar. While some students will not agree with his analysis of the data of every problem, all scholars will rejoice because of the fact that at long last a *systematic* attempt has been made to achieve the measurement of all political data. I know that the author will welcome criticism and comment from interested scholars everywhere.

Kenneth Colegrove.

PREFACE

Several years ago the author of this work was invited to prepare a course which was to bear the generic name of "Political Statistics" and which had as its objective the instruction of students of political science in the use of the statistical method. By fortuitous circumstance it happened that at that time the author had initiated a project which correlated with such a course. This project originated from certain observations presented in the final chapter of his *Analysis of Economic Time Series* (1941) and involved the exploration and interpretation of price, population, shipping, and other data over long periods of time. The purpose of such an analysis was to examine the relationship between great historical movements and economic variation. The hope was cherished that history might yield some of its secrets if it could be subjected to statistical scrutiny, its patterns mathematized, and its movements analyzed.

The magnitude of the project was not realized until after the work was well begun. The data of classical times were carefully studied, particularly with respect to the variation observed both in coinage and in weights and measures. As part of the task of interpretation, it was found necessary to prepare a volume on the history of Alexandria during nearly a thousand years of its existence. But the task of assembling statistical series to cover this long period of time was greatly simplified by the wealth of material available from the scholarly labors of a number of men to whom due credit will be rendered in the ensuing pages.

The problem of the Middle Ages was more difficult, since few statistical records for this dim period have survived the ravages of time. The *Doomsday Book* (1086) of William the Conqueror provided a bench mark from which one could proceed with a certain amount of confidence. In addition to this, various price series, principally for England and Spain, had been extended into some of the Mediaeval centuries and our debt to the scholars who have made them available will be acknowledged later in this book. Richer data became more abundant as one advanced into the Renaissance. Quite recently there was published a remarkable series extending over nearly three centuries, which gave extensive information about the volume and the nature of shipping into the North Sea. These data provided an unparalleled tool for interpreting the political movements of the sixteenth, seventeenth, and eighteenth centuries.

Although the original interest of the author was in the interpretation of political movements by statistical methods, the scope of the study has not been limited to this problem. Many other questions, such as that of political tenure, the problem of congressional apportionment, the voting behavior of electorates, the judgment of tribunals, cohesion in legislative processes, the analysis of opinion polls, forecasting elections, and numerous others, have been presented with appropriate data and analysis. The causes which underlie conflicts, both civil and foreign, have been examined. Political disturbances, which originate in the observed distribution of incomes, have been discussed and tentative theories have been presented to account for the "struggle of the classes" and its effect upon the political state.

Although many deductions have been made from the material which has been assembled, the author's purpose has not been to advance any particular political theory. It has been rather that of the scientist making a serious attempt to examine data and to create from this examination a consistent pattern of political behavior. While interpretations may differ, the data are always the final referent. No theory can survive which is inconsistent with the basic facts.

From his survey of this complex of data, it soon became evident to the author that the subject of political science might be divided conveniently into two parts, one dealing with static problems and the other with dynamic problems. A tentative division was thus suggested by the use of the terms "Political Statics" and "Political Dynamics." The material seemed to fit readily into one or the other of these categories.

Although the statistical method has been used for a number of years by certain well known political scientists, the problems of the subject, for the most part, have been approached through other channels. Since the statistical method thus has not been a traditional part of political science, it has seemed desirable to present certain elements of the subject. This has been done with a minimum of mathematics. The book has been made self-contained by an appendix which gives some of the elements of algebra which are necessary to the understanding of the formal presentation of statistics.

PREFACE

In conclusion the author should like to acknowledge the help which he has received from many individuals, who have contributed in one way or another to the development of this work. Their number is too large to make it practical to list the names of all who have been consulted about various parts of the text. But it should be stated that this work would never have been carried to its completed form without the constant encouragement and the lavish assistance of Professor Kenneth Colegrove of Northwestern University. He was the first to see the possibility of such a development as we have given here and to him belongs the credit for the initiation of the project. Professor Colegrove aided in the assembling of the data and guided the author to the works of those who in the past had used the statistical method in various parts of the subject. Special mention should also be made in this connection to Dr. Lynford A. Lardner, who devoted a considerable amount of time to an examination of the literature of political science for subjects which could be studied by the methods of statistics. He provided a wealth of data which has been used in connection with some of these problems. And finally the author wishes to acknowledge the substantial assistance which he received from Miss Vera Fisher in all parts of the production of this work. In particular, the excellent charts throughout the book were prepared by her.

H. T. Davis.

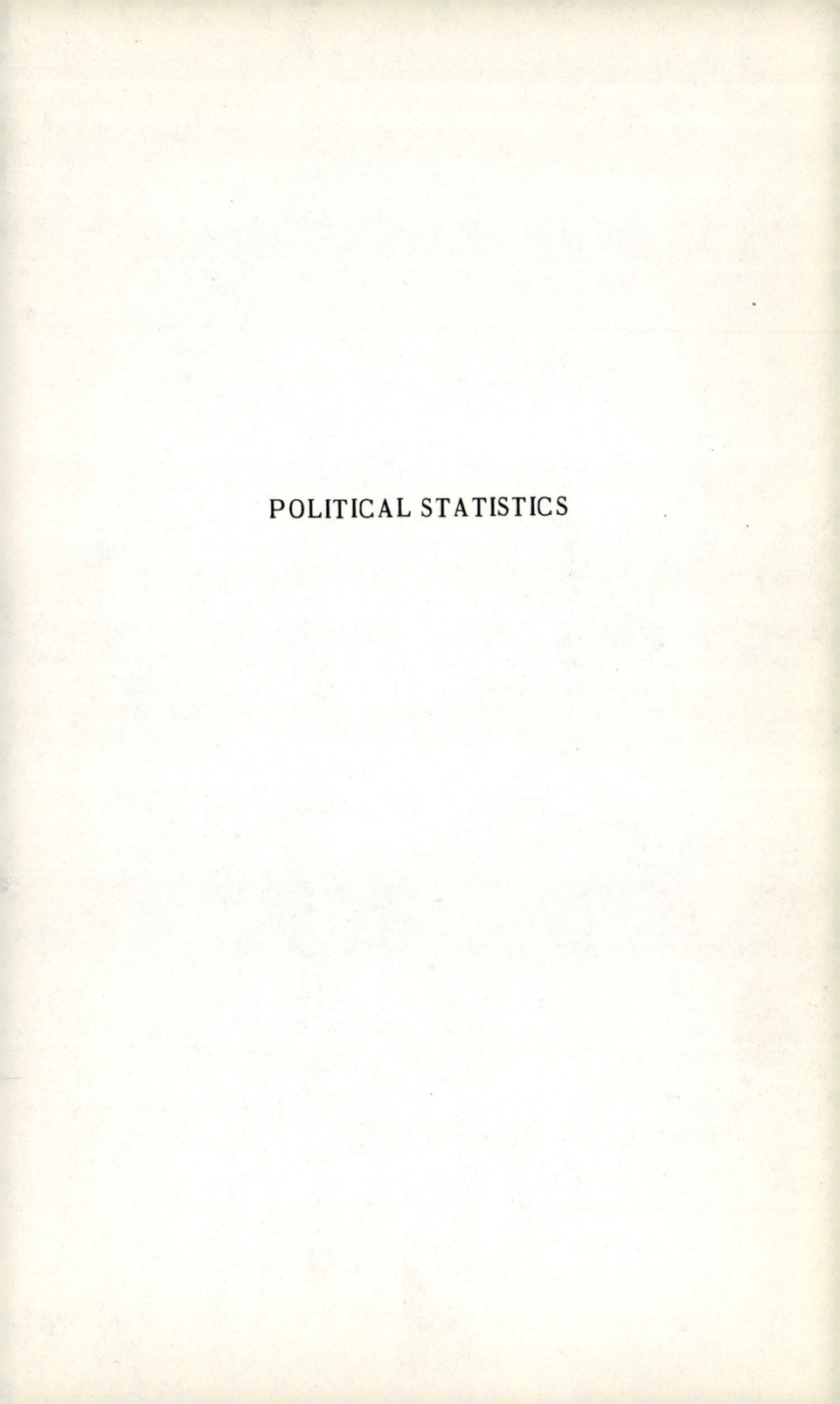

POLITICAL STATISTICS

CHAPTER 1
POLITICAL SCIENCE AS A STATISTICAL SCIENCE
1. *Historical Introduction.*

POLITICAL science in its broadest aspect is the study of the principles and conduct of government. On the one hand it devotes its attention to the origin of the various types of political state and to the rationales which have been proposed to account for them; on the other hand political science considers the executive, legislative, and judicial techniques which have been evolved to carry out the functions of the governing state.

If we consider the development of the subject historically we encounter first the greatest of a long line of utopian schemes, which have had as their objective the creation of an ideal state. This is the *Republic* of Plato (c. 427-347 B. C.), which sets forth and discusses many of the most fundamental problems encountered by established governments since Plato's time. While Plato put into the hands of an intellectual aristocracy all political controls, he also introduced a communism which went so far as to abolish the rights to private property and made all children the dependents of the state. In the *Republic* we find that government is based upon an abstract concept of justice, which diverges widely from the observed behavior of actual states. How great this divergence is may be apprehended from the following famous passage put into the mouth of Socrates: "Until philosophers are kings, or the kings and princes of this world have the spirit and power of philosophy, and the political greatness and wisdom meet in one, and those commoner natures who pursue either to the exclusion of the other are compelled to stand aside, cities will never have rest from their evils — no, nor the human race, as I believe — and then only will this our state have a possibility of life and behold the light of day."

The second contribution made by Greek thought to the problem of government was the *Politics* of Aristotle (384-322 B. C.). Since this philosopher was the pupil of Plato, it is natural that we should find considerable influence exerted by the earlier *Republic* upon this new work. But Aristotle vigorously opposed the communism of Plato and its abolition of private rights and the family. And instead of the philosopher king, he vests the power of the state in constitutional rule and the supremacy of law. Aristotle makes the first attempt at the classification of governmental forms, which may be described roughly by three types: (1) monarchial; (2) aristocratic; (3) democratic. But the delimitation of these three categories is not precise, and the area where one shades into another produces a penumbra which requires further definition. Within this shadow many of the various types of government: oligarchies, tyrannies, dictatorships, feudalisms, constitutional democracies, communes, socialisms, and the like, have developed in the centuries since Aristotle.

We shall omit description of other works in the ancient and medieval period for their contributions were largely of a philosophical nature. The *De Republica* of Cicero (106-43 B.C.) adds little to the earlier contributions of Plato and Aristotle. The dissertations of Marsilius of Padua (c. 1290-c. 1343), William of Occam (c. 1300-c. 1349), Duns Scotus (c. 1265- c. 1308), Saint Thomas Aquinas (c. 1225-1274), and their intellectual successors, valuable as these works were, considered the theory of states and the nature of society by philosophical arguments rather than by an appeal to economic or other influences.

But after the quickening of intellectual life in the sixteenth and seventeenth centuries a number of able philosophers entered the field of political theory. Foremost among these was Thomas Hobbes (1588-1679), whose classical work *Leviathan, or the Matter, Form and Power of a Commonwealth, Ecclesiastical and Civil* appeared in 1651. Hobbes was the first of a long succession of thinkers who advocated the principle of utilitarianism, namely, that people act in accord with those desires which appear to promote their greatest happiness. Thus the establishment of a government is an indispensable action in achieving this end. In his philosophy Hobbes conceived of government as a protective device established to preserve the peace which would otherwise be destroyed by man's general tendency toward war. "The final cause, end, or design of men," he says, "who naturally love liberty, and dominion over others in the introduction of that restraint upon themselves, in which we see them live in commonwealths, is the foresight of their own preservation, and of a more contented life thereby; that is to say, of getting themselves out from that miserable condition of war, which is necessarily consequent... to the natural passions of men, when there is no visible power to keep them in awe, and tie them by fear of punishment to the performance of their covenants."*

Hobbes was something of a mathematician and early came under the influence of Euclid's *Elements*, which made a deep impression upon his mind. He had a desire to bring social phenomena within the same framework of exact formulation so recently achieved by Sir Isaac Newton and his contemporaries. This is reflected in his insistence upon the precise definition of fundamental terms and their derivation of logical conclusions from carefully expressed assumptions. Thus we find the following statement, which is remarkable for its early appearance in a work on political philosophy:[†]

"Seeing that truth consisteth in the right ordering of names in our affirmations, a man that seeketh precise truth had need to remember what every name he useth stands for, and to place it accordingly, or else he will find himself entangled in words as a bird in lime twigs — the more he struggles the more belimed. And therefore in geometry, which is the only science that it hath pleased God hitherto to bestow on mankind, men begin at settling the significations they call definitions, and place them in the beginning of their reckoning... So that in the right definition of names lies the first use of speech, which is the acquisition of science; and in wrong or no definitions lies the first abuse; from which proceed all false and senseless tenets, which make these men that take their instruction from the authority of books, and not from their own meditations, to be much below the condition of ignorant men as men endued with true science are above it."

Following Hobbes, and his intellectual opponent in the matter of utilitarian belief, was John Locke (1632-1704). His principal contribution to political thought is found in his *Two Treatises on Government* (1690) wherein he argued for the democratic principle as a law of nature, or, to employ his interpretation, as a necessity of reason. He thus assumed that government is a creation of those governed and it is thus subservient to their will. Thus he says:[‡] "Men being by nature all free, equal, and independent, no one can be put out of this estate and subjected to the political power of another without his own consent. The only way whereby any one divests himself of his natural liberty, and puts on the *bonds of civil society*, is by agreement with other men to join and unite into a community."

---

*Leviathan, Chap. 17.   †*Ibid.*, Chap. 4.   ‡*On Civil Government*, c, viii.

Toward the end of the eighteenth century and the beginning of the nineteenth a new trend is to be observed in political theory. Abstract logic and pure philosophical inquiry began to yield to the more practical study of the relationships between the state and its economic system. The "revolt against reason" and the "return to nature" advocated by J. J. Rousseau (1712-1778) had culminated in the French Revolution. But it was soon evident to those whose hopes had been stirred by the doctrine of liberty, equality, and freedom, yet who had also been forced to witness the excesses of the French commune, that the problems of the state were also the problems of economic production and the distribution of this production. It was no accidental matter that the subject of economics was first called *political economy*.

A succession of brilliant writers began to explore the new domain. The first of these was Adam Smith (1723-1790) who produced in 1776 his *Inquiry into the Nature and Causes of the Wealth of Nations*. This celebrated treatise became authoritative in politics as well as economics and exerted an influence throughout the world equalled by few books. This was followed in due time by the work of David Ricardo (1772-1823), who published his *Principles of Political Economy and Taxation* in 1817. Ricardo's ideas were further explored by John Stuart Mill (1806-1873) in his *Principles of Political Economy* produced in 1848, which applied his theories to social as well as economic problems.

Toward the end of the nineteenth century there was an abundance of evidence to show that the theories advanced by earlier writers were in need of more scientific appraisal. W. S. Jevons (1835-1882) in 1871 put the modern position forcibly as follows: "The deductive science of economy must be verified and rendered useful by the purely inductive science of statistics. Theory must be invested with the reality and life of fact. Political economy might gradually be erected into an exact science, if only commercial statistics were more complete and accurate than they are at present, so that the formulas could be endowed with exact meaning by the aid of numerical data."

Most of the lingering suspicion with which social scientists had watched the intrusion of statistical methods and stubborn facts into their hitherto unblemished subject had almost disappeared by the beginning of the twentieth century. Alfred Marshall (1842-1924), whose

Principles of Economics (1890) had used mathematical methods in its exposition, wrote in 1907: "Disputes as to method have ceased. Qualitative analysis has done the greater part of its work... that is to say, there is general agreement as to the characters and durations of the changes which various economic forces tend to produce. Much less progress has been made towards the quantitative determination of the relative strength of different economic forces. That higher and more difficult task must wait upon the slow growth of thorough realistic statistics." In the same year, Vilfredo Pareto (1848-1923), author of *Cours d'économie politique* (2 volumes, 1896-1897), wrote: "The progress of political economy in the future will depend in great part upon the investigation of empirical laws, derived from statistics, which will then be compared with known theoretical laws, or will suggest derivation from them of new laws."

Concurrent with the trend toward political economy and statistical analysis, which we have just mentioned, another movement was under way that was to have dramatic consequences in the twentieth century. This was the development of socialistic theories, which sought to ameliorate the conditions of the poor and raise the general standard of living by what were called "more equitable" methods of distributing wealth and income. This movement had essentially three phases, the first devoted to the intellectual creation of ideal states, the second to the actual establishment of communal settlements, and the third, associated with a theory which asserted that the course of history is determined by natural factors external to political systems themselves.

Following the pattern first established by Plato to define the ideal commonwealth, Sir Thomas More had created his *Utopia* in 1516, and thereby contributed a new word to the language. More's political satire was followed in due time by Bacon's *New Atlantis* (1624-1629), Tommaso Campanella's *Civitas Solis* (1623), James Harrington's *Oceana* (1656), and works of lesser consequence. These pleasing inventions of the imagination have been imitated in more recent times by a number of writers. Thus we can mention Etienne Cabet's *Voyage en Icarie* (1840), Bulwer Lytton's *The Coming Race* (1871), Samuel Butler's *Erewhon* (1872) and *Erewhon Revisited* (1901), Edward Bellamy's *Looking Backward* (1888), and numerous works by H. G. Wells in the present century. While these pleasing fantasies mainly failed in their purpose of directing man to higher destiny, they stimulated an abundance of thought on the relationship between the political, social, and economic factors of government.

Closely related to the creation of utopias, we find movements to establish communities in accord with some of the theories advanced by the philosophers. Only two of the most celebrated will be mentioned here. The first of these was the communal settlement established by Robert Owen (1771-1858) at New Harmony, Indiana, in 1826; the other was the Brook Farm experiment in Massachusetts during the years 1841-1847 based upon the system of *phalansteries*, or cooperative organizations, initiated by F. M. C. Fourier (1772-1837). Unsuccessful as these adventures proved to be, they nevertheless focused the attention of many people upon the difficulties of government in solving social and economic problems.

The third movement was associated with what has come to be called the *mechanistic theory of history*, by which we mean that the events of history are not governed by the whims and actions of individuals, but rather are the results of the impact of economic and social events upon the political structure. This theory had its roots in the work of Jean Bodin (1530-1596) and was amplified in certain respects by Montesquieu (1689-1755) in his treatise *L'esprit des lois* (The Spirit of Laws), published in 1748, and in G. B. Vico's *Principi di una scienza nuova* (Principles of a New Science), which appeared in 1725. The determinism which permeates these writings was further explored by G. W. F. Hegel (1770-1831) in his *Philosophy of History*, published in 1837, by Thomas Buckle (1821-1862) in his *History of Civilization in England* (1857), and by Karl Marx and his school, who initiated their writings with Karl Marx's *Poverty of Philosophy*, published in 1847. Since the story of this movement will be treated more adequately in a later section of this book it will suffice for the present to indicate here the historical origins from which have come in recent times some of the most dramatic and explosive events in modern political history.

With this brief, and in many respects, inadequate survey of a few of the classical figures in the development of political science, we shall turn to a consideration of the tenets which underlie the writing of the present volume. This work belongs to what Quincy Wright in his *Study of War* (1942) has called the "Statistical School" of Political Scientists, which has had a "late development because of the resistance of most political phenomena to measurement."

2. *Politics as a Science.*

In the long history of political thought from Plato and Aristotle until very recent times, there is little evidence of the use of numerical measurement or of the methods of scientific inquiry. Politics was believed to be largely unmeasurable. The nature of the state, the character of community life, the role of the sovereign power, and similar concepts were not believed to be amenable to statistical methods. Clear definition of terms in a formulation which would lead to measurement is almost completely lacking; the subject thus was largely one of philosophical inquiry, and volumes were written both for and against the proposition that logical processes govern the organization and operation of communities. Where Thomas Hobbes advocated a doctrine of utilitarianism in interpreting community life, namely, that cooperation among its members is made necessary by the fact that as individuals they are governed by self interest alone, John Locke denied this premise and believed that communities work for the good of all under the regulations of government and its laws. All such arguments were based upon an *appeal to reason*, but they were never subjected to the scrutiny of actual human behavior as it is measured by statistical data.

Back of this appeal to reason, as contrasted with the *appeal to data*, lies the widely held belief that the problems of the social sciences, depending as they do upon the vagaries of human conduct, cannot be reduced to exact measurement. In the physical sciences there is an underlying determinism which is lacking in social phenomena. A distinguished jurist once said to the writer in a debate upon this point: "How can one hope to measure the love, the hope, and the fear of individuals, or of groups of individuals?" But he would not stop for an answer.

It is this postulate of determinism which cuts the deep chasm between the natural and the social sciences. Capricious nature, despite man's original assumption that her activities were governed by the whims of gods, was finally found to be reducible to rigid laws. The wind and the tides, the thunderbolt of Zeus, disease and pestilence, the moon and the planets, were all discovered to have predictable characteristics, which brought them within the scope of scientific determinism. But this demonstration, which finally destroyed the gods in nature, was a struggle waged through many centuries. For man bitterly resented the proposition that there existed an immutable order in the natural universe.

A similar and even more violent resentment has assailed the proposition that man himself is subject to external laws, that his social, economic, and political activities are governed by restraints beyond his own will. For how, he inquires, can the uncertainties of human life be brought within the domain of mathematical precision? How can man's loves and passions be formulated in terms of equations and subjected to interpretation by the cold logic of formal science?

Answers to such questions cannot be given categorically. Nevertheless one can approach the problem in a scientific spirit. By this we mean that we can set up tentative propositions regarding human conduct and then determine their reasonableness by comparing deductions derived from them with the actual behavior of the real world. This has been the method followed from the beginning by the exact sciences and in no other way can scientific laws be established.

But one should observe in this connection that there are orders of determinism. The law of supply and demand in economics, for example, has a very different status in science from the law of gravitation in astronomy. The degree of variation from the normal pattern is much greater in the one than in the other. Not only are the statistical measures of prices themselves subject to considerable error, but the influences which affect the underlying economic system are complex and variable. In contrast to this, the motion of a planet about the sun under the law of gravitation may be determined with such rare accuracy that tables can be constructed which give its position for many years in the future. And yet, exactly as in the case of prices, the elements in the planet's ephemeris are subject to numerous complex influences. The difference is merely that all other forces which affect the planet are small in comparison with the gravitational attraction of the sun, while all the factors which control prices are generally of the same order of magnitude. Whenever the gravitational influences other than that of the sun become significant, as they do in the motion of the moon, then the astronomer is beset by the same difficulties which face the economist.

From what has just been said we see that scientific disciplines lie somewhere between complete determinism on the one hand and a complete randomness on the other. This may be phrased otherwise by saying that some sciences are more exact than others.

For this reason, that is to say, the variability in determinism itself, we must content ourselves in social, political, and economic investigations with trends and correlations. The laws of social behavior, although many of them can be stated in the language of mathematics, are not exact. About them there always lies a haze of uncertainty. It is the goal of science to define with precision this uncertainty and to state the limitations that must be applied to the structural elements. Later in the book we shall formulate what may be called the law of legislative tenure, but it can never have the precision of the law of falling bodies in physics. By limiting its imperfections, however, this law has sufficient precision to serve as an interpreter of legislative efficiency. In this sense, and in this sense only, can meaning be given to the proposition that there exists a determinism in the propositions of political science.

3. *The Role of Postulates in Scientific Inquiry.*

Since we propose in this work to apply the methods of science to some of the problems of political science, it might be well for us to get some idea as to what these methods actually involve.

Perhaps the best single statement of the scientific point of view is that of Lord Kelvin (1824-1907) who said:* "I often say that when you can measure what you are speaking about, and express it in numbers, you know something about it; but when you cannot measure it, when you cannot express it in numbers, your knowledge is of a meager and unsatisfactory kind."

The importance of this point of view in political science is at once seen if we consider the nebulous character of such words as socialism, communism, fascism, etc. Without an adequate definition, actually reduced to one or more numerical measures, it would be impossible to say that a given government is so many per cent socialistic, or that the ratio of fascistic elements to socialistic elements is equal to a stated number.

As we have said before, some critics of the mathematical method in social problems believe that the erratic psychology of groups of individuals, and the behavior of political institutions, are not subjects suitable to scientific inquiry. But since definite structure is

---

*Popular Lectures and Addresses by Lord Kelvin. London, 1889, V.1, p.73.

visible in many series constructed from economic variables, and since political events appear to be largely influenced by the economic factor, the strongest evidence presents itself in favor of the proposition that certain sectors of political science may be reduced to measurement.

But measurement, while it is the heart of the scientific method, is not sufficient by itself. The heroic names in science are those of men who have observed some kind of structure in the measured variables. Thus Johann Kepler (1571-1630), examining the data on the paths of the planets, observed that these bodies moved essentially in elliptical orbits. K. F. Gauss (1777-1855), studying the distribution of measurements themselves, observed that they had a central tendency from which some varied much more than others, and was able to give a satisfactory mathematical form to account for this variation. Both Kepler's observation and Gauss's equations are examples of theories derived from statistical data. One formed the corner stone of modern gravitational astronomy; the other the basis of modern statistical science. Both are formulated within a framework of mathematics.

We thus see that exact measurement leads ultimately to some comprehensive theory of the quantities subjected to the measurement. It is the custom today to refer to these theories as *postulates*. By this we mean that science formulates its basic principles in terms of tentative propositions, not as inevitable truths of natural phenomena, but as statements which conform to the existing facts. In this way, when new facts present themselves, the postulates can be altered without introducing the fear that fundamental truths are being modified. This gives a kind of elasticity to the scientific method, which has prevented it from assuming a rigid and sterile form.

To many people, even in this day of enlightened scientific progress, the postulational nature of truth is a strange and often repugnant idea. But we shall use it in its scientific setting, where it now has universal approval.

The difficulty of the postulational approach to truth is found in two things, first, the problem of formulating postulates in exact form, that is to say, in terms of mathematical expressions which lend themselves to the mechanics of deduction and inference; second, the problem of accumulating data which will permit a realistic determination of the unknown parameters in the mathematical expressions.

A classical example which illustrates in a rather astonishing manner the nature of postulation is found in the three geometries. In an important segment of his *Elements* Euclid required either directly or indirectly the proposition that the sum of the angles of a triangle is equal to two right angles. This mathematical *truth* depended in turn upon the proposition that through a point external to a given line one and only one line could be drawn parallel to a given line. For more than twenty centuries after Euclid mathematicians made vain attempts to prove these propositions. And then, at last, it was discovered that these propositions were postulates, since an equally valid geometry with useful applications was constructed on the proposition that the sum of the angles of a triangle is less than two right angles. This in turn depended upon the postulate that through a point external to a given line more than one line could be drawn parallel to the given line. Astonished by this remarkable solution of an ancient problem, mathematicians soon discovered that the third possibility also had postulational validity, namely that a geometry could be founded upon the proposition that the sum of the angles of a triangle exceeds two right angles. And in this case no line parallel to a given line could be drawn through a point external to the line. Never before these remarkable discoveries in the first half of the nineteenth century had the postulational nature of truth been so clearly apprehended.

Hence science has learned to build its various disciplines upon a structure of postulates. These propositions do not permit debate as to their truth or falsity, for they are asserted as statements which appear to be consistent with the observed facts. Their defense, for the most part, does not lie in a logical demonstration of their validity, but in the fact that they are *isomorphic* with experience, that is to say, that they represent, or agree with, the observed data. Even though logic or prejudice be offended, the postulate stands or falls upon the evidence of the data themselves. There is no other court of appeal beyond the facts of experience, and this is why the true science is an objective one.

4. *The Role of Mathematics in Science.*

There is some confusion in the lay mind as to the role which mathematics plays in science. The widely used phrase "that a proposition has been proved mathematically" connotes a finality which is not always justified.

A science may be said to be approaching mathematical form when the objects of its investigation have been carefully defined, the relationships between them have been established in terms of equations, and the constants, or parameters, which enter into these equations have been determined by statistics.

Adolphe Quetelet (1796-1874), who, although a Belgian astronomer of note, is perhaps best known for his work in statistics and his attempt to define the "average man," made the following important observations:*

"The more advanced the sciences have become, the more they have tended to enter the domain of mathematics, which is a sort of center towards which they converge. We can judge of the perfection to which a science has come by the facility, more or less great, with which it may be approached by calculation... It has seemed to me that the theory of probabilities ought to serve as the basis of all sciences, and particularly of the sciences of observation... Since absolute certainty is impossible, and we can speak only of the probability of the fulfillment of a scientific expectation, a study of this theory should be a part of every man's education."

In order to understand the significance of the mathematical approach to knowledge we shall consider an example. Suppose that we take the term "a stable government." If one reads history he is soon impressed by the fact that some commonwealths are subject to frequent disorders, rapidly varying economic fluctuations, changes of rulers at short intervals either by election, usurpation, or assassination. In other segments of history the contrary is true. There is a steady advance in material prosperity, long periods in which the governing unit is unchanged. We may contrast, for example, the period between 212 A.D. to 306 A.D., when the Roman commonwealth had 21 emperors, with the period from 1837 to 1936, when England was governed by but three rulers.

There was obviously a great deal of difference between the Roman government under the later emperors and the English government of the last century. But it is not enough merely to make this statement. Some measure should be devised to present this fact in more absolute terms. In this way it would be possible to extend our analysis of the stability of governments to other countries, much as one can compare the climates of Norway and Italy by the average readings of a ther-

―――――――
*From Frank H. Hankins: "Adolphe Quetelet as Statistician," *Studies in History, Economics and Public Law*, Vol. 31, 1908, No. 4, 133 pp.

mometer. Later in this work we shall devise such a statistical measure for the comparison of different governments with respect to their stability, but it would be premature to describe it now. The point of the present discussion is to emphasize the need for exact measurement in all scientific inquiry combined with a mathematical device by means of which the measurements may be readily interpreted. This is the method of science.

But it is not enough merely to have systematic methods for presenting data. In physics, for example, galvanometers were invented for the purpose of measuring electrical currents. But it is a long way from the readings of galvanometers to the great mathematical structure of modern electromagnetic theory. After such quantities as electrical currents, potential differences, resistances, capacities, etc. had been carefully defined and reduced to exact measurement, a theory was necessary by means of which they could be connected with one another. Equations were discovered which expressed these relationships in exact form. From these equations new properties of the quantities were discovered, which in turn led to more complex relationships and further knowledge.

Let us consider a very important problem in political science as an illustration of this point. It was observed by Plato, and practically all writers since his time, that great political difficulties appear to arise out of the difference in income between various classes in the state. The demagogue is one who appeals to the prejudices of the *demos*, or the class of the common man. But where does one find in the history of political thought any attempt to define the demos? The problem is fundamentally related to the distribution of income. Only in recent times, in the work of Vilfredo Pareto (1848-1923), and other economists, has a measure of success been achieved in discovering the nature of the actual distribution of income in modern states. More recently attempts have been made to give an exact mathematical description of income distribution, and one may say that the facts are pretty well accounted for by the theory thus developed.

But much more than this is needed if the impact of income distribution upon political events is to be described. Are revolutions and civil wars the results of disturbances in the concentration of income? This requires an exact mathematical description of the term "concentration of income" and some adequate theory of how the variation in concentration is related to observed political disturbances.

5. *Political Science and Economics.*

In attempting to formulate a theory of political statistics, it is important at the outset to ascertain the reasons why one should believe such a theory possible. This is found in the fact that political events are closely related to economic events on the one hand, and to sociological facts on the other. It is sometimes difficult to mark the line where the domain of one of these disciplines ends and the domain of the other begins.

Thus, as we shall show in some detail later in the book, there is a very close connection between the variations of the business cycle and the trend of political events. The lack of popularity of Martin Van Buren in the presidential election of 1840, and the overwhelming defeat of Herbert Hoover in 1932, after he had won in 1928 by a plurality of more than six million votes, were consequences of disastrous drops in the business cycle, rather than blemishes in the characters of the candidates. The evidence from this and other countries confirms overwhelmingly the proposition that the rise and fall of political parties is closely correlated with economic trends, for the voice of the people is generally a cry against the disasters which come upon the common man through the strains and the stresses of economic crises.

From the time of the Greek historian Polybius (c.205 – c.125 B.C.) there has been an insistent theory that the events of history have a pattern governed by external events. This ancient theory is now known as the *mechanistic theory of history*. Formulated first by the philosophers of the subject, Bodin, Hegel, Buckle, and others, this theory has had an explosive development in recent times through the writings of Karl Marx and his school of political theorists. No longer is it confined to the meditations of the cloisters, but it has become a dynamic element in the political drama of our own times. At its core this theory is one of economics. The wages of the worker, the distribution of income and wealth, the products of the industrial machine, are all elements in this social and political philosophy. Hence, even more than in past times, it becomes a matter of great importance to examine economic events by statistical methods and relate them to the trends of political history.

We are thus led in our inquiry into the theory of what have been called *time series*, that is to say, series of data arranged successively in time. Since prices, production, and other economic variables are best represented by index numbers, that is to say, numbers which relate the level of one year or period to the level of another, it will be necessary to examine the origin and structure of these statistical measures.

One of the difficulties with the general application of the theory of economic variation to the interpretation of political events is found in the fact that very long time series are required. Political trends often extend over many years and the relationship between the political changes and the economic situations that accompany them require time series of unusual length. Thus the great revolution in ideas, the quickening tempo in the pulse of the world, the profound change in political and social institutions, which marked the transition from Medieval to Modern history, is readily apprehended from economic time series over the interval of a century and a half between 1500 and 1650. (See, for example, Figure 1, which shows the growth of Spanish trade in the sixteenth and seventeenth centuries.) The construction of such long series over this and similar lengths of time has been one of the major statistical achievements of economic historians. It will be found that the great political revolutions can be observed in the variations of the economic indexes and from these

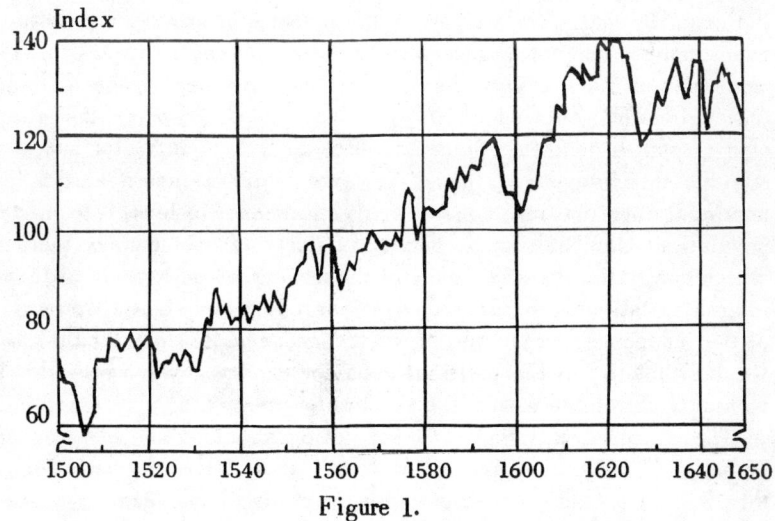

Figure 1.

Index of Spanish Trade, Based on Soetbeer's Treasure Series, 1501-1650 facts we can more readily understand the underlying reasons for the revolutions.

Most conspicuous of all causes of political change is that of war, for war is the great inflator. Under its impact the currencies of the belligerents always deteriorate and the universal measure of war-intensity is the index of prices. Hence prices will act as a kind of barometer for the political events which accompany these all-too-frequent cataclysms. The complete destruction of a government is often indicated by the complete destruction of its monetary system, and these events are fruitful creators of despotic regimes under harsh dictators.

6. *Political Science and Sociology.*

If we define sociology in its broadest sense to be "the science of the origin, development, and constitution of human society" then it is clear that a large segment of the phenomena considered by political science must have roots in the phenomena studied by sociology. Where the latter are measurable and can be related to the measurable elements of politics, then these phenomena will have direct interest for us.

Many examples of this intimate connection between the two disciplines come to mind. Let us consider, for example, the problems of the city. We shall see later, when the proper statistical methods have been applied, that the political status of a city can be gauged by the measures of its social welfare. Attempts have been made to define the various elements which, taken as a whole, determine the status of a city as a desirable place in which to live. One writer has segregated thirty-seven of these elements which measure health, educational opportunities, comfort of living, economic level, etc. of the population. Obviously in a complex of thirty-seven elements there is a high correlation between many of the measures and a study of these internal relationships might easily result in a substantial reduction of the independent measures of urban "goodness." However that may be, it is clear that the political behavior of city governments should be highly correlated with these social elements.

The standard of living of a population should also be a concern of political science, since, as we shall show later, the variation of this level has had great importance in political changes. The phenomenon of the Gracchi (c. 133 B.C.) in the old Roman Republic is identical with that in the recent Spanish civil war (1936-1939) and in the striking political change which developed in this country after the miseries of the depression of 1932. Political slogans such as "two chickens in every pot," "two cars in every garage" show the relationship between living standards and problems of government.

Demographic elements, which describe the well-being of the demos from the standpoint of health and mortality, its physical condition from the amount of disease, the number of births, marriages, and divorces, and its general progress from the statistics of population growth, have fundamental significance in the interpretation of political phenomena. In a classic volume on *Rats, Lice, and History* (1935) Hans Zinsser developed the thesis that typhus fever and other similar scourges more than generals have changed the course of history and the trend of political events. Thus he makes the following observations: "[The Black Death] carried in its wake moral, religious, and political disintegration... Swords and lances, arrows and machine guns and even high explosives have had far less power over the fate of nations than the typhus louse, the plague flea, and the yellow-fever mosquito. Civilizations have retreated from the plasmodium of malaria, and armies have crumbled into rabbles under the onslaught of cholera, spirilla, or of dysentery and typhoid bacilli... Even the greatest general of them all, Napoleon, was helpless when pitted against the tactics of epidemic disease." Certainly the course of history has been changed by the impact of these scourges upon the population and any appraisal of political history must take into account these vast influences.

In recent times, with the diminution of epidemic disease, the populations of the world, and in particular, the populations of Europe, have increased in a terrifying manner (See Figure 2). The old spectre of Malthus again appears in the political events of Europe, for population seems in a fair way to outrun its supply of food. In modern power-politics the number of bushels of wheat held by a country has more political importance than the number of pounds of gold in its vaults, or even the number of men in its armies.

Another important sociological problem which greatly affects the trend of legislation is the constantly increasing expectation of life. The distribution of ages in the population has shown a material alteration during the last half century, and this is creating new and disturbing problems in the legislation of employment.

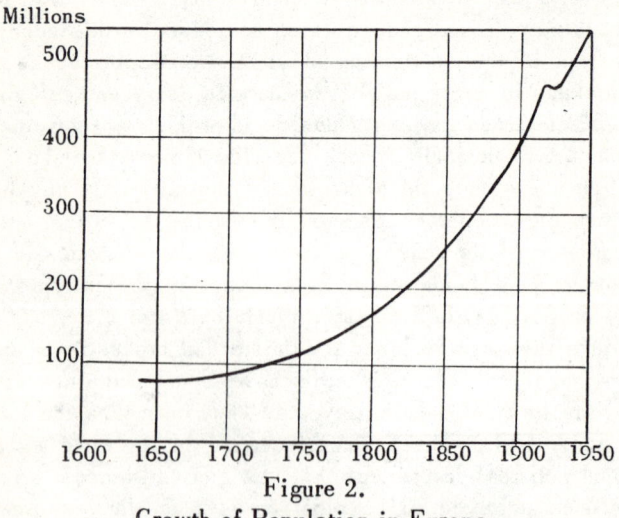

Figure 2.
Growth of Population in Europe.

We mention finally the importance of crime as a factor in the purview of sociology, which also has a significant relationship with the problems of government. When in the United States the total number of major crimes is annually in excess of one per cent of the number of citizens, it is clear that the problems thus presented are important functions not only of local, but of state and national governments as well. The decay of cities, which universally follows the same pattern of moving outward from the center, is intimately connected with the distribution of the criminal elements which it contains.

PROBLEMS

1. Name two or three problems which concern political questions, that might be treated by the statistical approach.

2. What assumption, or assumptions, underlie the collection of data on opinions about political matters? Specifically, what is the implication of the statement that 80 per cent of those polled favor some particular theory or course of action?

3. From the graph of American wholesale prices (Figure 6) determine approximately when our five major wars began and when they ended. Do wars end when actual belligerency stops?

4. Is it possible from the graph of prices to determine the respective intensities of the wars? How would the war of 1812 compare with the Civil War?

5. What political event caused the rise in prices around 1837? What caused the rise in 1855? what the rise in 1935?

6. In a general manner of speech the doctrine of Malthus asserts that populations will outrun their food supplies. Similarly Newton's law of gravitation states that material objects attract one another. But more precisely Newton's law of gravitation says that two bodies attract one another directly as their masses and inversely as the square of the distance between them. How can the doctrine of Malthus be put into this same precise form?

7. The following table gives the production of wheat for the year indicated and the total population of the United States as then determined over the period from 1870 to 1945:

Year	Production of Wheat Unit: 1,000,000 bu.	Population Unit:1,000,000	Year	Prod. of Wheat	Population
1870	235.9	38.558	1920	833.0	105.711
1880	498.6	50.156	1930	857.4	122.775
1890	378.1	62.948	1940	813.3	131.410
1900	602.7	75.995	1945	1,123.1	139.621
1910	635.1	91.972	1950	1,026.8	150.697

How does the increase in the production of wheat compare with the growth in population? Does the theory of Malthus seem to be in the way of fulfillment in the United States?

8. Discuss the following two postulates:
(a) Utility, defined as a measure of human wants, decreases as our stock of goods and services increases.
(b) Every individual strives to increase his utility.
Are these postulates consistent? What modifications or additions could one make to the system?

9. In the light of Lord Kelvin's statement about measurement, what would be your reaction to the proposition that the beauty of an object can be measured by the ratio, O/C, where O is defined to be the order observed in the object and C is its complexity?

10. If two cities A and B are said to have "indexes of goodness" equal respectively to 60 and 40, what interpretation can be made of such a statement? What further information would one desire about such an index? Would the index of a third city C, let us say 30, help one to interpret the meaning of the measure? Could such a measure conceivably have a zero value? Could it have a negative value?

11. In Figure 3 we find represented the distribution of members of the House of Representatives in the Indiana legislature with respect to the number of terms which they have held. Reading from the graph the number who have held office for two terms and those who have held office for three terms, what is the proportionate hold-over in office? How can one account for the value of this tenure-ratio? What relationship could it have to the problem of efficient legislation?

7. *The Problems of Political Statics.*

It is time to make an appraisal of our task and to see what problems in the field of politics we can consider with any hope of success. As in other parts of social science we find it convenient to divide the phenomena into what we may call those of *statics* and those of *dynamics*. These words are taken from the science of mechanics, which has been conveniently divided into these two categories. As the first of these words implies, the theory of statics deals with problems of equilibrium, wherein the variations occasioned by

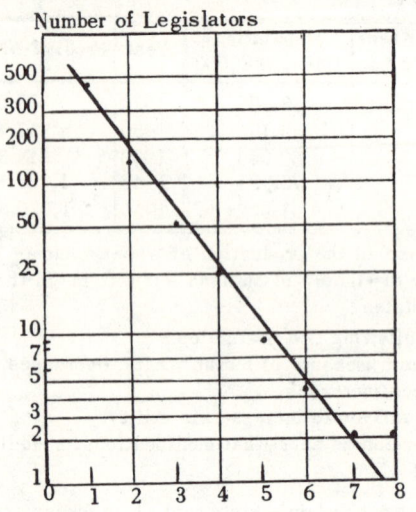

Number of Legislators

Number of Terms Served by Legislators

Figure 3.
Law of Legislative Tenure as Illustrated
by Terms in the Indiana House of Representatives.
Line shows theoretical tenure and dots actual tenure.

the flow of time are not considered. On the other hand the theory of dynamics treats of the motion of bodies (*kinematics*) and the action of forces which produce changes in the motion (*kinetics*). Thus we see that dynamics is essentially a theory of the variations which take place in time. As one may easily surmise, there is considerable interrelationship between statics and dynamics, although, for the most part, problems belonging to one of these disciplines are easily recognized from those belonging to the other.

Under the general classification of *political statics* we shall subsume those problems in which the element of time does not play a part. Such problems, for example, would relate to the size of state legislatures, to their composition, the average tenure of their members, and the occupational, educational, and other characteristics of the legislators. (See, for example, Figure 3.)

What we have called "the problem of the philosopher king" is another static problem. This problem considers the occupational, educational, and similar characteristics of public servants. From what class are presidents and governors chosen? Does the largest occupational class in the commonwealth provide the largest number of legislators, or are our laws made by a class selected from a small minority group in the demos? And what is the effect of such choices?

One of the most conspicuous patterns in political events is that of the struggle of the classes, called from time to time by different names, but embraced with sufficient accuracy for our present purpose, by the name of socialism. At heart this class-struggle revolves itself around the problem of the distribution of wealth and income. But since the production of income bears a fairly uniform ratio to the wealth which produces it, and since income is currently estimated, the problem reduces to that of studying the distribution of income. Although the relationship of the distribution of income to political events is a dynamic one, the actual determination of the pattern of the distribution of income among the people of a commonwealth is a problem in statics. The essential permanence of the pattern may be inferred from the fact that the distribution of incomes among the people of the Roman Republic in the time of Cicero was practically the same as among the people of the United States in the year 1929. This comparison is made in Figures 4 and 5.

It will thus be a matter of interest to us to study the characteristics of the pattern of income and to interpret its significance in the stability of different forms of government.

Since the days of the gerrymander (1812) the problem of legislative and congressional representation has been one of much interest to students of politics. What might seem at first sight to be a very simple matter, the allocation of representatives among the various states according to their populations, produced a problem which required more than half a century for its solution. This is again a problem in political statics, since it involves no element of time in its consideration.

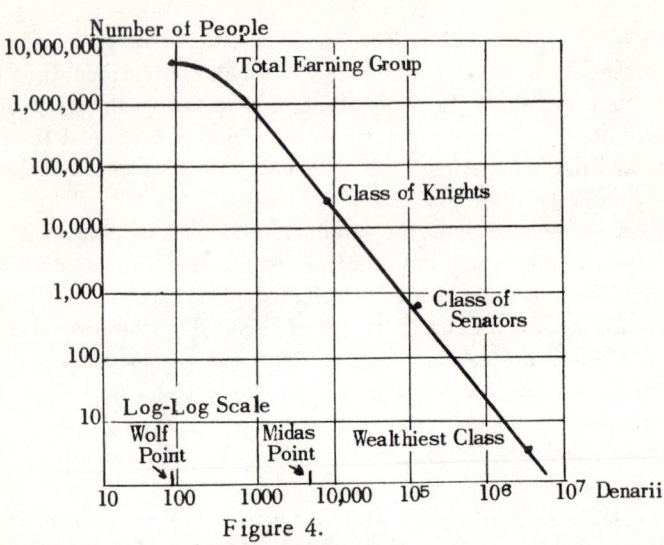

Figure 4.
Distribution of Incomes in Rome at the Time of Augustus Caesar.

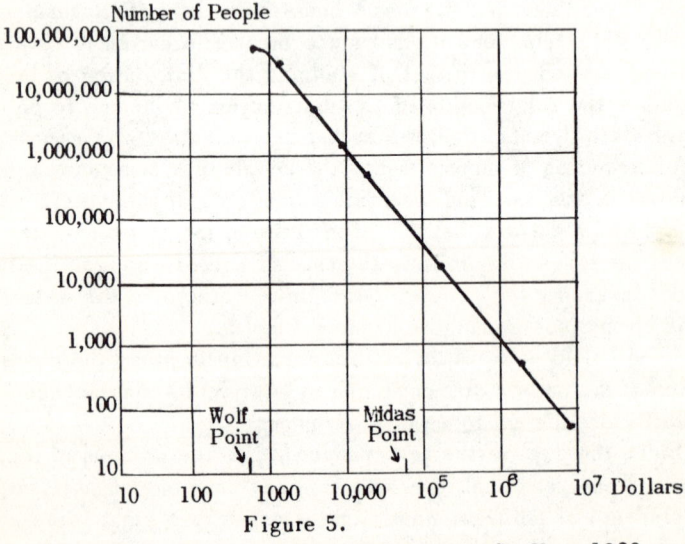

Figure 5.
Distribution of Income in the United States in the Year 1929.
The wolf point indicates the smallest sum that will maintain life. The Midas point indicates where great wealth begins, i.e., where 99% of earners have lower incomes.

In recent times there has been widespread interest in political polls designed to determine the general opinion of the people on current problems. Naturally the greatest interest has been shown in attempts to forecast the results of elections. Unfortunately the techniques developed have not always given satisfactory results. In appraising the problem involved in such forecasts we have been led into the theory of probability and its application.

8. *The Problems of Political Dynamics.*

Since the greatest interest in political science centers around the current events of governments, it is natural that the problems of political dynamics should challenge major attention. There appears to be one satisfactory way to approach such problems and that is through the use of statistical time series, which we have defined earlier as series of data observed successively in time. An example of such a series would be the population counts provided in its decennial enumeration by the Bureau of the Census.

In many cases there is no way of making a simple enumeration such as that of the population. Instead we must rely upon what are called index numbers, that is to say, numbers which compare the level of some statistical quantity at one time with the level of the same quantity at another time. One conspicuous example is that of price, or, more specifically some particular kind, such as wholesale price. Since a price level is determined from more than one item, it is impossible to designate price in terms of dollars per unit; hence the level is determined as a comparison of the weighted prices of a comparison date in relationship to the weighted prices at a given date, designated as the base. Thus if the price of wholesale goods is designated by 100 for the base year 1926 (usually written 1926 = 100), then the wholesale price in 1947 can be represented by the index 197. This means that the general level is 97 per cent higher on the average in 1947 than it was in 1926. We shall explore this subject more thoroughly later in the book, but it is important to observe that for the most part our measurement of political events depends upon a comparison of index numbers computed over some period of time. An example of such a time series is shown in Figure 6.

Among the most conspicuous problems in political dynamics is that of war, for this phenomenon of human society causes the most rapid and profound changes in governments. We shall be interested statistically in attempts to measure the intensity of wars, and to ascertain how they come about through the rupture of political relationships by a system of economic and cultural strains.

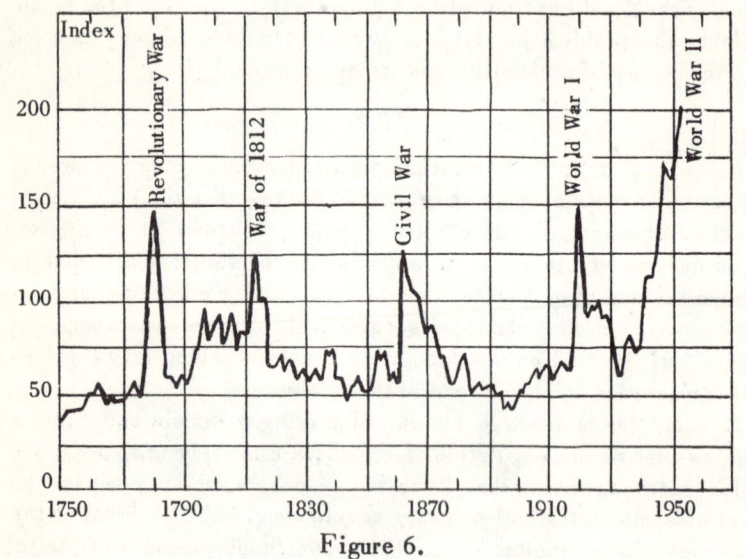

Figure 6.
Prices in America in Three Centuries
Index Numbers of Wholesale Prices in the United States, 1750-1950, 1926 = 100.

Since wars are of two distinct kinds, those of nation against nation, that is to say, external struggles, and those between classes of the same nation, commonly called civil wars, it will be necessary to examine the nature of these two types of conflict. For the most part it will be found that civil wars are concerned in some manner with the distribution of wealth and income. The interrelations here must be examined attentively with respect to what we have called the concentration ratio, a measure which we shall define later in the book.

In a broader way we are concerned also with what has been called the mechanistic theory of history. We have already mentioned this subject and its intimate relationship with the movements of economic time series. The rise and fall of prices, especially over long periods of time, supply a remarkable background for the interpretation of political revolutions. Now and then we observe in the course of history one of those devastating inflations which with tornadic force sweep away dynasties and even nations themselves. Thus the Ptolemaic rule of Egypt disappeared in the midst of a vast inflation which, over a period of years, substituted pure copper for pure silver in the common currency at a ratio of one hundred to one. The Roman empire fell into complete disorder in the wake of one of the most memorable inflations of history. The famous edict of Diocletian, issued in the year 301, established a price of 400 denarii for a bushel of wheat and ordered the penalty of death for those who violated the imperial decree. But this price was already more than 80 times that which prevailed under the stable government of Augustus Caesar, near the beginning of the Christian era, 40 times that in the age of Nero (c. 60 A. D.), and 20 times that in the reign of Decius (c. 250). There is evidence to show that the inflation proceeded with unabated violence until wheat reached the dizzy height of more than 300,000 denarii per bushel and was paid for by miserable bits of copper stamped with the value of talents (6,000 denarii) instead of the common unit. It is more than a chance event that the darkness of the Middle Ages followed in the wake of one of the greatest economic cataclysms of history.

The concept of utility which Hobbes and his successors introduced into political science has also dynamic consequences. In recent economic theory this concept has emerged from its obscurity as a vague plaything of the philosophers into a mathematically defined quantity. Although human satisfaction in its use of goods and services has never been precisely measured, its relationship to many economic phenomena is now clearly understood. In recent times there has been introduced a companion concept, that of erratic shocks, which may be regarded as events that reduce the sum total of the utility. And hence we can construct a theory of human behavior, political as well as economic, on the variation over a period of time of the difference between the utility, which measures satisfaction, and the shock, which tends to destroy this satisfaction. While it will be impossible to develop in this volume the mathematical formulation of this intriguing theory, since more mathematics is required than is assumed in this work, we must mention it as one of the dynamic outgrowths of the musings of the utilitarians. In this manner we are able, at least theoretically, to relate the problems of political behavior to the problems of economic variates.

9. Concluding Remarks.

In the foregoing pages of this chapter we have attempted to set the stage for the development of certain phases of political science as a mathematical discipline. We cannot hope to achieve in a short time, or perhaps ever, anything resembling the precision of the physical sciences. For we are dealing with the behavior of human beings, and where this behavior does not depend upon biometric measurements, but rather is a function of the group-will of many men, then we are faced by a complex of causes very difficult to reduce to exact formulation.

But the subject of statistics was developed for precisely this type of problem, where the exact relationships observed in the physical sciences are replaced by the erratic variation of many, and often obscure, factors. Hence our journey into the labyrinth must be along the thread of statistical analysis. Whenever this subject gives us partial relationships, more precisely known as correlations, then we can say with some assurance that we have made some progress in the description and understanding of political events.

It is thus necessary to begin with a study of the elements of statistics. We must achieve an understanding of the laws of probability, and must learn to use methods whereby relationships are discovered between variable factors, and hence are reduced to the precise language of mathematics. With this brief prelude we plunge into the more technical aspects of our subject.

PROBLEMS

1. From the graph of the growth of population in Europe (Figure 2), estimate how rapidly this population has increased during the past fifty years. Compare this with the growth in the first half of the eighteenth century. Is there any relationship between this graph and the estimates that military deaths during the Seven Years' War (1756-1763) totaled 360,000, during the Napoleonic Wars (1790-1815) totaled 2,300,000, and during World War I (1914-1918) totaled 8,500,000?

2. Estimate the annual rate of growth of the population of Europe between 1650 and 1800 from Figure 2. Compare this with the rate of growth since 1800.

3. The following data give the number of major crimes reported in the United States during the years indicated. Given the following population figures for the United States during the years indicated in the table, as respectively: 129,337,000: 131,108,000; 136,497,000; 139,621,000, would you say

POLITICAL SCIENCE AS A STATISTICAL SCIENCE

Nature of the Crime	1937	1939	1943	1945
Murder and non-negligent manslaughter	7,859	7,514	6,517	6,847
Manslaughter by negligence	5,705	4,394	3,464	4,387
Robbery	59,786	55,242	45,263	54,279
Burglary	292,870	311,104	271,894	321,672
Larceny	780,031	872,988	806,325	865,521
Auto theft	215,569	177,997	187,751	241,491
Totals	1,361,820	1,429,239	1,321,214	1,494,197

that there is a significant difference in crime between 1937 and 1939? between 1943 and 1945? How would one account for the per capita difference between the amount of crime reported for the four years given in the table? Is this a problem of political significance?

4. From the index of Spanish trade (Figure 1) make your own interpretation of the internal state of that nation from 1620 to 1650. Was the king, in your opinion, regarded as a great ruler? Compare your interpretation with that of actual history by surveying in some source the events of the reign of Philip IV (1621-1665). Can you account for some of the observed declines in the curve?

5. Referring to Figures 4 and 5, what conclusion would you draw from the similarity in the distribution of income in the Roman and American republics, separated as they are by a period of twenty centuries? Would you expect to find a similar distribution of income in other countries? Would you care to formulate a definite law on the basis of these two cases?

6. From Figures 4 and 5, would one conclude that the curve of the distribution of income depends upon the monetary unit employed in its description? Would it be possible to relate the monetary units of different political countries by giving the amounts necessary to purchase a bushel of wheat in each country? What limitation would such a comparison have? Could monetary units be compared more satisfactorily by giving, instead of wheat, the amount necessary to buy an ounce of gold or silver?

7. What would be your interpretation of the phrase "wolf point" in connection with the distribution of income? Would this wolf point be different for different countries, and for the same country, at different times? What is meant by the term "Midas point"?

8. What does Tolstoy mean by the phrase "homogeneous, infinitesimal, elements" when he says in *War and Peace* (Part xi, Chap. 1): "For, studying the laws of history, we must absolutely change the objects of our observation, leaving kings, ministers, and generals out of the account, and select for study the homogeneous, infinitesimal, elements that regulate the masses. No one can say how far it is given to me to alter by this path an understanding of the laws of history."

9. State two postulates which might belong to a system which defines what is meant by a mechanistic theory of history.

10. Do the words *statics* and *dynamics* have essentially the same meaning in the theory of the social sciences as they do in mechanics? Are there quantities which we might call political force and political energy which are analogous to mechanical force and mechanical energy?

CHAPTER 2
ENUMERATION AND FREQUENCY DISTRIBUTIONS
1. *Measurement.*

IN EVERY SCIENCE we must begin with measurement. The objects with which the science is concerned must be described in numerical terms if progress in understanding them and in determining their relationships with one another, is to be made. Thus, in economics, which is concerned basically with wealth and income, measure must be made of these two quantities. If they are described in terms of dollars, or other monetary units, then the fluctuations in these units must be measured numerically. In political science, the size of different governments is a matter of interest. Various attributes of this size can be described, one, for example, being the number of people governed, another the ratio of the parliamentary units to the population.

Any set of measurements or values, usually recorded in the form of a table, which is the object of scientific study may be referred to as *data*. This word is the plural of *datum*, the Latin for "a thing given"; hence we say: "The data are the basic facts with which any science deals."

No.	Population	No.	Population	No.	Population	No.	Population	No.	Population
1	5,671	14	3,402	27	3,306	40	3,213	53	4,145
2	2,873	15	6,255	28	9,044	41	3,533	54	10,193
3	12,752	16	2,875	29	6,385	42	14,390	55	3,511
4	12,648	17	8,487	30	3,804	43	19,220	56	14,294
5	3,821	18	10,045	31	3,238	44	4,410	57	17,571
6	4,921	19	13,188	32	3,719	45	4,497	58	6,591
7	2,580	20	3,803	33	2,885	46	11,659	59	4,819
8	3,765	21	10,557	34	2,872	47	4,055	60	21,073
9	2,629	22	3,524	35	30,013	48	7,194	61	67,833
10	10,142	23	4,375	36	11,565	49	3,376	62	7,246
11	3,185	24	6,285	37	7,244	50	11,048	63	114,966
12	4,518	25	2,607	38	8,507	51	2,762	64	9,506
13	17,355	26	2,554	39	121,458	52	3,979		
								Total	753,941

As an example, let us consider the above table which gives the population for the 1940 census of all cities in Kansas which exceed 2500. Instead of giving the names we have, for convenience, designated each city by a number.

A few elementary facts will now be derived from a study of this set of data. In the first place, if we observe that the total population of Kansas in 1940 was 1,801,028, then the ratio of the city population to the total population can be computed. This constant, called the *urban concentration,* has been watched with great interest by demographers since it has a vital significance in social, economic, and political changes in the commonwealth.

If we then compute: $c = 753,941/1,801,028 = 0.4186$, we see that approximately 42 per cent of the population dwells in urban communities. Since this is less than the national ratio of 0.5652, we may infer that the state of Kansas is more agricultural than industrial. This follows from the fact that urban concentration is a rough measure of industrial production as contrasted with agricultural production.

Since most data may be understood more readily if they are presented graphically, we now proceed to such a representation. To accomplish this it will be necessary to classify the data. For this purpose we first observe that all but five of the cities have populations under 20,000. We then select a *class range* from 2,500 to 20,000 and divide this into convenient *class intervals.* Although this division is entirely arbitrary, it depends to some extent upon the actual number of items, or the *total frequency,* of the data. Lacking other considerations, we may use the following table as a guide for the number of divisions into which a range is to be divided:

Number of Items	Divisions in Range	No. of Items	Divisions in Range
8	4	128	8
16	5	256	9
32	6	512	10
64	7	1024	11

There is a tendency, however, for the number of divisions of the range to increase with the frequency more rapidly than the one indicated. In the present instance, since there is a large concentra-

ENUMERATION AND FREQUENCY DISTRIBUTIONS

tion in the smaller cities, the class interval should be chosen to bring out this fact. Hence we select a unit of 1000 as the class interval. Since the total number of items is 64, we should have about seven divisions in the range. With intervals of 1000, this would give us a range from 2500 to 9500. But since 67% of the cities lie within this range, we are justified in our selection of the class interval, in spite of the fact that we shall actually divide the total range into 19 intervals.

The next step is to find the frequencies for each interval, and this is accomplished by arranging the items into classes as shown in the following table:

FREQUENCY TABLE

Class Mark	Interval in hundreds	Frequency	Class Mark	Interval in hundreds	Frequency
1	25- 34	15	11	125-134	3
2	35- 44	14	12	135-144	2
3	45- 54	3	13	145-154	0
4	55- 64	4	14	155-164	0
5	65- 74	4	15	165-174	1
6	75- 84	1	16	175-184	1
7	85- 94	2	17	185-194	1
8	95-104	4	18	195-204	0
9	105-114	2	19	over 204	5
10	115-124	2		Total	64

For convenience of designation it is often useful to denote a class interval by a *class mark*. This mark may be merely a number designating the class, or it may be a number which lies within the interval of the class itself. Thus we might have used conveniently the class marks 30, 40, 50, etc., which are mid-values of the respective intervals.

2. *Graphical Representation of Data.*

Whenever possible, it is desirable to represent data graphically. By this means one is able to see the data as a whole and grasp the significance of the collection of items which cannot be appreciated from single items. Numerous devices have been employed for this purpose, such, for example, as pie charts, bar charts, curves, maps, and so on.

The data of the example given in Section 1 are presented in the accompanying charts. Helpful as these devices sometimes are, how-

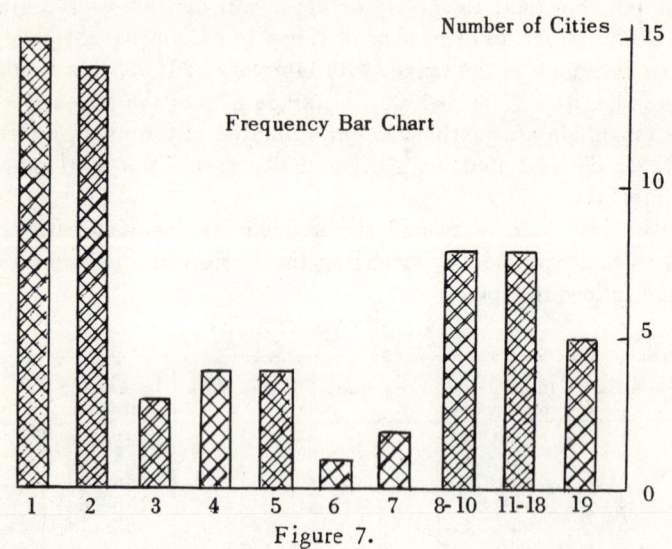

Figure 7.
Bar Chart Showing the Number of Cities in each Urban Class.

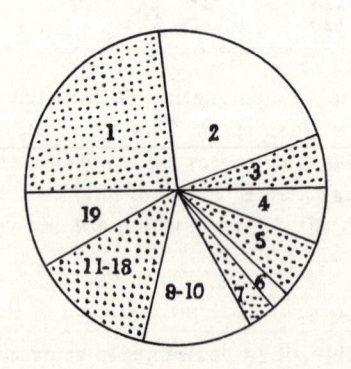

Figure 8.
Pie Chart Showing the Percentage of Cities in each Urban Class.

These per cents, obtained by dividing the number of cities in each class by the total number of cities, are as follows:
(1) 23%, (2) 22%, (3) 5%, (4) 6%, (5) 6%, (6) 2%, (7) 3%, (8) to (10) 12.5%, (11) to (18) 12.5%, (19) 8%.

ENUMERATION AND FREQUENCY DISTRIBUTIONS 33

ever, in the representation of statistical material, the ordinary method of graphing is more important in the ultimate analysis of the data.

The most common method of graphing is that of referring the quantities involved to mutually perpendicular, intersecting straight lines called *axes*. The horizontal axis is customarily referred to as the *x-axis*, the vertical axis as the *y-axis*, and their point of intersection as the *origin*. Convenient intervals are marked off on each axis.

A point is designated by the symbol (a,b), where a indicates the distance along the *x*-axis and b the distance along the *y*-axis. Negative values of a are taken to the left of the origin, and negative

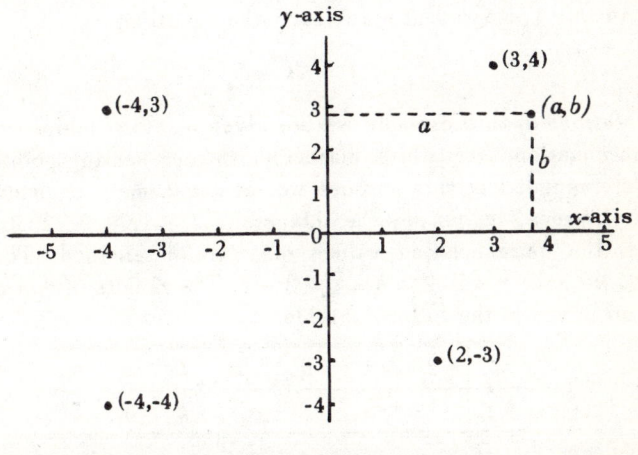

Figure 9.

values of b below the origin. In the figure four points are represented, one in each of the four quadrants into which the plane is divided by the axes.

The quantities a and b are called respectively the *abscissa* and *ordinate* of the point (a,b). The abscissa a and the ordinate b are called the *coordinates* of the point. They are sometimes referred to as *rectangular Cartesian coordinates* after René Descartes (1596-1650), who first introduced them in his famous essay *La Géométrie* published in 1637.

Letting $x_1, x_2, \ldots, x_n$, denote n values of x, and $y_1, y_2, \ldots, y_n$, the corresponding values of y, one may record them in tabular form:

Values of x	x_1	x_2	x_3	...	x_n
Values of y	y_1	y_2	y_3	...	y_n

The number pairs, (x_1,y_1), (x_2,y_2), (x_3,y_3),..., (x_n,y_n), may then be plotted as points, and this succession of points when connected by lines makes a graph. When there is some exact relationship between x and y, these points will not be entirely random ones, but will be found to be so arranged that a smooth curve can be drawn through them.

Let us consider a few examples, which will illustrate the theory and practice of graphical representation.

Example 1. Represent graphically the equation,

$$y = 2x - 3.$$

Solution: In this example we are given a relationship, expressed by an equation, from which number pairs representing points are to be determined. For this purpose we let x assume a sequence of arbitrary values, let us say the integers: $-2, -1, 0, 1, 2, 3, 4$, from which the corresponding values of y are determined. Thus when $x = 2$, we have $y = 2 \cdot 2 - 3 = 4 - 3 = 1$. The results of this computation are given in the following table:

x	-2	-1	0	1	2	3	4
y	-7	-5	-3	-1	1	3	5

When these points are graphed and connected by a line, we see that the equation represents the straight line shown in the accompanying Figure 10.

This example illustrates how equations can be given graphical representation. Many scientific laws are formulated in terms of equations and it is often convenient to present them in the form of a graph.

One should also observe that scales used on the two axes may be different. This will usually be the case in application since y and x in general will represent different quantities.

Example 2. Represent graphically the values given in the following table, where we assume that Y has the same value for $-t$ as for $+t$:

ENUMERATION AND FREQUENCY DISTRIBUTIONS

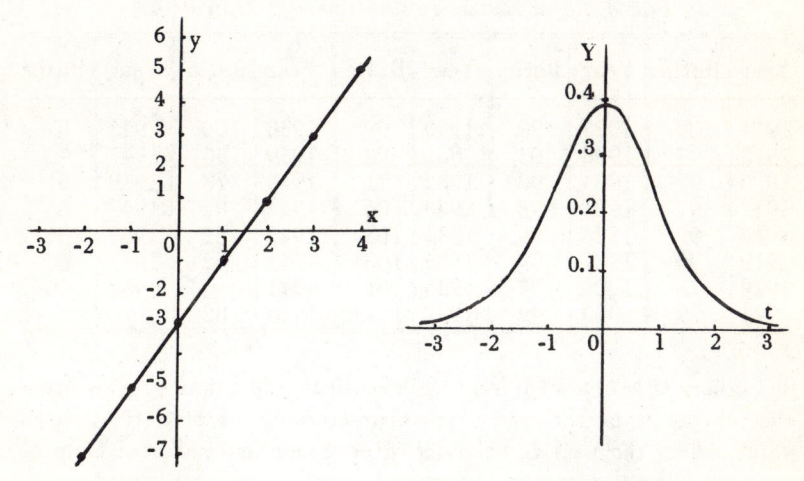

Figure 10.

Figure 11.

t	Y	t	Y	t	Y	t	Y
0.0	3.99	0.4	3.68	0.8	2.90	2.0	0.54
0.1	3.97	0.5	3.52	0.9	2.66	2.5	0.18
0.2	3.91	0.6	3.33	1.0	2.42	3.0	0.04
0.3	3.81	0.7	3.12	1.5	1.30	3.5	0.01

Solution: In this example the abscissa values are designated by t and the ordinates by Y. Convenient intervals are now selected to obtain a graph which has pleasing proportions, that is to say, where the greatest ordinate is not too large for the maximum width of the horizontal range. The points are now graphed and connected by a smooth curve as shown in Figure 11.

The curve thus represented is called the *normal curve of error*, since the deviations in the measurement of a given object were found to be represented by this mathematical figure.

Example 3. The following table gives the ratio of exchange between the English pound and the American dollar, reduced to a par value of 100 in 1914. Represent graphically the fluctuations in the exchange rate of the two currencies.

The graph in Figure 12 differs from those of the previous examples, since it is derived from a table of statistical data, whereas

POLITICAL STATISTICS

Pound-dollar Exchange Rate, par = 100 in 1914.

Year	Ratio	Year	Ratio	Year	Ratio	Year	Ratio	Year	Ratio
1914	100	1922	90	1930	99	1938	100	1946	82
1915	97	1923	93	1931	92	1939	90	1947	-
1916	97	1924	90	1932	71	1940	78	1948	81
1917	97	1925	98	1933	86	1941	82	1949	56
1918	97	1926	99	1934	103	1942	82	1950	56
1919	90	1927	99	1935	100	1943	82	1951	56
1920	75	1928	99	1936	101	1944	-	1952	56
1921	79	1929	99	1937	101	1945	82		

the others are obtained from mathematical expressions. The irregular character of the curve is characteristic of statistical data which reflect the varying behavior of economic and political factors.

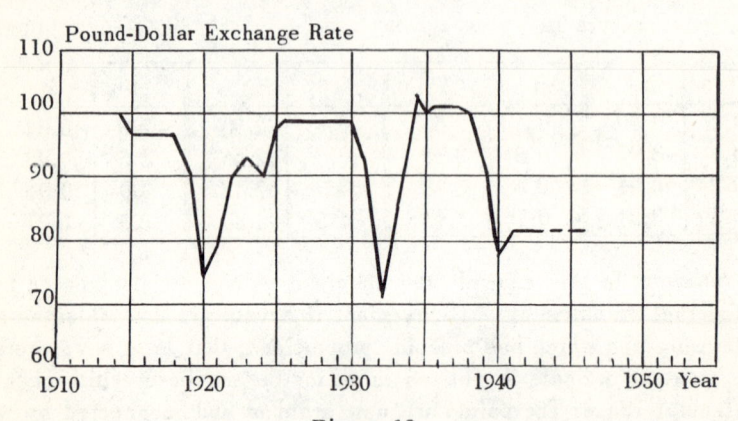

Figure 12.

From this graph one may derive at a glance an appreciation of the violent international events of the last third of a century. The first dip in the curve terminating in 1920 was a reflection of the impact of World War I upon international affairs, the second dip ending in 1932 shows the world-wide character of the great depression which began with the collapse of the American stock market in 1929, and the third dip marks the first phase of the economic effects of World War II. This graph is an example of a statistical *time series* which we shall study in more detail later.

PROBLEMS

1. The following table gives the population of the cities (designated by number) in Colorado which equal or exceed 2500 (1940 census):

No.	Population	No.	Population	No.	Population	No.	Population
1	5,613	9	5,887	17	7,040	25	52,162
2	3,437	10	9,680	18	4,445	26	3,494
3	12,958	11	2,632	19	3,232	27	4,969
4	4,029	12	12,251	20	4,774	28	7,411
5	6,690	13	4,884	21	7,406	29	13,223
6	36,789	14	3,175	22	6,145	30	5,855
7	3,717	15	12,479	23	3,208		
8	322,412	16	15,995	24	4,764	Total	590,756

Form a frequency table for these data and represent them by means of a bar chart.

2. Form a pie chart for the data of problem 1.

3. Given that the total population of Colorado in 1940 was 1,123,296 compute the urban concentration. Compare this with the urban concentration in Kansas. Does the difference seem significant? How can one account for the difference?

4. How many class marks should one choose for a frequency distribution of 100? of 300? of 500? of 2000? How does the range of the data modify the choice of the number of class marks?

5. If the range of 200 items was from $x = 10$ to $x = 60$, what would be the best choice for the number of class marks?

6. Given $y = 3x - 2$, form a table of values and graph the equation.

7. Show that the graphs of $y = 2x + 1$ and $y = -\frac{1}{2}x + 3$ are perpendicular straight lines.

8. In 297 cities the following number of telephones per 100 inhabitants was reported:

No. of telephones:	4	6	8	10	12	14	16	18	20	22	24
No. of cities:	5	19	37	60	70	39	35	17	10	3	2

Represent these data graphically.

9. Form a table for the equation: $y = 2x^2 - 3x + 1$ and represent it graphically.

10. The data below give the urban concentration in per cents since 1820:

Year	1820	1830	1840	1850	1860	1870	1880	1890	1900	1910	1920	1930	1940
% Urban	7.0	8.4	11.6	16.8	20.8	26.2	29.6	35.4	40.0	45.8	51.4	56.2	56.5

Represent these data graphically. Does urban concentration appear to be continuing? At its present rate when will the country be 80% urban? Does this increase in concentration have political significance?

3. Frequency Distributions.

In the first section of this chapter some preliminary ideas were presented about frequency distributions. Since this is one of the basic concepts of the statistical method we shall find it desirable to extend our knowledge of this subject.

In order that we may have a basic set of data to analyze we shall consider the following table which gives the percentages of the Republicans and the Democrats in the House of Representatives since the founding of the Republican party in 1856. The column marked R gives the per cent of Republicans in the House, the column marked D gives the per cent of Democrats, and the column x shows the difference R − D, which will be the special object of our study.*

Political Composition of the House of Representatives since the Thirty-Fifth Congress (1857) Expressed in Per Cent of Republicans (R) and Per Cent of Democrats (D) of the Total Membership.

Congress	Year	R	D	x = R - D	Congress	Year	R	D	x = R - D
35	1857	39	55	-16	58	1903	54	46	8
36	1859	48	43	5	59	1905	65	35	30
37	1861	60	24	36	60	1907	58	42	16
38	1863	55	40	15	61	1909	56	44	12
39	1865	78	22	56	62	1911	41	58	-17
40	1867	74	26	48	63	1913	29	67	-38
41	1869	66	34	32	64	1915	44	53	- 9
42	1871	56	42	14	65	1917	50	48	2
43	1873	65	31	34	66	1919	54	44	10
44	1875	39	61	-22	67	1921	69	30	39
45	1877	48	52	- 4	68	1923	52	48	4
46	1879	44	51	- 7	69	1925	57	42	15
47	1881	50	47	3	70	1927	54	45	9
48	1883	38	61	-23	71	1929	62	38	24
49	1885	37	63	-26	72	1931	49	50	- 1
50	1887	47	52	- 5	73	1933	27	72	-45
51	1889	52	47	5	74	1935	24	74	-50
52	1891	26	69	-43	75	1937	20	77	-57
53	1893	35	62	-27	76	1939	39	60	-21
54	1895	69	29	40	77	1941	37	61	-24
55	1897	58	38	20	78	1943	48	51	- 3
56	1899	52	46	6	79	1945	44	56	-12
57	1901	55	43	12	80	1947	57	43	14

*The percentages in this table do not always total 100, since in some years one or more minor parties polled a significant number of votes.

ENUMERATION AND FREQUENCY DISTRIBUTIONS

In this table we find the political composition of 46 Congresses and we observe that the sign of the quantity $x = R - D$ shows which of the two parties was in power. When the sign is negative the Democrats have a majority and when the sign is positive the Republicans dominate. The magnitude of x indicates the size of the majority.

We thus observe that the Democrats were in power in 20 Congresses and the Republicans in 26. The magnitude of x varies from −57 in 1937 to +56 in 1865. The total range is thus 113 and we now propose to make a frequency distribution for x which will show how the political power varied from one party to another. For this purpose we first set up 12 class intervals, 10 units in length, from −60 at one extreme to +60 at the other. We then distribute the congresses with respect to these classes with the result given in the following table:

Frequency Table of Per Cents (I)

Class Interval	Frequency	Class Interval	Frequency
−60 to −50	2	0 to 9	8
−49 to −40	2	10 to 19	8
−39 to −30	1	20 to 29	2
−29 to −20	6	30 to 39	5
−19 to −10	3	40 to 49	2
− 9 to 0	6	50 to 60	1
		Total (N)	46

But a survey of this table shows no characteristic frequency pattern and we thus reach the conclusion that we have used too many intervals. Consulting the Division Table of Section 1 we see that for a total frequency of 46 items we should not use more than 7 classes. Hence, we combine the classes by doubling the class interval and thus obtain the following table:

Frequency Table of Per Cents (II)

Class Mark	Class Interval	Frequency
1	−50 and lower	2
2	−49 to −30	3
3	−29 to −10	9
4	− 9 to 9	14
5	10 to 29	10
6	30 to 49	7
7	50 and over	1
	Total (N)	46

In the column of frequencies we now observe the existence of a *central tendency* of the data. By this we mean that there is a tendency for the frequencies to cluster about a class mark near the midpoint of the range. This characteristic of frequency distributions will be discussed later.

If the data are now represented graphically in a frequency chart, the central tendency is immediately evident. From the approximate symmetry of the figure we are able to conclude that there has been no marked tendency over the years for one political party to remain in control of the House of Representatives.

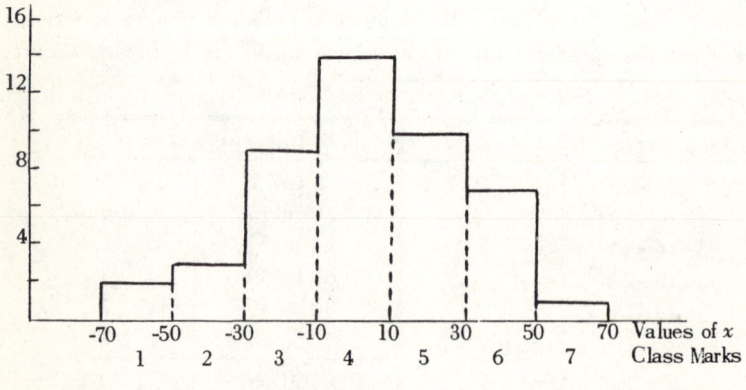

Figure 13.

In this representation of frequencies we observe a difference from the method of graphing discussed in Section 2, where ordinates are given by a single line. Here the frequencies are represented by a rectangle, the base of which is the class interval and the height is equal numerically to the value of the frequency. The diagram thus formed by these frequency rectangles is called a *histogram*. Such a diagram has the advantage that the area included by the figure is equal to the total frequency.

The reasonably symmetric frequency distribution exhibited by the preceding example is not always obtained from the measurement of quantities studied by statistical methods. One example of what is called a *skewed* frequency distribution is found in our previous study of urban populations. Another such tendency to skewness is exhibited by the data in the following table which gives the size of the State Legislatures in the various states.

ENUMERATION AND FREQUENCY DISTRIBUTIONS 41

Size of State Legislatures (1947)

Number	State	Senate	Repre.	Number	State	Senate	Repre.
1	Alabama	35	106	25	Nebraska	Unicameral	with 43
2	Arizona	19	58	26	Nevada	17	45
3	Arkansas	35	100	27	New Hampshire	24	400
4	California	40	80	28	New Jersey	21	60
5	Colorado	35	65	29	New Mexico	24	49
6	Connecticut	36	272	30	New York	56	150
7	Delaware	17	35	31	North Carolina	50	120
8	Florida	38	95	32	North Dakota	53	113
9	Georgia	52	105	33	Ohio	36	138
10	Idaho	44	59	34	Oklahoma	44	120
11	Illinois	51	153	35	Oregon	30	60
12	Indiana	50	100	36	Pennsylvania	50	208
13	Iowa	50	108	37	Rhode Island	44	100
14	Kansas	40	125	38	South Carolina	46	124
15	Kentucky	38	100	39	South Dakota	35	75
16	Louisiana	39	100	40	Tennessee	33	99
17	Maine	33	151	41	Texas	31	150
18	Maryland	29	123	42	Utah	23	60
19	Massachusetts	40	240	43	Vermont	30	241
20	Michigan	32	100	44	Virginia	40	100
21	Minnesota	67	131	45	Washington	46	99
22	Mississippi	49	140	46	West Virginia	32	94
23	Missouri	35	154	47	Wisconsin	33	100
24	Montana	56	90	48	Wyoming	27	55
	Totals (Omitting Nebraska)					1785	5550

From these data we observe that the size of the legislative bodies in the different states varies widely. Thus the House of Representatives is 35 in Delaware and 400 in New Hampshire, while the Senate varies from 17 in Nevada and Delaware to 67 in Minnesota. This difference can be shown readily by a frequency histogram.

In order to construct the histogram we first form the following table of frequencies for the House of Representatives:

Class Marks:	1	2	3	4	5	6	7	8	9
Class Intervals:	30-59	60-89	90-119	120-149	150-179	180-209	210-239	240-269	over 269
Frequencies:	6	6	17	8	5	1	0	2	2

When these frequencies are graphed as shown in Figure 14 we observe that, although there is a central tendency for the House to have

Figure 14.

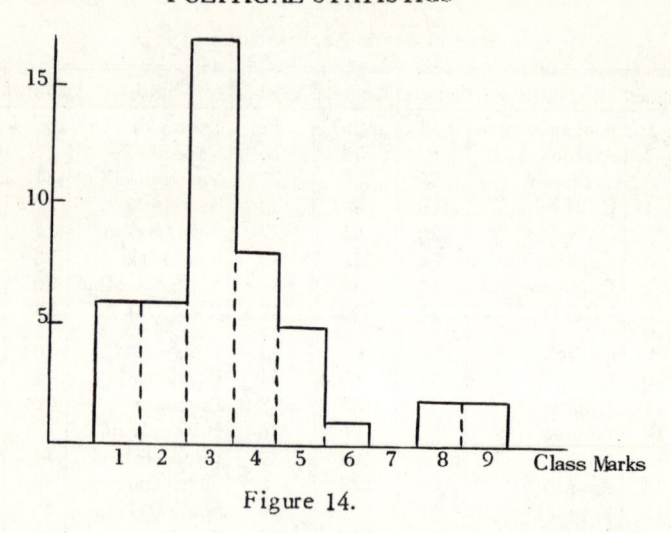

Histogram Showing Distribution in Size of State Houses of Representatives. Each Class Mark Corresponds to 30 Members.

a membership between 90 and 120, there is also a wide variation from this norm.

4. *Binomial Frequencies.*

A norm with which many statistical frequency distributions may be compared is derived from the terms of the expansion of the binomial

$$(a + b)^n.$$

A few expansions of this expression are given below as follows:

$(a + b)^2 = a^2 + 2ab + b^2,$
$(a + b)^3 = a^3 + 3a^2b + 3ab^2 + b^3,$
$(a + b)^4 = a^4 + 4a^3b + 6a^2b^2 + 4ab^3 + b^4,$
$(a + b)^5 = a^5 + 5a^4b + 10a^3b^2 + 10a^2b^3 + 5ab^4 + b^5,$
$(a + b)^6 = a^6 + 6a^5b + 15a^4b^2 + 20a^3b^3 + 15a^2b^4 + 6ab^5 + b^6.$

The coefficients of the terms in these expansions are called *binomial coefficients*. Thus the numbers 1, 4, 6, 4, 1 are the binomial coefficients corresponding to the *exponent* 4.

It is customary to designate the binomial coefficients corresponding to the exponent n by the symbol, $_nC_r$, where r has the succession

ENUMERATION AND FREQUENCY DISTRIBUTIONS 43

of values $0, 1, 2, \ldots, n$. Thus when $n = 4$, we have: $_4C_0 = 1$, $_4C_1 = 4$, $_4C_2 = 6$, $_4C_3 = 4$, $_4C_4 = 1$.

In the following table we record the binomial coefficients corresponding to values of n from 1 to 12:

TABLE OF BINOMIAL COEFFICIENTS, $_nC_r$

n/r	0	1	2	3	4	5	6	7	8	9	10	11	12	Total (N)
1	1	1												2
2	1	2	1											4
3	1	3	3	1										8
4	1	4	6	4	1									16
5	1	5	10	10	5	1								32
6	1	6	15	20	15	6	1							64
7	1	7	21	35	35	21	7	1						128
8	1	8	28	56	70	56	28	8	1					256
9	1	9	36	84	126	126	84	36	9	1				512
10	1	10	45	120	210	252	210	120	45	10	1			1024
11	1	11	55	165	330	462	462	330	165	55	11	1		2048
12	1	12	66	220	495	792	924	792	495	220	66	12	1	4096

If we introduce the factorial notation, then these coefficients can be expressed in a simple form. Thus we define $2!$ (read "factorial two") to equal $1 \cdot 2$; $3!$ (read "factorial three") $= 1 \cdot 2 \cdot 3 = 6$; $4! = 1 \cdot 2 \cdot 3 \cdot 4 = 24$; and, in general,

$$n! \text{ (read ``factorial } n\text{'')} = 1 \cdot 2 \cdot 3 \cdots n.$$

In terms of this notation the general binomial coefficient can be written:

$$_nC_r = \frac{n!}{(n-r)! \, r!}.$$

For example, we have

$$_7C_3 = \frac{7!}{(7-3)! \, 3!} = \frac{1 \cdot 2 \cdot 3 \cdot 4 \cdot 5 \cdot 6 \cdot 7}{(1 \cdot 2 \cdot 3 \cdot 4)(1 \cdot 2 \cdot 3)} = 35.$$

The relationship of the binomial coefficients to the subject of statistical frequency distributions is shown in the following diagram in which a histogram is formed from the binomial coefficients corresponding to $n = 8$. This histogram is a norm with which frequency distributions of 9 class marks can be compared.

Values of $_8C_r$

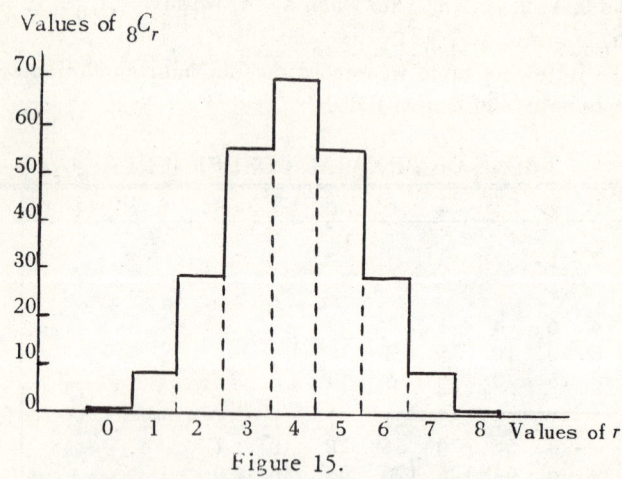

Figure 15.
Binomial Frequency Distribution.

In order to illustrate the comparison of a binomial frequency distribution with one obtained from statistical data, let us compare the first frequency table of Section 3 (Composition of the House of Representatives) with the binomial frequency distribution for $n = 6$. Since the total frequency in the statistical table is 46 and that for the binomial frequency distribution is 64, we reduce all the binomial frequencies in the ratio $46/64 = 0.71875$. We thus obtain the comparison shown in the following table:

Class Marks	Frequencies (Comp. of House)	Frequencies (Binomial Coeff.)
0	2	1
1	3	4
2	9	11
3	14	14
4	10	11
5	7	4
6	1	1
Total	46	46

PROBLEMS

1. The following table gives the number of representatives in the House of Representatives for each state (indicated by number). Make a frequency distribution for these 48 items and represent it graphically. Since 41 of the states have fewer than 15 representatives, what units should be used for the

ENUMERATION AND FREQUENCY DISTRIBUTIONS

State	Number of Representatives	State	Number of Repres.	State	Number of Repres.	State	Number of Repres.
1	9	13	8	25	4	37	2
2	2	14	6	26	1	38	6
3	7	15	9	27	2	39	2
4	23	16	8	28	14	40	10
5	4	17	3	29	2	41	21
6	6	18	6	30	45	42	2
7	1	19	14	31	12	43	1
8	6	20	17	32	2	44	9
9	10	21	9	33	23	45	6
10	2	22	7	34	8	46	6
11	26	23	13	35	4	47	10
12	11	24	2	36	33	48	1
						Total	435

range? Can those in excess of 15 representatives be placed in the class 15 or greater?

2. Make a frequency distribution for the data of problem 8, section 2. Compare this with the binomial frequency corresponding to $n = 10$ where the frequencies have been reduced by multiplying by the factor $297/1024 = 0.29$.

3. Compute the values of $_8C_3$, $_9C_5$, $_{11}C_4$.

4. Show that the sum of the binomial frequencies corresponding to an integral value n is equal to 2^n.

5. Ten coins were tossed 1024 times and the following frequencies observed. Graph this distribution. Compare it with the binomial frequency distribution corresponding to $n = 10$.

No. of heads	0	1	2	3	4	5	6	7	8	9	10
Frequencies	2	10	38	106	188	257	226	128	59	7	3

5. *Ogives or Cumulative Frequency Curves.*

One type of graphical representation of frequencies is the so-called *ogive* or *cumulative frequency curve*. The ordinates of such a curve are formed from a given frequency distribution by the addition of successive frequencies.

Thus the ogive corresponding to Table II of Section 3 is formed from the accumulated frequency distribution shown in the following table:

Class Mark	Frequency	Accumulated Frequency
1	2	2
2	3	5
3	9	14
4	14	28
5	10	38
6	7	45
7	1	46

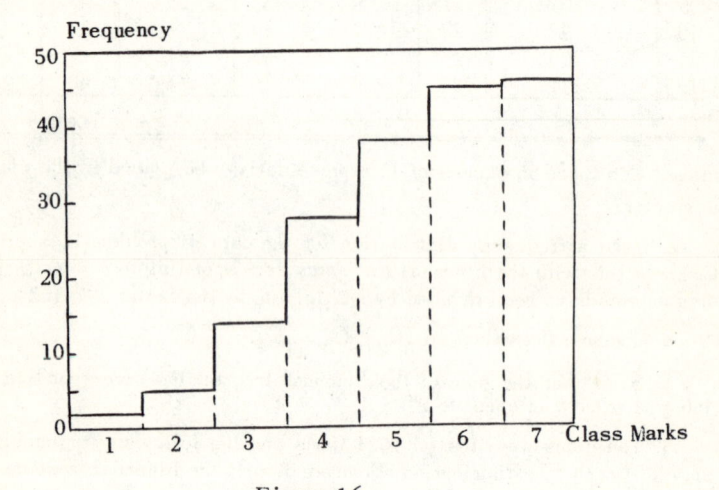

Figure 16.
Ogive of Composition of House of Representatives.

One may observe from this ogive that the frequencies of the original distribution are the differences of successive frequencies of the ogive. This is a useful property when an ogive is given and one desires to reconstruct the original set of frequencies.

A very useful form of ogive is that in which percentage frequencies are used. In this case each accumulated frequency is reduced to a per cent of the total frequency and these per cents are graphed. With such ogives it is possible to compare distributions in which the frequencies differ widely from one another in absolute values.

In some cases it is also desirable to reduce the class marks to a percentage basis. This would be the case where one wished to compare ogives with different ranges of the class marks. This reduction

ENUMERATION AND FREQUENCY DISTRIBUTIONS

to percentages is accomplished by dividing each class mark by the total range. An ogive in which both the frequencies and the class marks are given in per cents is called a *Lorenz curve*.

For illustration let us compare the ogive of the binomial frequency corresponding to $n = 10$ with the ogive of what is called a rectangular frequency distribution, namely, one in which all the frequencies are equal. The two frequency distributions, their ogive values, and the corresponding ratios of both the class marks and the accumulated frequencies are given in the following table:

Class Marks	Binomial Distribution				Rectangular Distribution		
Class Marks	Class Mark Ratios	Freq.	Accumulated Frequencies	Ratios of Acc. Freq.	Freq.	Accumulated Frequencies	Ratios of Acc. Freq.
0	0.091	1	1	0.001	100	100	0.091
1	0.182	10	11	0.011	100	200	0.182
2	0.273	45	56	0.055	100	300	0.273
3	0.364	120	176	0.172	100	400	0.364
4	0.455	210	386	0.377	100	500	0.455
5	0.545	252	638	0.623	100	600	0.545
6	0.636	210	848	0.828	100	700	0.636
7	0.727	120	968	0.945	100	800	0.727
8	0.818	45	1013	0.989	100	900	0.818
9	0.909	10	1023	0.999	100	1000	0.909
10	1.000	1	1024	1.000	100	1100	1.000

The two ogives are represented graphically in Figure 17. One observes from this that a rectangular frequency appears as a straight line which forms the diagonal of the square. The ogive of the binomial frequency, however, lies below this line in the first part of the diagram and above it in the second part.

In Figure 18 we have shown the percentage ogives or Lorenz curves for (1) the size of State Houses of Representatives and (2) the composition of the National House of Representatives. The second, as we have seen earlier, is nearly a binomial distribution, while the first is a skewed distribution. This departure from a binomial frequency distribution is immediately seen from the ogive.

PROBLEMS

1. Make an ogive for the binomial frequency distribution corresponding to $n = 6$. Does this correspond with the one given in the text for $n = 10$?

POLITICAL STATISTICS

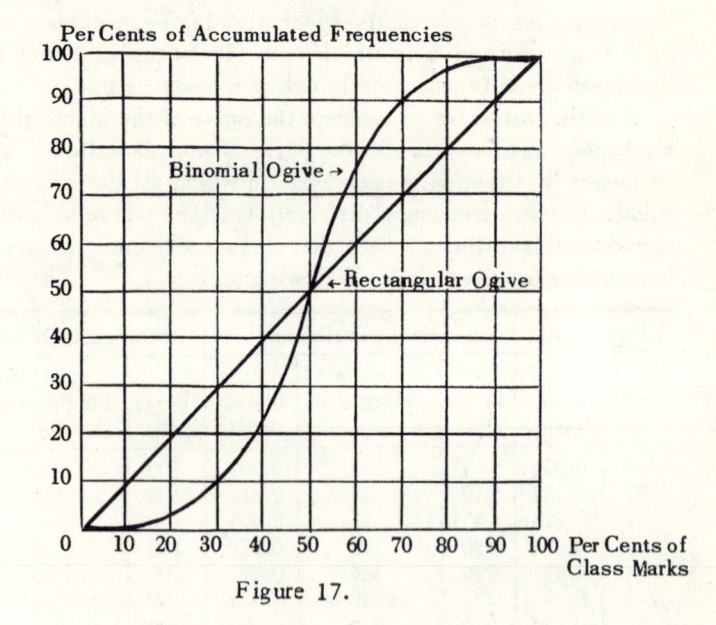

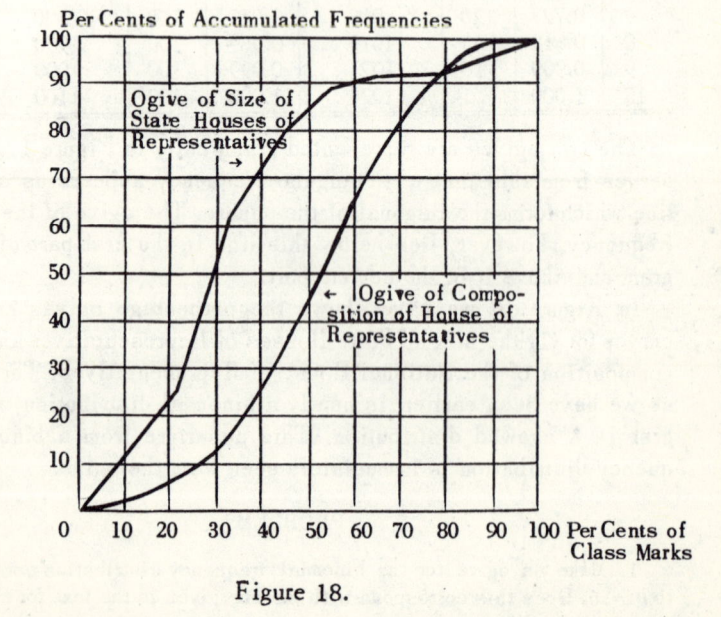

Figure 17.

Figure 18.

ENUMERATION AND FREQUENCY DISTRIBUTIONS

2. Make an ogive for the following rectangular distribution:

Class Marks	1	2	3	4	5	6	7	8	9	10
Frequencies	10	10	10	10	10	10	10	10	10	10

3. Construct an ogive for the data of problem 8, Section 2.

4. Make an ogive for the frequency distribution obtained from the data of problem 1, Section 4.

5. Make a pie chart showing the following original sources of funds for social services in Cook County, Illinois.*

Means of Financing	Funds
Taxes on Commodities, Sales or Services	$68,359,794.
Taxes Measured by Income	36,266,169.
Taxes Measured by Value of Property	27,483,494.
Other Revenues	7,141,007.
Other Means of Financing	29,953,985.

6. Represent by means of a bar chart the following data showing the percentage of revenue from specific sources for the state of Illinois.* Can small sources be put together in the one classification of miscellaneous?

Type of Tax with Percentage of Revenue from Specified Sources
(Illinois, 1938)

Gasoline Tax	20.74%	Property	0.70%	Severance	
Gross Receipts, Sales, etc.	42.80	Inheritance	4.44	Tobacco	
Net Income		Utilities	6.10	License	1.83%
Motor Vehicle	11.19	Insurance	4.66	Bank	
Alcoholic Beverage	5.84	Franchise	1.64	Stock Transfer	
				All Other	.06

*Source: *Who Pays for Social Services* by Carl H. Chatters.

CHAPTER 3
THE CENTRAL TENDENCIES OF DATA
1. *Averages.*

ONE OF THE FIRST problems in statistical analysis is to exhibit the central tendency of data, that is to say, the tendency of data to conform to some characteristic value or values. Thus, if a new state were admitted to the Union, it might be of interest to those framing its constitution to know what is the most characteristic size of the legislatures of the other states as a guide to their own decision in this matter. This characteristic size, if such exists, would be shown by the tendency of other legislative bodies to conform to it.

The measurement of central tendency is by means of *averages*. Although there are, in fact, a number of averages which are recognized in statistics, we shall consider only four of them. These are: (1) the *arithmetic mean*, which we shall designate by A; (2) the *median*, designated by M; (3) the *mode*, designated by Mo; (4) and the *root-mean-square*, or *quadratic mean*, designated by R.

These averages all have their own special uses, as will appear in the ensuing discussion. Other averages, which have a limited application in statistical analysis, are the *geometric mean* and the *harmonic mean*.

In order to have a common example to illustrate the various methods of averaging we shall use the frequency distribution discussed in Section 3 of the preceding chapter, namely, the political composition of the House of Representatives. For the sake of ready reference the values of x (Table A) and the table of frequencies derived from it (Table B) are repeated below:

Table A

Congress	x	Con.	x	Con.	x	Con.	x	Con.	x	Con.	x	Con.	x
35	-16	41	32	47	3	53	-27	59	30	65	2	71	24	77	-24
36	5	42	14	48	-23	54	40	60	16	66	10	72	-1	78	-3
37	36	43	34	49	-26	55	20	61	12	67	39	73	-45	79	-12
38	15	44	-22	50	-5	56	6	62	-17	68	4	74	-50	80	14
39	56	45	-4	51	5	57	12	63	-38	69	15	75	-57
40	48	46	-7	52	-43	58	8	64	-9	70	9	76	-21

THE CENTRAL TENDENCIES OF DATA

Table B

Class Interval	Class Mark (x)	Frequency (f)
-50 and lower	-60	2
-49 to -30	-40	3
-29 to -10	-20	9
- 9 to 9	0	14
10 to 29	20	10
30 to 49	40	7
50 and over	60	1

2. *The Arithmetic Mean.*

The arithmetic mean is the most commonly used average and is generally what is referred to when one speaks of the average price, average size, average income, etc. The arithmetic average of a set of items is merely their sum divided by their number. Thus the arithmetic average of the numbers 2, 4, 7, 12, and 15 is $2 + 4 + 7 + 12 + 15 = 40$, divided by 5, that is, $A = 8$.

More generally, for the items in the following table:

Class Marks	x_1	x_2	$x_3 \cdots x_n$
Frequencies	f_1	f_2	$f_3 \cdots f_n$

the *arithmetic mean* is, by definition, the value of the class mark obtained from the formula:

$$A = \frac{f_1 x_1 + f_2 x_2 + f_3 x_3 + \cdots + f_n x_n}{N} \tag{1}$$

where N, the total frequency, is the sum: $N = f_1 + f_2 + f_3 + \cdots + f_n$.

It will be convenient for us to make use of the symbol Σ, the Greek letter capital sigma, which is employed throughout mathematics to denote summation. Thus we may write $\Sigma f_i x_i$, or simply Σfx, to designate the sum: $f_1 x_1 + f_2 x_2 + f_3 x_3 + \cdots + f_n x_n$, or the symbol $\Sigma f_i x_i^2$, sometimes abbreviated to Σfx^2, to represent: $f_1 x_1^2 + f_2 x_2^2 + f_3 x_3^2 + \cdots + f_n x_n^2$. The subscript, i, is used in the summation symbol to designate the quantities to which the summation applies. Thus, if the frequencies were all equal, let us say to a constant f, then we would have: $\Sigma f_i x_i = \Sigma f x_i = f \Sigma x_i$.

It is sometimes convenient in the summation symbol to indicate the beginning term and the final term. Thus the symbol

$$\sum_{i=1}^{n} f_i x_i$$

means that the summation starts with $i = 1$ and ends with $i = n$, that is to say, $f_1 x_1$ is the first term and $f_n x_n$ is the last term. Thus we can indicate the sum: $3^3 + 4^3 + 5^3 + \cdots + 20^3$ by the symbol

$$\sum_{x=3}^{20} x^3.$$

When no ambiguity exists as to the quantity which is being summed, or as to the first and last terms, it is usually convenient to omit the limits of summation from the symbol.

In terms of the summation symbol we can write the arithmetic mean as follows:

$$A = \frac{\Sigma f_i x_i}{N}.$$

Example 1. Compute the average value of x given in Table A.

Solution. We add the values of x and divide by 46, the number of items. That is,

$$A = \frac{\Sigma x}{N} = \frac{-16 + 5 + 36 + \cdots + 14}{46} = \frac{59}{46} = 1.28.$$

Example 2. Compute the average value of x from the values in Table B.

Solution. In this case we make use of formula (1) in which the class marks are the average values of the class intervals. The work can be arranged in tabular form as follows:

Class Marks (x)	Frequency (f)	Product (fx)
-60	2	-120
-40	3	-120
-20	9	-180
0	14	0
20	10	200
40	7	280
60	1	60
Totals	46	120

THE CENTRAL TENDENCIES OF DATA   53

The arithmetic mean is then computed from the totals as follows:

$$A = \frac{120}{46} = 2.61.$$

We observe that there is a small difference between the averages as determined from the two tables. This difference is occasioned by the fact that mean values for the class intervals are substituted for the actual values of the items within the intervals. If the choice of class intervals has been properly made this difference is not statistically significant. A more precise interpretation of this statement will be made later in the book.

PROBLEMS

1. Write in contracted form the series: $1^2 + 2^2 + 3^2 + 4^2 + 5^2$.

2. Expand the symbol: $\sum_{n=1}^{5} n$.

3. Find the arithmetic average of the numbers: 5, 7, 5, 8, 6, 4, 4, 4, 3, 1.

4. Find the arithmetic average of the numbers in Problem 3, first arranging them in the form of a frequency table.   *Ans. A = 4.7.*

5. Compute the arithmetic average of the following data:

Frequency	2	4	8	10	10	6	3
Class Marks	-4	-2	-1	0	2	3	5

Ans. A = 0.67.

6. Arrange the following data in the form of a frequency table and compute the arithmetic average:

1	14	16	18	12	18	11	13	18	19
0	2	4	5	6	8	5	15	15	20
7	1	12	13	1	10	0	9	10	18
8	7	17	6	14	13	2	4	13	12
4	11	8	6	5	1	8	6	0	6
2	9	17	17	3	20	16	1	17	13
9	3	19	5	2	6	11	16	9	9
4	9	8	11	15	9	14	15	9	20

Ans. A = 9.63.

7. Nevada in 1940 had five cities over 2500 population in size. From these populations compute the average size of the five cities: 4,094; 4,140; 8,422; 21,317; 5,318.   *Ans. 8,658.*

8. Twenty-seven states impose limits upon the length of their legislative session. These limits in days are as follows: 70, 60, 60, 130, 60, 60, 70, 60, 61, 50, 60, 60, 90, 90, 60, 60, 60, 60, 60, 40, 60, 75, 60, 60, 60, 60, 40. Find the average length of the sessions.   *Ans. 64.30.*

9. In Problem 8, Section 2, Chapter 2, the number of telephones per 100 inhabitants in 297 cities was reported. From the data given there compute the average number per city. *Ans.* 12.11.

10. In Section 3, Chapter 2, the following table of frequencies for the House of Representatives is given:

Class Marks	1	2	3	4	5	6	7	8	9
Class Interval	30-59	60-89	90-119	120-149	150-179	180-209	210-239	240-269	over 269
Frequencies	6	6	17	8	5	1	0	2	2

From this table compute the average value of the class marks. *Ans.* 3.53.

3. Simplifications in the Computation of the Arithmetic Mean.

Certain simplifications can be effected in the computation of the arithmetic mean by changing the class marks to ones more convenient for computation.

Thus, if a constant quantity denoted by X is subtracted from each class mark, and if an average is computed in terms of the new class marks, namely $x_i - X$, the arithmetic mean of the original data is merely the computed average increased by X. In symbolic form this statement becomes,

$$A = X + \frac{\Sigma f_i(x_i - X)}{N}. \tag{1}$$

The proof follows from the identity,

$$\frac{\Sigma f_i(x_i - X)}{N} = \frac{\Sigma f_i x_i}{N} - \frac{X \Sigma f_i}{N} = A - X,$$

since $\Sigma f_i = N$.

By choosing X to be some value near the mean, the labor of calculation is often materially reduced. Also, if one wishes to avoid the use of negative class marks, the selection of a proper value for X, since it can be any number positive or negative, will convert all the class marks into positive quantities. Thus in Table B, let us add 60 to each class mark, which is, in effect, subtracting $X = -60$ from each of the values. We then compute A as follows:

THE CENTRAL TENDENCIES OF DATA

Class Mark (x_i)	Frequency (f_i)	$x_i - X$	$f_i(x_i - X)$
-60	2	0	0
-40	3	20	60
-20	9	40	360
0	14	60	840
20	10	80	800
40	7	100	700
60	1	120	120
Totals	46		2880

From these totals we then compute:

$$A = -60 + \frac{2880}{46} = -60 + 62.61 = 2.61,$$

which agrees with our previous calculation.

It is also convenient sometimes to change from one set of class marks to another. If we denote the first class marks by x_i and the second class marks by y_i, the frequency table would appear as follows:

Class Marks (x_i)	x_1	x_2	x_3	$x_4 \ldots x_n$
Class Marks (y_i)	y_1	y_2	y_3	$y_4 \ldots y_n$
Frequencies (f_i)	f_1	f_2	f_3	$f_4 \ldots f_n$

We should then have two values for the arithmetic average, namely,

$$A_x = \frac{\Sigma f_i x_i}{N}, \qquad A_y = \frac{\Sigma f_i y_i}{N}.$$

Now, as is often the case, if there exists a linear relationship between the class marks represented by the formula

$$x_i = ay_i + b, \qquad (2)$$

where a and b are constants, then the first average, A_x, is related to the second average, A_y, by the following formula:

$$A_x = aA_y + b. \qquad (3)$$

To prove this we substitute x_i from (2) in the formula for A_x and thus obtain:

$$A_x = \frac{\Sigma f_i(ay_i + b)}{N} = \frac{a\Sigma f_i y_i}{N} + \frac{b\Sigma f_i}{N}$$
$$= aA_y + b.$$

Thus, in the example given above, let us compute the average using the class marks: $y_i = 1, 3, 5, 7, 9, 11, 13$. Since the original class marks are the following: $x_i = -60, -40, -20, 0, 20, 40, 60$, we seek a relationship of the form given by equation (2) above.

To find a and b we choose two pairs of class marks, let us say $x = -60, y = 1$, and $x = -40, y = 3$, and substitute these in (2) to obtain two equations as follows:

$$-60 = a + b,$$
$$-40 = 3a + b.$$

Subtracting the first from the second, we have: $2a = 20$, that is, $a = 10$. When this value is substituted in the first equation, we also find: $b = -70$. Equation (2) thus reduces to

$$x_i = 10y_i - 70.$$

Since we merely assumed that such a linear relationship existed between the two sets of class marks, it is necessary to check our result. This can be done either by checking one set of class marks by the other, or by representing them graphically.

Since we have already found earlier in this section that $A_x = 2.61$, we now find from equation (3) that

$$A_x = 10A_y - 70,$$

that is,

$$A_y = \frac{A_x + 70}{10} = \frac{2.61 + 70}{10} = 7.261.$$

This result can be checked directly by computing the average using the y-class marks.

PROBLEMS

1. Express in the form: $x_i = ay_i + b$
the relationship between the following sets of class marks:

x:	5	10	15	20	25	30	35	40
y:	17	32	47	62	77	92	105	122.

THE CENTRAL TENDENCIES OF DATA   57

2. If the arithmetic average of a frequency distribution with respect to the x-class marks of Problem 1 is 16.3, what is the corresponding arithmetic average with respect to the y-class marks?

3. Using the answer to Problem 4, Section 2, compute the arithmetic average of the numbers obtained from those of Problem 3 of Section 2 through multiplication of each number by 3 and the addition of 2, that is to say, of the numbers: 17, 23, 17, 26, etc.

4. Find the answer to Problem 9, Section 2, if the "number of telephones" were replaced by the sequence: 1, 2, 3, 4, 5, etc.

5. Problem 10, Section 2 computes the average value of the class marks, but the information really desired is the average number of members in the state House of Representatives. If we replaced the class marks by the average number in each class range, namely, by the numbers 45, 75, 105, 135, 165, 195, 225, 255, 285, what would the average then equal? Compare this with the average of 118 determined directly from the table of values given in Section 3 of Chapter 2.   *Ans.* 121.

6. Use the simplification suggested in this section to compute the answer to Problem 9, Section 2.

7. Solve Problem 5, of Section 2, first replacing the class marks by the numbers: 0, 2, 3, 4, 6, 7, 9.

8. Compute the arithmetic average for Problem 10, Section 2, replacing the class marks by the class marks $x_i - X$, where $X = 4$.

4. *The Root-Mean-Square or Quadratic Mean — The Standard Deviation.*

Next to the arithmetic mean, the *root-mean-square*, or *quadratic mean*, plays the most important role in statistics because of its fundamental connection with dispersion. It may be defined as the square root of the arithmetic mean of the squares of the class marks. In symbols this definition becomes:

$$R = \sqrt{\frac{(f_1 x_1^2 + f_2 x_2^2 + f_3 x_3^2 + \cdots + f_n x_n^2)}{N}} \qquad (1)$$

$$= \sqrt{\frac{\Sigma f_i x_i^2}{N}}.$$

The quadratic mean gives special weight to large class marks, since they enter into the formula as squares. Hence it is an effective average to use in the study of the dispersion of data and this is its principal use in statistics.

A *deviation* from the mean is defined as the difference between a class mark and the arithmetic mean, namely, $(x_i - A)$.

The *standard deviation* of a frequency distribution is defined to be the root-mean-square of the deviations of the values of the class marks from their arithmetic mean. The Greek letter σ (sigma) is commonly used to denote the standard deviation.

By the *variance* of a distribution we shall mean the square of the standard deviation. That is to say, the variance is σ^2. Because the variance does not involve the square-root symbol it is easier to manipulate mathematically.

Both the standard deviation and the variance are defined in symbols by the following formula:

$$\sigma^2 = \frac{f_1(x_1 - A)^2 + f_2(x_2 - A)^2 + \cdots + f_n(x_n - A)^2}{N} \qquad (2)$$

where A is the arithmetic mean defined in Section 2 and N is the total frequency.

The formula for σ^2 may be written more compactly as follows:

$$\sigma^2 = \frac{\Sigma f_i(x_i - A)^2}{N}. \qquad (3)$$

Since the arithmetic average is generally some fractional part of a class mark, the deviation $(x_i - A)$ is usually an awkward quantity with which to compute. Hence the following formula, in which X is any arbitrarily chosen number, is generally used in computation:

$$\sigma^2 = \frac{f_1(x_1 - X)^2 + f_2(x_2 - X)^2 + \cdots + f_n(x_n - X)^2}{N} - (A - X)^2. \qquad (4)$$

This formula may also be written more compactly as follows:

$$\sigma^2 = \frac{\Sigma f_i(x_i - X)^2}{N} - (A - X)^2. \qquad (5)$$

The proof that (4) is identical with (2) may be given as follows:
We first observe that when $X = A$, formula (4) reduces to (2). If, then, we can show that (4) is actually a constant independent of X, it must follow that this constant is σ^2. To show this we write:

THE CENTRAL TENDENCIES OF DATA

$$\sigma^2 = \frac{\Sigma f_i(x_i - X)^2}{N} - (A - X)^2 = \frac{\Sigma f_i(x_i^2 - 2Xx_i + X^2)}{N} - (A - X)^2$$

$$= \frac{\Sigma f_i x_i^2}{N} - 2X \frac{\Sigma f_i x_i}{N} + X^2 \frac{\Sigma f_i}{N} - (A^2 - 2AX + X^2). \qquad (6)$$

Recalling now that $\Sigma f_i x_i / N = A$ and $\Sigma f_i = N$, we see that (6) becomes

$$\sigma^2 = \frac{\Sigma f_i x_i^2}{N} - 2AX + X^2 - A^2 + 2AX - X^2$$

$$= \frac{\Sigma f_i x_i^2}{N} - A^2.$$

Since this last expression is independent of X, we have thus established the identity of formulas (4) and (2).

As an example, let us compute the standard deviation and the variance for the data of Table B, Section 1. As in our computation of A for these same data in Section 3, we shall choose for X the value $X = -60$. The computation may then be arranged as in the following table:

Class Mark (x_i)	Frequency (f_i)	$x_i - X$	$(x_i - X)^2$	$f_i(x_i - X)^2$
-60	2	0	0	0
-40	3	20	400	1200
-20	9	40	1600	14400
0	14	60	3600	50400
20	10	80	6400	64000
40	7	100	10000	70000
60	1	120	14400	14400
Totals	46			214400

From the totals, and recalling that $A = 2.61$, we obtain from formula (4) the following values:

$$\sigma^2 = \frac{214400}{46} - (2.61 + 60)^2 = 4660.8696 - 3920.0121 = 740.8565,$$

$$\sigma = \sqrt{740.8565} = 27.22.$$

We thus see that the variance is 740.8565 and the standard deviation is 27.22.

As in the case of the arithmetic mean it is sometimes convenient to change from one set of class marks to another. Let us assume, as in Section 2, that one set of class marks (x_i) is related to a second set of class marks (y_i) by means of the formula,

$$x_i = a y_i + b, \qquad (7)$$

where a and b are constants.

Under this assumption if we designate the standard deviation with respect to (x_i) by σ_x and the standard deviation with respect to (y_i) by σ_y, it is not difficult to prove that we have,

$$\sigma_x = |a|\, \sigma_y, \qquad (8)$$

where $|a|$ means the *absolute value*, that is to say, the positive numerical value, of a.

To prove this we first recall from Section 3 that the respective averages, A_x and A_y, are connected by the equation,

$$A_x = a A_y + b. \qquad (9)$$

Then in the formula,

$$\sigma_x^2 = \frac{\sum f_i (x_i - A_x)^2}{N},$$

we replace x_i by $a y_i + b$ from (7) and A_x by $a A_y + b$ from (9) to obtain

$$\sigma_x^2 = \frac{\sum f_i (a y_i + b - a A_y - b)^2}{N}$$

$$= a^2 \frac{\sum f_i (y_i - A_y)^2}{N}$$

$$= a^2 \sigma_y^2.$$

Since σ_x and σ_y are always positive numbers, while a may be either positive or negative, we must replace $\sqrt{a^2}$ by $|a|$ when we take the square root of the last equation. Hence we have $\sigma_x = |a|\, \sigma_y$, which was to be proved.

Thus if, as in the example of Section 3, we replace the class marks x_i = -60, -40, -20, etc. by the class marks y_i = 1, 3, 5, etc.

THE CENTRAL TENDENCY OF DATA

such that
$$x_i = 10 y_i - 70,$$
we have immediately,
$$\sigma_x = 10 \sigma_y;$$
and since $\sigma_y = 27.22$, it follows that $\sigma_y = 2.72$.

The standard deviation is used in statistical analysis to indicate the spread of the data about the mean, or in more technical language, its *dispersion*. In most frequency distributions nearly all the frequencies correspond to class marks between the limits $A - 2\sigma$ and $A + 2\sigma$. For the particular distribution under discussion we see that these limits are respectively -53 and $+57$. Referring to the data of Table A, Section 1, we see that only one item lies outside of this range.

PROBLEMS.

1. Compute the standard deviation for the data of Problem 3, Section 2.
Ans. $\sigma = 1.9$.

2. Show that the standard deviation for the data of Problem 5, Section 2, is 2.19.

3. Find the standard deviation for Problem 6, Section 2. *Ans.* 9.66.

4. Find the standard deviation for the limits upon the length of state legislature sessions, Problem 8, Section 2. *Ans.* 17.55.

5. Given that the standard deviation for the data of Problem 9, Section 2, is 3.84, find what this would be if the "number of telephones" were replaced by the sequence: 1, 2, 3, 4, 5, etc.

6. Given that the standard deviation corresponding to the data of Problem 10, Section 2 is 1.94, find the standard deviation if the class marks are replaced by the sequence: 45, 75, 105, 135, etc. *Ans.* 58.2.

7. If $\sigma = 5.2$ for the following set of class marks: 5, 7, 9, 11, 13, 15, 17, 19, 21, 23, what would the standard deviation be if these were replaced by the sequence: 15, 14, 13, 12, 11, 10, 9, 8, 7, 6?

5. *The Coefficient of Variability.*

The *coefficient of variability* is defined as the ratio of the standard deviation to the arithmetic mean, that is,
$$v = \frac{\sigma}{A},$$
and is used as a measure of the uniformity of data.

If one had, for example, two sets of data, the arithmetic means of which were the same, but where the items of one set varied considerably in magnitude, while the items of the second set varied little in magnitude, this would be shown by the standard deviation alone which would be larger in the first case than in the second. But if the arithmetic means were different, let us say because the class range in one set of items was greater than in the second, a comparison of standard deviations would not reveal the relative variability. In this case we should require the coefficient defined above.

A very interesting example of the use of this coefficient is found in a study of the stability of political governments. Thus we may assume that the length of duration of a ruling power has a conspicuous relationship with the stability, or the lack of stability, of a nation in both its economic and its political life.

The governing power assumes many forms and cannot always be fully recognized. Frequently it has been vested in a king or an emperor, sometimes in a prime minister, often in a parliament, or, as in the United States, in a president, a legislative body, and a judiciary. The power may sometimes change abruptly from one group to another, as in the case of elections or revolutions. But if the central authority, whatever its form, can be recognized, and its length of tenure measured, then the coefficient of variability, which we have defined above, can be used to measure this stability.

The following table, giving the average tenure of the governing authority in years for several nations, the standard deviation of the tenure, and the coefficient of variability, shows what information is afforded by such an analysis. A considerable amount of historical fact is contained in this table of values. The presence of political turmoil with its accompanying economic difficulties is revealed by large values of the coefficient of variation. For example, any student of ancient history is impressed by the difference in the political stability of the Ptolemaic dynasty and the Roman rule which followed it. All historians of this period comment about the constant rioting which was a conspicuous pattern of the rule of the prefects. In contrast with this, only one riot of serious consequence has been reported during the entire reign of the Ptolemies. The coefficient of variability of 1.13 for the first period and the value of 0.43 for the second period give striking statistical evidence in support of the comments of the historian. That Alexandria declined both in popula-

THE CENTRAL TENDENCIES OF DATA

The Governing Unit	Average in years of tenure, (A)	Standard Deviation (σ)	Coefficient of Variability ($v = \sigma/A$)
The Rulers in Alexandria			
The Ptolemies (omitting Eupator and Neos Dionysius (323 B.C. to 30 B.C.)	24.82	10.74	0.43
Prefects in the period of the Empire (30 B.C. to 578 A.D.)	3.00	3.39	1.13
Rulers of the Roman Empire			
Roman Emperors (31 B.C. to 476 A.D.)	7.91	9.08	1.15
Roman Emperors of the East (491 to 1205)	12.31	12.04	0.98
English Rulers			
English Rulers (827 to 1937)	17.90	15.55	0.87
Saxons and Danes (827 to 1066)	11.95	10.33	0.86
Rulers after the Norman Conquest (1066 to 1937)	20.74	16.77	0.81
Rulers of France			
Rulers of France (840 to 1940)	16.92	15.75	0.93
The Carlovingians (840 to 987)	13.36	12.28	0.92
Capets to the First Republic (987 to 1793)	24.42	17.19	0.70
First Republic to the Occupation of France (1793 to 1940)	7.00	5.55	0.79
Presidents and Political Parties of the United States			
Presidents (1789 to 1944)	4.88	2.53	0.52
Political Parties (1789 to 1944)	9.18	6.51	0.71
Political Parties since Lincoln (1861 to 1944)	8.40	4.80	0.58

tion and in economic prosperity during the first three centuries of Roman rule is well known.

The uneasy state of the Roman empire itself under the autocratic sway of the Emperors is shown by the high value of v. Being the ruler of Rome was a hazardous occupation; the average tenure was less than eight years. Toward the end of the Western Empire the situation became even more uncertain and the period from 212 A. D. to 305 A. D. produced twenty-one emperors, many of whom met violent death.

In contrast with this we find unusual stability in the government of the United States as measured either by the tenure of presidents, or by the tenure of political parties. While we have seen that the balance of power has been almost evenly distributed between the two major parties, the swing from one to the other has never been so decisive that the coefficient of variability has been large.

PROBLEMS

1. Compute the coefficient of variability for the data of Problem 3, Section 2.
Ans. 0.40

2. Compare the coefficients of variability of the data of Problems 6 and 8, Section 2. *Ans.* 0.60 and 0.27, respectively.

3. Can you account by an inspection of the frequency patterns of the data in Problems 6 and 8, Section 2, for the difference in the coefficients of variability?

4. Compute the variability for the data of Problem 9, Section 2.
Ans. 0.32.

5. What is the variability for the data of Problem 10, Section 2?
Ans. 0.55.

6. Does the variability for the data of Problem 10, Section 2 change if we replace the given class marks by the sequence: 45, 75, 105, etc.?

6. *The Median.*

An average which is closely related to the arithmetic mean is the *median,* which we shall designate by the letter M. By the median is meant that value on the scale above and below which half the data lie. When the items of the series have been arranged in order of size, the median is the class mark belonging to the middle item. Thus the

THE CENTRAL TENDENCIES OF DATA

median of the numbers 5, 7, −4, 2, 10 is 5, since this is the central number of the series: −4, 2, 5, 7, 10.

When the items of a series are arranged by class marks in a frequency table, it is usually found necessary to interpolate for the value of the median, since the frequency table gives only the limits between which the median lies. This is done by means of the following formula:

$$M = L + \frac{C[\frac{1}{2}(N + 1) - \Sigma f_i]}{F},$$

where L is the lower limit of the median class, C is the class interval, N the total frequency, Σf_i the total number of items below L, and F the frequency of the median class.

As an example, let us determine the medians of both Table A and Table B in Section 1.

In the first case we arrange the items in Table A in their order of magnitude as shown in the following array:

x	Congress	x	Cong.	x	Cong.	x	Cong.	x	Cong.	x	Cong.	x	Cong.	x	Cong.
-57	75	-26	49	-16	35	-3	78	5	51	12	61	20	55	39	67
-50	74	-24	77	-12	79	-1	72	6	56	14	42	24	71	40	54
-45	73	-23	48	- 9	64	2	65	8	58	14	80	30	59	48	40
-43	52	-22	44	- 7	46	3	47	9	70	15	38	32	41	56	39
-38	63	-21	76	- 5	50	4	68	10	66	15	69	34	43		
-27	53	-17	62	- 4	45	5	36	12	57	16	60	36	37		

Since there are 46 items in this table, there is no middle item, but items 23 and 24 are median values. Since the first of these is 4, corresponding to the 68th Congress, and the second is 5, corresponding to the 36th Congress, we can take as our median value their arithmetic average, or $\frac{1}{2}(4 + 5) = 4.5$.

Turning next to Table B, we see that the median class corresponds to the frequency 14. Hence we have $F = 14$, $N = 46$, $L = -9$, $C = 20$, and $\Sigma f_i = 9 + 3 + 2 = 14$. Substituting these values in formula (1), we then obtain

$$M = -9 + \frac{20(23.5 - 14)}{14} = -9 + 13.57 = 4.57,$$

which differs very slightly from the value determined from Table A.

One advantage of the median as an average is found in the simplicity with which it can be computed. Another resides in the fact that no undue influence is exerted upon the average by extreme values in the data. Thus the median just computed would have been unchanged if the first value in the table had been −100, although such an extreme item would have influenced the value of the arithmetic mean.

A third advantage of the median is found in the fact that it can be determined even when some of the data are non-arithmatic, or mere estimates, provided only that they can be arranged in order of magnitude. Thus the median is 5 for the following items: Lower than 3, very high, very low, 5, 10.

PROBLEMS

1. Compute the median for the data of Problem 3, Section 2. *Ans.* 4.5.

2. Find the median for Problem 5, Section 2.

3. Obtain the difference between the median of Problem 6, Section 2 and the arithmetic average obtained for these data. *Ans.* -0.37.

4. Compute the median for the data of Problem 8, Section 2. *Ans.* 61.47.

5. Find the median for the data of Problem 9, Section 2. *Ans.* 11.8.

6. Using the class intervals instead of the class marks, show that the median for Problem 10, Section 2 is 111.2.

7. *The Mode.*

Nearly all frequency distributions show a tendency toward the accumulation of frequencies at one or more values of the class marks. By the *mode*, which we designate Mo, is meant that value of the class mark which corresponds to the largest frequency, that is to say, that value which is the most fashionable. When a distribution has but one mode, it is called *uni-modal*, when it has two modes, *bi-modal*, etc.

Since the mode is some average value in the modal class, that is to say, the class to which the highest frequency belongs, it is necessary to estimate this value by means of an interpolation formula. For this purpose we shall use the following:

$$Mo = L + \frac{CF}{F + f}, \qquad (1)$$

where L is the lower limit of the modal class, C the class interval,

THE CENTRAL TENDENCIES OF DATA

F the frequency of the class just above the mode, and f the frequency of the class just below the mode.

As an example, let us compute the mode for the data on the size of State Legislatures, given in Section 3 of Chapter 2.

From the table of frequencies we see that the modal class corresponds to the frequency 17. The lower limit of this class is $L = 90$, the class interval is $C = 30$, the frequency of the class above the mode is $F = 8$, and the frequency of the class below the mode is $f = 6$. Hence we have for the mode the value:

$$Mo = 90 + \frac{30 \times 8}{8+6} = 90 + 17.14 = 107.14.$$

One important use of the mode is in the measurement of the *skewness* of a frequency distribution, that is to say, its unsymmetrical character. It not infrequently happens that the frequencies of a distribution will tend to pile up at one end or the other of the class range, instead of diminishing symmetrically from a normal modal value. In such cases the mode will not correspond to the arithmetic mean, but will deviate from it by a significant amount.

The skewness (S) of a distribution can be conveniently measured by the formula:

$$S = \frac{A - Mo}{\sigma} \qquad (2)$$

where A is the arithmetic mean, Mo the mode, and σ the standard deviation of the distribution.

When the sign of S is positive the skewness is to the right, and when the sign is negative the skewness is to the left, as indicated in the accompanying figure.

For the data on the size of State Legislatures, where the skewness to the right is readily observed in the frequency chart, we obtain the following value for S:

$$S = \frac{120.96 - 107.14}{58.00} = 0.2382.$$

PROBLEMS

1. Compute the mode for Problem 8, Section 2. *Ans.* 6.2.
2. Find the modal value for Problem 9, Section 2. *Ans.* 11.93.
3. Obtain the mode for Problem 10, Section 2. *Ans.* 108.

POLITICAL STATISTICS

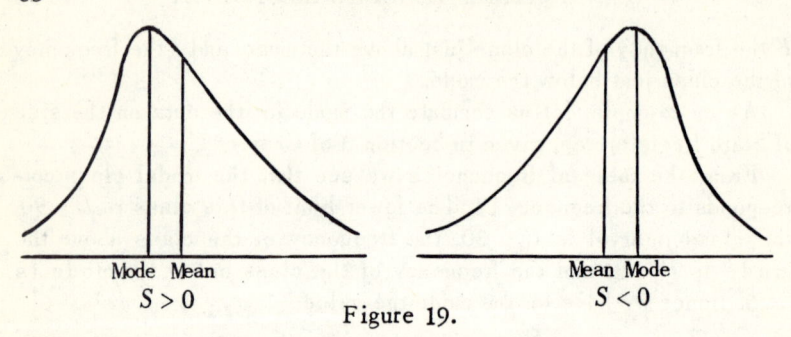

```
   Mode Mean              Mean Mode
    S > 0                  S < 0
```
Figure 19.

4. Compute the skewness for the frequency distribution of Problem 8, Section 2.

5. Determine whether there is any skewness in the data on the political composition of the House of Representatives, Section 1.

8. *Minor Averages — Concluding Remarks.*

As we have said earlier the geometric and harmonic means also have statistical application. But since this application is limited in scope, they are regarded as minor averages. We shall, however, find it convenient to define them.

By the *geometric average*, designated by G, of a set of items: $x_1, x_2, \ldots, x_N$, we mean the value

$$G = \sqrt[N]{x_1\ x_2 \ldots x_N}.$$

This average can be put in convenient form by taking logarithms of both sides. We thus obtain

$$\log G = \frac{\log x_1 + \log x_2 + \cdots + \log x_N}{N}.$$

In other words the logarithm of the geometric average is the arithmetic average of the logarithms of the class marks.

The geometric average finds special application in the averaging of ratios.

By the *harmonic average*, designated by H, of a set of items: $x_1, x_2, \ldots, x_N$, we mean the value

$$H = \frac{N}{\frac{1}{x_1} + \frac{1}{x_2} + \cdots + \frac{1}{x_N}}.$$

This average also has limited application in such problems as finding the average values of rates, although it is also used in certain types of index numbers.

Since so many different averages have been defined, it might appear at first sight that the term "average value" does not have precise meaning. This is not, indeed, the case for each average has its domain of usefulness and this domain is not arbitrary. Thus, frequency distributions of the types discussed above require an arithmetic mean in their interpretation, or, under certain conditions, the median, which is usually a value approximating the arithmetic average. The root-mean-square is used almost entirely in connection with the computation of the standard deviation, the significance of which will be given in more detail later. The mode applies when modal characteristics of a distribution are important, or when there is obvious skewness in the data.

PROBLEMS

1. Find the harmonic mean of the numbers: 2, 3, 7, 9, 10.

2. Compute the geometric mean of the values: 5, 6, 9, 10, 12.

3. Compute the arithmetic, geometric and harmonic means of the numbers 1, 2, 3 and show that these values satisfy the inequalities: $A > G > H$. This is a general property of these averages when the numbers averaged are positive and unequal.

CHAPTER 4
ELEMENTS OF THE THEORY OF PROBABILITY
1. *Definition of Probability.*

IN THE MEASUREMENT of human events there is always an erratic element which is due to chance and hence unpredictable. However, even here, it is possible to introduce estimates which measure the chances in these variable elements. Thus, if one tosses a coin, there is no way before the event to know whether it will fall heads. But the only alternative is that the coin will fall tails and hence we say that the chance of obtaining heads is even, or fifty-fifty. Similarly, before an election, one cannot say that a given candidate will be successful, but there may be events during the campaign which increase his chances of election. It is often possible to measure these chances and reduce them to a numerical indicator.

A study of the phenomenon of chance led many years ago to the formulation of what has been called the theory of probability. Since this theory is fundamental to a proper understanding of statistics we shall give a brief resume of some of its most conspicuous elements.

The following definition has been generally adopted as a mathematical measure of probability:

Definition. If an event can happen in m ways and fail in n ways, and if each of these ways is equally likely to happen, then the *probability*, or *chance*, of its happening, which we designate by p, is the ratio: $p = m/(m + n)$. Similarly, the probability of its failing to happen which we denote by q, is the ratio: $q = n/(m + n)$. This is frequently expressed by saying that the odds are m to n that the event will happen, or n to m that it will fail to happen.

Thus the probability that a coin will fall heads is ½; that two coins will fall heads is ¼. This second case illustrates what is meant by the phrase "equally likely" in the definition. For two coins can fall in three ways, namely, two heads, two tails, or one head and one tail. But these three ways are not equally likely since the case "heads, tails" happens twice as often as the other two cases. The probabilities in the three cases are thus respectively: ¼, ¼, and ½.

ELEMENTS OF THE THEORY OF PROBABILITY

Another aspect of the theory of probability is found in the classification of probabilities into two categories, namely, those designated as *a priori,* or mathematical, and those designated as *a posteriori,* or experimental. Thus the probabilities produced by the tossing of two coins are *a priori,* since we can determine them without recourse to experiment. On the other hand, the probability that a man, age 25, will survive to age 26 can be determined only by the observation of a large group of individuals. This probability also has been observed to increase materially during the present century as the result of advances in medical science. It thus depends upon external events and is determined entirely by observation. Most of the probabilities interesting to political science are *a posteriori* since they are obtained from polls and other sets of statistical data. All attempts to measure political opinion, to forecast the results of elections, etc. belong to this category of the theory of probability.

However, a study of *a priori* probability is a necessary preliminary to a proper understanding of the subject, since it furnishes a mathematical model against which we can measure empirical probabilities. Thus we know that the probability of obtaining a head in one toss of a coin is ½, but if we should actually toss 100 coins and observe the number of heads thus obtained, the probability computed from the observations would not in general equal ½. Or repeated for 1,000 or 10,000 tosses, the observed probability, while very close to ½, would not necessarily equal this *a priori* ratio.

If p_N is the empirical probability computed from N observations, and if p is the *a priori* probability, then it is customary to say that the difference

$$D_N = p_N - p$$

tends toward zero as N is indefinitely increased.

But this difference does not necessarily decrease in a regular manner. Thus, if we are considering the problem of computing the probability of obtaining a head by tossing a large number of coins (or by tossing one coin a large number of times), we should find sequences of heads and tails which would increase or decrease the observed probability. On the whole, however, as N increases the probability will tend toward the theoretical value of 0.50. This is illustrated in the accompanying figure which shows the results of tossing a coin 1000 times and computing the probability of obtaining heads

Figure 20.

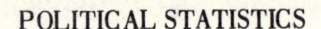

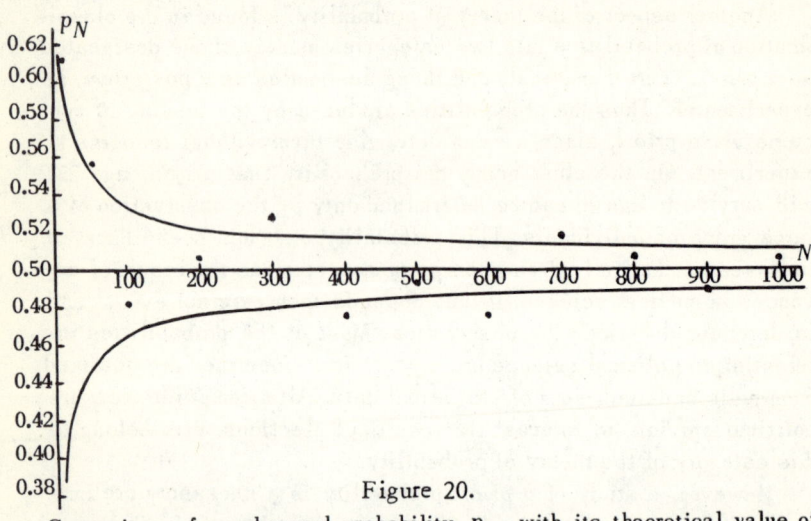

Comparison of an observed probability, p_N, with its theoretical value of 0.50 for various values of N. The theoretical limits are the curved lines and the observed probabilities are indicated by the solid circles: •.

from the frequencies observed at the end of the 10th, 50th, 100th, etc. tosses. The two curved lines in the figure define a region between them within which half the observations lie. It is observed that these lines are converging slowly toward one another and if N is chosen large enough the distance between them could be made as small as one desired. This is a typical situation for all empirically determined probabilities.

The values from which the theoretical limits are computed are given in the following table. The explanation of the derivation of these values will be found in Example 2 of Section 7.

Value of N	Upper limit of p_N (0.50 + k)	Lower limit of p_N (0.50 - k)	Value of k
10	0.6124	0.3876	0.1124
50	0.5477	0.4522	0.0477
100	0.5337	0.4663	0.0337
200	0.5238	0.4762	0.0238
300	0.5195	0.4805	0.0195
400	0.5169	0.4831	0.0169
500	0.5151	0.4849	0.0151
600	0.5138	0.4862	0.0138
700	0.5127	0.4873	0.0127
800	0.5119	0.4881	0.0119
900	0.5112	0.4888	0.0112
1000	0.5107	0.4893	0.0107

ELEMENTS OF THE THEORY OF PROBABILITY

The following examples will illustrate the computation of probabilities.

Example 1. Three coins are tossed. What is the probability that they will all fall heads?

Solution: Since the fall of one coin is independent of the fall of another, and since each can fall in two ways, there are altogether 8 different ways for them to fall. Since only one way is represented by a fall of 3 heads, the probability is $1/8$.

Example 2. Show that the probability of obtaining exactly 2 heads in one toss of 3 coins is $3/8$. What is the probability of obtaining at least 2 heads?

Solution: Let us make a table of the eight possibilities, regarding each coin as having been separately thrown. We thus get the following:

HHH, HHT, HTH, THH, TTH, THT, HTT, TTT.

We thus see that there are three cases where exactly 2 heads appear, and hence the desired probability is $3/8$. When we ask for the probability of obtaining at least 2 heads we must add the case HHH, and hence the probability is $4/8 = 1/2$.

Example 3. The following table is formed from the American Experience Table of Mortality and shows the number of people surviving at different ages out of an initial group of 100,000 age 10 years:

Age	No. Living	Deaths in 5-yr. Period	Age	No. Living	Deaths in 5-yr. Period
10	100,000		35	81,822	3,619
15	96,285	3,715	40	78,106	3,716
20	92,637	3,648	45	74,173	3,933
25	89,032	3,605	50	69,804	4,369
30	85,441	3,591	55	65,563	5,241

From this table compute the probability of living from age 20 to 25.

Solution: Since from the table 89,032 persons are alive at age 25 out of 92,637 at age 20, the desired probability is

$$p = 89,032/92,637 = 0.961.$$

We also could have computed the probability of not surviving, that is,

$$q = 3,605/92,637 = 0.039,$$

and hence obtained: $p = 1 - q = 0.961$, since a person either survives or doesn't and the respective probabilities must total unity.

PROBLEMS

1. Show that the probability of obtaining exactly 2 heads in one toss of 4 coins is 3/8. Compare this with the probability of obtaining at least two heads.

2. What is the probability of obtaining 7 in a single throw with two dice? What is the probability of obtaining at least 7 in a single throw with two dice?

3. What is the most probable throw with two dice?

4. Six balls numbered from 1 to 6 are placed in a bag and two are drawn at random. What is the probability that they are numbers 1 and 2? *Ans.* 1/15.

5. Six balls numbered from 1 to 6 are placed in a bag and three are drawn at random. What is the probability that they are numbered 4, 5, 6? *Ans.* 1/20.

6. Compare the chances of throwing 4 with one die and 8 with two dice.

7. Toss five coins 128 times and estimate the probabilities that in a single throw one should get: 0 Head, 1 Head, 2 Heads, 4 Heads, and 5 Heads. From these probabilities estimate the chance of getting 3 heads in a single throw.

8. Using the table given in Example 3 above, compute the probability of living from age 10 to age 15.

9. Using the table of Example 3, compare the probability of living from 15 to 20 with the probability of living from 40 to 45.

10. What is the probability that a letter selected at random in an English book, is the letter e? *Hint*: Take a selection of not less than 500 letters from some book and count both the number of letters and the number of e's.

11. In *The Gold Bug* Edgar Allan Poe asserts that the letter a is next in frequency to the letter e in English. Test this by the number of times a is found in 1,000 letters with the corresponding frequencies for a, o, and i. *Ans.* In a count of 20,000 letters the following percentages were found. For e, 12.7; for a, 9.0; for o, 7.5, and for i, 7.4. It was found, however, that t has a higher frequency than a, the percentage being 9.8.

12. A group of scientific men reported 1705 sons and 1527 daughters. If this is a fair sample from the general population, what is the probability that a child to be born will be a boy?

2. *The Multiplication and Addition of Probabilities.*

Two laws of combination of probabilities aid in the solution of problems in the theory of probability. The first of these, called the multiplication law, involves the probabilities of *independent events;* the second, called the addition law, is concerned with the probabilities of *mutually exclusive events.*

When two or more events can occur in connection with one another, the joint occurrence is called a *compound event*. If these

ELEMENTS OF THE THEORY OF PROBABILITY

events are *independent of one another*, then the following theorem is to be used in calculating this *joint probability:*

If the respective probabilities for the occurrence of n independent events are $p_1, p_2, ..., p_n$, *then the probability that all the events will occur is given by the product*

$$p = p_1 \cdot p_2 \cdot p_3 \cdots p_n.$$

The proof of this proposition can be derived from a consideration of two events. Thus let us assume that the probability for the occurrence of the first event is m/M, and that for the occurrence of the second is n/N. Since the events are independent of one another, a total of mn favorable cases exists out of a total of MN possibilities. This is true from the readily apprehended proposition that if one thing can be done in m ways and another thing in n ways, there will be mn different ways in which both things can be done. Hence the compound probability is (mn/MN), that is, the product of the two probabilities. This same reasoning can then be extended to any number of independent events.

A few examples will illustrate the application of this theorem.

Example 1. A bag contains 4 white balls and 5 black balls. If three balls are drawn from the bag, what is the probability that they are all white?

Solution. The probability of drawing a white ball on the first draw is $4/9$; hence, if a white ball has been drawn, the probability of drawing a white ball on the second draw is $3/8$; finally, if two white balls have been drawn, the probability of drawing a third white ball is $2/7$. Since these are all events independent of one another, the joint probability will be

$$p = \frac{4}{9} \cdot \frac{3}{8} \cdot \frac{2}{7} = \frac{1}{21}.$$

Example 2. What is the probability that if a die is thrown three times it will come up 2, 3, and 4 in succession? What is the probability that if three dice are thrown they will come up 2, 3, 4?

Solution. In the first question the probability for each event is $1/6$. Since the events are independent the desired probability will be

$$p = \frac{1}{6} \cdot \frac{1}{6} \cdot \frac{1}{6} = \frac{1}{216}.$$

Considering the second question, we see that the order is not important as it was in the first case. Thus if we think of the three dice as being thrown separately, the probability of getting one of the numbers on the first throw is $3/6$, then the probability of getting one of the remaining numbers on the next throw is $2/6$, and finally, the probability of getting the last number on the third throw is $1/6$. Since these are independent events, we have as the joint probability,

$$p = \frac{3}{6} \cdot \frac{2}{6} \cdot \frac{1}{6} = \frac{1}{36}.$$

Example 3. If a candidate's chance to be elected to office is always ½ at each election, how many consecutive terms can he expect to serve before his chance of defeat is greater than 99 in 100?

Solution. Since each election is an independent event, the candidate's chance of election in x successive campaigns is $(\frac{1}{2})^x$. Since his chance for defeat is greater than 0.99, his chance for election successively is less than 0.01. Hence we must find x such that $(\frac{1}{2})^x < 0.01$. Since $(\frac{1}{2})^6 = 1/64$ and $(\frac{1}{2})^7 = 1/128$, his chance of holding office for $x = 7$ terms is less than one in 100.

If a set of events is of such a nature that, when one of them happens, the others cannot happen, the set is said to be *mutually exclusive*. Thus, if three candidates run for a given office, the election of any one of them excludes the other two. Any events contingent upon the results of the election are mutually exclusive.

The theorem connected with the probabilities of mutually exclusive events is as follows:

If the probabilities of n mutually exclusive events are respectively $p_1, p_2, ..., p_n$, *then the probability that some one of these events will occur is given by the sum*

$$p = p_1 + p_2 + p_3 + \cdots + p_n.$$

We can prove this proposition by supposing that all the probabilities have been reduced to a common denominator, so that

$$p_1 = \frac{n_1}{N}, \quad p_2 = \frac{n_2}{N}, \quad p_3 = \frac{n_3}{N}, ..., p_n = \frac{p_n}{N}.$$

Since the events are mutually exclusive, the total number of cases favorable to the occurrence of some one of the events is the sum, $n_1 + n_2 + n_3 + \cdots + n_n$. Hence, since N is the total number of cases, the probability that some one of the events will happen is given by

$$p = \frac{n_1 + n_2 + n_3 + \cdots + n_n}{N}$$

$$= p_1 + p_2 + p_3 + \cdots + p_n.$$

Example 1. A bag contains 10 black balls, 9 white balls, 4 red balls, and 7 green balls. What is the probability that if one ball is drawn it will be either black or white?

Solution. The probability of drawing a black ball is $p_1 = 10/30$, and that of drawing a white ball is $p_2 = 9/30$. Since these are mutually exclusive events the desired probability is

$$p = p_1 + p_2 = \frac{10}{30} + \frac{9}{30} = \frac{19}{30}.$$

Example 2. Three candidates, A, B, and C are running for different offices, and their respective probabilities of election are estimated from a straw vote to be $\frac{1}{3}$, $\frac{1}{4}$, and $\frac{1}{5}$. What is the probability that at least one of them will be elected?

Solution. We first form the following set of mutually exclusive events together with their respective probabilities:

$A, B,$ and C all win: $\quad p_1 = \frac{1}{3} \cdot \frac{1}{4} \cdot \frac{1}{5} \qquad\qquad = \frac{1}{60},$

A, B win; C loses: $\quad p_2 = \frac{1}{3} \cdot \frac{1}{4} \cdot (1 - \frac{1}{5}) \qquad = \frac{4}{60},$

A, C win; B loses: $\quad p_3 = \frac{1}{3} \cdot \frac{1}{5} \cdot (1 - \frac{1}{4}) \qquad = \frac{3}{60},$

B, C win: A loses: $\quad p_4 = \frac{1}{4} \cdot \frac{1}{5} \cdot (1 - \frac{1}{3}) \qquad = \frac{2}{60},$

A wins; B, C lose: $\quad p_5 = \frac{1}{3} \cdot (1 - \frac{1}{4}) \cdot (1 - \frac{1}{5}) = \frac{12}{60},$

B wins; A, C lose: $\quad p_6 = \frac{1}{4} \cdot (1 - \frac{1}{3}) \cdot (1 - \frac{1}{5}) = \frac{8}{60},$

C wins; A, B lose: $\quad p_7 = \frac{1}{5} \cdot (1 - \frac{1}{3}) \cdot (1 - \frac{1}{4}) = \frac{6}{60}$

$$p = \frac{36}{60} = \frac{3}{5}.$$

This result is rather surprising since it shows that, in spite of the low individual probabilities of the candidates, the actual probability that at least one will be elected is considerably better than ½.

It should also be observed that the final probability could have been obtained in another way, namely by first finding the probability that all candidates fail to be elected. This probability is

$$q = (1 - \tfrac{1}{3}) \cdot (1 - \tfrac{1}{4}) \cdot (1 - \tfrac{1}{5}) = \tfrac{24}{60} = \tfrac{2}{5}.$$

Since $p + q = 1$, we obtain $p = \tfrac{3}{5}$.

PROBLEMS

1. Three runners enter a race and the probabilities that they will win are respectively 1/2, 1/4, 1/6. What is the probability that the race will be a tie?

2. In a certain election A and B are running for different offices. If A's chance is 2/3 and B's chance is 1/4, what is the probability that exactly one of them will be elected?

3. Under the conditions of Example 2, what is the probability that at least two will be elected?

3. *Binomial Frequency Distributions and the Theory of Probability*

In Section 4 of Chapter 2 binomial frequency distributions were introduced by graphing the values of the binomial coefficient, $_nC_r$, for some fixed value of n and variable values of r. An illustrative histogram was given for $n = 8$. Since these distributions are closely related to the theory of sampling which will concern us in this chapter, we shall consider them in connection with the theory of probability.

Thus let us suppose that n coins are tossed a total of N times, and on each toss the number of heads observed is recorded. When the experiment is concluded we shall find certain frequencies which correspond to the cases: 0 head, 1 head, 2 heads, etc. to n heads. Since the probability of getting a head in one toss of one coin is ½, the probability of getting n heads (or n tails, that is, 0 head) is $(½)^n$, because the probability of getting n heads with one toss of n coins is the same as getting n successive heads in n tosses of a single coin. Hence the total frequency corresponding to n heads (or 0 head) in N tosses of n coins is theoretically equal to $N(½)^n$. Similarly the

ELEMENTS OF THE THEORY OF PROBABILITY

probability of getting 1 head (or $n-1$ heads) will be $n(\frac{1}{2})^n$, for we see that we are concerned with the probability of getting $n-1$ tails and one head, but the one head may appear for any one of the n coins. In the case of 2 heads (or $n-2$ heads), the probability is $\frac{1}{2}n(n-1)(\frac{1}{2})^n$ = $_nC_2(\frac{1}{2})^n$, since now we combine with the probability of getting $n-2$ tails the probability of getting 2 heads; but the two heads will be distributed among the n coins in $\frac{1}{2}n(n-1)$ ways. In general, pursuing the same argument, it will turn out that the probability of getting x heads (or $n-x$ heads) is $_nC_x(\frac{1}{2})^n$.

Thus we reach the conclusion that the frequency distribution for the number of heads, designated by x, in N tosses of n coins, is given theoretically by the formula:

$$y = N \,_nC_x (\tfrac{1}{2})^n. \tag{1}$$

To illustrate, suppose that $n = 10$ coins are tossed $N = 1024$ times and that the frequencies corresponding to 0 head, 1 head, 2 heads, etc. to 10 heads are recorded. Then if x represents the number of heads, and since $1024 = (2)^{10}$, we obtain from the binomial frequency distribution the following:

$$y = 1024(\tfrac{1}{2})^{10} \,_{10}C_x = \,_{10}C_x. \tag{2}$$

Letting $x = 0, 1, 2$, etc. and referring to the table of binomial frequencies in Section 4, Chapter 2 we obtain the following table, for which we also give the computations basic to the determination of both the arithmetic average and the standard deviation.

No. of Heads (x)	Frequencies (y)	xy	x^2y
0	1	0	0
1	10	10	10
2	45	90	180
3	120	360	1080
4	210	840	3360
5	252	1260	6300
6	210	1260	7560
7	120	840	5880
8	45	360	2880
9	10	90	810
10	1	10	100
	1024	5120	28160

From the totals we then compute the arithmetic average, the variance, and the standard deviation as follows:

$$A = \frac{5120}{1024} = 5, \quad \sigma^2 = \frac{28160}{1024} - A^2 = 27.5 - 25 = 2.5, \quad \sigma = \sqrt{2.5} = 1.58.$$

It can be proved that for the general binomial frequency defined by equation (1) above, the arithmetic average is given by $A = \frac{1}{2}n$. Similarly, the standard deviation is found from the formula: $\sigma = \frac{1}{2}\sqrt{n}$. In the present case we have: $A = \frac{1}{2} \cdot 10 = 5$, and $\sigma = \frac{1}{2}\sqrt{10} = 1.58$.

4. *The Normal Frequency Distribution.*

In the discussion of most statistical problems it has been found generally convenient to replace the binomial frequency distribution by what is called the *normal frequency distribution,* which approximates very closely the values given by equation (1) in the preceding section.

The normal frequency distribution is given by the points on the curve defined by the following formula:

$$y = \frac{N}{\sigma} \frac{1}{\sqrt{2\pi}} e^{-\frac{1}{2}\frac{(x-A)^2}{\sigma^2}}, \tag{1}$$

where N is the total frequency of the distribution, A is the arithmetic average, and σ is the standard deviation. The number e which enters the formula is called *Napier's number,* and it has, to 4-place approximation, the value 2.7183.

Since the points given by equation (1) for various values of x are somewhat difficult to calculate, recourse is had to tabular values. To simplify the tabulation, we make the abbreviation:

$$t = \frac{x - A}{\sigma} \tag{2}$$

and hence write (1) in the form:

$$y = \frac{N}{\sigma} z, \tag{3}$$

where z is defined to be

$$z = \frac{1}{\sqrt{2\pi}} e^{-\frac{1}{2}t^2}. \tag{4}$$

Tables are then made for z, the following being sufficiently extensive for the purposes of the present book:

ELEMENTS OF THE THEORY OF PROBABILITY

Table of Values of the Ordinates of the Normal Frequency Curve

t	z	t	z	t	z
0.0	0.39894	0.6	0.33322	2.0	0.05399
0.1	0.39695	0.7	0.31225	2.5	0.01763
0.2	0.39104	0.8	0.28969	3.0	0.00443
0.3	0.38139	0.9	0.26609	3.5	0.00087
0.4	0.36827	1.0	0.24197	4.0	0.00013
0.5	0.35207	1.5	0.12952	5.0	0.00000

In order to illustrate the use of the normal curve we shall compare the values obtained from it with those of the binomial histogram discussed in Section 3. For this purpose we introduce into equation (3), making use of equation (2), the values obtained in the computation of the binomial frequency of Section 3, namely: $A = 5$, $\sigma = 1.58$, $\sigma^2 = 2.5$, $N = 1024$.

Thus, from (2) we get:

$$t = \frac{x - A}{\sigma} = \frac{x - 5}{1.58}, \text{ that is, } x = 5 + 1.58t.$$

Introducing the value $N/\sigma = 1024/1.58 = 648.7$ into equation (3), and making use of the values of the table given above, we obtain the following:

t	$x = 5 + 1.58t$	$y = 648.1\,z$	t	$x = 5 + 1.58t$	$y = 648.1\,z$
0.0	5.00	259	0.0	5.00	259
0.2	5.32	253	-0.2	4.68	253
0.4	5.63	239	-0.4	4.37	239
0.6	5.95	216	-0.6	4.05	216
0.8	6.26	188	-0.8	3.74	188
1.0	6.58	157	-1.0	3.42	157
1.5	7.37	84	-1.5	2.63	84
2.0	8.16	35	-2.0	1.84	35
3.0	9.74	3	-3.0	0.26	3

In forming this table one should observe that the normal curve is symmetric about the axis through $t = 0$, since $(-t)^2 = t^2$. Hence the values of z computed for positive values of t are used for negative values of t as well.

The values of the ordinates of the normal curve which we have just computed are compared graphically with those of the histogram of the binomial frequency distribution in the accompanying figure.

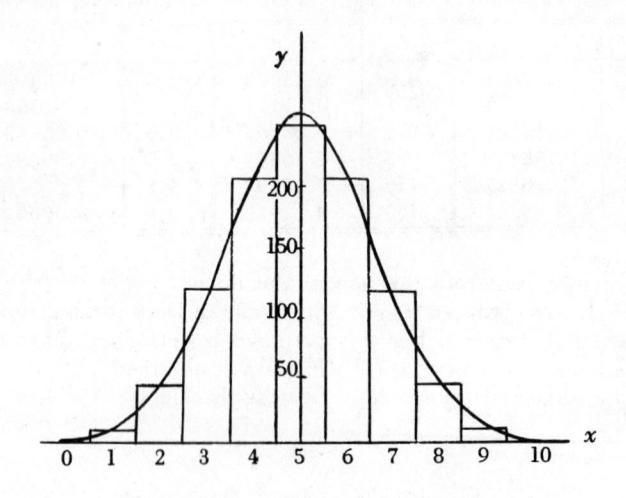

Figure 21.

Normal curve compared with the histogram of binomial frequency distribution.

If we desire to compare the values of the ordinates of the normal curve with those of the histogram of the binomial frequency over the range $x = 0, 1, 2$, etc., we must first form a table of the values of t from the formula: $t = (x - 5)/1.58$. From this, by interpolation, we then compute the corresponding values of z. Multiplying z by N/σ, we then obtain the desired ordinates. The following table shows this computation:

x	$t = (x-5)/1.58$	z	$648.1\,z$	Values of binomial frequencies
0	-3.16	0.00271	2	1
1	-2.53	0.01625	11	10
2	-1.90	0.06562	43	45
3	-1.27	0.17810	115	120
4	-0.63	0.32713	212	210
5	0.00	0.39894	259	252
6	0.63	0.32713	212	210
7	1.27	0.17810	115	120
8	1.90	0.06562	43	45
9	2.53	0.01625	11	10
10	3.16	0.00271	2	1

… ELEMENTS OF THE THEORY OF PROBABILITY 83

PROBLEMS

1. What is the standard deviation for a binomial frequency corresponding to $n = 6$? to $n = 8$?

2. If in a distribution x has the values $10, 15, 20, 25$, etc. to 50, and if $A = 32, \sigma = 10$, compute the corresponding values of t.

3. From the values of t obtained in Problem 2, compute the corresponding ordinates of the frequency table if $N = 1,000$.

4. Assuming that the distribution of frequencies given in Table II, Section 3, Chapter 2 is essentially normal, compute values of t corresponding to the class marks given there. Observe that we found in Chapter 3 the following values: $A = 2.61, \sigma = 27.22$.

5. From the results of Problem 4, compute the ordinates of the normal curve corresponding to the distribution of frequencies given in Table II. Exhibit the computations graphically.

5. *Areas Under the Normal Curve.*

In most statistical work on frequency distributions it is desirable to use areas instead of ordinates to represent frequencies. Thus in the histograms which we have introduced earlier in this book, the total frequency will be observed to equal the total area contained within the histogram, and the area of each individual rectangle is equal numerically to the frequency which corresponds to the class mark attached to it.

In a similar way the total area under the normal curve is equal to the total frequency of the data represented by it, and the area included between the ordinates corresponding to $x = x_1$ and $x = x_2$ will be numerically equal to the sum of the frequencies corresponding to the class marks between x_1 and x_2.

For convenience the area under the curve,

$$y = \frac{1}{\sqrt{2\pi}} e^{-\frac{1}{2}t^2}, \tag{1}$$

is tabulated for values of t from 0 to 4 in Table 3 at the end of this book. We shall use the symbol $I(t)$ to designate the area included under the curve from 0 to t. Thus $I(2)$, which is found from Table 3 to equal 0.47725, is the area under (1) from $t = 0$ to $t = 2$. Since the total area under the normal curve is equal to 1, the value of $I(t)$ for large values of t, that is, when t is 4 or greater, will approximate ½, since it represents half the area under the curve.

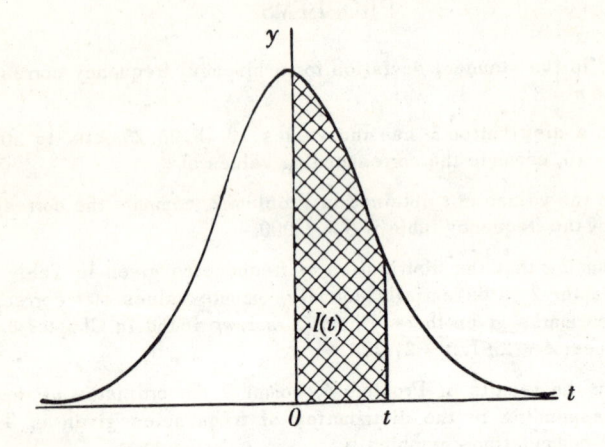

Figure 22.

To find the area between any two values of x in a distribution of total frequency N, let us say between x_1 and x_2, where we assume that $x_2 > x_1 > A$, we first compute:

$$t_1 = \frac{x_1 - A}{\sigma} \text{ and } t_2 = \frac{x_2 - A}{\sigma}.$$

The desired area is then given by the difference,

$$I = N I(t_2) - N I(t_1).$$

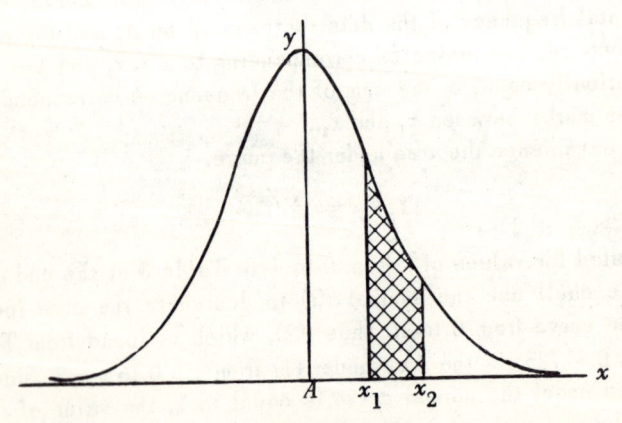

Figure 23.

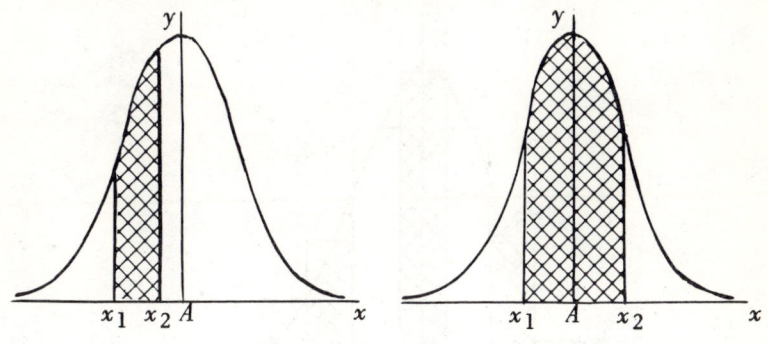

Figure 24.

If x_1 and x_2 are less than A, we compute t_1 and t_2 as before, but in this case they will both be negative numbers. Since, however, the normal curve is symmetric about the arithmetic average, the area corresponding to negative values of t is equal to the area for numerically equivalent positive values of t. Hence, we get the absolute values of t_1 and t_2, which we designate respectively by t_1' and t_2', and thus compute the desired area:

$$I = N I(t_1') - N(t_2').$$

Finally, if x_1 and x_2 are on different sides of A, and if the value of t corresponding to x_2 is t_2, and the absolute value of t corresponding to x_1 is t_1', then the desired area is given by

$$I = N I(t_2) + N I(t_1').$$

As an example, let us compute the areas under the normal curve considered in the preceding section which correspond to the areas of the rectangles in the accompanying histogram. An inspection of the figure shows that the ordinates which bound these areas have the abscissas: 0.5, 1.5, 2.5, etc. The areas which we desire to compute are those alternately shaded and unshaded in Figure 25.

Since the arithmetic average is 5, that is, $A = 5$, and $\sigma = 1.58$, we first find the values of t corresponding to $x = 0.5$, 1.5, etc. from the formula:

$$t = \frac{x - 5}{1.58}.$$

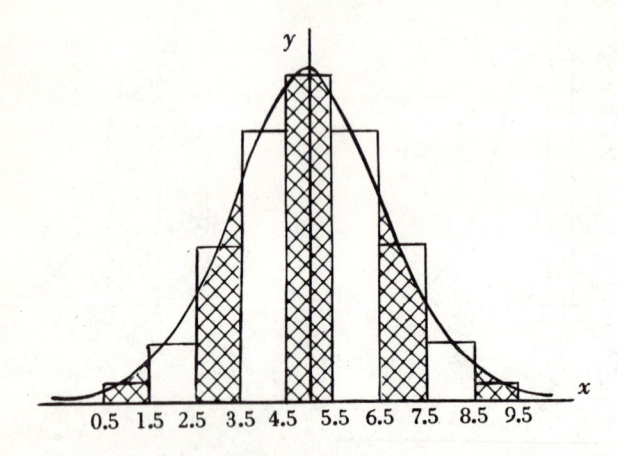

Figure 25.

These are given in the following table:

x	t	x	t
0.5	-2.85	5.5	0.32
1.5	-2.22	6.5	0.95
2.5	-1.58	7.5	1.58
3.5	-0.95	8.5	2.22
4.5	-0.32	9.5	2.85

Noting that $N = 1024$, we see that the area between 5.5 and 6.5 is given by

$$I = 1024\ I(0.95) - 1024\ I(0.32)$$
$$= 1024 \times 0.32894 - 1024 \times 0.12552$$
$$= 336.83 - 128.53 = 208.30 \sim 208.$$

Similarly, the area between 2.5 and 3.5 is found to be,

$$I = 1024\ I(1.58) - 1024\ I(0.95)$$
$$= 453.58 - 336.83 = 116.75 \sim 117.$$

In the same manner we compute the area between 4.5 and 5.5 to be

$$I = 1024\ I(0.32) + 1024\ I(0.32) = 2048\ I(0.32) = 257.06 \sim 257.$$

Proceeding in this way for all the areas we obtain the following table of areas under the normal curve, which are compared with the frequencies in the original histogram of the binomial distribution:

x	Areas under Normal Curve	Frequencies of Histogram
0	2.2	1
1	11.7	10
2	44.5	45
3	116.8	120
4	208.3	210
5	257.0	252
6	208.3	210
7	116.8	120
8	44.5	45
9	11.7	10
10	2.2	1
Totals	1024.0	1024

PROBLEMS

1. Calculate the values of the following: $I(1.42)$, $I(2.31)$, $I(-1.14)$, $I(0.333)$, $I(-1.234)$.

2. Compute the area under the normal curve between the limits of 1.32 and 2.32 if $N = 1,000$.

3. Answer problem 2 if the limits are -1.32 and $+2.32$.

4. Answer problem 2 if the limits are -2.22 and -1.11.

5. Graduate the data of Table II, Section 3, Chapter 2, using the method of this section.

6. *Probable and Standard Errors.*

The *probable error* of a normal distribution is defined to be the value

$$\text{p.e.} = 0.6745\,\sigma, \tag{1}$$

where σ is the standard deviation of the distribution. Its usefulness in statistics is found in the fact that half of the total frequencies correspond to class marks lying between $A - \text{p.e.}$ and $A + \text{p.e.}$

The probable error can be obtained readily by interpolation from the table of areas (Table 3) under the normal curve, since, if x_0 designates the probable error, then x_0/σ will be equal to that value of t

for which the area, $I(t) = \frac{1}{4} = 0.2500$. From Table 3 the following values are obtained:

$$I(0.67) = 0.24857$$
$$0.00318 \text{ (first difference)}$$
$$I(0.68) = 0.25175.$$

By interpolation, we get

$$t = 0.67 + \frac{0.25000 - 0.24857}{0.00318} = 0.6745.$$

Hence, since $x_0/\sigma = t$, we get $x_0 = 0.6745\sigma$ as the value of the probable error.

Since 0.6745 is very close to $0.6667 = \frac{2}{3}$, it is often convenient to use the approximate value $\frac{2}{3}\sigma$ for the probable error.

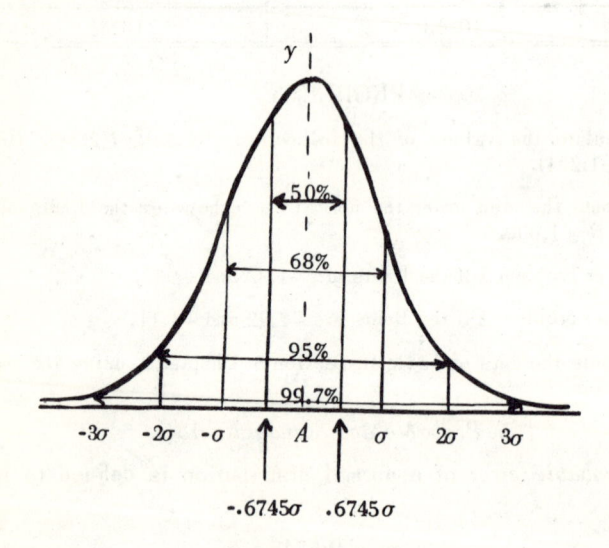

Figure 26.

The standard deviation is sometimes called the *standard error* of the normal distribution. We see from the above graph that 68% of the frequencies lie between $A - \sigma$ and $A + \sigma$. This figure is found from the fact that $2I(1) = 0.68268$. Similarly 95% of the frequencies are included between $A - 2\sigma$ and $A + 2\sigma$, and 99.7% of the frequencies between $A - 3\sigma$ and $A + 3\sigma$. It is thus highly improbable that items of any normal data will lie outside the 3σ range. Since three probable errors are very close to two standard errors, the 68% range is bounded very nearly by $A \pm 1.5$ p.e. and the 95% range by $A \pm 3$ p.e.

Probable and standard errors have been computed for most statistical variables. The theory of these derivations is beyond the scope of this book, but a few of them may be listed for convenient reference.

Errors of the arithmetic average, A:

$$\sigma_A = \sigma/\sqrt{N}, \quad \text{p.e.} = 0.6745\,\sigma_A, \qquad (2)$$

where σ is the standard deviation of the original distribution from which A is computed, and N is the total frequency.

Errors of an observed probability, p:

$$\sigma_p = \sqrt{\frac{p(1-p)}{N}}, \quad \text{p.e.} = 0.6745\,\sigma_p, \qquad (3)$$

where N is the number of observations used to compute p.

Errors of an observed frequency, f:

$$\sigma_f = \sqrt{f(1 - \frac{f}{N})}, \quad \text{p.e.} = 0.6745\,\sigma_f, \qquad (4)$$

where N is the total number of frequencies in the distribution which contains f.

7. *Sampling and the Use of Probable and Standard Errors.*

By sampling we mean the technique by which information about a large group of things, sometimes called the *statistical universe*, is obtained from a smaller group picked at random from a larger one. Thus, large shipments of merchandise are examined to see whether specifications have been complied with by the selection of samples picked randomly throughout the total collection of goods. Industrial production uses sampling extensively under what is called the technique of *quality control* in order to determine whether or not the quality of the things manufactured remains within the tolerance limits set by the engineers. In political science we are familiar with the use of polls to determine the opinion of large groups of individuals from the opinions of small samples.

The use of probable and standard errors is essential in the technique of sampling if we are to be able to interpret the significance of the sample. The following examples will serve as characteristic illustrations.

Example 1. The members of a class of 50 students are asked to toss 100 coins and count the number of heads that turn up. A sample of one toss is chosen at random. Within what limits should the number of heads lie?

Solution. The standard error of the expected frequency, $f = 50$, is given by formula (4), Section 6, that is,

$$\sigma_f = \sqrt{50(1 - \frac{50}{100})} = 5.$$

From this we can infer that in 95% of the samples the number of heads will lie within the range, $50 \pm 2\sigma_f$, that is, between 40 and 60. In a class of 50 only two or three students should report heads outside of these limits. Since the probable error is $0.6745 \times 5 = 3.37$, slightly less than half the class will report heads within the range 47 and 53, inclusive.

Example 2. One hundred coins are tossed and the probability of obtaining heads in a single toss is computed from the observed number of heads. Within what limits should this probability lie?

Solution. Using formula (3) of Section 6, we get

$$\sigma_p = \sqrt{\frac{½(1 - ½)}{100}} = 0.05;$$

the probable error is thus,

$$0.6745\,\sigma_p = 0.0337.$$

Hence we conclude that the probability is ½ that the probability obtained from our experiment will lie within the range $0.5 + 0.0337 = 0.5337$ and $0.5 - 0.0337 = 0.4663$.

We are now able to explain the table introduced in Section 1 of this chapter, which gives the upper and lower limits of an observed probability, p_N, with theoretical value 0.50, for various values of N. The limits of p_N, as recorded in this table, are $0.50 \pm k$, where k is the probable error of p_N, namely,

ELEMENTS OF THE THEORY OF PROBABILITY

$$k = 0.6745 \sqrt{\frac{\frac{1}{2}(1-\frac{1}{2})}{N}} = \frac{0.3372}{\sqrt{N}}.$$

Thus for $N = 100$, we get the limits just computed above. For $N = 200$, we have $k = 0.3372/\sqrt{200} = 0.0238$; for $N = 900$, we get $k = 0.3372/\sqrt{900} = 0.0112$, and so on.

Example 3. In Example 1 of Section 1, Chapter 3, an arithmetic average based on a frequency of $N = 46$ items was found to be 1.28. In Example 2 of that same section and chapter, by a rearrangement of the data, an average of 2.61 was found. Are these values significantly different from one another?

Solution. The standard deviation for the problem in question was found to be 27.22. Hence the standard error of the arithmetic average is given by

$$\sigma_A = \frac{27.22}{\sqrt{46}} = 4.01,$$

and the probable error of A is

$$\text{p.e. of } A = 0.6745\,\sigma_A = 2.70.$$

Since the difference between the two averages, namely $2.61 - 1.28 = 1.33$, is less than half the probable error, it is clear that no significant difference exists.

Example 4. Two candidates A and B are running for office in a city ward which polls 10,000 votes. In a straw vote of 100 chosen at random from the electorate, A is found to have 60 votes and B 40 votes. How could the election be forecast from this result?

Solution. The standard errors of 60 and 40, designated respectively by σ_A and σ_B, are respectively

$$\sigma_A = \sqrt{60(1-0.60)} = \sqrt{24} = 5\text{-},\qquad \sigma_B = \sqrt{40(1-0.40)} = 5\text{-}.$$

Adding and subtracting twice the standard error from the sample we get the following limits for any other sample:

	For A	For B
Upper limit:	70	50
Lower limit:	50	30

Hence, if the original sample has been carefully chosen so that no bias exists in it, the most probable forecast for the election will be a vote between 5,000 and 7,000 for A and a vote between 3,000 and 5,000 for B. We might interpret this to mean that B has a slender chance for election, but the odds are heavily in A's favor.

PROBLEMS

1. Given $A = 30$, $\sigma = 10$, $N = 1000$, compute the probable error of A. Explain the meaning to be attached to the value thus obtained.

2. What is the standard error of $p = 0.35$, if this value has been found from a sample of 500 items?

3. In a binomial distribution of 256 frequencies, one observes a frequency of 50. What is the probable error of this frequency?

4. One hundred coins are tossed and a frequency of 70 heads is observed. What is the probability of obtaining such a value if the coins are not biased?

5. In an election poll it was found that the probability of election for a certain candidate was 0.55. If 100 people were interviewed in obtaining this probability, and if they may be regarded as representative of the electorate, what is the standard error of the figure obtained?

8. *Distributions Which are not Normal.*

All statistical frequency distributions are not normal, and there are cases where this abnormality is large. Hence, it is always a matter of importance in making estimates from sampling to know, if possible, from what kind of a distribution the sample is taken.

It will be impossible for us in this brief treatment to investigate many types of distribution, but the description of two or three will suffice to indicate the nature of the problem which they present.

One of the simplest of these is the rectangular distribution, which we have discussed in Section 5 of Chapter 2. This distribution is one in which all the frequencies are equal throughout the range.

In the accompanying figure we have shown a rectangular distribution, equal in total frequency to the binomial distribution exhibited with it. Observing that the total number of class marks is $2n + 1$, we know from Section 3 that the standard deviation of the binomial distribution, designated by σ_B, is given by the formula: $\sigma_B = \frac{1}{2}\sqrt{2n}$. It can be proved that the standard deviation of the rectangular distribu-

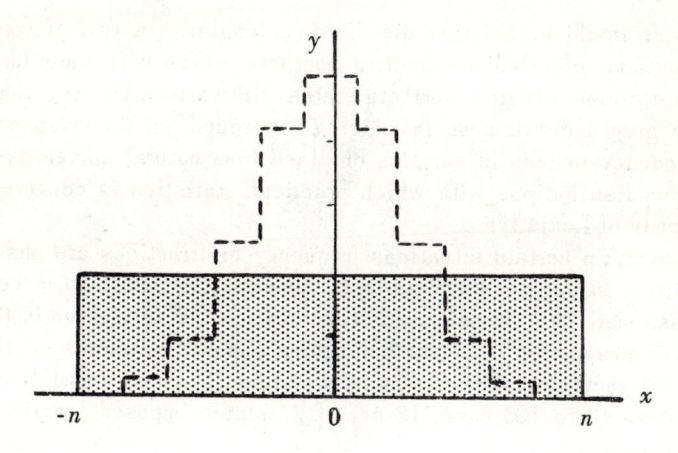

Figure 27.

tion, which we shall designate by σ_R, is given similarly by the formula: $\sigma_R = \sqrt{n(n+1)/3}$.

If we form what is called the *Lexis ratio*, namely the ratio,

$$L = \frac{\sigma_R}{\sigma_B},$$

we obtain the value:

$$L = \sqrt{\frac{n(n+1)}{3} \cdot \frac{2}{n}} = \sqrt{\frac{2(n+1)}{3}}.$$

Hence L is always greater than unity and increases as n increases. This means that the dispersion of the rectangular distribution is always greater than that of the binomial distribution with which we have compared it.

Any frequency distribution in which L exceeds unity, when the comparison is made with a binomial distribution, is said to be of *Lexis type*, the name being taken from that of the German statistician, W. Lexis (1837-1914). It can be shown that frequency distributions formed by the addition of frequencies obtained from sets of data with different underlying probabilities are of this kind. Thus, if the leaves from several different trees are gathered and a distribution formed by measurements of their length of stem it is likely that

94 POLITICAL STATISTICS

the result would be a Lexis distribution. Similarly, a poll of votes on a national election, taken from Southern states with their large Democratic bias and from Northern states with various biases, would usually give a distribution in which L exceeded unity. Because of this tendency to bias in samples obtained from natural universes of data, the distributions with which practical statistics is concerned are usually of Lexis type.

However, in certain situations frequency distributions are observed with a strong tendency toward concentration about some central class mark. An example of this is found in the data given in the preceding chapter on the legal limitations imposed by states on the length of their legislative sessions. Although these legal limits varied from 40 to 130 days, 18 out of 27 states imposed lengths of 60 or 61 days.

For series of the kind just described the standard deviation is less than the corresponding binomial distribution. Thus the Lexis ratio is less than unity. Such distributions are said to be of *Poisson type*, the name being taken from that of the French mathematician, S. Poisson (1781-1840), who studied a special distribution of this kind.

As an illustration let us consider the following two distributions of which the first, designated by B, is the binomial distribution corresponding to $n = 10$, and the second, designated by P, is one in which there is an unusual concentration of values about the mean:

Class Marks (x):	0	1	2	3	4	5	6	7	8	9	10
Frequencies (B):	1	10	45	120	210	252	210	120	45	10	1
Frequencies (P):	1	5	20	96	190	400	190	96	20	5	1

These data are graphically represented in Figure 28, the shaded area corresponding to the distribution P, and the other to the binomial distribution B. Computing the respective standard deviations we obtain, $\sigma_P = 1.30$ and $\sigma_B = 1.58$. Hence the Lexis ratio has the value:

$$L = \frac{\sigma_P}{\sigma_B} = \frac{1.30}{1.58} = 0.82,$$

which is less than unity.

It is also customary to speak of frequency distributions with the characteristics described above as being *hypernormal*, if their disper-

Figure 28.

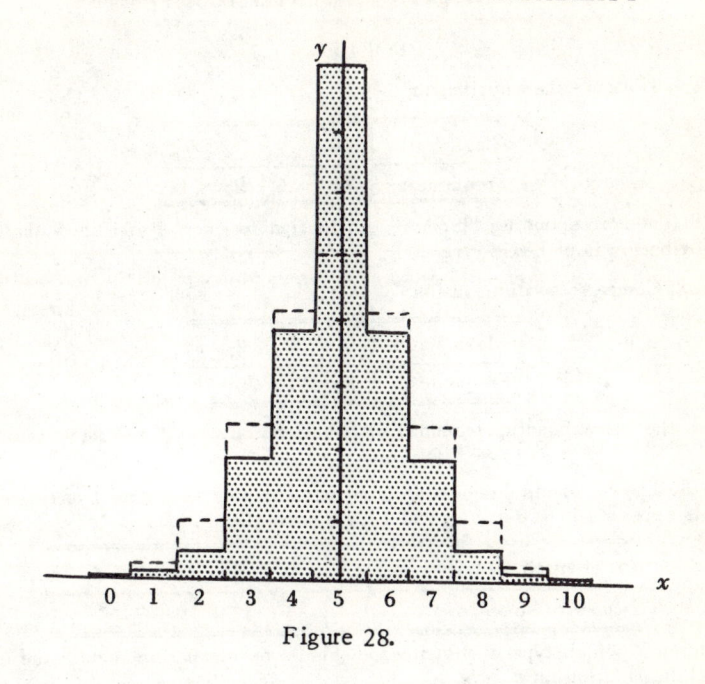

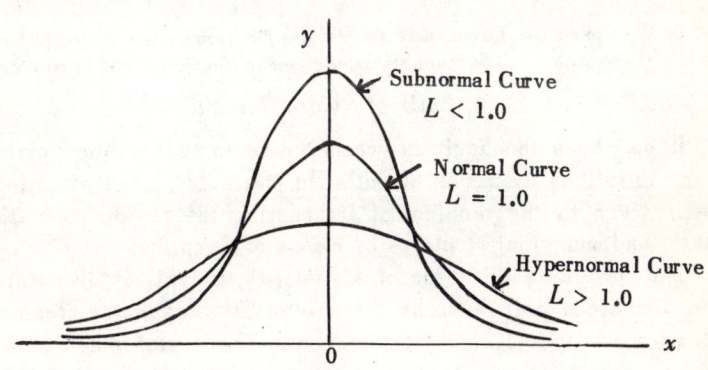

Figure 29.

sion is greater than that of the normal (or binomial) distribution and *subnormal* if their dispersion is less than that of the normal distribution. This situation is graphically portrayed in Figure 29.

PROBLEMS

1. Compare the distribution

Class Marks	0	1	2	3
Frequencies	11	25	25	11

with the corresponding binomial distribution for $n = 3$ and show that this distribution is of Lexis type.

2. Compare the distribution:

Class Marks	0	1	2	3
Frequencies	8	28	28	8

with the corresponding binomial distribution for $n = 3$ and show that this distribution is of Poisson type.

3. The following frequency distribution records the number of times ten tails appeared in 100 samples of 1024 tosses of ten coins:

No. of times 10 tails appeared	0	1	2	3	4	5
Number of samples	34	37	19	7	2	1

Determine which type of distribution this is by comparing it with the binomial distribution for $n = 5$.

4. Determine the Lexis ratio for the distribution of the political composition of the House of Representatives given in Section 3 of Chapter 2.

9. *Polls of Public Opinion.*

It has been the habit in recent years to test public opinion on many questions by means of polls. In particular, much attention has been given to the problem of forecasting the results of national, state, and municipal elections by means of sampling.

The hazard in this type of statistical analysis is illustrated by the disastrous poll taken by the *Literary Digest* in the presidential election of 1936. Hitherto this magazine had established an excellent accuracy in such prediction. It forecast the election in 1924 with an error of one per cent, in 1928 with an error of 4.4%, and in 1932 with an error of less than one per cent. But in 1936 it predicted that the Republican candidate would win with a majority of 56 per cent of the popular vote. As a matter of fact he received only 37 per cent of the ballots cast. So disastrous was this fiasco that the publication of the *Literary Digest* was discontinued.

The interesting fact about this forecast was that it was made on the basis of one of the largest polls of public opinion ever made. Of ten million ballots sent out, 2,376,523 were returned. Yet in spite of a sample of this size, a completely erroneous picture of the opinions of the electorate was obtained.

An analysis of the poll afforded at least a partial explanation of its failure. As we shall show later in this volume there is a close relationship between political and economic events. In 1936 the nation was emerging from the effects of the depression; large numbers of people were still on relief rolls, and the country was conscious of its economic ills. Under these conditions the *Literary Digest* relied for its samples principally upon lists of telephone subscribers and automobile owners. The effect of this selection was to poll the opinion of people in the higher income brackets, but it left largely untouched the opinion of those more heavily burdened with economic problems. Other polls of similar high income groups showed approximately the same ratios as those obtained by the *Literary Digest*.

Technically stated, the error in the *Literary Digest* poll was one of *stratification*. By this we mean that all groups were not sampled proportionately to their numerical strength. The problem of stratification is one well known in the applications of sampling and the necessity of taking it into account is illustrated by the care which one must exercise in not judging the contents of a bushel of apples from the size of those on the first layer. Some of the most careful sampling techniques, designed to remove this statistical error, have been developed by industrial organizations to test the quality of their products. An extensive survey of the problem of sampling has recently been published by W. E. Deming.*

In spite of the disastrous fate of the *Literary Digest*, the problem of forecasting public opinion was continued by several agencies. Prominent among these was the poll of the American Institute of Public Opinion conducted by G. H. Gallup, the *Fortune* poll by E. Roper, and that of Crossley Incorporated by A. M. Crossley. The results of these agencies for the presidential elections for the years 1936, 1940, and 1944 were as shown in the table on the next page.

Encouraged by these successful predictions, the pollsters enlarged their field of operation. Political and social questions of many kinds were investigated and the opinions of the public were sought

---

***Some Theory of Sampling*. New York, 1950.

| | Democratic and Republican Ratios in Presidential Vote |||
		1936	1940	1944
Gallup:	D	54	52.0	51.5
	R	46	48.0	48.5
Roper:	D	62	55.2	53.6
	R	38	44.8	46.4
Crossley:	D	54	50.4	52.2
	R	46	49.6	47.8
Actual Vote:	D	62.2	55.0	53.8
	R	37.8	45.0	46.2

by the route of polls. In most of these cases there was no way to check independently the accuracy of the opinion, as in election forecasts, since the poll merely estimated the collective views of a group of citizens on some problem of public interest. The highly subjective character of such polls was shown by the fact that there was usually a considerable percentage of those questioned who had no settled opinion on the matter under review. But this was, perhaps, one of the most important aspects of the poll, since it measured the magnitude of the indecision of the population and hence the magnitude of the task of propagandists and lobbyists, who wished to confirm by legislation or other action the opinions expressed.

Since no independent check was available in most polls of public opinion, unusual interest was directed to those polls which forecasted elections; a comparison of the prediction with the actual vote was a measure of the reliability of polls in general. But disaster again overtook this method of determining public opinion and the results obtained in forecasting the election of 1948 were almost as bad as those which had overwhelmed the *Literary Digest* twelve years before. On the eve of the election the three forecasting agencies mentioned above agreed on the results which were to be expected in the vote. The situation was complicated by the revolt of the Southern Democrats and the formation of a Progressive party, but the same element of high economic activity prevailed, which had been a large factor in the three previous elections. However that may be, the three polls gave as their final estimates of the situation the following forecasts of the percentage of the total vote which would be obtained respectively by the Republican and Democratic parties. It is interesting to observe that Roper, who had had phenomenal success in

ELEMENTS OF THE THEORY OF PROBABILITY

almost perfect prediction of the three previous elections, was in error by more than twelve per cent in this election.

	Gallup	Roper	Crossley	Actual Vote
Republican:	49.5	52.8	50.1	45.2
Democratic:	44.5	37.5	45.0	49.6

With this disastrous result before them, the pollsters showed undue caution in their analysis of the election of 1952. Making use of the same technique which had been so successfully employed by the oldest forecasting organization in history, the oracle of Delphi, the forecasters gave their polls with so generous a margin of probable error that the election could be won by either candidate. As we have remarked before, in polling subjective opinions there is always a large margin of error. Many people contacted have reached no firm opinion and the undecided vote is usually a substantial part of the poll. In the election of 1952 the pollsters agreed that the results depended upon this undecided vote, which on election day would necessarily crystallize and thus decide the fate of the candidates. It is a curious matter that the polls were unable to predict the landslide character of the presidential vote, 55.1% for the Republican candidate and 44.3% for the Democratic candidate. There is evidence to show, however, that in spite of the presidential vote, there still existed a prevailing Democratic majority in the electorate. For if the percentage is computed on the basis of the total vote for governors in the 29 states in which there were contests between Republican and Democratic candidates, the vote stood 49.8% for the Republicans and 50.2% for the Democrats. Undoubtedly the polling agencies encountered much of this opinion, which would be reflected in a large measure of indecision in stating party preferences.

10. *Forecasting the Election of 1944.*

It will be of interest statistically to study the reliability of election polls, assuming that due care has been given to securing the sample. We shall consider the results obtained by the Gallup poll in its successful forecast of the political election of 1944.

In the following table we give the percentages forecasted by the poll for each state as of November 1st, together with the actual figures in the official count.

		Poll Forecast		Actual Count	
State	Number of Electoral Votes	Republican Percentage	Democratic Percentage	Republican Percentage	Democratic Percentage
Alabama	11	22	78	18.3	81.7
Arizona	4	42	58	41.0	59.0
Arkansas	9	28	72	29.9	70.1
California	25	47	53	43.2	56.8
Colorado	6	56	44	53.4	46.6
Connecticut	8	48	52	47.3	52.7
Delaware	3	49	51	45.4	54.6
Florida	8	29	71	29.7	70.3
Georgia	12	19	81	17.4	82.6
Idaho	4	49	51	48.3	51.7
Illinois	28	51	49	48.3	51.7
Indiana	13	55	45	52.9	47.1
Iowa	10	56	44	52.3	47.7
Kansas	8	64	36	60.6	39.4
Kentucky	11	46	54	45.4	54.6
Louisiana	10	22	78	19.4	80.6
Maine	5	52	48	52.5-	47.5+
Maryland	8	47	53	48.1	51.9
Massachusetts	16	49	51	47.1	52.9
Michigan	19	54	46	49.5-	50.5+
Minnesota	11	53	47	47.2	52.8
Mississippi	9	11	89	2.3	97.7*
Missouri	15	51	49	48.5+	51.5-
Montana	4	46	54	45.3	54.7
Nebraska	6	62	38	58.6	41.4
Nevada	3	46	54	45.4	54.6
New Hampshire	4	49	51	47.9	52.1
New Jersey	16	52	48	49.3	50.7
New Mexico	4	51	49	46.5-	53.5+
New York	47	50+	50-	47.5-	52.5+
North Carolina	14	29	71	33.2	66.8
North Dakota	4	62	38	54.2	45.8
Ohio	25	52	48	50.2	49.8
Oklahoma	10	49	51	44.3	55.7
Oregon	6	49	51	47.5+	52.5-
Pennsylvania	35	49	51	48.6	51.4
Rhode Island	4	44	56	41.3	58.7
South Carolina	8	11	89	4.8	95.2
South Dakota	4	64	36	58.3	41.7
Tennessee	12	36	64	39.4	60.6
Texas	23	22	78	19.9	81.1
Utah	4	44	56	39.5-	60.5+
Vermont	3	55	45	57.1	42.9
Virginia	11	36	64	37.6	62.4
Washington	8	46	54	42.6	57.4
West Virginia	8	49	51	45.1	54.9
Wisconsin	12	56	44	50.9	49.1
Wyoming	3	53	47	51.2	48.8
	531				

*Votes cast for other than the party candidates included 9,964 Regular Democrats and 7,859 Independent Republicans. If these are added to their respective parties, the percentages would be respectively 6.4 and 94.6.

ELEMENTS OF THE THEORY OF PROBABILITY

In the total popular vote of 48,026,170 the Republicans had a total of 22,006,616 and the Democrats 25,603,152. Hence, their respective percentages of the total were 45.8 and 53.1. Since, however, the figures in the table are computed on the basis of the Republican and Democratic votes alone, we shall use the percentages based on the totals of these two parties only. Thus we have out of a total of 47,609,768 votes cast, 46.2 per cent for the Republican party and 53.8 per cent for the Democratic party.

Our interest in these results is in making a statistical appraisal of the efficiency of the forecast. To do this we must have some idea as to the standard error in the percentage estimate. In the first place we observe that the percentages do not form a normal distribution, since the Southern states maintain their traditional bias and give abnormal majorities in favor of the Democratic party. This shows that we are dealing with a distribution of Lexis type. In the second place, although the figures in the table are percentages, they represent probabilities and can be analyzed as such.

We shall consider first the problem of determining the national average forecasted by the distribution and the size of its standard error. It would appear logical, at first sight, to weigh each probability by the electoral vote which it represents. But this, unfortunately, will give undue bias to the data since states vary greatly in the per cent of votes cast by the total population. Thus Illinois, with a population of 7,897,241 (1940) cast a total vote in 1944 of 4,036,061, while Alabama, with a population of 2,832,961, cast a total vote of only 244,743. That is to say, with a population equal to 6% of the national total, Illinois cast a vote equal to 8.4% of the national total, while Alabama, with 2.15% of the population, cast a vote of 0.51% of the total. In the electoral college of 531 members Alabama has 11 votes (approximately 0.0215×531), while Illinois has 28. But if representation were based upon the percentage of vote, as it must be in statistical analysis, these figures should be revised to 3 (approximately 0.0215×531) and 45 (approximately 0.084×531) respectively. It is this system of revised weights which we shall use in our computation. These revised weights, shown in the third table below, are denoted by w_i.

Since the weights enter linearly into our computation, they can be combined for states with the same probabilities. Thus, for the probability 0.89, we find two states, Mississippi and South Carolina, with a combined weight of 3. Hence to the probability 0.89 we give the weight 3. In this manner we obtain the following table:

p_i	w_i	$p_i w_i$	p_i	w_i	$p_i w_i$	p_i	w_i	$p_i w_i$
0.89	3	2.67	0.56	6	3.36	0.48	60	28.80
0.81	4	3.24	0.54	23	12.42	0.47	13	6.11
0.78	18	14.04	0.53	46	24.38	0.46	24	11.04
0.72	2	1.44	0.52	31	16.12	0.45	19	8.55
0.71	15	10.65	0.51	69	35.19	0.44	33	14.52
0.64	10	6.40	0.50	70	35.00	0.38	8	3.04
0.58	2	1.16	0.49	64	31.36	0.36	11	3.96
						Totals	531	273.45

From the totals we obtain the average probability to be

$$p = \frac{273.45}{531} = 0.515-,$$

which is observed to agree with the probability announced by Gallup.

In order to obtain the variance corresponding to this probability, we must compute the sum

$$\sigma^2 = \frac{\Sigma w_i (p_i - p)^2}{\Sigma w_i}. \tag{1}$$

This computation is given in the following table where we take $p = 0.51$.

p_i	w_i	(p_i-p)	$w_i(p_i-p)^2$	p_i	w_i	(p_i-p)	$w_i(p_i-p)^2$
0.89	3	0.38	0.4332	0.51	69	0.00	0.0000
0.81	4	0.30	0.3600	0.50	70	-0.01	0.0070
0.78	18	0.27	1.3122	0.49	64	-0.02	0.0256
0.72	2	0.21	0.0882	0.48	60	-0.03	0.0540
0.71	15	0.20	0.6000	0.47	13	-0.04	0.0208
0.64	10	0.13	0.1690	0.46	24	-0.05	0.0600
0.58	2	0.07	0.0098	0.45	19	-0.06	0.0684
0.56	6	0.05	0.0150	0.44	33	-0.07	0.1617
0.54	23	0.03	0.0207	0.38	8	-0.13	0.1350
0.53	46	0.02	0.0184	0.36	11	-0.15	0.2475
0.52	31	0.01	0.0031	Totals	531		3.8096

From the totals we then obtain

$$\sigma^2 = \frac{3.8096}{531} = 0.007174,$$

and consequently, $\sigma = 0.085$.

In spite of the obvious skewness of the distribution we shall consider that this value of σ represents the standard error of the distribution itself.

But the standard error of the average, which we shall denote by σ_P, will be given approximately by the formula:

$$\sigma_P = \frac{\sigma}{\sqrt{531}} = \frac{0.085}{\sqrt{531}} = 0.0037. \tag{2}$$

Hence, if the poll is reliable, the actual probability should lie within the limits:

$$p \pm 2\sigma_P = 0.515 \pm 0.007 = 0.522 \text{ and } 0.508.$$

The observed probability was actually 0.538, a value which does not lie within the computed range. As a matter of fact it exceeds the estimated value of 0.515 by an amount equal to about six times the standard deviation. This might be partially explained by the fact that we are analyzing a distribution which is far from normal, but the existence of so great a difference between estimated and observed values should have been a matter of some concern. Either the size of the sample from which the computations were made was too small, or the uncertainty of the subjective vote was too great to make the sample reliable. Excellent as the forecast appeared to be, an analysis of the kind just made would indicate the existence of difficulties in the technique.

If we now examine the poll forecast for the electoral vote, we see that the sum of the weights for values of p above 0.50 total 292 and for values of p below 0.50 total 239. The actual vote in the electoral college was 432 Democratic and 99 Republican.

But we observe that many of the probabilities are close to 0.50; and the question is how great an error exists in the probabilities for individual states. To answer this we must appeal to the actual state percentages, since we have no information as to how large the sample was in determining the percentages in the poll.

Hence we form the following table of values. Then from the two totals we can compute the variance of the error which we shall designate by σ_E^2, that is,

$$\sigma_E^2 = \frac{0.5392}{531} = 0.001015.$$

State	w_i	$\bar{p}_i$ (poll)	p_i (actual)	$\bar{p}_i - p_i$	$w_i(\bar{p}_i - p_i)^2$
Alabama	3	0.78	0.82	-0.04	0.0048
Arizona	2	0.58	0.59	-0.01	0.0002
Arkansas	2	0.72	0.70	0.02	0.0008
California	39	0.53	0.57	-0.04	0.0624
Colorado	6	0.44	0.47	-0.03	0.0054
Connecticut	9	0.52	0.53	-0.01	0.0009
Delaware	1	0.51	0.55	-0.04	0.0016
Florida	6	0.71	0.70	0.01	0.0006
Georgia	4	0.81	0.83	-0.02	0.0016
Idaho	2	0.51	0.52	-0.01	0.0002
Illinois	45	0.49	0.52	-0.03	0.0405
Indiana	18	0.45	0.47	-0.02	0.0072
Iowa	12	0.44	0.48	-0.04	0.0192
Kansas	8	0.36	0.39	-0.03	0.0072
Kentucky	10	0.54	0.55	-0.01	0.0010
Louisiana	4	0.78	0.81	-0.03	0.0036
Maine	3	0.48	0.48	0.00	0.0000
Maryland	7	0.53	0.52	0.01	0.0007
Massachusetts	22	0.51	0.53	-0.02	0.0088
Michigan	24	0.46	0.51	-0.05	0.0600
Minnesota	12	0.47	0.53	-0.06	0.0432
Mississippi	2	0.89	0.95	-0.06	0.0072
Missouri	17	0.49	0.51	-0.02	0.0068
Montana	2	0.54	0.55	-0.01	0.0002
Nebraska	6	0.38	0.41	-0.03	0.0054
Nevada	1	0.54	0.55	-0.01	0.0001
New Hampshire	3	0.51	0.52	-0.01	0.0003
New Jersey	22	0.48	0.51	-0.03	0.0198
New Mexico	2	0.49	0.53	-0.04	0.0032
New York	70	0.50	0.53	-0.03	0.0630
North Carolina	9	0.71	0.67	0.04	0.0144
North Dakota	2	0.38	0.46	-0.08	0.0128
Ohio	35	0.48	0.50	-0.02	0.0140
Oklahoma	8	0.51	0.56	-0.05	0.0200
Oregon	5	0.51	0.52	-0.01	0.0005
Pennsylvania	42	0.51	0.51	0.00	0.0000
Rhode Island	3	0.56	0.59	-0.03	0.0027
South Carolina	1	0.89	0.95	-0.06	0.0036
South Dakota	3	0.36	0.42	-0.06	0.0108
Tennessee	6	0.64	0.61	0.03	0.0054
Texas	11	0.78	0.81	-0.03	0.0099
Utah	3	0.56	0.61	-0.05	0.0075
Vermont	1	0.45	0.43	0.02	0.0004
Virginia	4	0.64	0.62	0.02	0.0016
Washington	10	0.54	0.57	-0.03	0.0090
West Virginia	8	0.51	0.55	-0.04	0.0128
Wisconsin	15	0.44	0.49	-0.05	0.0375
Wyoming	1	0.47	0.49	-0.02	0.0004
	531				0.5392

ELEMENTS OF THE THEORY OF PROBABILITY 105

From this we then obtain: $\sigma_E = 0.032$, which is the standard error of the error in the forecasted probabilities. Thus any actual probability, $\bar{p}_i$, should differ from the forecasted probability p_i by not more than $2\sigma_E = 0.064$.

It is very interesting to observe that if we place in the Republican column all those states which had a Democratic probability of 0.47 or less, that is, where the probability was at least one σ_E below 0.50, then we get an electoral vote of 99, exactly equal to the one observed. If we place in the Democratic column those with a probability of 0.53 or greater we get an electoral vote of 198. Between the limits $50 \pm \sigma_E = 53$ to 47, we find the doubtful electoral vote of 234. The actual election count showed 7 states, electoral total 44, with Democratic percentages 47 or lower and 22 states, electoral total 297, with Democratic percentages 53 or higher. This left a total electoral vote of 190 between these limits. In this way we observe again the hazardous statistical situation faced by the election polls, which would sooner or later result in the error that upset the forecasts for the year 1948.

11. *Forecasting the Election of 1948.*

The statistical difficulties which we have described in the preceding section finally caught up with the forecasters in 1948. Since this failure of the polls is a matter of much interest, it will be worth while to examine the details of one of them by the analysis which we have applied to the data for the election of 1944.

In this election the vote was divided among four principal candidates, those nominated by the Republican, the Democratic, the States' Rights, and the Progressive parties. The actual percentages of the total vote received by these candidates compared with the forecast by the Gallup poll are recorded in the following table:

	Republican	Democrat	States' Rights	Progressive
Forecast Percentage:	49.9	44.5	2.2	3.4
Actual Percentage:	45.2	49.6	2.4	2.3

By an analysis similar to that already given, we find that the standard deviation of the Republican probabilities, distributed with respect to states, as computed by formula (1) of Section 10, has the value: $\sigma = 0.08$. From this quantity we obtain by means of formula (2) of Section 10 the following estimate of the standard deviation of the computed probability p, namely, $\sigma_p = 0.0035$.

The measure of the unreliability of the poll is obtained from the fact that the difference between the computed probability $p = 0.499$ and the observed probability 0.452, that is to say, $0.499 - 0.452 = 0.047$ was of the order of $13\sigma_p$. From the point of view of statistical estimation, this is an intolerable difference.

In the analysis of the forecasts of the probable votes by states, a similar situation is found to prevail. Applying the methods described in Section 10, we obtain for the value of the standard deviation σ_E the estimate, $\sigma_E = 0.055$. Using as our measure the value $2\sigma_E = 0.11$, we see that the actual probability p_i for the state vote should not differ from the estimated probability $\bar{p}_i$ by more than 0.11. But this is a very large error and would make the forecasting of the electoral vote essentially impossible.

Thus, if we place in the Democratic column all the states which have a Republican probability of 0.44 or less, that is, where the probability was at least one σ_E below 0.51, then we get an electoral vote of 124. And if, similarly, we place in the Republican column all the states with a Republican probability of 0.56 or greater, then we can forecast a minimum electoral vote of 42. As a matter of fact, one of the seven states which met this test was Wisconsin, which actually showed a Democratic majority. On this method of forecasting the final electoral vote, in which the observed standard deviation is used as the measuring rod, it is clear that an electoral vote of 365 is doubtful. The difficulty of making a safe forecast in the face of this statistical analysis is quite evident.

12. *Concluding Remarks.*

In this chapter we have considered some of the elements of the theory of statistical sampling. Beginning with the concept of probability, we have shown the connection between the theory of chance and the theory of frequency distributions. Different types of such distributions have been exhibited and two classes have been defined which vary significantly from the normal distribution, used as the fundamental norm in most statistical sampling analysis.

As an example illustrating the techniques of sampling, the problem of forecasting public opinion by means of polls was discussed. This very difficult subject was shown to have had a thorny history.

After a period of successful prediction, the *Literary Digest* poll was completely wrong in its forecast of the election of 1936 and twelve years later succeeding polls ran into disaster.

As a result of this lack of reliability in measuring public opinion, many people reached the conclusion that there was a flaw in the theory of statistics and that the entire subject should be regarded with suspicion. This is a very unfortunate conclusion and is clearly untenable as is shown by the high success obtained by production enterprises in the application of quality control to their manufacturing processes. Quality control is fundamentally a technique for the securing of proper samples and the analysis of these samples to determine the *tolerance limits* which they define.

A careful statistical appraisal has been made of one of the national polls for the elections of 1944 and 1948. This analysis showed that the forecasted probabilities were outside the tolerance limits defined by the analysis and that conclusions reached by way of the samples were not to be trusted.

But criticism of the polls should be tempered by respect for the courage of those who have pioneered in this interesting adventure of measuring public opinion. The difficulties are quite obvious. In the first place, public opinion is a highly subjective matter. People change their opinions readily and many have no firm convictions at any time. There is thus a considerable element of uncertainty in the original data. In the second place, the opinion of a large group of people, let us say of the order of the entire electorate, is to be determined by the opinion of a very small group of people. No matter how much care is exercised in determining the sample, it appears almost impossible to prevent bias from entering such a pattern. In the third place, the time factor is important. Public opinion is a very fluid thing and convictions held in July may be very different from those held in November. While there remains a certain inertia in the underlying fabric of public opinion in the sense that many people have fixed beliefs and fixed prejudices which are not easily changed, there exists, nevertheless, a large population easily influenced by the turn of events. It is this population which makes hazardous the lives of those who attempt to measure public opinion.

CHAPTER 5

THE THEORY OF CORRELATION

1. *Functional Relationships.*

IN MATHEMATICS and the exact sciences the concept of a functional relationship is a basic one. A *function* may be defined as follows: *If two variables x and y are so related that when a value of x is given, y can be determined, then y is said to be a function of x.*

By a *variable* we mean any quantity which, under the conditions of the problem in which it enters, may assume different values.

For example, we may define a function by the equation: $y = 2x$. Thus when $x = 1$, $y = 2$, when $x = 10$, $y = 20$, etc. Although most functional relationships in mathematics can be expressed in the form of equations, this is not always the case. Thus we might say that y is 1 when x is a prime number (namely, one divisible only by itself and unity), but $y = 0$ when x is not a prime number. Thus, when $x = 5$, $y = 1$, but when $x = 6$, $y = 0$.

Functions, as we have just said, are commonly defined by equations between the variables. Thus we might have: $y = 3x + 2$, $y = x^2 + 2x - 1$, etc. From such expressions it is possible to compute tables of related values. Thus, considering the first function, namely, $y = 3x + 2$, we let x assume integral values from $x = -3$ to $x = 3$. For example, if $x = 2$, $y = 6 + 2 = 8$; for $x = -2$, $y = -6 + 2 = -4$. In this way we obtain the following table:

x	-3	-2	-1	0	1	2	3
y	-7	-4	-1	2	5	8	11

Similarly for the second equation, namely, $y = x^2 + 2x - 1$, over the same range of values of x we obtain the following set of related values:

x	-3	-2	-1	0	1	2	3
y	2	-1	-2	-1	2	7	14

Since in this manner we have converted equations into tables of related values, it is clear that functional relationships may also be given directly by tables of values. This is the case in many applications where the actual equation may not be known.

Functions of a variable x are commonly designated by the symbol $f(x)$, which is read "f of x." Thus, for example, we can write $f(x) = x^2$, in which case $f(2) = 2^2 = 4$, $f(-3) = (-3)^2 = 9$, etc. We have already introduced a symbol in Chapter 4 where we designated by $I(t)$ the area under the normal curve between the ordinates at 0 and t.

PROBLEMS

1. Compute a short table of values for the function: $y = -3x + 4$.

2. Compute the values of the function $y = -3x^2 + 2x + 5$, for values of x from $x = -4$ to $x = +4$, using only integral values of x. Does the function change sign over this range of values? What interpretation do you give for this?

3. Given $f(x) = \sqrt{2x}$, compute $f(0)$, $f(2)$, $f(6)$, $f(-2)$.

4. If $f(x) = 1/x$, compute $f(3) + f(2) + f(1)$.

5. If $f(x) = \dfrac{1}{2x - 1}$, show that $f(x + 1) - f(x) = \dfrac{2}{1 - 4x^2}$.

6. The table in Section 4 of Chapter 4 gives the value of the function: $f(x) = \dfrac{1}{\sqrt{2\pi}} e^{-\frac{1}{2}t^2}$. Find $f(1.3)$, $f(2.22)$, $f(-2.5)$.

7. In the table of Example 3, Section 1, Chapter 4, is the "number of living" a function of age? If so, compute this function for $x = 20$, $x = 33$, $x = 47$, where x is the age. Is age a function of the number of living? If so, compute this function for $y = 89,032$, $y = 75,000$, where y is the number of living.

2. *The Graphical Representation of Functions.*

At the threshold of the subject we find the problem of the graphical representation of the functions. While there are many ways in which statistical data are exhibited, the most common method of representing functions is by the Cartesian graph which was described in Section 2 of Chapter 2.

Since an adequate description of this method was presented in Chapter 2, we shall not review it here, but proceed to the discussion of the linear functions which will be useful to the purposes of this chapter.

3. *The Linear Function*

One of the most frequently encountered functions is defined by the equation,

$$y = ax + b, \qquad (1)$$

where a and b are constants.

The graphical representation of this function is a straight line and it is for this reason that it is called the *linear function*.

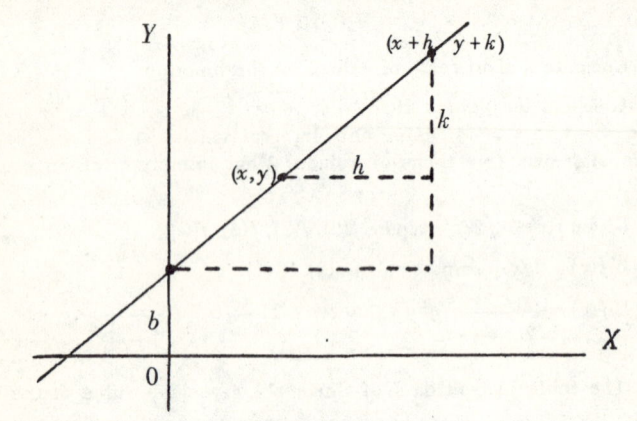

Figure 30.

That equation (1) represents a straight line can be established as follows: At any point (x,y), let x be increased by h and y by k, that is to say, let us consider the neighboring point $(x+h, y+k)$.

Since both points lie on the graph of equation (1), they satisfy simultaneously the equations:

$$y + k = a(x + h) + b \qquad (2)$$
$$y = ax + b.$$

Subtracting (3) from (2), we then have

$$k = ah,$$

from which it follows that

$$\frac{k}{h} = a.$$

THE THEORY OF CORRELATION

Hence the ratio, k/h, called the *slope* of the curve, is equal to the constant a. Since the only curve which has a constant slope is a straight line we are able to conclude that (1) is linear.

We also observe that when $x = 0$, then $y = b$. This value is called the *y-intercept* and is shown in Figure 30.

4. *Fitting a Straight Line to Data*

In statistical work one is usually more concerned with a problem inverse to that discussed in the preceding section. That is to say, we are often interested in solving the problem of finding the equation of a straight line which represents approximately a given set of data.

To illustrate the procedure, consider the following data:

x	2	3	4	7	10	12
y	1	4	6	9	14	15

If these points are represented graphically, they will be found to lie approximately, but not exactly, upon a straight line. The problem is to calculate the coefficients a and b of the straight line

$$y = ax + b,$$

determining them in such a way that the straight line will pass as near as possible to all the given points.

One method of achieving this is first to substitute the given values of x and y in the equation. We thus obtain the following sys-

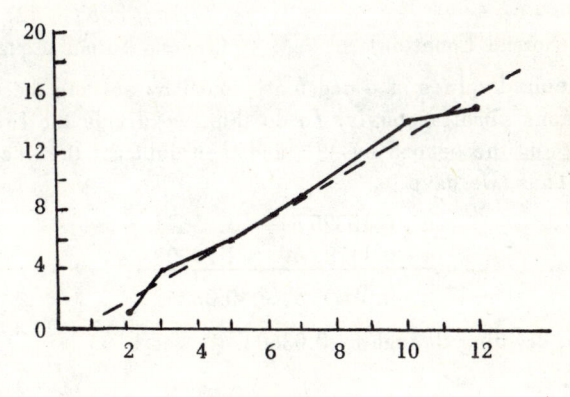

Figure 31.

tem of equations:

$$2a + b = 1$$
$$3a + b = 4$$
$$5a + b = 6$$
$$7a + b = 9$$
$$10a + b = 14$$
$$12a + b = 15.$$

It will be readily seen that no values of a and b can be found which will satisfy simultaneously all six equations. Hence, one must find one set of values which is the *best approximation* to a solution of the equations. The words *best approximation* are used in a particular sense here which it is not convenient to explain at this point.

In order to approximate the values of a and b, the equations just given are added. We thus have a single equation in the two unknowns, which is called the *first normal equation* of the system. To find the *second normal equation* we multiply each equation in turn by the coefficient of a and then add the set thus obtained. For the present example, we obtain the following:

$$2a + b = 1 \qquad\qquad 4a + 2b = 2$$
$$3a + b = 4 \qquad\qquad 9a + 3b = 12$$
$$5a + b = 6 \qquad\qquad 25a + 5b = 30$$
$$7a + b = 9 \qquad\qquad 49a + 7b = 63$$
$$10a + b = 14 \qquad\qquad 100a + 10b = 140$$
$$\underline{12a + b = 15} \qquad\qquad \underline{144a + 12b = 180}$$
$$39a + 6b = 49 \qquad\qquad 331a + 39b = 427$$

(First Normal Equation) \qquad (Second Normal Equation)

The desired values of a and b are found by solving the two normal equations simultaneously. To do this, we divide the first equation by 39 and the second by 331, and then subtract the second from the first. Thus, we have

$$a + 0.15385\,b = 1.25641$$
$$\underline{a + 0.11782\,b = 1.29003}$$
$$0.03603\,b = -0.03362.$$

Hence, dividing through by 0.03603, we get

$$b = -0.9331.$$

THE THEORY OF CORRELATION

Substituting this value in the first equation and solving for a, we obtain

$$a = 1.25641 - (-0.14356) = 1.25641 + 0.14356 = 1.39997.$$

Since we have more decimal points than necessary we reduce both values to $a = 1.40$ and $b = -0.93$. Hence the desired line becomes

$$y = 1.40x - 0.93. \qquad (1)$$

Substituting the given values of x in this equation we obtain the corresponding values of y as shown in the following table:

x	y (data)	$\bar{y}$ (computed)	$\|y - \bar{y}\|$	$(y - \bar{y})^2$
2	1	1.87	0.87	0.7569
3	4	3.27	0.73	0.5329
5	6	6.07	0.07	0.0049
7	9	8.87	0.13	0.0169
10	14	13.07	0.83	0.6889
12	15	15.87	0.87	0.7569
			Total	2.7574

The values of y and the line of best fit are graphically portrayed in Figure 31. The excellence of the approximation is easily seen.

From the last column in the above table it is possible to explain in what sense the line just computed is the line of best approximation to the data. The differences between the items of the data and the corresponding values of the line, if squared and summed, will be *smaller than for any other line*. For this reason, it is customary to call the line just computed the best approximation in the sense of *least squares*.

For example, suppose that the line

$$y = 1.44x - 1.13 \qquad (2)$$

were suggested as a better approximation.

In order to test this hypothesis, we compute the values corresponding to the data and form the sum $\Sigma(y - \bar{y})^2$, where y represents the data and $\bar{y}$ the values computed from (2). We then get the accompanying table of values.

The sum of the squared differences in this case exceeds the sum of the squared differences obtained from the original line described above. Hence the second line cannot be the best fit in the sense of least squares.

x	y (data)	$\bar{y}$ (computed)	$\|y - \bar{y}\|$	$(y - \bar{y})^2$
2	1	1.75	0.75	0.5625
3	4	3.19	0.81	0.6561
5	6	6.07	0.07	0.0049
7	9	8.95	0.05	0.0025
10	14	13.27	0.73	0.5329
12	15	16.15	1.15	1.3225
			Total	3.0814

PROBLEMS

1. What are the slopes of the following lines: $y = 5x + 2$; $3x + 2y = 5$; $x = 2y - 4$?

2. Represent graphically the function: $y = -3x + 7$.

3. Compute a table for the function: $y = -3x^2 + 2x + 5$ and represent it graphically.

4. Show graphically that the lines: $y = \frac{1}{2}x - 1$ and $y = -2x + 4$ are perpendicular to one another.

5. Given the following data:

x	1	2	3	4	5
y	7	5	5	2	0

determine the straight line, $y = ax + b$, which best represents them. Show this representation by graphing both the points and the line obtained.

6. Given the same data as in problem 5 but with the values for x and y interchanged, namely the data,

x	7	5	5	2	0
y	1	2	3	4	5

compute the straight line, $y = ax + b$, which best represents them. Is this the same straight line which was obtained in problem 5? Explain the difference.

THE THEORY OF CORRELATION

5. *General Formulas for Fitting a Straight Line to Data*

It will be of interest to us later to have a more general formula for evaluating the coefficients a and b in the equation

$$y = ax + b,$$

where x and y are given by the following set of data:

x	x_1	x_2	x_3	...	x_N
y	y_1	y_2	y_3	...	y_N

Proceeding as before, we form the following sets of equations:

$$x_1 a + b = y_1 \qquad\qquad x_1^2 a + x_1 b = x_1 y_1$$
$$x_2 a + b = y_2 \qquad\qquad x_2^2 a + x_2 b = x_2 y_2$$
$$x_3 a + b = y_3 \qquad\qquad x_3^2 a + x_3 b = x_3 y_3$$
$$\cdots \qquad\qquad\qquad \cdots$$
$$x_N a + b = y_N \qquad\qquad x_N^2 a + x_N b = x_N y_N$$

(First Normal Equation) \qquad (Second Normal Equation)

To solve these equations for a we multiply the first normal equation by Σx_i and the second by N, and subtract the first equation thus obtained from the second as follows:

$$(\Sigma x_i)^2 a + N \Sigma x_i b = \Sigma x_i \Sigma y_i$$
$$N \Sigma x_i^2 a + N \Sigma x_i b = N \Sigma x_i y_i$$
$$\overline{[N \Sigma x_i^2 - (\Sigma x_i)^2] a = N \Sigma x_i y_i - \Sigma x_i \Sigma y_i.}$$

Hence, dividing by the coefficient of a, we get

$$a = \frac{N \Sigma x_i y_i - \Sigma x_i \Sigma y_i}{N \Sigma x_i^2 - (\Sigma x_i)^2}. \tag{1}$$

Similarly to determine b we multiply the first normal equation by Σx_i^2, and the second by Σx_i and subtract the second equation thus obtained from the first as follows:

$$\Sigma x_i \Sigma x_i^2 a + N \Sigma x_i^2 b = \Sigma x_i^2 \Sigma y_i$$
$$\Sigma x_i \Sigma x_i^2 a + (\Sigma x_i)^2 b = \Sigma x_i \Sigma x_i y_i$$
$$\overline{[N \Sigma x_i^2 - (\Sigma x_i)^2] b = \Sigma x_i^2 \Sigma y_i - \Sigma x_i \Sigma x_i y_i.}$$

Hence dividing by the coefficient of b, we get

$$b = \frac{\Sigma x_i^2 \Sigma y_i - \Sigma x_i \Sigma x_i y_i}{N \Sigma x_i^2 - (\Sigma x_i)^2}. \qquad (2)$$

Example. Let us use these formulas to find the straight line corresponding to the data of Section 4, namely the following values:

x	2	3	5	7	10	12
y	1	4	6	9	14	15

To find a and b by the formulas we need the sums:

$\Sigma x_i = 2 + 3 + \cdots + 12 = 39,\quad \Sigma x_i^2 = 2^2 + 3^2 + \cdots + 12^2 = 331,$
$\Sigma y_i = 1 + 4 + \cdots + 15 = 49,\quad \Sigma x_i y_i = 2 \cdot 1 + 3 \cdot 4 + \cdots + 12 \cdot 15 = 427.$

Observing that $N = 6$, we then compute

$$a = \frac{6 \cdot 427 - 39 \cdot 49}{6 \cdot 331 - (39)^2} = \frac{2562 - 1911}{1986 - 1521} = \frac{651}{456} = 1.40.$$

$$b = \frac{331 \cdot 49 - 39 \cdot 427}{6 \cdot 331 - (39)^2} = \frac{16219 - 16653}{1986 - 1521} = -\frac{434}{465} = -0.93.$$

These values are seen to agree with those previously computed in Section 4.

PROBLEMS

1. Given the data of Problem 5, Section 4, determine a and b by the formulas of this section.

2. Using the data of Problem 6, Section 4, determine a and b by the formulas of this section.

3. If we designate Σy_i by m_0 and $\Sigma x_i y_i$ by m_1, compute the values of a and b, formulas (1) and (2) provided x has the values 1, 2, 3, 4, 5.

4. Noting the formulas:

$$1 + 2 + 3 + 4 + \cdots + n = \frac{n(n+1)}{2}$$

$$1^2 + 2^2 + 3^2 + 4^2 + \cdots + n^2 = \frac{n(n+1)(2n+1)}{6}$$

compute the values of a and b by formulas (1) and (2), using the abbreviations $\Sigma x_i = m_0$, $\Sigma x_i y_i = m_1$, provided x has the value $1, 2, 3, \ldots, n$.

6. *Correlations.*

In the applications of mathematics to problems in the world of experience one method of procedure is to discover relationships between two or more measured variables. Thus one finds that the intensity of light upon an object varies as the intensity of the illumination of the source and inversely as the square of the distance of the object from the source. Volumes of spheres vary as the cubes of their radii and the areas of circles as the squares of their diameters.

But there are many cases where the relationships are not as exact as those which we have just cited. Thus in economics we have the law that the demand for a quantity varies inversely with its price. But this variation is not an exact one. Where it has been tested statistically, there has been discovered a considerable variability in the law. Another example is found in the change of temperature with the number of minutes of daylight at a given place. From year to year the mean temperature of July 4 will show a considerable fluctuation although every July 4 at a specified location will have approximately the same number of minutes of daylight. But this variation is about an average value established for many July 4ths and a temperature curve can be established throughout a year from the total set of these mean values for every day. While a strict functional relationship thus does not exist between temperature and minutes of daylight, we can say that the two variables are *correlated*.

We may thus define the theory of correlation as the *theory of the concomitant variation of two or more attributes of a group of individual entities, the attributes being measured with respect to each entity*.

In an earlier chapter we found a wide variation in the size of the legislatures of individual states. We might suspect that this variation is accounted for by the variation in population in different states. Whether this is a tenable hypothesis or not may be tested by the methods of correlation. That it is not an exact relationship is seen from the fact that the state of New Hampshire with a population of less than half a million has a House of Representatives of 400 members, while New York with a population of nearly 13.5 millions has a House of 150 members.

A very satisfactory theory of correlation has been evolved by statisticians, which on the one hand exhibits its existence between two or more variables, and on the other defines a measure for it. We shall consider here only the case of linear correlation between two variables, that is to say, the theory and measurement of correlation where a linear relationship exists between the variables. More advanced treatises on statistics develop the theory of linear correlation between two or more variables as well as the theory of non-linear correlation.

7. The Correlation Coefficient.

In order to make the idea of correlation more precise, let us assume that we are considering two sets of related measurements which, for convenience, may be recorded in parallel rows as follows:

x-data: $\quad x_1 \quad x_2 \quad x_3 \ldots x_N$

y-data: $\quad y_1 \quad y_2 \quad y_3 \ldots y_N$.

Since a relationship is supposed to exist between the x-data and the y-data, we graph the points $(x_1, y_1), (x_2, y_2), \ldots, (x_N, y_N)$ in order to observe the character of this assumed relationship.

If the points group themselves about a straight line, then the two sets of data are said to be *linearly correlated*. If they tend to follow a curve other than a straight line, then the sets are *non-linearly correlated*. If the points assume no statistical pattern, but are randomly distributed over the paper, then they are *un-correlated*.

In order to measure the degree of linear correlation between the points, the *correlation coefficient* has been devised. This coefficient is given by the following formula:

$$r = \frac{\Sigma (x_i - A_x)(y_i - A_y)}{N \sigma_x \sigma_y} \qquad (1)$$

which reduces to

$$r = \frac{1/N \Sigma x_i y_i - A_x A_y}{\sigma_x \sigma_y}, \qquad (2)$$

where A_x and σ_x are the arithmetic average and the standard deviation respectively, of the x-series, A_y and σ_y are the same constants for the y-series, and N is the total number of pairs of items.

The correlation coefficient can be either positive or negative. In the first case the variables are said to be *positively correlated* and in the second *negatively correlated*. When two variables are negatively correlated then one will be found to increase as the other de-

THE THEORY OF CORRELATION

creases. For example, if the temperatures observed in two cities, one in the southern hemisphere and the other in the northern hemisphere, are correlated, the correlation coefficient will be found to be negative.

As a simple illustrative example of the computation of the correlation coefficient, let us consider the set of values introduced in Section 4, namely, the following:

x	2	3	5	7	10	12
y	1	4	6	9	14	15

That these data are not functionally related is clear from the graph of the points given in Section 4. In the theory of correlation this graph of points is called a *scatter diagram*. But it is also evident that there is a high linear correlation between the points since they lie close to a straight line.

To exhibit the correlation we make the following computations:

x	y	x^2	y^2	xy
2	1	4	1	2
3	4	9	16	12
5	6	25	36	30
7	9	49	81	63
10	14	100	196	140
12	15	144	225	180
39	49	331	555	427

From these figures we then compute:

$$A_x = \frac{39}{6} = 6.5, \qquad A_y = \frac{49}{6} = 8.1667,$$

$$\sigma_x^2 = \frac{331}{6} - A_x^2 \qquad \sigma_y^2 = \frac{555}{6} - A_y^2$$

$$= 55.1667 - 42.25 = 12.9167, \qquad = 92.5 - 66.6944 = 25.8056,$$

$$\sigma_x = 3.5940, \qquad \sigma_y = 5.0799,$$

$$r = \frac{\tfrac{1}{6}(427) - A_x A_y}{\sigma_x \sigma_y} = \frac{71.1667 - 53.0833}{18.2572} = \frac{18.0834}{18.2572}$$

$$= 0.9905.$$

POLITICAL STATISTICS
PROBLEMS

1. Find the correlation coefficient of the following set of values:

x	1	3	4	6	5	8
y	10	8	3	3	4	2

Ans. -0.89.

2. Given the following sets of values:

```
a:  632  924  128   70  1002  400   50  700
b:  100  209   52   30   382  150   40  252
```

arrange the values in each row in ascending order of magnitude, that is, 50, 70, 128, etc. for the first row and 30, 40, 52, etc. for the second row. To each number assign its proper rank in the sequence, that is, assign to 50, 70, 128, etc. the numbers 1, 2, 3, etc. respectively and to 30, 40, 52, etc. the same numbers. Now compute the correlation coefficient of the rank numbers as they appear in the original sequences given above. This computation is an example of what is called *rank correlation*. Ans. 0.93.

3. The following table gives the number of police per 1000 population and the number of crimes per 1000 population in 30 cities of the United States:

Police per 1000 pop.	Crimes per 1000 pop.	Police per 1000 pop.	Crimes per 1000 pop.	Police per 1000 pop.	Crimes per 1000 pop.
0.8	1.3	2.6	1.8	1.6	0.9
2.2	0.7	3.3	1.5	2.8	0.6
1.0	1.8	1.2	2.8	1.3	1.1
2.3	1.3	1.6	2.8	2.8	1.8
1.2	2.7	3.6	0.4	1.5	2.9
1.5	1.9	1.6	2.0	1.7	1.3
1.7	2.0	1.2	1.0	1.9	0.8
2.0	2.7	2.0	1.0	2.2	2.2
1.1	1.5	1.4	1.8	2.4	1.5
1.5	2.2	1.5	3.4	2.9	3.2

Designating number of police by P and number of crimes by C, we have as the respective averages and standard deviations the following values:

$$A_P = 1.880, \quad \sigma_P = 0.690; \quad A_C = 1.763, \quad \sigma_C = 0.795.$$

Compute the correlation coefficient. Ans. $r = -0.2372$.

4. In a study of the influence of business upon national elections, L. Bean in his book on *How to Predict Elections* (1948) gave the following table. The column marked x gives the percentage change in business activity between October of the election year and October two years before the election as measured by the Index of the Cleveland Trust Company. The column

Year	x	y	Majority Party	Year	x	y	Majority Party
1856	-10	-7	R	1904	-8	+11	R
1868	-8	-4	R	1908	-21	-2	R
1876	-5	-8	D	1920	-13	-14	D
1884	-18	-7	D	1924	-2	5	R
1892	-7	-8	D	1928	-1	7	R
1896	-12	-11	R	1932	-20	-24	R
1900	-4	+4	R	1944	-3	-3	D

marked y gives the percentage change in the membership of the majority party in the House of Representatives. Compute the correlation coefficient r_{xy}. Would this value tend to support the proposition that business activity plays a significant part in deciding the swing of elections?

8. Properties of the Correlation Coefficient

In order to understand the significance of the correlation coefficient, it is necessary to examine some of its properties. A few of these are given below as follows:

(1) If either or both of the sets of values $\{x_i\}$ and $\{y_i\}$ are related linearly to two other sets of values $\{x'_i\}$ and $\{y'_i\}$, the correlation coefficient is unchanged in absolute value.

Thus, by assumption, we replace x_i and y_i as follows:

$$x_i = ax'_i + b, \qquad y_i = cy'_i + d,$$

where a, b, c, and d are constants.

From Sections 3 and 4 of Chapter 3 we then have,

$$A_x = aA_{x'} + b, \quad A_y = cA_{y'} + d, \quad \sigma_x = |a|\sigma_{x'}, \quad \sigma_y = |c|\sigma_{y'}.$$

Substituting in formula (1) of Section 7, that is, in

$$r_{xy} = \frac{\Sigma(x_i - A_x)(y_i - A_y)}{N\sigma_x\sigma_y}$$

we get

$$r_{xy} = \frac{a\Sigma(x'_i - A_{x'})c(y'_i - A_{y'})}{N|a||c|\sigma_{x'}\sigma_{y'}}$$

$$= \frac{ac}{|a||c|} \frac{\Sigma(x'_i - A_{x'})(y'_i - A_{y'})}{N\sigma_{x'}\sigma_{y'}} = r_{x'y'},$$

where the sign is to be determined from the sign of the product $a \cdot c$. Hence the absolute value of the correlation coefficient is unchanged.

(2) The absolute value of the correlation coefficient cannot exceed unity. To prove this we make the transformations:

$$x_i = \sigma_x x'_i + A_x, \quad y_i = \sigma_y y'_i + A_y.$$

We then have $A_{x'} = A_{y'} = 0$ and $\sigma_{x'} = \sigma_{y'} = 1$.

The original correlation coefficient remains unchanged but reduces to the simple form

$$r = \tfrac{1}{N} \Sigma x'_i y'_i.$$

But it is readily proved that

$$(\Sigma x'_i y'_i)^2 \leq \Sigma x'^2_i y'^2_i.*$$

But since $A_{x'} = A_{y'} = 0$, and from our hypothesis, we have

$$\sigma^2_{x'} = \tfrac{1}{N}\Sigma x'^2_i = 1, \text{ and } \sigma^2_{y'} = \tfrac{1}{N}\Sigma y'^2_i = 1.$$

It thus follows that $r^2 = \tfrac{1}{N^2}(\Sigma x'_i y'_i)^2 \leq \tfrac{1}{N^2}\Sigma x'^2_i \Sigma y'^2_i = 1.$

From this inequality we conclude that $r^2 \leq 1$, and hence r lies between -1 and +1.

(3) The significance of the correlation coefficient can be understood from the following proposition which we shall state without proof.

If the two sequences X and Y are affected by $m+n$ equally probable causes of which m are common to both, then the correlation coefficient is equal to

$$r = \frac{m}{m+n},$$

or, in other words, *the correlation coefficient is the ratio of the common causes of the variation to the total number of causes, if these common causes are equal in the sense of probability.*

While this is a very satisfactory interpretation of the correlation coefficient, it must be used with caution, since one seldom knows what the causes of variation in X and Y really are, and

---

*This is derived from the inequality

$$\Sigma(ax'_i + by'_i)^2 = a^2 \Sigma x'^2_i + 2ab \Sigma x'_i y'_i + b^2 \Sigma y'^2_i \geq 0.$$

Since this is a quadratic expression in a and b which holds for all values of these quantities, it follows that

$$(\Sigma x'_i y'_i)^2 \leq \Sigma x'^2_i \Sigma y'^2_i.$$

generally the effective probabilities are not equal. In the early history of the subject nonsense correlations were obtained by correlating the number, let us say, of Chinese laundries and divorces observed each year over a period of time in a large city. Since both were a function of the increase in population, the correlations obtained were high.

But as an interpretation of the correlation coefficient, the theorem just cited is in many cases an excellent guide.

(4) If the correlation coefficient is not too large, let us say less than 0.5, or if N is sufficiently large, then the expression:

$$\sigma_r = \frac{1-r^2}{\sqrt{N}}$$

can be used as the standard deviation of r in estimating its significance.

Thus if $r = 0.2$, computed from $N = 100$ items, $\sigma_r = (1 - .04)/\sqrt{100} = 0.096 \sim 0.1$. Since 0.2 is thus twice the standard error, the probability is high that the correlation coefficient is significantly greater than zero.

PROBLEMS

1. Using the values: $x_i = 2, 3, 4, 5$; $y_i = 1, 4, 2, 6$, show that

$$(\Sigma x_i y_i)^2 < \Sigma x_i^2 y_i^2.$$

2. If $r = 0.4$ and $N = 200$, what is the standard deviation of r? How can this value be used in interpreting the significance of r?

3. Two series of values, x and y, are known to be affected by 4 common causes, out of 12. What correlation coefficient is to be expected? What standard error would it have if each series had 144 items?

4. Ten coins, of which three are marked, are tossed and the number of heads is observed. The three marked coins are left as they fell and the other seven again tossed and the total number of heads is again observed. If a series of such double tosses is obtained, what should the correlation be between the two series of tosses?

9. *Lines of Regression*

In order to complete a correlation analysis the linear character of the data under discussion should be exhibited graphically by what are called *lines of regression*. The first of these lines, called the *line of regression of y on x*, is given by the formula:

$$y - A_y = r\frac{\sigma_y}{\sigma_x}(x - A_x), \tag{1}$$

and the second, called the *line of regression of x on y*, is given by the formula:

$$y - A_x = \frac{1}{r}\frac{\sigma_y}{\sigma_x}(x - A_x). \tag{2}$$

When the data are graphically represented by plotting the points $(x_1,y_1), (x_2,y_2),..., (x_r,y_r)$, the two lines will conform closely to the graph thus obtained provided there is high correlation between the x-series and the y-series.

Both lines pass through the point (A_x, A_y), and the angle between them is a measure of the correlation that exists. If the correlation is perfect, that is if $r = \pm 1$, the two lines coincide; if, however, there is no correlation, that is, if $r = 0$, then the lines are perpendicular to one another.

In order to understand better the nature of these lines, let us examine (1) more closely. We first write it in the form

$$y = \frac{r\sigma_x\sigma_y}{\sigma_x^2}x + A_y - \frac{r\sigma_x\sigma_y}{\sigma_x^2}A_x,$$

$$y = \frac{r\sigma_x\sigma_y}{\sigma_x^2}x + \frac{\sigma_x^2 A_y - r\sigma_x\sigma_y A_x}{\sigma_x^2}. \tag{3}$$

In the coefficient of x we now replace r by its explicit formula given by equation (2) in Section 7 and σ_x^2 by its explicit formula, (see Section 4, Chapter 3), namely,

$$\sigma_x^2 = \frac{1}{N}\Sigma x_i^2 - A_x^2.$$

We thus obtain

$$\frac{r\sigma_x\sigma_y}{\sigma_x^2} = \frac{{}^1/_N \Sigma x_i y_i - A_x A_y}{\sigma_x^2} = \frac{{}^1/_N \Sigma x_i y_i - A_x A_y}{{}^1/_N \Sigma x_i^2 - A_x^2}.$$

Finally, we replace A_x by $\Sigma x_i/N$, A_y by $\Sigma y_i/N$ and multiply both numerator and denominator of the fraction by N^2. There thus results

THE THEORY OF CORRELATION

$$\frac{r\sigma_x\sigma_y}{\sigma_x^2} = \frac{N\Sigma x_i y_i - \Sigma x_i \Sigma y_i}{N\Sigma x_i^2 - (\Sigma x_i)^2}. \tag{4}$$

Similarly for the second term in (3), we get

$$\frac{\sigma_x^2 A_y - r\sigma_x\sigma_y A_x}{\sigma_x^2} = \frac{\sigma_x^2 A_y - (1/N \Sigma x_i y_i - A_x A_y)A_x}{\sigma_x^2}$$

$$= \frac{(1/N \Sigma x_i^2 - A_x^2)A_y - (1/N \Sigma x_i y_i)A_x + A_x^2 A_y}{\sigma_x^2}$$

$$= \frac{1/N \Sigma x_i^2 A_y - (1/N \Sigma x_i y_i)A_x}{1/N \Sigma x_i^2 - A_x^2}.$$

As before we replace A_x by $\Sigma x_i/N$, A_y by $\Sigma y_i/N$, and multiply both numerator and denominator by N^2. We thus get

$$\frac{\sigma_x^2 A_y - r\sigma_x\sigma_y A_x}{\sigma_x^2} = \frac{\Sigma x_i^2 \Sigma y_i - \Sigma x_i y_i \Sigma x_i}{N\Sigma x_i^2 - (\Sigma x_i)^2}. \tag{5}$$

If we now compare equations (4) and (5) with formulas (1) and (2) in Section 5, where we computed the va l u e of a and b in the line $y = ax + b$, we see that they are identical.

From this we reach the conclusion that *the line fitted to the data by the method of Section 5 is identical with the first regression line given above in* (1).

The second regression line, given by (2), is similarly obtained merely by reversing the roles of x and y.

In illustration we return to the illustrative example of Section 7, where we had the values:

$A_x = 6.5$, $A_y = 8.1667$, $\sigma_x = 3.5940$, $\sigma_y = 5.0799$, $r = 0.9905$.

The first regression line is thus

$$y - 8.1667 = 0.9905 \cdot \frac{5.0799}{3.5940}(x - 6.5) = 1.4000(x - 6.5)$$

which may also be written in the form

$$y = 1.40x - 0.93. \tag{6}$$

This is seen to agree with the results of our computation in Section 4 of this chapter.

The second regression line is computed as follows:

$$y - 8.1667 = \frac{1}{0.9905} \frac{5.0799}{3.5940} (x - 6.5) = 1.4270(x - 6.5),$$

which may also be written in the form

$$y = 1.43 x - 1.11. \tag{7}$$

Over the range of the data equations (6) and (7) do not differ significantly from one another. This is because the correlation coefficient is so close to unity.

PROBLEMS

1. Compute and graph the lines of regression for the data of Problem 1, Section 7.

2. Compute the two lines of regression for the set of data of Problem 3, Section 7.

3. Compute the two regression lines for the data of Problem 4, Section 7.

4. It has been shown that the angle θ between two lines of regression can be computed from the formula:

$$\tan \theta = \frac{\sigma_x \sigma_y}{(\sigma_x^2 + \sigma_y^2)} \left(\frac{1 - r^2}{r} \right).$$

Find the angle between the regression lines of Problem 3, Section 7.

10. *The Size of State Legislatures.*

Earlier in this chapter we raised the question whether a significant correlation existed between the number of representatives in state legislatures and the population of the states. We might also ask whether there is a similar relationship between the size of state Senates and the population of states. A third question would be to ascertain the correlation between the sizes of state Senates and state Houses of Representatives.

Since these three questions are closely related we shall answer all of them. In the accompanying table the first column, marked R, gives the number of representatives, the second column, marked S, gives the number of senators, and the third column, marked P, gives

THE THEORY OF CORRELATION

the state population in units of 100,000 as of 1940. There are 47 items in each column since Nebraska with its unicameral legislature is omitted.

In order to illustrate the computation of the correlation coefficient let us consider the one between R and P, which, for convenience of identification, we shall designate by r_{RP}. We first compute the squares of R and P, namely, the columns designated respectively by R^2 and P^2. We then compute the products: $R \cdot P$. From the totals of the five columns, R, P, R^2, P^2, and $R \cdot P$, we can now obtain the desired correlation coefficient.

Beginning with the totals of the first two columns, R and P, we first compute:

$$A_R = \frac{5550}{47} = 118.0851, \qquad A_P = \frac{1295}{47} = 27.5532.$$

Thus the average number of state representatives was 118 and the average state population was 2,755,000, facts of interest in themselves. On the average each representative served a district of 23,347 people.

We next compute the variances from the totals of the columns R^2 and P^2, thus,

$$\sigma_R^2 = \frac{853418}{47} - A_R^2 = 18157.8300 - 13944.0908 = 4213.7392,$$

$$\sigma_P^2 = \frac{69565}{47} - A_P^2 = 1480.1064 - 759.1788 = 720.9276,$$

from which we obtain the standard deviations:

$$\sigma_R = 64.9133, \qquad \sigma_P = 26.8500.$$

Both of these values are large, indicating a wide dispersion in the data.

Finally we compute the correlation coefficient making use of the total of the column $R \cdot P$ as follows:

$$r_{R \cdot P} = \frac{\frac{169623}{47} - A_R A_P}{\sigma_R \sigma_P} = \frac{3609 - 3253.6224}{64.9133 \times 26.8500} = \frac{355.3776}{1742.9221} = 0.2039.$$

This is a small correlation and indicates the great disparity be-

POLITICAL STATISTICS

R	S	P	R^2	S^2	P^2	$R \cdot S$	$R \cdot P$	$S \cdot P$
106	35	28	11236	1225	784	3710	2968	980
58	19	5	3364	361	25	1102	290	95
100	35	19	10000	1225	361	3500	1900	665
80	40	69	6400	1600	4761	3200	5520	2760
65	35	11	4225	1225	121	2275	715	385
272	36	17	73984	1296	289	9792	4624	612
35	17	3	1225	289	9	595	105	51
95	38	19	9025	1444	361	3610	1805	722
105	52	31	11025	2704	961	5460	3255	1612
59	44	5	3481	1936	25	2596	295	220
153	51	79	23409	2601	6241	7803	12087	4029
100	50	34	10000	2500	1156	5000	3400	1700
108	50	25	11664	2500	625	5400	2700	1250
125	40	18	15625	1600	324	5000	2250	720
100	38	28	10000	1444	784	3800	2800	1064
100	39	24	10000	1521	576	3900	2400	936
151	33	8	22801	1089	64	4983	1208	264
123	29	18	15129	841	324	3567	2214	522
240	40	43	57600	1600	1849	9600	10320	1720
100	32	53	10000	1024	2809	3200	5300	1696
131	67	28	17161	4489	784	8777	3668	1876
140	49	22	19600	2401	484	6860	3080	1078
154	35	38	23716	1225	1444	5390	5852	1330
90	56	6	8100	3136	36	5040	540	336
45	17	1	2025	289	1	765	45	17
400	24	5	160000	576	25	9600	2000	120
60	21	42	3600	441	1764	1260	2520	882
49	24	5	2401	576	25	1176	245	120
150	56	135	22500	3136	18225	8400	20250	7560
120	50	36	14400	2500	1296	6000	4320	1800
113	53	6	12769	2809	36	5989	678	318
138	36	69	19044	1296	4761	4968	9522	2484
120	44	23	14400	1936	529	5280	2760	1012
60	30	11	3600	900	121	1800	660	330
208	50	99	43264	2500	9801	10400	20592	4950
100	44	7	10000	1936	49	4400	700	308
124	46	19	15376	2116	361	5704	2356	874
75	35	6	5625	1225	36	2625	450	210
99	33	29	9801	1089	841	3267	2871	957
150	31	64	22500	961	4096	4650	9600	1984
60	23	6	3600	529	36	1380	360	138
241	30	4	58081	900	16	7230	964	120
100	40	27	10000	1600	729	4000	2700	1080
99	46	17	9801	2116	289	4554	1683	782
94	32	19	8836	1024	361	3008	1786	608
100	33	31	10000	1089	961	3300	3100	1023
55	27	3	3025	729	9	1485	165	81
5550	1785	1295	853418	73549	69565	215401	169623	54381

THE THEORY OF CORRELATION

tween states in the construction of their legislatures. The correlation is significantly greater than zero, however, as may be seen from the standard error,

$$\sigma_r = \frac{1 - (0.2039)^2}{\sqrt{47}} = 0.1398.$$

Proceeding to similar correlations between S and P, and R and S, we obtain the following:

$$A_S = \frac{1785}{47} = 37.9787, \quad \sigma_S^2 = 122.4907, \quad \sigma_S = 11.067,$$

$$r_{SP} = \frac{\frac{54381}{47} - A_S A_P}{\sigma_S \sigma_P} = \frac{110.6079}{297.1624} = 0.3722,$$

$$r_{RS} = \frac{\frac{215401}{47} - A_R A_S}{\sigma_R \sigma_S} = \frac{98.2814}{718.4229} = 0.1368.$$

From these correlation coefficients we infer first that there is greater uniformity in state legislatures between the size of state Senates and population than between the size of state Houses of Representatives and population. This is a curious fact, since the number of representatives is generally supposed to be related more closely to population than the number of senators. Secondly, we see that there is very little relationship between the size of the Senates and the size of the Houses of Representatives, a rather natural inference.

In order to exhibit these relationships graphically, we proceed to the construction of scatter diagrams and regression lines. Thus, in the case of R and P, we have for the first regression line (R on P) the following:

$$R - A_R = r_{RP} \frac{\sigma_R}{\sigma_P} (P - A_P),$$

$$R - 118.09 = 0.2039 \frac{64.9133}{26.8500} (P - 27.55) = 0.4930 (P - 27.55);$$

which reduces to,

$$R = 0.4930 P + 104.51. \qquad (1)$$

POLITICAL STATISTICS

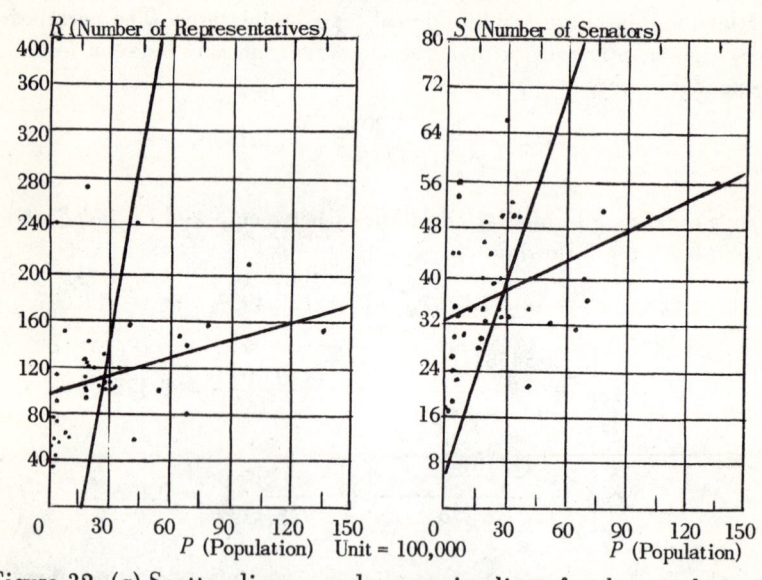

Figure 32. (a) Scatter diagram and regression lines for the correlation between the number of state representatives and the state population. (b) Scatter diagram and regression lines for the correlation between the number of state senators and the state population.

Similarly for the second regression line (P on R), we have

$$R - A_R = \frac{1}{r_{RP}} \frac{\sigma_R}{\sigma_P} (P - A_P),$$

$$R - 118.09 = \frac{1}{0.2039} \frac{64.9133}{26.8500} (P - 27.55) = 11.8569 (P - 27.55);$$

which reduces to

$$R = 11.8569 P - 208.57. \qquad (2)$$

The scatter diagram of the data and the two regression lines are graphically portrayed in Figure 32(a). We observe that the lines intersect at the point (A_P, A_R) and that the low correlation is easily inferred from the large angle between the two regression lines.

Similarly we compute the two regression lines for the relationship between S and P. We thus get for the regression of S on P,

THE THEORY OF CORRELATION

$$S - 37.98 = 0.3722 \, \frac{11.0675}{26.8500} \, (P - 27.55) = 0.1534 \, (P - 27.55);$$

which reduces to

$$S = 0.1534 P + 33.75. \tag{3}$$

Similarly, for the regression of P on S, we get

$$S - 37.98 = \frac{1}{0.3722} \, \frac{11.0675}{26.8500} \, (P - 27.55) = 1.1075 \, (P - 27.55);$$

which reduces to

$$S = 1.1075 P + 7.47. \tag{4}$$

The scatter diagram for the data and the graphical representation of the two regression lines are shown in Figure 32 (b).

In spite of the low correlations with which we have been concerned the regression lines might still have some practical application since they represent the data better than any other lines. For example, suppose that Puerto Rico, with a population of 1,869,255 in 1940, was admitted as a new state and desired to form a legislature in relative conformity with those of the other states. Equations (1) and (2) might be used to determine the sizes of the House of Representatives and the Senate respectively. Thus we would let $P = 19$ and hence compute:

$$R = 0.4930 \times 19 + 104.51 = 113.88,$$

$$S = 0.1534 \times 19 + 33.75 = 36.66.$$

Thus the House of Representatives might have approximately 114 members and the Senate 37. Arkansas with a population about equal to that of Puerto Rico has a legislature of comparable size, namely, $R = 100$ and $S = 35$. As one can see from the scatter diagram, a number of other states are in the immediate neighborhood of these figures. At present Puerto Rico has a House of Representatives of 39 and a Senate of 19.

PROBLEMS

1. Represent graphically the data of Problem 3, Section 7 and the two lines of regression obtained in Problem 2, Section 9.

2. Represent graphically the data of Problem 4, Section 7 and the two lines of regression obtained in Problem 3, Section 9.

3. The quantities,

$$\sigma_y \sqrt{1-r^2} \quad \text{and} \quad \sigma_x \sqrt{1-r^2},$$

are called the *standard errors of forecast*, the first for the line of regression of y on x [Formula (1), Section 9] and the second for the line of regression of x on y [Formula (2), Section 9]. They give the standard error of any value computed by the respective formulas.

Find the standard errors of forecast for the illustrative example of this section. How do you interpret your results?

4. If Hawaii with a population (1940) of 423,330 were to become a state, what should be recommended as the size of its legislature?

11. *The Traffic Problem.*

The problem of motor traffic can be studied in many of its features by means of correlation. The large number of accidents which occur within a metropolitan area has been a matter of much concern to police departments and their affiliated traffic organizations. These agencies can learn, and have learned, a great deal about traffic problems by use of the statistical method. Variations in the per capita accidents between different cities and different districts within cities can be studied by means of correlation. The effects of changes in the handling of traffic can be estimated by comparing the patterns of one year with those of another.

As an example of how correlations can be used in the study of traffic problems we shall compare the motor vehicle accidents and the resulting death rate observed in the city of Chicago according to the hour of occurrence for the two years 1938 and 1946. The pertinent data are given in the table on the next page.

Several questions are suggested by these data: (a) Is there any significant difference in the pattern of accidents between the two years? (b) How closely is the number of accidents which result in fatalities related to the total number of accidents? That is to say, are the accidents of one hour likely to be more serious than those of another hour? (c) Does the number of fatalities of one year correspond to the number of fatalities in another year?

It is clear that these questions can be answered by means of correlation. If we denote by x and y the number of accidents and the

THE THEORY OF CORRELATION

Motor Vehicle Accidents and Resulting Fatalities in the City of Chicago According to the Hour of Occurrence

Time of Day A.M.	Number 1946 (x)	Fatalities in 1946 (y)	Number 1938 (u)	Fatalities in 1938 (v)	Time of Day P.M.	Number 1946 (x)	Fatalities in 1946 (y)	Number 1938 (u)	Fatalities in 1938 (v)
12-1	613	16	589	27	12-1	743	18	678	22
1-2	562	21	564	29	1-2	690	9	716	18
2-3	503	20	450	14	2-3	765	11	770	15
3-4	410	21	351	18	3-4	1,029	19	1,037	21
4-5	298	13	242	19	4-5	1,287	32	1,149	28
5-6	241	8	207	10	5-6	1,573	36	1,516	63
6-7	241	9	243	19	6-7	1,225	34	1,223	69
7-8	423	13	439	14	7-8	1,029	41	1,217	49
8-9	515	13	515	11	8-9	949	32	1,147	37
9-10	382	7	422	10	9-10	769	34	934	42
10-11	448	8	619	10	10-11	632	30	880	34
11-12	627	11	584	18	11-12	649	18	739	37
					Totals	16,603	474	17,231	634

number of fatalities respectively in 1946 and by u and v the number of accidents and the number of fatalities respectively in 1938, then we can compute the following significant quantities:

$$A_x = 691.8, \quad \sigma_x = 334.8; \quad A_y = 19.8, \quad \sigma_y = 10.2;$$
$$A_u = 718.0, \quad \sigma_u = 346.7; \quad A_v = 26.4, \quad \sigma_v = 15.9.$$

Making use of these values, we compute, by means of formula (2), Section 7, the following correlation coefficients:

$$r_{xy} = 0.7528, \quad r_{xu} = 0.9601, \quad r_{yv} = 0.8451, \quad r_{uv} = 0.7968.$$

From these coefficients we are now able to answer the three questions asked above. With respect to (a), since r_{xu} is very close to unity, it is clear that the patterns of the two years do not show a significant difference. The actual frequency of traffic accidents for each hour of the day is shown in Figure 33 (a), and we can infer that a similar graph will be obtained for any other year during the recent past. A maximum value will occur between 5 and 6 in the afternoon. With respect to question (b), we learn from the coefficient: $r_{xy} = 0.75$ that fatal accidents correlate highly with total accidents, but that

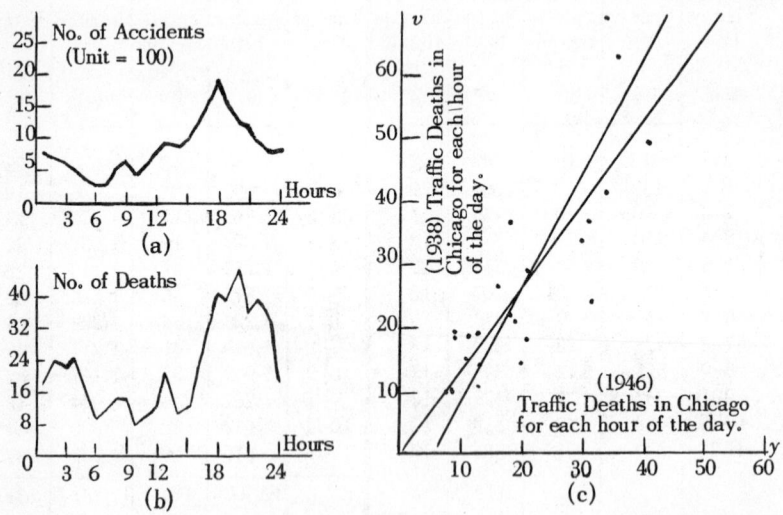

Figure 33. (a) Number of Traffic Accidents in Chicago (1946) for each Hour after Midnight (Unit = 100). (b) Number of Traffic Deaths in Chicago for each Hour after Midnight. (c) Regression Lines Showing Relationship between Traffic Deaths in Different Years.

there is some variation with respect to the ratio of fatal accidents to total accidents for different hours in the day. This conclusion is substantiated for the correlation coefficient r_{uv}, which does not differ significantly from r_{xy}. This is also shown by a comparison of Figure 33 (b) with Figure 33 (c).

That the fatality pattern does not change greatly from year to year, the question asked in (c), is shown from the high value of the correlation coefficient r_{yv}. While this is not as great as r_{xu}, we infer from its value of 0.85 that approximately 85 per cent of the causes which lead to fatal accidents in one year are effective also in other years. The significance of this relationship is shown in the graphical representation of the two regression lines given in Figure 33 (b). The equations of the two lines are as follows:

$$v = 1.84\,y - 9.9, \qquad v = 1.31\,y + 0.5.$$

THE THEORY OF CORRELATION

12. Applications to the Problem of Voting Behavior.

The problem of voting behavior has been extensively studied by correlation. This investigation was initiated by H. F. Gosnell, who has given his results in several books and a number of papers.* It illustrates in an excellent way how the theory of correlation can be used to study problems which involve a number of different factors.

In one of Gosnell's studies the voting behavior of the residents of 147 voting districts in the city of Chicago was made the subject of the investigation. The districts varied from those predominantly Democratic to those predominantly Republican. Seventeen different variables were introduced which were designed to measure both the vote itself and various factors assumed to have an influence upon the vote. The primary object was to ascertain the influences which contributed to the vote obtained in these districts by Alfred Smith in 1928 and by F. D. Roosevelt in 1932. Using the notation of the author, we shall denote these votes by the letters a and c respectively. Thus x_a will mean the percentage of the total vote obtained by Smith in each of the 147 districts and x_c will represent the percentage of the vote obtained by Roosevelt.

In addition to these primary variables, we shall consider six others, chosen from the original group of 17, which may be described as follows: The first of these, denoted by d, is the per cent who were women in the total number of registered voters in October 1930. The second, denoted by g, is the per cent of the "yes" vote cast in the 1930 public opinion referendum calling for repeal of the eighteenth amendment. The third, denoted by j, is the per cent of the total population which was born, or whose parents were born, in a selected group of foreign countries that are primarily Catholic. The fourth variable, denoted by k, is the median rental in the districts measured in dollars. The fifth variable, denoted by m, is the per cent of unemployed in 1921 of the gainful workers ten years of age or over. The sixth variable, denoted by u, is the per cent of the population 18 years of age that had completed more than ten grades of school. The

---

*See, for example, (a) *Machine Politics: Chicago Model.* Chicago, 1937, xx + 229 pp. (b) *Grass Root Politics.* Washington, D. C., 1942, ix + 195 pp. (c) *Democracy — The Threshold of Freedom.* New York, 1948, vii + 316 pp. (d) "Factorial and Correlation Analysis of the 1934 Vote in Chicago," *Journal American Statistical Soc.*, Vol. 31, 1936, pp. 507-518.

six factors were assumed to measure respectively (1) the women's vote; (2) the "wet" vote; (3) the Catholic vote; (4) the economic level of the voters; (5) the factor of unemployment; and (6) the influence of education.

The significance of these various factors on the voting behavior of the residents of the 147 districts is shown in the following table which gives both the averages and the standard deviations of the correlation coefficients between each of them:

| Variable | \multicolumn{8}{c|}{Table of Correlation Coefficients: r_{ij}} | Mean | σ |
	a	c	d	g	j	k	m	u		
a	1.00	0.94	−0.57	0.64	0.78	−0.62	0.69	−0.62	51.7%	15.0%
c	0.94	1.00	−0.66	0.62	0.78	−0.68	0.76	−0.73	63.4	31.1
d	−0.57	−0.66	1.00	0.34	−0.54	0.58	−0.68	0.65	40.4	6.8
g	0.64	0.62	−0.34	1.00	0.34	−0.34	0.36	−0.30	78.4	5.7
j	0.78	0.78	−0.54	0.34	1.00	−0.74	0.78	−0.73	34.1	21.0
k	−0.62	−0.68	0.58	−0.34	−0.74	1.00	−0.80	0.88	$47.50	$18.50
m	0.69	0.76	−0.68	0.36	0.78	−0.80	1.00	−0.84	28.3%	12.5%
u	−0.62	−0.73	0.65	−0.30	−0.73	0.88	−0.84	1.00	24.8	15.6

Some interesting results can be read immediately from the table of correlation coefficients. Thus, observing that $r_{ac} = 0.94$, we see that the districts which voted for Smith in 1928 were substantially the same that voted for Roosevelt in 1932. But we can also infer that, while the voting pattern remained the same, the percentage polled by Smith was lower than that polled by Roosevelt since the averages were respectively 51.7% and 63.4% of the total vote.

It is also evident from the values $r_{ak} = -0.62$ and $r_{ck} = -0.68$, that the voters in the upper levels of income tended quite strongly to vote Republican rather than Democratic. This conclusion was substantiated in the *Literary Digest* poll of 1936, described in Chapter 4, which went astray in its forecast by including too great a percentage of people in the high income brackets.

That unemployment was a greater factor in 1932 than in 1928 is easily seen from the fact that $r_{am} = 0.69$ while $r_{cm} = 0.76$. Although the unemployment data were taken from the year 1921, there is a natural inference that districts which had a relatively high unemployment in 1921 would continue to show such a pattern in 1932.

One can construct readily various regression lines between the factors from the data given in the table. Thus, observing the values: $A_a = 51.7$, $\sigma_a = 15.0$; $A_c = 63.4$, $\sigma_c = 13.1$; and $r_{ac} = 0.94$, we obtain the following regression lines by proper substitution in formulas (1) and (2) of Section 9:

$$x_c = 0.821\, x_a + 21.0; \quad x_c = 0.929\, x_a + 15.4. \quad (1)$$

If we have the additional fact that x_a varied between 24 and 88 per cent and that x_c varied between 43 and 92 per cent, the regression lines can be graphed between their proper limits. An excelcellent idea can thus be obtained as to the relationship between the two elections.

PROBLEMS

1. Compute the standard error for the coefficient r_{xy} given in Section 11 and decide whether the difference $r_{uv} - r_{xy}$ is significant.

2. Compute the regression lines between the variables x and y given in Section 11 and represent them graphically.

3. Compute the regression lines between the factors k and u in the table of Section 12. With the additional information that the factor k varies between 15 and 129 and the factor u between 6 and 67, represent the regression lines graphically between their proper limits.

4. State two inferences in addition to those given earlier about the voting behavior of Chicago from the information contained in the table of correlation coefficients given in this section.

5. Represent graphically between proper limits the regression lines given by (1) of this section. Discuss the significance of these lines.

6. Make use of the formula stated in Problem 4 of Section 9 to compute the angle between the regression lines connecting the variables x_a and x_m of this section.

CHAPTER 6
SOME PROBLEMS IN POLITICAL SCIENCE
1. Introduction.

IN THIS CHAPTER we shall discuss by mathematical and statistical arguments some problems which pertain to political science itself. In this way we can illustrate the application of the methods which we have discussed in preceding sections of this book.

The first of these problems is one pertaining to the appointment of representatives in Congress, a problem that at first sight seems very simple, but which has given surprising difficulty in actual application.

2. The Problem of Representation.

According to the Constitution of the United States, representation in Congress is to be apportioned according to the population of the states except that every state is to have at least one representative and the number shall not exceed one representative from every 30,000 population. Now in the 77th Congress (1941) the total number of representatives was 435 and the total population 132 million so that the actual size of a congressional district was on the average slightly in excess of 300,000. Hence New York, with a population of 13,479,000, would be entitled to approximately 45 representatives, a figure which agrees with the one actually observed.

But we note that difficulties arise when the congressional ratio for a state is some number between two integral values, let us say 45.5. Should a representative be added to this state and taken from another whose ratio is just below an integral value, let us say, a ratio which has fallen from 25.0 to 24.8?

This problem of apportionment was studied extensively by E. V. Huntington and finally his solution called "the method of equal proportion" was adopted as Public Law 291 (H.R. 2665) on Nov. 15, 1941. *

---

*The method was first proposed by Huntington in 1921: "A New Method of Apportionment of Representatives," *Quarterly Publication of the American Statistical Association*, Sept. 1921, pp. 859-870. This was followed by a "Report upon the Apportionment of Representatives," prepared by a joint committee of the American Statistical Association and the American Eco-

SOME PROBLEMS IN POLITICAL SCIENCE   139

Since there is considerable mathematical and statistical interest in this problem we shall give a brief resume of its operation.

3. Measure of Inequality of Representation.

Because of the absence of any provision for fractional representation in Congress, it is clear that inequalities of representation must prevail. For example, in the 77th Congress we had the following Congressional apportionment and the following distribution of population among the states:

State	No. of Repres.	Population	State	No. of Repres.	Population
Alabama	9	2,832,961	Nebraska	4	1,315,834
Arizona	2	499,261	Nevada	1	110,247
Arkansas	7	1,949,387	New Hampshire	2	491,524
California	23	6,907,387	New Jersey	14	4,160,165
Colorado	4	1,123,296	New Mexico	2	531,818
Connecticut	6	1,709,242	New York	45	13,479,142
Delaware	1	266,505	North Carolina	12	3,571,623
Florida	6	1,897,414	North Dakota	2	641,935
Georgia	10	3,123,723	Ohio	23	6,907,612
Idaho	2	524,873	Oklahoma	8	2,336,434
Illinois	26	7,897,241	Oregon	4	1,089,684
Indiana	11	3,427,796	Pennsylvania	33	9,900,180
Iowa	8	2,538,268	Rhode Island	2	713,346
Kansas	6	1,801,028	South Carolina	6	1,899,804
Kentucky	9	2,845,627	South Dakota	2	642,961
Louisiana	8	2,363,880	Tennessee	10	2,915,841
Maine	3	847,226	Texas	21	6,414,824
Maryland	6	1,821,244	Utah	2	550,310
Massachusetts	14	4,316,721	Vermont	1	359,231
Michigan	17	5,256,106	Virginia	9	2,677,773
Minnesota	9	2,792,300	Washington	6	1,736,191
Mississippi	7	2,183,796	West Virginia	6	1,901,974
Missouri	13	3,784,664	Wisconsin	10	3,137,587
Montana	2	559,456	Wyoming	1	250,742

It will be observed from this list that Arkansas with 7 representatives and a population of 1,949,387 elects from a Congressional dis-

nomic Association to advise the Director of the Census, and published *Ibid.*, Dec. 21, pp. 1004-1013. This report, favorable to the *Method of Equal Proportions*, was reprinted in the *Congressional Record* for April 7, 1926, pp. 6840-6842. A full account of the method is given in "The Apportionment of Representatives in Congress," *Transactions of the American Math. Society*, Vol. 30, 1928, pp. 85-110. See also *Congressional Record* for March 2, 1927, pp. 5327-5332, and *U. S. Statutes at Large*, Vol. 55, 1941-1942, Part 1, pp. 761-762.

trict of 1,949,387/7 = 278,484, while Michigan with 17 representatives and a population of 5,256,106 elects from a Congressional district of 5,256,106/17 = 309,183. There is an inequality here which may be said to be of the order of 11.02 per cent, since, comparing Congressional districts, we have

$$\frac{309,183}{278,484} = 1.1102.$$

But if one representative is taken from Arkansas and transferred to Michigan, then the Congressional districts would be respectively:

$$1,949,387/6 = 324,898 \quad \text{and} \quad 5,256,106/18 = 292,006.$$

The inequality would then be of the order of 11.26 per cent, since we have
$$\frac{324,898}{292,006} = 1.1126.$$

Hence no transfer should take place, since the inequality would be increased by the change.

The observation which we have just made is basic to the method of equal proportion. To put the matter in symbolic language, let us say that the populations of two states are respectively A and B and that the numbers of their representatives are respectively a and b. Let us further assume that A/a is smaller than B/b. Thus the inequality of representation is represented by the fraction

$$R = \frac{\frac{B}{b} - \frac{A}{a}}{\frac{A}{a}} = \frac{Ba}{Ab} - 1.$$

Let us now inquire what would happen if one representative is transferred from A to B. For this purpose we shall assume that $a = x + 1$ and $b = y$.

Before the transfer we then have

$$R_1 = \frac{B(x+1)}{Ay} - 1;$$

but after the transfer has been made, that is to say when $x + 1$ has been reduced by one and y increased by one, the inequality is reversed and we have

$$R_2 = \frac{A(y+1)}{Bx} - 1.$$

SOME PROBLEMS IN POLITICAL SCIENCE

Now if the inequality is actually increased by the transfer of one representative from A to B, we should have R_2 greater than R_1. That is to say:

$$R_2 - R_1 = \frac{A(y+1)}{Bx} - \frac{B(x+1)}{Ay} > 0.$$

Hence we find that

$$\frac{A(y+1)}{Bx} > \frac{B(x+1)}{Ay};$$

or, multiplying both sides of this inequality by $AB/(x+1)(y+1)$, we get

$$\frac{A^2}{x(x+1)} > \frac{B^2}{y(y+1)}, \text{ that is, } \frac{A}{\sqrt{x(x+1)}} > \frac{B}{\sqrt{y(y+1)}}.$$

Thus, in the example of Arkansas and Michigan given above, we see that if $A = 1,949,387$, $x + 1 = 7$, $B = 5,256,106$, $y = 17$, then

$$\frac{1,949,387}{\sqrt{6 \cdot 7}} = 300,797 > \frac{5,256,106}{\sqrt{17 \cdot 18}} = 300,472;$$

but if $x + 1 = 8$ and $y = 16$, we have

$$\frac{1,949,387}{\sqrt{7 \cdot 8}} = 260,492 < \frac{5,256,106}{\sqrt{16 \cdot 17}} = 318,698.$$

The inequality which we have just derived can be used to derive a simple and useful method of apportioning representatives. Thus we proceed in the following manner.

We first construct a table of multipliers, where the multiplier M is given in terms of a serial number k by the formula:

$$M = \frac{1}{\sqrt{(k-1)k}}.$$

Serial No (k)	Multiplier (M)	Serial No. (k)	Multiplier (M)	Serial No. (k)	Multiplier (M)
1	--	8	0.1336306	15	0.0690066
2	0.7071068	9	0.1178511	16	0.0645497
3	0.4082483	10	0.1054093	17	0.0606339
4	0.2886751	11	0.0953463	18	0.0571662
5	0.2236068	12	0.0870388	19	0.0540738
6	0.1825742	13	0.0800641	20	0.0512989
7	0.1543033	14	0.0741249	21	0.0487950

Serial No. (k)	Multiplier (M)	Serial No. (k)	Multiplier (M)	Serial No. (k)	Multiplier (M)
22	0.0465242	32	0.0317500	42	0.0240981
23	0.0444554	33	0.0307729	43	0.0235310
24	0.0425628	34	0.0298541	44	0.0229900
25	0.0408248	35	0.0289886	45	0.0224733
26	0.0392232	36	0.0281718	46	0.0219793
27	0.0377426	37	0.0273998	47	0.0215066
28	0.0363696	38	0.0266690	48	0.0210538
29	0.0350931	39	0.0259762	49	0.0206197
30	0.0339032	40	0.0253185	50	0.0202031
31	0.0327913	41	0.0246932	51	0.0198030

We then use the following rules according to Huntington:

(1) Assign one representative to each state (here 48 in number).

(2) Make out a set of cards containing (a) the name of the state, (b) a serial number, k, starting with 2 and running up to a number somewhat greater than the number of representatives that the state is expected to receive, (c) a "rank index" found by multiplying the population of the state by the multiplier M.

(3) Distribute the cards into a single series arranged in order of "rank index" from the highest to the lowest, thus forming what is called a "priority list" for the given population and any size of House of Representatives.

Finally assign additional members (after the first) to the several states in the order in which the cards occur in this "priority list" continuing the assignment as far as is necessary to fill up a House of any desired size.

As an example, let us consider the following four states for which a House of 17 members is to be formed, each state to have at least one member.

State	Population (P)
A	729
B	535
C	346
D	90
Total	1700

Making the indicated computation from $k = 2$ to $k = 8$ for A, we obtain the following "priority table":

P·M	State	Value of k	P·M	State	Value of k
515.48	A	2	119.63	B	5
378.30	B	2	112.49	A	7
297.61	A	3	99.88	C	4
244.66	C	2	97.68	B	6
218.41	B	3	97.42	A	8
210.44	A	4	82.55	B	7
163.01	A	5	77.37	C	5
154.44	B	4	63.64	D	1
141.26	C	3	36.74	D	2
133.10	A	6			

To each state there is now assigned one member. Then from the table we see that A deserves 2 representatives before any other. Hence we assign an additional representative to A. We next see that B deserves an additional representative before one is added to any other state. Hence we add another to B. Proceeding in this manner until we get a legislature of 17 members, we have the following table:

State	Population	Representation
A	729	7
B	535	5
C	346	4
D	90	1
Total	1700	17

Let us check directly the figures for B and C. Since the average value for a Congressional district is 100, we obtain for B the value $\frac{535}{5} = 107$ and for C the value $\frac{346}{4} = 86.5$. But if we reduce the representatives of C by one and add this to B, we have $\frac{535}{6} = 89.2$ and $\frac{346}{3} = 115.3$. The respective inequalities are represented by the ratios $\frac{107}{86.5} = 1.24$ and $\frac{115.3}{89.2} = 1.30$. Since the former is smaller than the second, we conclude that the first distribution, namely 5 for B and 4 for C, is the more equitable.

PROBLEMS

1. From the table of representatives we see that the state of California elects from a Congressional district of 300,321. Show that in spite of this size, no representative should be given to California from Arkansas with a Congressional district of 324,898.

2. In the illustrative example above find the representation of the states A, B, C, D if a legislature of 25 were desired.

3. Apportion representatives for a legislature of 10 among three states, $A, B,$ and C, with respective populations of 5,000, 3,000, and 2,000.

4. The Problem of the Philosopher King.

We have already quoted in the first chapter of this work the famous statement of Plato, which extols the virtues of the philosopher as king. But unfortunately history shows very few rulers who could be classified as philosophers, so we have no possibility of testing Plato's proposition by statistical means. The most famous example is probably Marcus Aurelius Antoninus (121-180), who ruled as Emperor of the Romans for nearly twenty years (161-180). His classical *Meditations* has given him a distinguished place among philosophers, and the work is widely read even to this day after a lapse of seventeen centuries. The advice of Plato in this single instance is verified by the words of Gibbon, who, speaking of him and his predecessor, Antoninus Pius, said: "Their united reigns are possibly the only period of history in which the happiness of a great people was the sole object of government."

The problem of the philosopher king is that of determining what should be the characteristics of the ideal ruler. What should be his training? From what class of society should he be chosen? What profession is most desirable as a background?

While such a problem is scarcely amenable to the statistical method, it is possible, nevertheless, to determine the professional background of those who actually function as our executive, legislative, and judicial leaders.

We shall begin our inquiry with a study of the composition of state legislatures, since these will give an excellent cross-section of the opinion of the electorate as to the general classes from which our law-makers should be chosen. We base this investigation upon studies made by C. S. Hyneman and E. F. Ricketts,* whose evidence seems to be quite conclusive.

In the study of the occupational interests of the members of the Indiana Legislature during six sessions from 1925 to 1935, Hyneman obtained the accompanying table. Some interesting conclusions are derived immediately from this table. If one wishes to enter politics

---

*"Tenure and Turnover of the Indiana General Assembly," by C. S. Hyneman, *American Political Science Review*, Vol. 32, 1938, pp. 51-67, 311-331. "Tenure and Turnover of the Iowa Legislature," by C. S. Hyneman and E. F. Ricketts, *Iowa Law Review*, Vol. 24, 1939, pp. 673-696. "Who Makes our Laws?" by C. S. Hyneman, *Political Science Quarterly*, Vol. 55, 1940, pp. 556-581.

Occupation	Senate No.	Senate %	House No.	House %	Occupational Population of State	Positions held, both houses, per 1000 population
1. Lawyers	103	34.3	141	23.5	3,747	65.1
2. Business men	61	20.3	108	18.0	-	-
3. Insurance and real estate	24	8.0	40	6.7	11,714	5.5
4. Newspaper men and publishers	23	7.7	15	2.5	942	40.3
5. Bankers and brokers	18	6.0	12	2.0	4,220	7.1
6. Farmers	44	14.7	144	24.0	223,882	0.8
7. Others	27	9.0	140	23.3	-	-
Totals	300	100.0	600	100.0	955,606	0.9

his best chance will be found in the legal profession. Thus, using six-year totals, the probability of any given male citizen of age 20 years or more who is gainfully employed becoming a member of the legislature is 0.0009, or 9 chances in 10,000. But if he is a lawyer, his chance increases to 651 in 10,000.

The sharpest contrast is seen in a comparison of the class of farmers with the class of lawyers. Although farmers outnumber lawyers approximately sixty to one, lawyers outnumber farmers in the senate by about 2½ to 1, and in the house maintain approximate equality with the farmers.

A more extensive study published in 1940 by Hyneman gives the distribution according to occupations of all members of thirteen lower chambers and twelve senates during the years 1925-1935. The states included were: Arkansas, California (House only), Illinois, Indiana, Iowa, Louisiana, Maine, Minnesota, Mississippi, New Jersey, New York, Pennsylvania, and Washington. The numbers in each occupational class, together with percentages, are given in the accompanying table. From this table we see again the preponderance of lawyers (28%) and farmers (21.5%) over other classes. Lawyers, farmers, and business men comprise nearly 60% of all legislative personnel.

Hyneman reaches the following conclusions: "At least four facts emerge conspicuously from the mass of data concerning occupations which has been compiled; (1) our bicameral system is not producing senates which differ from the lower houses, so far as means of liveli-

Occupations	No.	%	No. of chambers in which each occupational group occupied a given position of importance				
			First	Second	Third	Fourth	Fifth
1. Farmers	2,722	21.5	8	11	2		2
2. Lawyers	3,555	28.0	17	7	1		
3. Newspaper men	369	2.9			2	2	1
4. Other professional men	639	5.0		1	1	7	5
5. Bankers and brokers	352	2.8		1		3	
6. Contractors	273	2.2			1		
7. Manufacturing and industry	445	3.5		1	1	4	1
8. Insurance	484	3.8			2	3	1
9. Real estate	385	3.0			2		1
10. Merchants and other business men	1,263	10.0		3	12	7	2
11. Engineers and machinists	184	1.5		1		1	1
12. Salesmen and clerks	525	4.1					
13. Laborers	205	1.6					
14. Not otherwise classified	704	5.5			2	1	10
15. Unknown	584	4.6					
Totals	12,689	100.0	25	25	26*	28*	24*

*These apparent discrepancies come about through "the fact that when two occupations were equal in importance, they were accorded the same rank."

hood is concerned; (2) the farmer is not, as commonly supposed, in possession of too many seats in legislative chambers; (3) the lawyer is representative for all population groups — our professional representer; and (4) that part of our population which, under any definition, could be called the industrial proletariat enjoys very little membership."

Should this be a matter of concern? "It must be stated emphatically," says Hyneman, "that this *over-membership* of lawyers in the legislature cannot be viewed as a matter of *over-representation* of the legal profession. The attorney is the accepted agent of all politically effective groups of the American people. As a lawyer is habitually the representative of the grasping and the abusive in litigation, as he is increasingly the negotiator between business men with conflicting interests, and as he is more and more the spokesman of individual and corporation in public relations — so is the lawyer today depended upon to represent citizens in the lawmaking body."

We turn next to a consideration of the professional interests of the executives who rule us. We begin with an examination of the training of 32 presidents of the United States. Of these 22 would classify as lawyers, from which we obtain the remarkable percentage of 69. Hence, the answer to the problem of the philosopher king, as far as the chief executive of the country is concerned, is that the highest American political life is dominated by the lawyer king.

Turning to the professional training of the governors of the states, we find three adequate studies of this problem. The first of these,* considering the governors over the period from 1900 to 1910, provides the following table:

Occupation	Number	Per Cent	Occupation	Number	Per Cent
Lawyers	89	48	Newspaper men	10	5
Merchants	18	10	Physicians	6	3
Manufacturers	15	8	Contractors	3	2
Farmers	14	7	Others	20	11
Bankers	12	6			
				187	100

The second study,** concerning governors over the years from 1915 to 1930, gives the following distribution:

Occupation	Number	Per Cent	Occupation	Number	Per Cent
Law	86	43	Engineering	6	3
Education	18	9	Editing	5	2.5
Finance	15	7.5	Printing	4	2
Farming	10	5	Real estate	4	2
Ranching	7	3.5	Others	37	19
Manufacturing	7	3.5			
				199	100

A similar preponderance of lawyers appears in a third study, ǂ which considers governors over the decade between 1930 and 1940.

---

*"American Governors," by A. F. MacDonald, *National Municipal Review*, Vol. 16, 1927, pp. 715-719. **"American Governors since 1915," by S. R. Solomon, *National Municipal Review*, Vol. 20, 1931, pp. 152-158.

ǂ "American Governors — 1930 to 1940," by J. A. Perkins, *Ibid.*, Vol. 1940, pp. 178-184.

Occupation	Number	Per Cent	Occupation	Number	Per Cent
Lawyers	88	52	Ranchers	4	2
Merchants	15	9	Oil producers	4	2
Farmers	12	7	Career politicians	3	2
Financiers	8	5	Nurserymen	3	2
Manufacturers	8	5	Realtors	3	2
Educators	6	3	Others	16	9
				170	100

We thus see again that the most conspicuous group in American politics is that of the lawyer. High executive offices are filled in approximately 50% of the cases by members of the legal profession, and the legislatures, which are perhaps more representative of the total population, derive close to 30% of their membership from the lawyer class. It goes without saying that the judicial branch is derived almost entirely from those who receive their training in schools of law. Since there is little likelihood of substantial variations from these figures in the future, one should look with special care to the training provided in the law schools of the country. This training should certainly be broad enough to provide the lofty point of view required by Plato in his definition of the philosopher king.

PROBLEMS

1. Make a pie chart showing the composition of legislatures.
2. Show the professional distribution of governors by means of a bar chart.

5. The Problem of Legislative Tenure.

In most business and industrial activities, experience, as measured by length of employment, is a factor of great importance. Industries watch with much care the rate of labor turn-over, since production is certain to drop if this rate becomes too great.

It is but natural to infer that efficiency in government will also suffer if there is too great a change in legislative personnel. A House of Representatives, for example, in which most of the members appear for the first time would almost certainly function less efficiently than one with a more stable membership.

The problem with which this section deals is that of legislative tenure. C. S. Hyneman and E. F. Ricketts in their study previously cited have provided adequate information on this subject. They investigated the tenure and turnover of the Iowa legislature for the six sessions from 1925 to 1935. Their results confirm a similar study made by Hyneman for the Indiana legislature over the same years.

Our problem will be to discover the approximate law of tenure in the House of Representatives as shown by the accompanying table for the Iowa legislature. For this purpose we shall assume that the distribution has the form

$$y = ar^x, \tag{1}$$

where y is the number of members who have served in x sessions; and where a and r are constants to be determined. The function which we have given is called the *simple exponential*, and is readily fitted to proper data by several methods.

Legislative Tenure in Iowa

	Percentage of all members having a given amt of experience in sessions						Data on Six Combined Sessions	
	1925	1927	1929	1931	1933	1935	Total No of Members	Percentage
House Members								
1st session	50.0	34.2	47.3	47.2	63.9	53.7	320	49.4
2nd session	31.4	38.0	23.1	25.9	22.2	31.5	186	28.7
3rd session	13.9	19.4	14.8	10.2	7.4	6.5	78	12.0
4th session	2.8	6.5	11.1	6.5	1.9	3.7	35	5.4
5th to 9th sessions	1.9	1.9	3.7	10.2	4.6	4.6	29	4.5
Totals	100.0	100.0	100.0	100.0	100.0	100.0	648	100.0
Senate Members								
1st session	24	16	20	16	44	28	74	24.7
2nd session	16	26	18	18	18	42	69	23.0
3rd session	32	8	30	10	12	10	51	17.0
4th session	18	34	10	34	10	10	58	19.3
5th to 9th sessions	10	16	22	22	12	8	45	15.0
10th or more sessions	0	0	0	0	4	2	3	1.0
Totals	100	100	100	100	100	100	300	100.0

We now propose to see how well a function of this type can be fitted to the data under discussion. In the first place we see that we lack complete information on the actual number of members who were serving from five to nine terms, although we have the total in these sessions, namely, 29. We shall arbitrarily assume that for these sessions the number 29 is partitioned into 16 for the fifth, 7 for the sixth, 3 for the seventh, 2 for the eighth, and 1 for the ninth. This division is made from the observation that in the preceding cases each frequency is of the order of half of the one which precedes it. We thus obtain for our investigation the following table:

x	y	x	y
1	320	6	7
2	186	7	3
3	78	8	2
4	35	9	1
5	16		
		Total	648

In order to fit equation (1) to the data we first take logarithms of both sides and thus obtain:

$$\log y = \log a + x \log r,$$

which is seen to be a linear equation in x. The determination of $\log a$ and $\log r$ thus reduces to the problem discussed in Section 4 of Chapter 6.

To solve the problem we form the following table:

x	y	x^2	$\log y$	$x \log y$
1	320	1	2.50515	2.50515
2	186	4	2.26951	4.53902
3	78	9	1.89209	5.67627
4	35	16	1.54407	6.17628
5	16	25	1.20412	6.02060
6	7	36	0.84510	5.07060
7	3	49	0.47712	3.33984
8	2	64	0.30103	2.40824
9	1	81	0.00000	0.00000
45	648	285	11.03819	35.73600

From the totals we now form the following normal equations:

$$\begin{aligned} 9 \log a + 45 \log r &= 11.03819 \\ 45 \log a + 285 \log r &= 35.73600. \end{aligned} \quad (2)$$

Multiplying the first equation by 5 and subtracting the second from the first, we then obtain:

SOME PROBLEMS IN POLITICAL SCIENCE 151

$$45 \log a + 225 \log r = 55.19095$$
$$45 \log a + 285 \log r = 35.73600$$
$$-60 \log r = 19.45495$$
$$\log r = -0.32425 = 9.67575 - 10.$$

From this value we get: $r = 0.47397$, or since our data do not warrant more than two place accuracy, we write: $r = 0.47$.

The value of $\log a$ is determined from either of equations (2). Let us choose the first, from which we get

$$9 \log a = 11.03819 - 45 \log r$$
$$\log a = 1.22647 - 5 \log r$$
$$= 1.22647 + 1.62125 = 2.84772.$$

From this we find: $a = 704.21$.

Hence the law of tenure in the House of Representatives for the state of Iowa has the approximate form:

$$y = 704.21 \cdot (0.47)^x. \qquad (3)$$

In order to check this result we form a table of values by letting x assume successively the numbers 1, 2, etc. to 9. We then get the following table:

x	y (observed)	$\bar{y}$ (computed)	$\bar{y}$ (adjusted)	$y - \bar{y}$
1	320	331	343	-23
2	186	156	162	24
3	78	73	76	2
4	35	34	35	0
5	16	16	17	-1
6	7	8	8	-1
7	3	4	4	-1
8	2	2	2	0
9	1	1	1	0
	648	625	648	0

The adjusted values are obtained by multiplying the computed frequencies by the factor 648/625 so that the final computed values will total 648. This means that we should also correct (3) by this factor. Hence multiplying by 1.0368, we get as the final law of tenure the function:

$$y = 730.12 \cdot (0.47)^x.$$

POLITICAL STATISTICS

It is significant to compare this result with one derived from legislative tenure in Indiana. The following table gives the pertinent information:

Legislative Tenure in Indiana

	Percentage of all members having a given amt. of experience in sessions						Data on Six Combined Sessions	
	1925	1927	1929	1931	1933	1935	Total No. of Members	Percentage
House Members								
1st session	69	55	50	62	63	62	361	60.1
2nd session	21	29	27	20	27	22	146	24.3
3rd session	4	12	11	10	5	10	52	8.7
4th session	4		8	4	3	3	22	3.7
5th to 9th sessions	2	4	4	4	1	3	18	3.0
10th or more sessions					1		1	0.2
Totals	100	100	100	100	100	100	600	100.0
Senate Members								
1st session	26	26	30	24	34	36	88	29.4
2nd session	26	28	18	30	38	30	85	28.3
3rd session	20	12	16	8	2	22	40	13.3
4th session	18	14	14	16	8		35	11.7
5th to 9th sessions	8	18	20	22	18	10	48	16.0
10th or more sessions	2	2	2			2	4	1.3
Totals	100	100	100	100	100	100	300	100.0

Using a technique similar to the one employed in the case of Iowa, we find that the following function represents the law of tenure for the members of the House of Representatives:

$$y = 863 \cdot (0.41)^x.$$

The comparison between the computed and observed values shows the close approximation given by the formula:*

x	y (observed)	$\bar{y}$ (computed)	$y - \bar{y}$	x	y (observed)	$\bar{y}$ (computed)	$y - \bar{y}$
1	361	354	7	6	4	4	0
2	146	145	1	7	2	2	0
3	52	60	-8	8	2	1	1
4	22	24	-2	9	1	0	1
5	9	10	-1	10	1	0	1
					648	648	0

*From the 5th to the 9th sessions inclusive the data give a total of 18. This figure has been arbitrarily distributed in the sessions.

SOME PROBLEMS IN POLITICAL SCIENCE

It is unsafe, of course, to generalize from two examples, but if one assumed that the probability of any man succeeding himself is $\frac{1}{2}$, then the probability that he will be elected for x sessions is the value of the function: $(\frac{1}{2})^x$. Hence, if we consider a group of N legislators, out of this number only $N(\frac{1}{2})^x$ will have been elected for x terms. In this case we should have as the law of legislative tenure:

$$y = N(\tfrac{1}{2})^x.$$

The two formulas empirically found are seen to approximate this *a priori* expression except that the probability of reelection appears in the case of Indiana to be somewhat lower than $\frac{1}{2}$.

In the case of the senate the same law appears to hold if we note the modification that senators in both Iowa and Indiana are elected for two terms instead of one as in the case of representatives. From the tables given earlier we combine the sessions in pairs and thus obtain the following table:

Senatorial Tenure in Iowa and Indiana

Sessions	Class number x	Iowa Number	Iowa Per Cent	Indiana Number	Indiana Per Cent
1 - 2	1	143	47.7	173	57.7
3 - 4	2	109	36.3	75	25.0
5 - 6	3	30	10.0	30	10.0
7 - 8	4	12	4.0	14	4.7
9 - 10	5	6	2.0	8	2.6
		300	100.0	300	100.0

The Indiana data are almost exactly represented by the function: $y = 405(0.43)^x$. The distribution for Iowa is more imperfectly represented by the function: $y = 346(0.47)^x$. From these data it is clear that tenure in the Senate follows much the same pattern as that for the House of Representatives.

PROBLEMS

1. Find the law of legislative tenure if a legislature of 240 members has the following distribution:

   Session: 1   2   3   4   5   6   7   8
   Number: 125 58 28 16   7   3   2   1

2. If the law of tenure for a given legislature was $y = 200(0.40)^x$, how large is the legislative body? *Hint:* Find the values of y corresponding to values of x until $y = 1$. Then add the members in each category to obtain the total membership. *Ans.* 133.

6. *The Judgment of Tribunals.*

As an example of the direct application of the theory of probability to political science we shall consider the problem of the judgment of tribunals. This problem is one that has long interested the philosophers of jurisprudence, since it is a matter of common knowledge that justice occasionally miscarries. From time to time a belated confession will show that an innocent person has become the victim of circumstance, despite the fact that twelve good men and true condemned him on the basis of evidence.

But in spite of this danger of error, tribunals must reach conclusions, and defendants before the court must be condemned, for the protection of society. But if the probability that an error will be reached in the verdict is greater than the probability that society will be harmed if the accused is freed, then it is evident that some better method of trial should be devised.

It thus becomes a matter of considerable interest to find the answer to certain questions pertaining to the probability that a correct verdict is attained in a trial based upon testimony and decided by a tribunal. The questions are specifically: (a) How large should the tribunal be to assure a safe limit to the probability of obtaining a correct verdict? Should it be, for example, as large as the Athenian dicasts, which, in the case of the trial of Socrates, consisted of 501 members? or should it be no larger than one judge, as in most of the Roman trials? (b) What should be the ratio of the votes of the tribunal in favor of a certain verdict, in order to assure a safe probability that the verdict is correct? Should it be, for example, a majority vote as in the case of the Athenian dicasts, or a unanimous verdict of 12 jurors, as in the English system, or the decision of a single judge, as in the Roman courts? Is it probable that Socrates would have been condemned by an American jury, in view of the fact that he was condemned by a vote of 281 to 220 in the Athenian court?

The problem of the judgment of tribunals was apparently first considered by the French philosopher N. C. de Condorcet (1743-1794) in an essay published in 1785. Perhaps the principal result of his studies was that judges must be enlightened men if confidence is to be placed in their decisions, although there is no attempt to define the term "enlightened men." Condorcet advocated the abolition of capital punishment on the basis of the proposition that, since the probability of error in court decisions could never be reduced to zero, a certain number of innocent people must be condemned in the course of many decisions.

The next writer to consider the problem was the French mathematician P. S. de Laplace (1749-1827), who devoted part of the first supplement of his classical treatise on the *Theory of Probabilities* (1812-1820) to the subject. His conclusions will be the main source for the discussion of this section. But the formulas and argument of Laplace were not wholly acceptable to his distinguished colleague, S. D. Poisson (1781-1840), who produced in 1837 a volume entitled: *Researches upon the probability of judgments in criminal matters.* However, Poisson added little to the work of Laplace, since he merely substituted one set of assumptions for another, and both discussions of the problem were derived necessarily from *a priori* reasoning. Apparently no other contributions were made to the subject after these preliminary adventures, although J. Bertrand (1822-1900) devotes a chapter to it in his *Calculus of Probabilities,* published in 1889.

It will not be possible here to discuss in detail the arguments used by Laplace in attaining his results, since they depend upon what is called the theory of *inverse probability,* which we have not developed in this volume. Essentially his computation depended upon the assumption that "when the probability of the offense of an accused person is such that the citizens have more to fear the consequences which would arise from his impunity than the errors of the tribunal, then the interest of society requires the condemnation of the accused." Laplace called this degree of probability a, and supposed that the judge who condemns the accused person pronounces thereby that the probability of his offense is at least as great as a. Designating this probability of the opinion of the judge by x, Laplace assumed that it must be at least equal to ½ and can increase by small degrees to 1. Hence, if the tribunal is composed of $n = p + q$ judges, of which p condemn the accused person and q absolve him, then the probability that the opinion of the tribunal is just will be proportional to $x^p(1 - x)^q$, and the probability that the opinion of the tribunal is not just will be proportional to $(1 - x)^p x^q$.

Invoking now the principle of inverse probability, Laplace derived the following formula for the probability (P) that the judgment of the court is in error:

$$P = \frac{1}{2^{n+1}}[1+\frac{(n+1)}{1!}+\frac{(n+1)n}{2!}+\frac{(n+1)n(n-1)}{3!}+\cdots+\frac{(n+1)n(n-1)\cdots(n-q+2)}{q!}], \quad (1)$$

where we use the abbreviation: $p + q = n$.

Since this fraction is difficult to evaluate when n is large, Laplace gives two additional formulas. The first provides the approximate value of P when $p-q$ is large, and the second when $p-q$ is small.

The first of these, namely, for the case where $p-q$ is large, is as follows:

$$P = \frac{n^{n+1}\sqrt{n}}{(\sqrt{2})^{3n} p^p q^q \sqrt{\pi pq}(p-q)} [1 - \frac{n}{(p-q)^2} - \frac{n^2 - 13pq}{12pqn}]. \quad (2)$$

The second formula, namely, when $p-q$ is small, is the following:

$$P = \tfrac{1}{2} - l(s), \quad (3)$$

where s is defined by the expression:

$$s^2 = \frac{(p-q)^2 n}{4pq}, \quad (4)$$

and $l(s)$ is the function defined in Chapter 4 and evaluated in Table 3 in the Appendix.

We shall apply formula (1) to compute the probability of error in a verdict obtained by a jury of twelve persons for the following cases: (a) unanimous verdict; (b) one dissenting vote; (c) two dissenting votes, etc. The results are given in the following table:

Number in Division of Opinion	Probability of Error	Number in Division of Opinion	Probability of Error
Unanimous	0.00012	8 to 4	0.13342
11 to 1	0.00171	7 to 5	0.29053
10 to 2	0.01123	6 to 6	0.50000
9 to 3	0.04614		

From this table we see that the English and American jury system, under the assumption of Laplace, leads to a miscarriage of justice in only 12 out of 10,000 cases. The actual fraction is 1/8192. But if the plurality is reduced to 8 votes out of 12, then the probability of error is 1092/8192, or approximately one-eighth.

It is readily seen from formula (4) that the probability of error in a verdict increases with the number of jurors on the tribunal, if the difference between the number in favor of the verdict and the number

SOME PROBLEMS IN POLITICAL STATISTICS

against remains constant. For this means that $p-q$ is a constant, let us say, k. Then $4pq$ is nearly equal to n^2, if n is sufficiently large, and we thus have s approximately equal to $k/\sqrt{n}$. Hence, as n increases, s decreases and so also does $l(s)$. Thus P approaches the value ½.

PROBLEMS

1. Name some of the difficulties underlying any attempt of the kind discussed here to approximate the error in court judgments.

2. Make a table of the probability of error for the case where the jury contains 8 members. Verify from this the statement of Laplace that the probability of an error in the verdict is greater than ¼ when the required majority is 5 to 3.

3. Show that when the required majority is 4 to 2 in a jury of six, the probability of error is less than ¼.

4. Compute the probability of error in the verdict of condemnation of Socrates, where the vote stood at 281 to 220, was approximately 0.003. Since the opinion of history appears to have rejected the verdict of the Athenian dicast, what conclusions can you derive from this result?

5. Verify the statement of Laplace that in a vote of 112 to 100, the probability of an incorrect verdict having been reached is 0.20454.

6. Laplace states that in the case of a vote of 90 to 54, the probability of error is 1/773. Verify this statement.

CHAPTER 7
THE STATISTICS OF TIME SERIES
1. *Origin of the Problem.*

IN THE MATERIAL so far presented we have confined our attention almost exclusively to the problem of frequency distributions. The statistics of these important models lies at the heart of sampling theory, averages, the central tendency of data, and similar applications. But frequency statistics is essentially a static theory in the sense that time plays no part in the analysis.

In recent years there has been an increasing attention paid to what are called *time series*. By this we mean collections of data arranged serially with respect to time. For example, any one who has lived in the present century is very much aware that prices are not static phenomena. Great inflations have been observed in connection with both World War I and World War II. The price of wheat which prevailed in 1900 is very different from the price of wheat in 1952 (in excess of $2.00), but the price of wheat in 1932 (47 cents in Nov. and Dec.) at the bottom of what has been called the great depression was actually lower than at the beginning of the century.

The subject of time series is one that can be treated adequately only in a large volume, since it has many ramifications and presents a number of perplexing problems that are still in an unsettled condition. However, it will be possible to discuss some of the most salient features of these series. This will be necessary to the purpose of this book, since the phenomena which are described by time series are, in general, those which have the greatest influence upon political events. Periods of political stability are those in which certain fundamental time series show small variation, but disruptive periods are characterized by great and often violent movements in the same time series.

2. *Index Numbers.*

Before we can make progress in the theory of time series it is first necessary to define a measure by means of which the level of some activity at a given time can be compared with the same activity at another time. Thus we speak of the level of prices in 1900 and compare it with the level of prices in 1940. Attempts to make such comparisons led finally to the construction of index numbers.

By an *index number* we shall understand a ratio, generally expressed as a percentage, which is designed to indicate the level at any given date of the items of a time series. We shall illustrate some of the considerations which enter into the making of index numbers by forming the index numbers of prices.

For this purpose we shall designate price by p and quantity by q, using the subscript 0 to denote the base, or comparison year, and the subscript 1 to denote the year for which the index is desired. It has been customary in the application of index numbers to select as base some year not too remote from the present, a year, perhaps, which might be regarded as a reasonably normal one. In earlier work the year 1913 was employed as a base; in more recent times 1926 has been similarly designated, and many series today use 1939, or the average of several years in the period between 1930 and 1940.

Once the comparison year has been selected, we may assume that the following prices and quantities, n in number, are known for it:

Prices for the base year: $\quad p_0, p_0', p_0'', \ldots, p_0^{(n-1)}$

Quantities for the base year: $q_0, q_0', q_0'', \ldots, q_0^{(n-1)}$.

Similarly, for the year which is to be compared with the base year, we shall have the following prices and quantities:

Prices for the second year: $\quad p_1, p_1', p_1'', \ldots, p_1^{(n-1)}$,

Quantities for the second year: $q_1, q_1', q_1'', \ldots, q_1^{(n-1)}$.

It will be convenient to employ the abbreviation,

$$\Sigma pq = pq + p'q' + p''q'' + \cdots + p^{(n-1)}q^{(n-1)},$$

and to specify the four possible product sums by the following letters:

$$I = \Sigma p_0 q_0; \quad I' = \Sigma p_1 q_0; \quad J = \Sigma p_0 q_1; \quad J' = \Sigma p_1 q_1.$$

The problem of index numbers is to construct out of the $2n$ prices and the $2n$ quantities an expression which describes exactly and uniquely the level of prices in one year, when this level is compared with that of the other year.

3. Types of Index Numbers

In his treatise on *The Making of Index Numbers* (1922) Irving Fisher (1867-1947) listed 134 different formulas which have been suggested for the construction of index numbers. Of these it will be sufficient for our present purpose to mention only three. The first of these was used by E. Laspeyres in Germany as early as 1864 and is the ratio

$$i = I'/I. \qquad (1)$$

The second was formulated by H. Paasche (1851-1925) in 1874 and is the ratio

$$j = J'/J. \qquad (2)$$

The third was called the "ideal" formula by Irving Fisher and is the geometrical mean of the indexes of Laspeyres and Paasche, that is,

$$k = \sqrt{i \cdot j} \,. \qquad (3)$$

In order to illustrate these three indexes numerically, let us compute the agricultural price index for the year 1930 with 1926 as base. Using production and price data for ten agricultural commodities, we first construct the following table of values for pq:

Values of pq for the Years 1926 and 1930

Crops	p_0	p_1	q_0	q_1	$p_0 q_0$	$p_1 q_1$	$p_0 q_1$	$p_1 q_0$
Corn	0.75	0.84	2692	2060	2019.0000	1730.4000	1545.0000	2261.2800
Wheat	1.45	0.87	831.0	858.2	1204.9500	746.6340	1244.3900	722.9700
Oats	0.41	0.39	1247	1278	511.2700	498.4200	523.9800	486.3300
Cotton	0.175	0.136	8989	6966	1573.0750	947.3760	1219.0500	1222.5040
Potatoes	1.420	0.904	354.3	333.2	503.1060	301.2128	473.1440	320.2872
Hay	23.41	19.89	96.07	74.21	2248.9987	1476.0369	1737.2561	1910.8323
Sugar	0.043	0.034	12952	13169	556.9360	447.7460	566.2670	440.3680
Tobacco	0.182	0.144	1298	1635	236.2360	235.4400	297.5700	186.9120
Barley	0.64	0.52	184.9	304.6	118.3360	158.3920	194.9440	96.1480
Rye	0.92	0.61	40.80	45.38	37.5360	27.6818	41.7496	24.8880
Totals					9009.4437	6569.3395	7843.3507	7672.5195

In this table all prices are expressed in dollars. The quantities are in units of 1,000,000, where the measures are bushels of corn, wheat, oats, potatoes, barley, and rye; pounds for cotton, sugar and tobacco; and tons for hay. The products are thus in millions of dollars.

THE STATISTICS OF TIME SERIES 161

From the totals given in this table we immediately have the following values:

$I = 9009.4437$, $I' = 7672.5195$, $J = 7843.3507$, $J' = 6569.3395$.

Introducing these values into formulas (1), (2), and (3), we at once obtain the following values:

$$i = \frac{7672.5195}{9009.4437} = 0.8516; \quad j = \frac{6569.3395}{7843.3507} = 0.8376;$$

$$k = \sqrt{0.8516 \times 0.8376} = 0.8446.$$

Thus we see that while all three indexes vary slightly from one another, they indicate a drop in the price level between 1926 and 1930. This drop was of the order of 16 per cent, since, if the index for 1926 was taken as 100, the index for 1930 was 84.

PROBLEMS

1. Assuming the following sets of prices and quantities:

p_0	.20	.30	.40	.50	p_1	.30	.40	.30	.60
q_0	4	5	3	6	q_1	5	6	2	8

compute the values of I, I', J, and J' defined in Section 2.

2. Using the values found in Problem 1, compute the index numbers i and j as defined by formulas (1) and (2).

3. Using the data of Problem 1, compute the value of the "ideal" index number.

4. Employing the data of Problem 1, compute and compare with one another the following two index numbers:

$$\frac{1}{n} \Sigma \left(\frac{p_1}{p_0}\right) \text{ and } \frac{\Sigma p_1}{\Sigma p_0}.$$

Making use of the value obtained in Problem 3 for the "ideal" formula, compare your computations with this value. How well do these index numbers define the relative level of prices established by the "ideal" formula?

5. Using the data on agricultural prices introduced in the illustrative examples, compute the following two indexes:

$$P = \Sigma \left(\frac{p_1}{p_0}\right) \text{ and } Q = \Sigma \left(\frac{q_1}{q_0}\right).$$

Compare the product, PQ, with the index number J'/I.

4. Index Number Tests.

As we have seen in the preceding section, the three index numbers computed from the same data by different formulas varied from one another. We have also stated that Irving Fisher discovered the existence of 134 different formulas for computing index numbers. Fisher undertook the task of segregating from this list the most perfect index number. His line of attack was the formulation of two tests which index numbers should satisfy and the elimination of formulas which failed to meet one or both of them.

The first criterion was called the *time reversal test*, and it may be defined as follows:

If P_{ab} is the index number for year b with year a as base, and if P_{ba} is the index number for year a with year b as base, then P_{ab} and P_{ba} should satisfy the equation:

$$P_{ab} \times P_{ba} = 1. \tag{1}$$

If the product $P_{ab} \times P_{ba}$ is greater than 1, then an *upward bias* is said to exist; if the product is less than 1, the bias is *downward*.

It is clear from this definition that the time reversal test reduces to a study of the product of an index number by the same number in which the subscripts "0" and "1" of p and q have been interchanged.

As an example, let us apply the time reversal test to the number

$$P_{01} = \frac{I' + J'}{I + J},$$

where we make use of the abbreviations I, I', J and J' given in Section 2.

Interchanging the subscripts of p and q, we obtain

$$P_{10} = \frac{J + I}{J' + I'}.$$

Hence, we get

$$P_{01} \times P_{10} = \frac{(I' + J')}{(I + J)} \times \frac{(J + I)}{(J' + I')} = 1.$$

Neither formula (1) nor formula (2) satisfies the time reversal test. In general, the first will show an upward bias and the second a downward bias. For example, using the illustrative data of Section 3, we have for the first formula:

$$P_{01} = \frac{I'}{I} = \frac{7672.5195}{9009.4437} = 0.8516, \quad P_{10} = \frac{J}{J'} = \frac{7843.3507}{6569.3395} = 1.1939.$$

Hence we get,
$$P_{01} \times P_{10} = 0.8516 \times 1.1939 = 1.0167 > 1.$$

Similarly for the second formula,
$$P_{01} = \frac{J'}{J} = \frac{6569.3395}{7843.3507} = 0.8376, \quad P_{10} = \frac{I}{I'} = \frac{9009.4437}{7672.5195} = 1.1742.$$

Forming the product of these two numbers we have,
$$P_{01} \times P_{10} = 0.8376 \times 1.1742 = 0.9835 < 1.$$

Of the 134 formulas tested by the criterion of the time reversal test, 41 were found to satisfy the imposed condition. These were then subjected to a second criterion called the *factor reversal test*. This may be described as follows: Suppose that an index of prices, P, and an index of quantity change, Q, have been constructed. The factor reversal test then requires that the product of P and Q shall equal the ratio of the expenditure in the comparison year, namely $\Sigma p_1 q_1$, to the expenditure in the base year, namely $\Sigma p_0 q_0$. That is to say, in symbols we require that

$$P \cdot Q = \frac{\Sigma p_1 q_1}{\Sigma p_0 q_0} = \frac{I'}{I}. \tag{2}$$

Since the quantity index is obtained from the price index merely by interchanging p and q, leaving the subscripts unchanged, the factor reversal test consists in showing that the product of the price index by the same formula, in which the p's and q's have been interchanged, is equal to the ratio of the expenditures.

Thus the ideal index, formula (3) of Section 3, satisfies the factor reversal test. For we have,

$$P = \sqrt{ij} = \sqrt{\frac{I' J'}{I J}};$$

and, interchanging p and q, we get

$$Q = \sqrt{\frac{J J'}{I I'}} = \frac{J'}{I} \frac{1}{\sqrt{ij}}.$$

Hence, forming the product, we obtain

$$P \cdot Q = \frac{I'}{I} = \frac{\Sigma p_1 q_1}{\Sigma p_0 q_0}.$$

Neither formula (1) nor formula (2) of Section 3 satisfies the factor reversal test.

Of the 41 formulas out of the original 134 which had survived the time reversal test, only 13 were found also to satisfy the criterion of factor reversal. From this group Fisher selected his "ideal formula" as being the simplest.

But Fisher also observed that the formula

$$P = \frac{I' + J'}{I + J}, \qquad (3)$$

known as the *Edgeworth-Marshall aggregative* index number, was a close approximation to the ideal for normal ranges of the price and quantity variables. Since it is easier to compute than the ideal it is thus an excellent index number to use in practical applications.

For example, using the data of Section 3, we find by (3) that

$$P = \frac{I' + J'}{I + J} = \frac{7672.5195 + 6569.3395}{9009.4437 + 7843.3507} = \frac{14241.8590}{16852.7944} = 0.8451,$$

which differs from the value given by the ideal by only five units in the last place.

Unfortunately the ideal formula does not meet a third criterion, which has been called the *circular test*. If we designate by P_{ab} the index number for the year b with a as base, then the circular test requires the following equality for any value of n:

$$P_{1n} = P_{12} \cdot P_{23} \cdot P_{34} \cdots P_{n-1,n}.$$

The amount by which the circular test fails has been called by Fisher the *circular gap*. The following index number,

$$P = \frac{p_1{}^a (p_1')^a (p_1'')^a \cdots (p_1{}^{(n+1)})^a}{p_0{}^a (p_0')^a (p_0'')^a \cdots (p_0{}^{(n-1)})^a},$$

where a is any number, satisfies the circular test. This index number also satisfies the time reversal criterion, but it fails to satisfy the factor reversal test.

As an example, we shall compute the circular gaps obtained by the Laspeyres, Paasche, and ideal formulas given respectively by (1), (2), and (3) in Section 3. We shall use for this comparison agricultural

THE STATISTICS OF TIME SERIES

prices and quantities for the years 1926, 1927, 1928, and 1929, represented respectively by p_1, p_2, p_3, p_4 and q_1, q_2, q_3, q_4.

We shall require values of the sums

$$I_{ij} = \Sigma p_i q_j.$$

These values necessary for calculation are recorded in the following table:

Values of $I_{ij} = \Sigma p_i q_j$.

j	$i = 1$	2	3	4
1	9009.4	8891.2	9278.8	9169.3
2	9292.4	9060.8	9422.9	9848.7
3	...	9304.0	9636.6	9584.4
4	8432.1	...	8675.0	8556.6

Using the above data and the formula of Laspeyres we compute:

$$P_{12} = \frac{I_{21}}{I_{11}} = 0.9869, \quad P_{23} = \frac{I_{32}}{I_{22}} = 1.0400, \quad P_{34} = \frac{I_{43}}{I_{33}} = 0.9946.$$

Hence, we obtain by the circular method,

$$P_{14}^{(1)} = P_{12} \times P_{23} \times P_{34} = 1.0208.$$

This value is to be compared with the index obtained directly from the Laspeyres formula, namely,

$$P_{14}^{(2)} = \frac{I_{41}}{I_{11}} = \frac{9169.3}{9009.4} = 1.0177.$$

The circular gap is thus seen to be equal numerically to the difference between these two values, that is to say, 0.0031.

Using next the formula of Paasche we compute

$$P'_{12} = \frac{I_{22}}{I_{12}} = 0.9751, \quad P'_{23} = \frac{I_{33}}{I_{23}} = 1.0357, \quad P'_{34} = \frac{I_{44}}{I_{34}} = 0.9864.$$

Hence, as before, we obtain by the circular method,

$$P_{14}^{(3)} = P'_{12} \times P'_{23} \times P'_{34} = 0.9962.$$

This value is to be compared with the index obtained directly from the Paasche formula, namely,

$$P_{14}^{(4)} = \frac{I_{44}}{I_{14}} = \frac{8556.6}{8432.1} = 1.0148.$$

In this case the circular gap is numerically equal to 0.0186 and the sign is reversed from that in the first computation.

Finally, for the ideal formula, we compute:

$$P_{12}'' = \sqrt{P_{12}\cdot P_{12}'} = 0.9810, \quad P_{23}'' = \sqrt{P_{23}\cdot P_{23}'} = 1.0379, \quad P_{34}'' = \sqrt{P_{34}\cdot P_{34}'} = 0.9905.$$

Hence, we obtain by the circular method,

$$P_{14}^{(5)} = P_{12}'' \times P_{23}'' \times P_{34}'' = 1.0084.$$

This value we compare with the index number obtained directly from the ideal formula, namely,

$$P_{14}^{(6)} = \sqrt{P_{14}^{(2)} P_{14}^{(4)}} = 1.0163.$$

In this case the circular gap is numerically equal to 0.0079, a value between the gaps obtained from the other two formulas.

No formula has been found which satisfies all three criteria. Ingenious attempts have been made to obtain measures of comparison between price levels by means of economic considerations rather than by formal index numbers. But as yet these methods have not been put into satisfactory statistical form.

PROBLEMS

1. Assuming the data of Problem 1, Section 3, apply the time reversal test to formula (1) of Section 3. What is its bias?

2. Apply the factor reversal test to formula (2), Section 3, assuming the data of Problem 1, Section 3.

3. The following set of prices and quantities is added to those given in Problem 1, Section 3:

p_2	.40	.40	.60	.70
q_2	2	5	8	6

Using formula (1) of Section 3, compute the index numbers: P_{01}, P_{12}, and P_{02}. Hence, determine the circular gap by computing the difference:

$$P_{01} P_{12} - P_{02}.$$

4. Show that the "ideal" index number (3) of Section 3 satisfies the time reversal test.

5. Compare the value of k, formula (3), Section 3, using the data of Problem 1, Section 3, with the value of the aggregative index number, formula (3) of Section 4. Show that the two values differ very little from one another.

6. Compare the level of agricultural prices in 1926, 1927, 1928, and 1929, using the aggregative index formula.

5. *The Problem of Trends.*

From the standpoint of political science there is probably no feature of a time series which is of greater importance than the trend. By the *trend* we mean that characteristic of the series which tends to extend consistently throughout the entire range of time under consideration. This characteristic is also often called the *secular trend*, to distinguish it from shorter movements frequently observed in long time series.

For the last four centuries there has been a general tendency for series representing population and production to increase. During the last century this growth has been so phenomenal that one who contemplates the possible political stability of the world must have grave apprehensions lest these series should show too sudden a reversal in their trends at some future time.

Trends are of various kinds, the most usual being a *linear trend*. By this we mean that the data tend to follow along a straight line fitted to them. An example of this is shown in Figure 34 where the prices of railroad stocks in the United States over the century between 1830 and 1930 are graphically portrayed, together with the linear trend about which they have tended to fluctuate during the period.

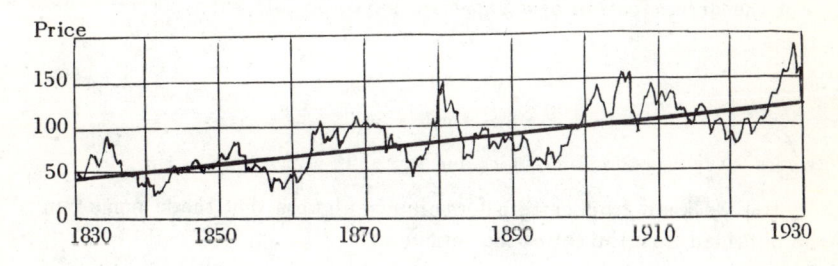

Figure 34. Prices of Railroad Stocks in the United States, 1830-1930.

If we examine the figure we see that over the century covered by the data the average price of railroad stocks has increased by the difference in the ordinates of the line at its two extremes, namely, by about $90. Hence the slope of the line is 90/100 = 0.90, from which we can infer that the price of railroad stocks has had an average annual appreciation of approximately 90 cents.

The determination of a linear trend is made by a method described in Section 4 of Chapter 5. A certain simplification is often possible in the computation since the items of a time series are usually given at uniformly spaced intervals of time, such as, by days, months, years, etc. Hence these intervals can be represented by the sequence of integers, namely, 1, 2, 3, etc. to n.

Thus, let us suppose that we have the following data:

Time (t)	t_1	t_2	t_3	t_4	...	t_n
Data (y)	y_1	y_2	y_3	y_4	...	y_n

Let us denote the linear trend by the equation:

$$y = at + b, \tag{1}$$

where a and b are to be determined.

Since by assumption the time intervals are constant, we can replace the values t_1, t_2, t_3, etc. by the integers 1, 2, 3, etc. We then denote by m_0 and m_1 the following sums:

$$m_0 = y_1 + y_2 + y_3 + y_4 + \cdots + y_n,$$
$$m_1 = 1 \cdot y_1 + 2 \cdot y_2 + 3 \cdot y_3 + 4 \cdot y_4 + \cdots + n \cdot y_n.$$

For the determination of a and b we have the following normal equations:

$$s_1 a + nb = m_0, \tag{2}$$
$$s_2 a + s_1 b = m_1,$$

where $s_1 = 1 + 2 + 3 + \cdots + n$, and $s_2 = 1^2 + 2^2 + 3^2 + \cdots + n^2$.

But we know from certain formulas in algebra that these sums can be obtained from the following formulas:

$$s_1 = \tfrac{1}{2}n(n+1) \quad \text{and} \quad s_2 = \tfrac{1}{6}n(n+1)(2n+1). \tag{3}$$

Hence these values can be substituted in the normal equations, from which we then have the following:

$$\tfrac{1}{2}n(n+1)a + nb = m_0$$
$$\tfrac{1}{6}n(n+1)(n+2)a + \tfrac{1}{2}n(n+1)b = m_1. \tag{4}$$

THE STATISTICS OF TIME SERIES

If these equations are solved by the methods indicated in Chapter 5, we then obtain the explicit values for a and b:

$$a = -\frac{6}{n(n-1)} m_0 + \frac{12}{n(n^2-1)} m_1, \quad b = \frac{2(2n+1)}{n(n-1)} m_0 - \frac{6}{n(n-1)} m_1. \quad (5)$$

As an example, let us approximate the trend to the railroad stock prices given in the figure. To simplify the computation we shall take the average values prevailing at the beginning of each ten-year period. We thus obtain the following table of values:

Year	Stock Price (y)	t	ty
1830	51	1	51
1840	36	2	72
1850	53	3	159
1860	38	4	152
1870	100	5	500
1880	105	6	630
1890	84	7	588
1900	102	8	816
1910	132	9	1188
1920	88	10	880
1930	161	11	1771
Totals	950		6807

From the totals we have: $m_0 = 950$, $m_1 = 6807$. Noting that $n = 11$, we then compute from formula (5):

$$a = -\frac{6}{11 \times 10} m_0 + \frac{12}{11 \times 120} m_1 = -0.054545 \times 950 + 0.009091 \times 6807 = 1.01$$

$$b = \frac{2 \times 23}{11 \times 10} m_0 - \frac{6}{11 \times 10} m_1 = 0.418182 \times 950 - 0.054545 \times 6807 = 25.98.$$

Hence the trend given in the figure is approximated by the line:

$$y = 1.01t + 25.98.$$

An inspection of the figure shows that we have estimated the slope, that is to say, the coefficient of t, to be somewhat higher than the actual slope computed from the complete time series.

As one might readily surmise, the linear trend is not the only kind observed in time series. Thus in Figure 35, we show the ratio of population to representation in the House of Representatives since the

170   POLITICAL STATISTICS

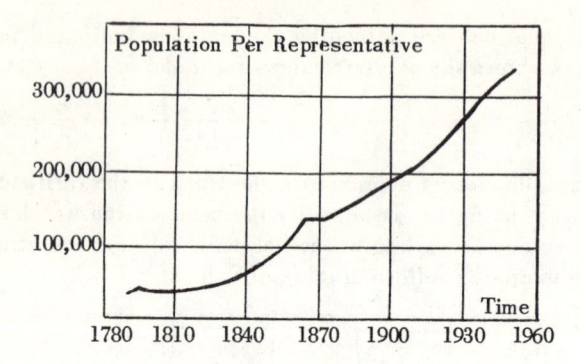

Figure 35. Ratio of Population to Representatives
in the House of Representatives.

time of the first Congress. The constitution originally provided that there should be one representative for each 30,000 population, but as the country expanded this ratio could not be maintained. At the present time the ratio is increasing at a rate of approximately 30,000 per decade. Over the time interval represented by the data, the trend is not linear. Since the present membership in the House of Representatives is held fixed at 435, the ratio portrayed in the graph is actually $P/435$, where P is the population of the United States, and hence increases proportionally to the population. This increase is known to be non-linear.

We shall indicate as another unusual trend the rate of divorce shown in Figure 36. The data show the number of divorces per 1,000 population. Sociologists in particular, and political scientists who are interested in the changes caused in government by changing social patterns, have long been interested in the obvious upward trend in the curve of divorce. The disruption caused by World War I is visible in the sudden increase of the curve around 1920. The more serious dislocations of World War II are shown in the abrupt rise from a rate of 2 in 1940 to a rate of 4.3 in 1946. When these facts are combined with the observation that the marriage rate has shown no corresponding change, except in 1946 when it rose to 16.4, but has remained slightly in excess of 10 per 1,000, with minor variations, for many years, the seriousness of the social problem is readily understood.

THE STATISTICS OF TIME SERIES

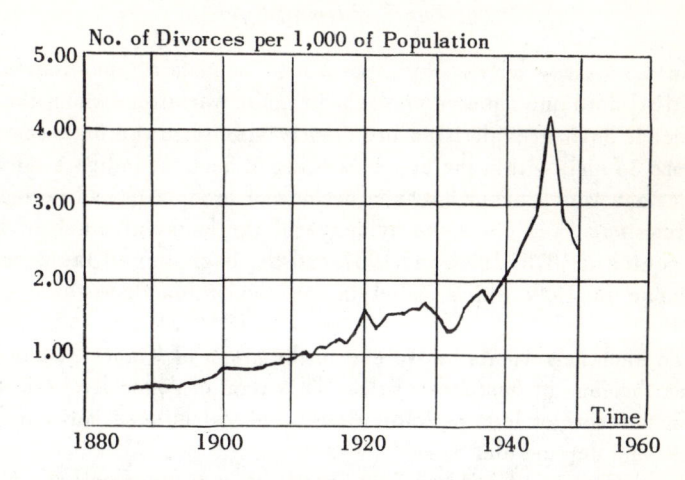

Figure 36. Rate of Divorce in the United States.

PROBLEMS

1. Find the sum of the first 100 integers.
2. Show that the sum of the squares of the first 100 integers is 338,350.
3. Find the sum of the first 100 odd integers.
4. Given the following series:

t	1	2	3	4	5
y	4	3	6	7	10

fit a linear trend by the method of this section.

5. The following table gives the ratio of population to the representation in the House of Representatives (Unit = 1,000), the data used in the construction of Figure 35.

Year	Ratio	Year	Ratio	Year	Ratio	Year	Ratio
1793	33	1833	48	1873	131	1913	211
1803	33	1843	71	1883	152	1923	243
1813	35	1853	93	1893	174	1933	282
1823	40	1863	127	1903	197	1943	301

Fit a linear trend to the first five items and a second linear trend to the last five items of the table. Compare the slopes of the two lines. What conclusion can one draw from this comparison?

6. *The Problem of Cycles.*

In most time series which pertain to economic, sociological, or political data one observes certain irregular variations about the line of trend. Such irregularities are clearly visible in the data shown in Figure 34 and, within the scope of railroad finance, indicate the wide variations which occur between periods of prosperity and periods of depression. Thus one sees evidence of the financial crash of 1837, the panics of 1873, 1893, and 1907, and the beginning of the economic collapse in 1929 which ended in the memorable depression of the 1930's.

To such movements as we see in the graph of Figure 34 has been given the name of *business cycles*. This term is generally assumed to mean the more or less periodic alterations of business between prosperity and depression.

It will not be possible for us here to discuss in detail the statistical methods by means of which true cycles, as contrasted with random variations, are distinguished in statistical data, since these methods are of more interest to economic statistics than to political statistics. We shall be interested mainly in what are called *long cycles*, as contrasted with *short cycles* from one to five years in length. Thus, for example, the existence of a seasonal variation, such as one finds in the price of eggs, or in the monthly index of freight-car loadings, is of little value to students of politics, however useful to economic theory, since these seasonal movements have no bearing upon the trend of political events. But the great drop in the index of prices following the inflations of major wars has peculiar significance in political science, since changes of government and shifts in the trend of political events usually follow these exceptional movements.

As an example of a series with large and definite cyclical properties we show in Figure 37 the composite index of building activity in the United States since 1830. One sees from this graph that there has been in the construction industry a more or less regular cycle, with an approximate interval of 18 years between successive tops and successive bottoms of the curve. One can also infer that the existence of such wide variations in this fundamental series must have considerable economic and political effect. Moreover, inspecting the graph, and noting that the top of the last cycle came in 1925, we are able to conclude that the top of the next cycle should have appeared

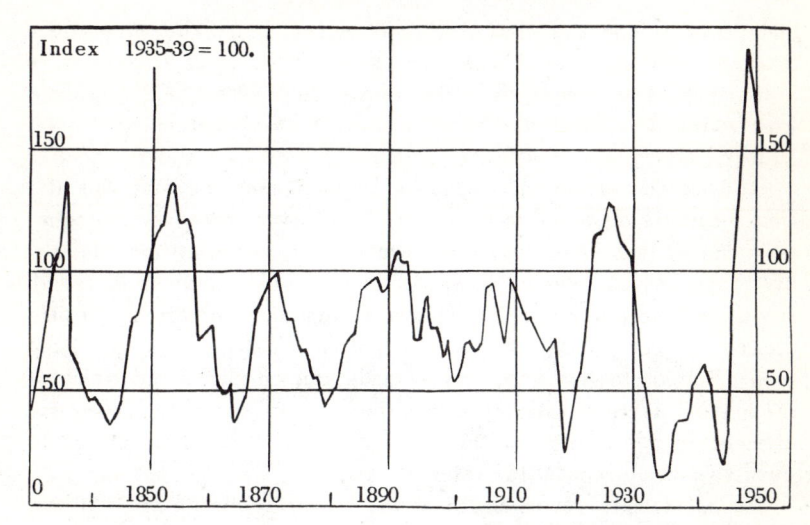

Figure 37. Composite Index of Building Activity, 1830-1951.

in 1943. But because of the dislocations caused by World War II, and the deterrent effects of both material shortages and the high cost of building, the anticipated boom in construction failed to develop until 1950. The impact of these disturbances of the normal cycle upon the body politic is evident in many directions. The crowded housing conditions which prevail not only in cities, but in the smallest villages, are certainly responsible in part for the rapid increase in the divorce rate, and this in turn must bear its share of responsibility for the increase in juvenile delinquency.

In the statistical study of time series it is often important to remove the cyclical element from the series and thus exhibit the trend and the elements of the erratic *movement* which appear as a residual of the statistical process. Various methods have been devised for this purpose, but perhaps the simplest is the method of moving averages.

If the items of a time series are represented by the quantities: $y_1, y_2, y_3, \ldots, y_n$, then a *moving average* of length m is the successive arithmetic averages of m of these items. That is, the series of moving averages consists of these items:

$$x_1 = \frac{y_1 + y_2 + \cdots + y_m}{m}, \quad x_2 = \frac{y_2 + y_3 + \cdots + y_{m+1}}{m}, \quad x_3 = \frac{y_3 + y_4 + \cdots + y_{m+2}}{m}$$

and so on to the end of the original series. Since the values of x represent the m items which form the average, it is customary in graphing them to center each one on the middle item of the average from which it is derived. Thus if m is 5, then x_1 corresponds to y_3, x_2 to y_4, etc.

The method of moving averages depends upon the fact that if a time series is observed to have a cyclical movement of period equal to m units, that is to say, there are m time units between successive tops and successive bottoms, then a moving average of length m will remove these cyclical elements. Hence, to obtain the erratic element in the series, one merely applies a moving average of the proper length to the time series, and then compares the items of the moving average with the trend line. Sometimes, when the erratic element is not too great, the moving averages themselves can be used as a trend line for the original series.

As an example let us consider the following series of 21 items, which are graphically represented in Figure 38.

Time Units	Items of Series	Time Units	Items of Series	Time Units	Items of Series
1	230	8	324	15	154
2	335	9	164	16	254
3	307	10	182	17	347
4	133	11	287	18	381
5	103	12	377	19	207
6	206	13	299	20	184
7	360	14	183	21	287

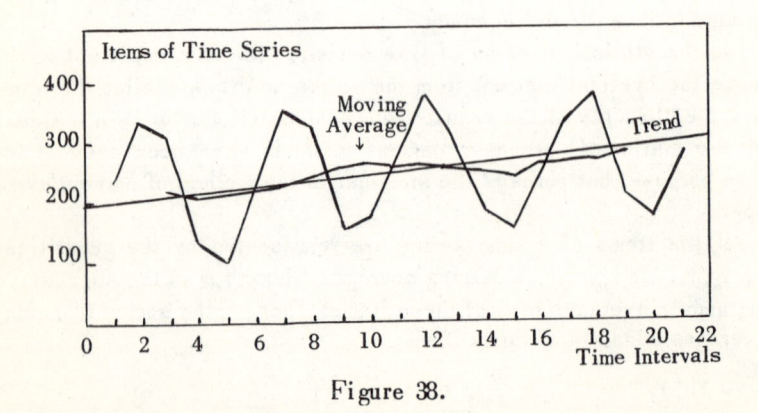

Figure 38.

Figure 39.

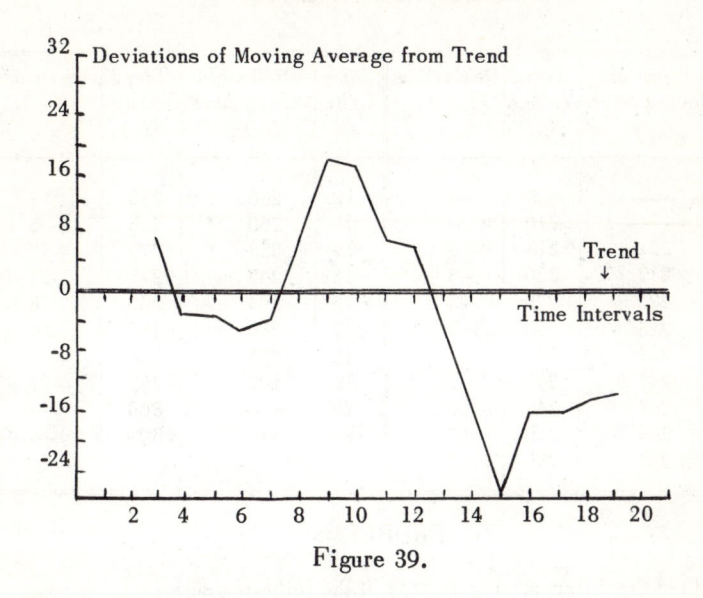

We now observe that the cyclical structure of the series consists of a single cycle of period 5, since there are five time units between successive tops and successive bottoms. Hence we apply a moving average of length 5 to the items of the series, centering each item on the middle item of the five used in the average. Thus the number corresponding to 307 will be 222, since we have

$$x_1 = \frac{230 + 335 + 307 + 133 + 103}{5} = \frac{1108}{5} = 222.$$

In this manner we obtain the items given in the table on the next page. In this table we also give the values of the trend line and the deviations of the moving averages from the trend, namely, the values: $x_i - T_i$, where T_i are the items of the trend.

The moving averages and the trend are represented in Figure 38, which illustrates graphically the efficacy of the moving average in removing the cyclical element from the time series. The residuals, after this technique has been applied, are exhibited in Figure 39, where the trend is represented as the horizontal line and the deviations of the moving averages are graphically portrayed as variations from the line.

POLITICAL STATISTICS

Time Units	Items of Moving Aver. (x_i)	Trend Values (T_i)	Deviations $x_i - T_i$	Time Units	Items of Moving Aver. (x_i)	Trend Values (T_i)	Deviations $x_i - T_i$
1	——	205	——	12	266	260	6
2	——	210	——	13	260	265	−5
3	222	215	7	14	253	270	−17
4	217	220	−3	15	247	275	−28
5	222	225	−3	16	264	280	−16
6	225	230	−5	17	269	285	−16
7	231	235	−4	18	275	290	−15
8	247	240	7	19	281	295	−14
9	263	245	18	20	——	300	——
10	267	250	17	21	——	305	——
11	262	255	7				

PROBLEMS

1. Find the 3-item moving average of the following series:

Item Number	1	2	3	4	5	6	7	8	9	10	11	12	13	14	15
Item Value	1	5	6	2	0	3	7	1	1	4	9	2	8	8	9

Graph the series and the series of moving averages derived from it.

2. Toss one die 24 times and record the value of each throw. The series thus obtained is a random series of numbers from 1 to 6. Apply a moving average of 6 items to the data and compare both sets of data graphically.

3. Graph the following data, which represent a cyclical series with a trend and an erratic element:

Time Units	Items of Series	Time Units	Items of Series	Time Units	Items of Series
1	340	8	364	15	121
2	420	9	179	16	214
3	377	10	184	17	279
4	195	11	283	18	309
5	166	12	367	19	121
6	262	13	282	20	88
7	410	14	160	21	183

Apply to this series a moving average of 5 units and observe how the cyclical element is removed.

4. Establish a trend for the data of Problem 3, and graph the deviations from the trend of the moving averages.

5. From Figure 6 of Chapter 1, would one conclude that there has been an upward or downward trend in the level of American prices? Are cyclical variations observed and if so, what is the average length of the cycle?

7. *Population and Production Trends.*

Among all the time series with which social science deals the most uniform is that of population growth. In Figure 2 of Chapter 1 we showed the curve of population growth in Europe since the early part of the seventeenth century and in Figure 40 of this chapter we give the same curve for the population of the United States. In both of these figures there can be observed the uniform rate of growth and the absence from the curve of the variations so characteristic of most time series.

The nature of the curve of population growth has been the object of much study by statisticians, especially since its regularity, in contrast to other statistical series, gives hope of estimating correctly the size of populations at future times. Thus, in Figure 40, the curve, which was computed from census figures prior to and including 1920, is projected into the future for more than a century. There is considerable hope that the extended curve will give a close approximation to the actual growth of the population through a number of census periods beyond 1920 as it has already done for the censuses of 1930, 1940, and 1950. Thus, the estimated population for 1950, a forecast of 30 years, was 148.35 million and the actual census count was 150.70 million.

The study of various kinds of biological growths, such as the increase of yeast cells and the growth of populations of fruit flies, shows that in the beginning the rate of growth is proportional to the size of the population. But after a time some mechanism begins to operate which decelerates growth. In the case of national populations it is obvious that eventually territorial limitations must put a bound upon the number of people who can be supported within them. This is another way of stating the famous proposition first argued by the English economist, Thomas R. Malthus (1766-1834), who thought to find this controlling agency of population growth in the assumption

178   POLITICAL STATISTICS

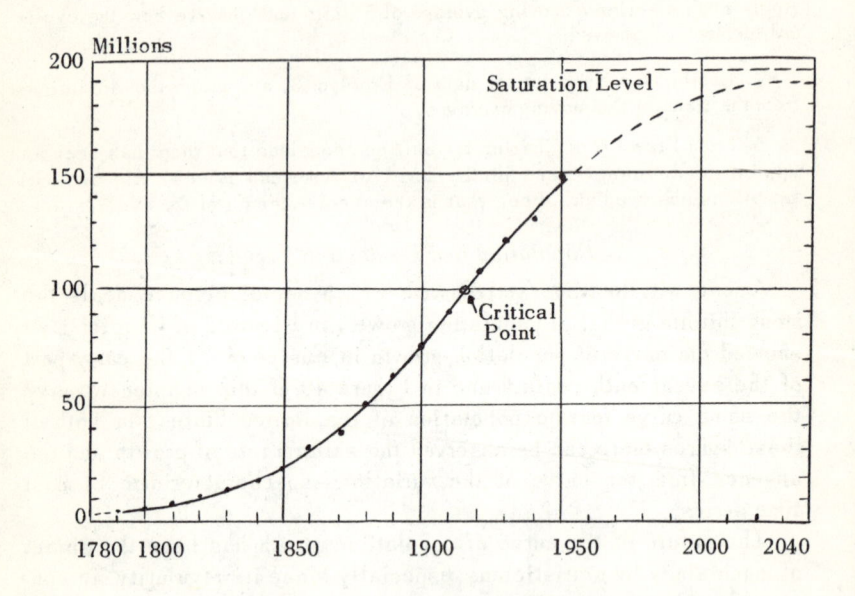

Figure 40. Growth of Population of the United States, 1790-1950.

"that population has a tendency to increase faster than food." Data for modern populations do not tend to confirm this explanation, however, as one may see from the fact that deceleration in the growth of the United States is observed while the country still has a supply of food far in excess of its needs.

But whatever the explanation, decelerating agencies are apparently present in population growth and these eventually must bring the population to a stable size, which is indicated in Figure 40 as the *saturation level*. Somewhere between this level and the origin of the population, there exists a point in time where the acceleration of growth, that is the rate of the rate of growth, changes to a deceleration. This we have called the *critical point* of the growth curve, and once it has been established the magnitude of the saturation level can be estimated. Usually this critical point is well defined and for the population of the United States can be estimated so accurately that one can place it approximately in March, 1914, when the population of the country was just under 98,000,000 people.

The curve which we have been describing is called the *logistic curve* and was given currency in biological and population studies by Raymond Pearl (1879-1940) and L. J. Reed. The curve was employed as early as 1844 by P. F. Verhulst. Its equation is as follows:

$$y = \frac{k}{1 + b e^{-at}}, \qquad (1)$$

where a, b, and k are quantities determined from the data of the population growth, t is time and e is the number 2.7183, which we encountered earlier in Chapter 4 in connection with the normal frequency law.

The quantity k in the equation is equal to the size of the population when it has reached the saturation level. The coordinates of the critical point may be shown to have the values:

$$t = \frac{1}{a} \log_e b, \qquad y = \tfrac{1}{2} k. \qquad (2)$$

Thus, when the curve is adjusted to the population of the United States, we find $k = 196.6$ and $t = 134.22$, where k is measured in millions and t in the years since 1780. From these values we can then compute that the critical point for this curve was in the year 1780 + 134.22 = March, 1914, and that the population was then approximately 98.2 millions, a value slightly in excess of the estimate 97,927,516 made by the Bureau of the Census as of July 1, 1914.

Similar in form to the curve of population is that of the trend of industrial production. This would be a natural inference since a growing population would impose demands upon the industries of the country and the two would thus tend to increase together. But along with this concomitant growth of the two series, we find another factor, namely, the increase in the standard of living. This would be measured by the per capita increase in the index of industrial production. Carl Snyder (1869-1946), who devoted a lifetime to the study of this problem, reached the following conclusion: "The picture that these measures [the per capita growth of production and trade in the United States from about 1800 to 1929 ... varying but little from an average of about 2.8 per cent per annum ...] gives is that of an amazingly even rate of growth not merely from generation to generation, but actually of *each separate decennium* throughout the last century. As if there was at work a kind of momentum or inertia that sweeps on in spite of all obstacles." Although we shall consider in a later chapter this problem of the increase in the standard of living as the result of the increase in production, it is significant to observe that the average return on a day's labor at the present time, measured in terms of the amount of wheat which it will purchase, is of the order of 350 pounds, whereas the same day's labor during the period of the Roman empire was approximately 10 pounds of wheat, in England at the beginning of the seventeenth century was 16 pounds, and in this country in 1882 was no greater than 64 pounds.

As measures of industrial production in the United States we shall exhibit the graphs of two time series which resemble one another in some respects, but in others are quite different. The first of these is the production of pig iron shown graphically in Figure 41, and the second is the growth of electrical power portrayed in Figure 42.

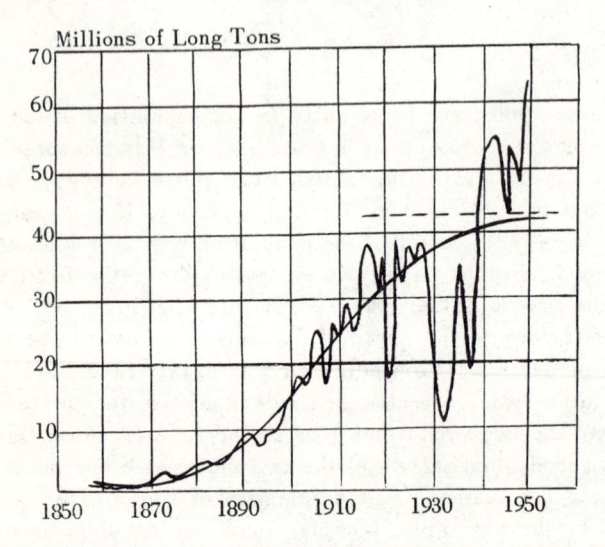

Figure 41.   Production of Pig Iron.

The first of these curves shows the amazing development of the steel industry from its output of 700,000 long tons in 1855 to its astonishing production of 55.5 million long tons under the stimulus of World War II, and its recent production in excess of 60 million long tons. The second of the curves shows similarly the rapid growth of electrical production from less than five billion kilowatt hours in 1903

THE STATISTICS OF TIME SERIES 181

to more than 230 billion in 1944. But the structures of the two curves exhibit striking differences. The first is ragged in appearance. Great drops from the trend appear, which in the case of the depression period around 1932 carried the curve to a level just equal to that which prevailed in 1896. As the average production reaches higher and higher values, the tendency to perturbation appears to increase as is shown by the range of the dips which occurred in 1921, 1932, and 1937. But the second curve is much smoother in appearance, resembling in this respect the logistic of population. The drops visible in 1921, 1932, and 1937 are insignificant percentage-wise when compared with those of the production of pig iron.

Since the use of iron and steel is essential in all heavy industry, it is obvious that the production of pig iron is a good barometer of industrial activity and forms one of the most essential components

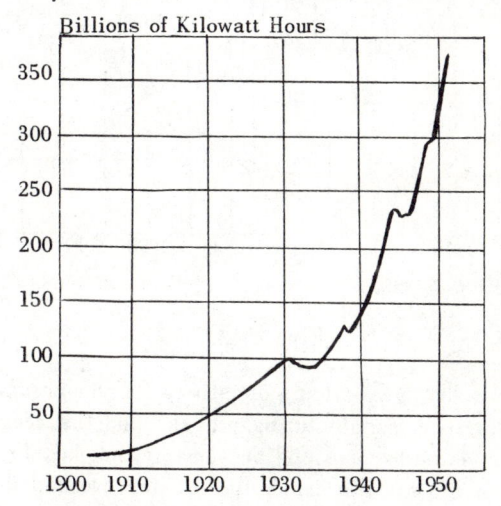

Figure 42. Electrical Production.

of industrial production in general. It is interesting to observe that a logistic curve appears to fit the data fairly well and might be relied upon as a guide to business in determining whether production was dangerously high or exceptionally low.

One or two interesting questions can be asked about these curves. In the first place, if the logistic trend exhibited for the production of pig iron is realistic, then the critical point, where the deceleration of the rate of growth appears, is found to be as early as 1907. Hence, one can infer that normal production is already approaching its maximum value. But the growth of population still continues at a rapid rate and the saturation level will not be reached for another century. Does this mean that the standards of living of the people must become lower as time goes on and the level of production falls below the level of population? Is the deceleration in the rate of growth, assuming the reality of the logistic, dependent upon the limits to the available supply of raw materials? or is it a function of the behavior and limitations of the economic system itself?

Production of Wheat   Production of Corn

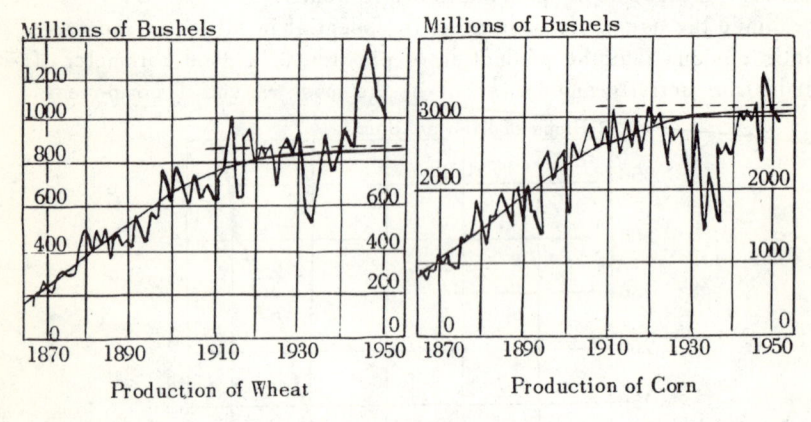

Figure 43.

It is difficult to answer these questions for the production of pig iron, since that is a manufacturing process and the creation of new mills and blast furnaces can add presumably indefinitely to the factors of production. Only the exhaustion of iron ore and the materials used in the process of refinement of the ores can put a limit to the expansion. But in the case of agricultural production it is possible to get a clearer view of the situation and give tentative answers to the questions asked above. Thus, let us examine the curves in Figure 43, the first of which shows the production of wheat in continental United States and the second the production of corn.

The story told by each of these graphs is clear. They indicate that we are approaching the top of production in these grains. In spite of the great need for food during World War II and the use of all available acreage, the production of wheat showed no such increase as that observed in the production of pig iron, while corn barely exceeded the limit of its logistic. Only an increase in the fertilization of the soil, the reclamation of marginal land, and new developments in genetics such as those which underlie the production of hybrid corn, will make any substantial alteration in the picture. If the logistic curves are found ultimately to be realistic forecasts of the trend, then the critical points in the production of wheat and corn, where the deceleration of the rate of growth began, were in the years 1882 and 1885 respectively.

8. *Concluding Remarks.*

In the preceding sections of this chapter the theory of index numbers has been developed as a necessary introduction to the study of time series. The nature of these important numbers was examined and the difficulties in the theory of their construction explained. Since they have become of much importance in recent times in many types of political and economic argument, the sense in which they may be said to compare the level of some variable quantity, measured at one time, with the level of the same quantity at another time, is a matter that should be carefully understood.

The elements of the theory of time series have also been developed and it was found that two significant patterns are recognized in many of the series. The first of these patterns is the trend, which shows the characteristic tendency of the series either to increase, or to decline, during the range of time under consideration. The second is the cyclical variation, which is a pronounced characteristic of some series, but is entirely lacking in others. The cycle is seldom regular in period, but changes of significant magnitude are easily recognized and often accompany profound economic, social and political revolutions.

The significance of what we have seen in the characteristics of certain time series as far as political science is concerned will be discussed in greater detail in later chapters of this work. It is sufficent for our present purpose to define these series and to indicate some elementary techniques by means of which their characteristic features can be determined.

PROBLEMS

1. If the United States were to export 300,000 million bushels of wheat annually, and if the balance of the wheat production were just sufficient to maintain the standard of living of 140 million people, approximately when would the per capita consumption of wheat be reduced by 20 per cent? Use the population curve (Figure 40) for your computation.

2. The following data give the number of patents (new and reissued) issued in the United States. Represent these data graphically. How does the curve compare with the curve of the growth of electrical production? Is there a necessary relationship between the two curves?

Year	Number	Year	Number	Year	Number	Year	Number
1831		1861	3,187	1891	22,408	1921	38,124
1832		1862	3,337	1892	22,472	1922	38,670
1833		1863	4,008	1893	22,867	1923	38,860
1834		1864	4,886	1894	18,939	1924	42,789
1835		1865	6,395	1895	20,942	1925	46,716
1836		1866	9,164	1896	21,928	1926	45,023
1837	436	1867	12,701	1897	22,163	1927	42,055
1838	521	1868	12,964	1898	20,464	1928	42,714
1839	417	1869	13,491	1899	23,388	1929	45,656
1840	468	1870	12,596	1900	24,741	1930	45,608
1841	496	1871	12,151	1901	25,639	1931	52,159
1842	501	1872	12,729	1902	27,246	1932	53,864
1843	505	1873	12,117	1903	31,163	1933	49,117
1844	485	1874	12,713	1904	30,377	1934	44,898
1845	486	1875	12,922	1905	29,913	1935	41,031
1846	579	1876	14,793	1906	31,340	1936	40,213
1847	509	1877	13,488	1907	36,031	1937	38,077
1848	607	1878	12,854	1908	32,925	1938	38,424
1849	1,018	1879	12,621	1909	36,734	1939	44,340
1850	911	1880	13,432	1910	35,291	1940	42,618
1851	782	1881	16,019	1911	33,074	1941	41,429
1852	910	1882	18,406	1912	36,389	1942	38,715
1853	875	1883	21,363	1913	34,105	1943	31,245
1854	1,787	1884	19,263	1914	40,135	1944	28,243
1855	1,853	1885	23,460	1915	43,389	1945	25,823
1856	2,398	1886	21,913	1916	44,168	1946	21,940
1857	2,783	1887	20,528	1917	41,248	1947	20,279
1858	3,593	1888	19,671	1918	38,734	1948	24,084
1859	4,396	1889	23,435	1919	37,075	1949	35,265
1860	4,595	1890	25,406	1920	37,397	1950	43,201

CHAPTER 8
POLITICAL SCIENCE AND THE DISTRIBUTION OF INCOME
1. *Historical Summary.*

ONE OF THE MOST manifest patterns in history is the ever-present conflict between what we might call the plebeian and the patrician elements in the state. This conflict is evident from ancient times as we see from the following comment by J. P. Mahaffy (1839-1919) in his *History of Egypt under the Ptolemaic Dynasty:*

"That famous Greek settlement [Cyrene], famous since the days of Pindar, and so isolated that it could be really independent, had exchanged its voluntary submission to Alexander for the sweets of autonomy, which in those days usually meant an internecine struggle between the rich who had most property and the poor who had most votes. As soon as one party had force enough to exile its opponents, these opponents appealed to any foreign nation to avenge them of their enemies."

The struggle which began in Rome under Tiberius Gracchus (163-133 B. C.) and his brother Gaius (153-121 B. C.) was one of the most prominent examples in ancient history of this class conflict. After the deaths of the Gracchi, the champion of the plebeian class was Gaius Marius (155?-86 B. C.) who carried out one of the most savage proscriptions in ancient times against the aristocratic class. A civil war was precipitated in 88 B. C. with Lucius Cornelius Sulla (138-78 B. C.) as the leader of the patricians. The eventual triumph of Sulla resulted in the destruction either by exile or death of the Marian party and the establishment of the power of the patricians. It was upon this ascendancy of the aristocratic party that Julius Caesar (100-44 B. C.) and later Augustus Caesar (63 B. C. - 14 A. D.) established the central authority which resulted in the Roman empire.

A similar sequence of events is to be observed in the period of the French Revolution. The growing misery of the French common people during the reign of Louis XV from 1715 to 1774 precipitated the expected "deluge." After a tempestuous reign from 1774 to 1792, Louis XVI was executed in 1793, together with his queen, the celebrated Marie Antoinette. This precipitated a proscription of the nobles, known to history as the French "Reign of Terror," which bore striking resemblance to the Marian horror nineteen centuries earlier. This "bath of blood" and the rule of the French Commune soon yielded to the dictatorship of Napoleon and the establishment of his imperial government.

In more recent times both the Spanish Revolution and the Bolsheviks' Revolution in Russia have established similar patterns. In Spain an uprising of the common people against both the monarchy, headed by King Alfonso XIII, and the clergy, who had great economic strength, resulted in the establishment of a republic in 1931 and the confiscation of the property of the nobility and the church. Flight from Spain of the Royal family and many of the monarchist party perhaps prevented the proscription which usually accompanies such revolutions. But the socialistic experiment again failed, for a Civil War began in 1936 with Nationalists, under the leadership of General Francisco Franco, opposing the Popular Front. This resulted, after the characteristic "bath of blood," in a complete victory in 1939 for the Nationalists, who had been given mercenary aid by Italy and other countries. Franco then established a virtual dictatorship which has provided a stable government since that time and attained the remarkable achievement of surviving the political ravages of World War II.

The events which led Russia from the autocratic aristocracy of the Czars to the iron dictatorship of Stalin and the communist party follow the same sanguinary pattern. The Revolution began with the execution of Czar Nicholas II, his entire family, and an unknown number of Russian nobles in 1918 by the Bolsheviks. After an uneasy period marked by proscriptions of such political opponents as Trotsky, Zinoviev, Kamenev, Bukharin, Rykov, and others, Stalin established himself as virtual dictator of the Soviet Republics. The rigid character of his rule, which terminated in 1953, is ascertained from the sobriquet of the "Iron Curtain" behind which it operated.

These classical examples are sufficient to illustrate the pattern which has always been observed in such conflicts between the plebeian and the patrician classes. But the philosophies upon which they rest have been the product of some of the most high-minded thinkers of the race. The reason for this great gulf between the ideals of socialism and its actual attainments of blood-shed, anarchy, and dictatorship is a matter of unusual scientific interest.

Let us first approach the problem by considering what is meant by the word *socialism*. The most commonly accepted definition is that socialism means "a political and economic theory of social organization based on collective or governmental ownership and management of the essential means of the production and distribution of goods." The distinction between socialism and *communism* is found in the fact that the latter implies in addition the collective or governmental ownership of consumers' goods as well as the ownership of producers' goods.

These ideas are very old, being found in the political theories of Plato, as we have indicated in Chapter 1. The word communism appears in the teaching of Apollonius of Tyana. Thus says Philostratus in his *Life of Apollonius* [1, iv, 3]: "His other discourses he delivered under the trees which grew hard by the cloisters; and in there he sometimes dealt with the question of communism, and taught that they ought to support and be supported by one another."

Since these early attempts to organize the philosophy of the conflict between wealth and poverty, many theories have been developed and some notable efforts have been made to put them into practical application. Thus we find the experiment of Robert Owen (1771-1858), English industrialist, who established a communal settlement at New Harmony, Indiana. Similarly F. M. C. Fourier (1772-1837) developed a theory of socialistic government in France, which was based upon the formation of coöperative organizations, called *phalansteries*, each one large enough to allow for the industrial and social needs of the group. This theory resulted in the Brook Farm experiment in Massachusetts during the years 1841-1847. Other variants of the general thesis, the collective ownership of goods, are to be found in Fabianism organized in England in 1883, Saint-Simonianism in France, Nationalism in the United States following the ideas of Edward Bellamy (1850-1898), Syndicalism in France, state socialism and social democracy in Germany. The most extensive experiment was that of Bolshevism in Russia developed under the explosive political socialism of Karl Marx and his followers. Since authoritative statistics are lacking, there is no reliable way of judging the success of this experiment, although in recent times it has given way to an absolute dictatorship quite remote from the idealistic state envisaged by Marx.

From this brief summary of socialistic theory, only one clear fact emerges. That is, that underlying every experiment one finds the problem of the distribution of wealth and income. Hence, what seems at heart a political problem reduces essentially to one in economics. In the next section we shall examine the statistics of the distribution of income.

2. *The Distribution of Income.*

Although most if not all utopian states had as a cardinal principle a distribution of material things more uniform than the one commonly observed, it has only been in recent times that any attempt has been made to describe the actual distribution of wealth and income.

It is a matter of more than usual interest, however, to observe that Solon (638-559 B. C.), the great law-giver of ancient Greece, recognized the significance of the distribution of wealth and income in the problem of the stable state. Thus we read in Plutarch's *Life of Solon* the following statement: "There was a saying of his [Solon], that when things are *even* there never can be war, and this pleased both parties, the wealthy and the poor; the one conceiving him to mean, when all have their fair proportion, the others, when all are absolutely equal."

Solon divided the population into four classes according to their income. First, those whose wealth produced corn, oil and wine equal to 500 measures (*medimni*) per year; Second, those, called knights or keepers of one horse, whose wealth produced 300 measures; Third, those called yoemen, whose wealth produced 200 measures. Fourth, all others, who were referred to as the servants. Since one medimnus of that date was equal approximately to our modern bushel, the first three classes had incomes equivalent respectively to 750 bushels, 450 bushels, and 300 bushels of grain per year. The extent of this wealth is readily estimated from the fact that in those days the daily wages of a laborer were equivalent to about 20 pounds of grain, or one-third of a bushel. The average income of a family was of the order of 80 bushels of grain per year and the amount necessary for the maintenance of life was about 35 bushels of grain per year. Although no figures are given as to the range of income in the wealthy class, nor as to the number of the population in this class, it is not unlikely that the range of income between that of the poorest laborer and that of the wealthiest citizen was not far different from the range observed in later economic systems.

The first comprehensive study of the problem of the distribution of wealth was made by the Italian engineer and economist, Vilfredo

Pareto (1848-1923), who published his results in his *Cours d'Economie Politique* which appeared in two volumes in 1896-97.

Pareto made a startling discovery which is now known as *Pareto's law* of the distribution of income. This law, following Pareto's statement with one exception, namely the insertion of the words "in a stable economy," may be given precisely in the following statement:

In all places and at all times the distribution of income in a stable economy, when the origin of measurement is at a sufficiently high income level, will be given approximately by the formula

$$N_x = \frac{A}{x^a}, \qquad (1)$$

where N_x is the number of people having the income x or greater, A is a constant depending on the size of the economy, and a is approximately 1.5.

Pareto was well aware of the importance of this discovery, as is proved by the following comment which he made about it:

"These results are very remarkable. It is absolutely impossible to admit that they are due only to chance. There is most certainly a *cause*, which produces the tendency of incomes to arrange themselves according to a certain curve. The form of this curve seems to depend only tenuously upon different economic conditions of the countries considered, since the effects are very nearly the same for the countries whose economic conditions are as different as those of England, of Ireland, of Germany, of the Italian cities, and even of Peru."*

As an example of Pareto's law we represent in Figure 44 the income distribution observed in the United States in 1918. In that year $a = 1.70$. To represent the distribution we first take logarithms of both sides of equation (1) and hence we obtain

$$\log N_x = \log A - a \log x. \qquad (2)$$

If then we let $y = \log N_x$ and $X = \log x$, this equation assumes the form

$$y = \log A - aX, \qquad (3)$$

which we recognize to be a straight line of slope $-a$. Hence if we graph the logarithms of N_x on the vertical axis and the logarithms of

Cours, Vol. 2, p. 312.

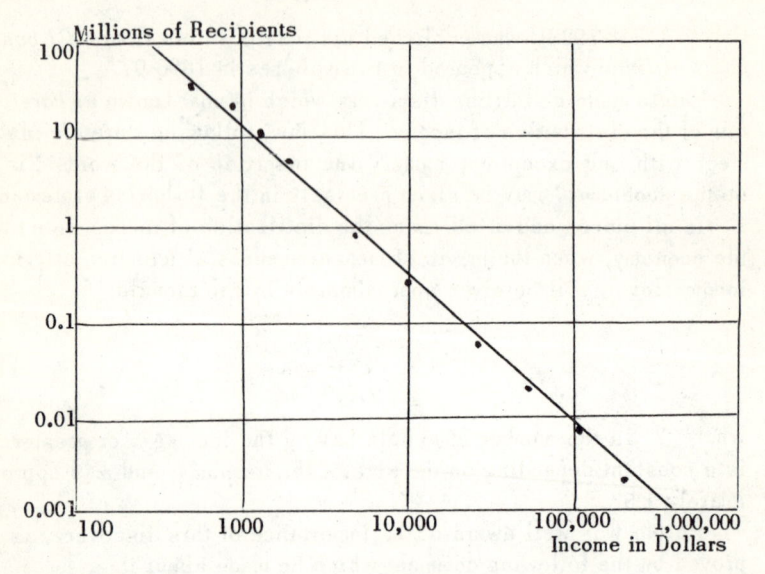

Figure 44. Cumulative Frequency Distribution of Incomes in United States, 1918, on Double Logarithmic Grid.

x on the horizontal axis, the resulting figure will be a straight line. This relationship is shown in the figure, the line representing Pareto's theoretical law and the points the actually observed distribution.

As a corollary to Pareto's law it can be shown that the income possessed by the number N_x is given by the formula:

$$I_x = \frac{B}{x^{a-1}}. \qquad (4)$$

Eliminating x between equations (1) and (4), we find

$$N_x = k(I_x)^\delta, \qquad (5)$$

where k is a constant and $\delta = a/(a - 1)$. Since a is very nearly equal to 1.5, we see that δ is very nearly equal to 3.

Another way, then, to express Pareto's law is to say that the number possessing income x, or greater, varies as the cube of the amount of income possessed by the group having income x or greater.

Since we are dealing here with an accumulated frequency it is very illuminating to form a percentage ogive similar to those constructed in Section 5 of Chapter 2.

POLITICAL SCIENCE AND THE DISTRIBUTION OF INCOME 191

To get the percentage of accumulated frequency, that is to say, the percentage of the number having income x or less, we let N represent the whole population, and then form the fraction:

$$P_x = \frac{N - N_x}{N} = 1 - \frac{N_x}{N}. \tag{6}$$

Similarly, to get the percentage of income possessed by those with income x or less, we let I be the total income and form the fraction:

$$q_x = \frac{I - I_x}{I} = 1 - \frac{I_x}{I}. \tag{7}$$

Now since $N_x = k(I_x)^\delta$, we also have $N = k(I)^\delta$, and hence we find

$$\frac{N_x}{N} = \left(\frac{I_x}{I}\right)^\delta. \tag{8}$$

From (6) we have,

$$\frac{N_x}{N} = 1 - P_x$$

and from (7) we get

$$\frac{I_x}{I} = 1 - q_x.$$

Hence from (8) we find

$$1 - P_x = (1 - q_x)^\delta,$$

that is to say,

$$P_x = 1 - (1 - q_x)^\delta. \tag{9}$$

This equation is to be compared with one in which there is the same number of persons in each income class. This leads to the equation

$$P_x = q_x. \tag{10}$$

In the accompanying figure we show the graphs of equation (9) in which $\delta = 3$, and equation (10).

If one contrasts the ogive given in Figure 45 with that of Section 5, Chapter 2 showing the binomial ogive, one will be impressed by

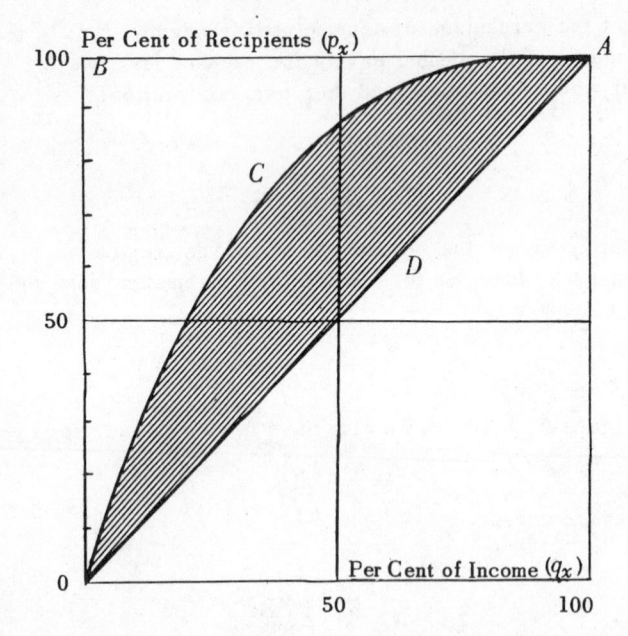

Figure 45. Ogive of Income Distribution.

the abnormality of the distribution of income. It is clear that there is no relationship between this distribution and that observed in the general theory of errors.

It is this fact which has so disturbed philosophers from the time of the Greeks. Thus Plato says in the *Republic*, [555]: "There can be no doubt that the love of wealth and the spirit of moderation cannot exist together in citizens of the same state to any considerable extent; one or the other will be disregarded." Similar statements are to be found in most political and social writers. The curve of distribution which thus exhibits the vast gulf between the very poor and the very rich is essentially the reason for all theories of socialism. These strive to create some mechanism by means of which the observed distribution of income can be reduced to a pattern more in conformity with the normal (or binomial) distribution.

In our mathematical and statistical appraisal of political science we are not concerned so much with these idealistic states as with the real world. Thus we first exhibit the character of the distribution of income and then appraise the consequences of a change in it.

POLITICAL SCIENCE AND THE DISTRIBUTION OF INCOME

PROBLEMS

1. In equation (3) of this section, assume that $\log a = 9.33459$ and $a = 1.5$. Make a graph of the line between the limits $X = 1$ and $X = 4$.

2. In the equation of Problem 1, compute the values of y corresponding to $X = 1, 1.5, 2, 2.5, 3, 3.5,$ and 4. Observing that $y = \log N_x$, find from the computed values of y the corresponding values of N_x.

3. Using the values of X given in Problem 2, compute x from the equation: $\log x = X$. Assuming that unit values of x correspond to $100, form a table showing the relationship between x and N_x.

4. Assuming that $a = 2$, compute δ, and make a graph of equation (9).

5. Solve equation (9) for q_x as a function of p_x.

6. Assuming that $N_x = 100 - x^2$, for values of x between 0 and 10, and that $I_x = \frac{2}{3}(1000 - x^3)$, show that the ogive has the form: $p_x = \frac{2}{3}q_x$.

7. In a large corporation it was found in 1936 that the following distribution of salaries prevailed:

Salary (x)	Number Having Salary x or Greater (y)	Salary (x)	Number Having Salary x or Greater (y)
$ 5,000	1,678	$ 50,000	20
10,000	315	60,000	12
15,000	142	70,000	11
20,000	75	80,000	3
30,000	33	100,000	2
40,000	24		

Graph $\log y$ as a function of $\log x$ for this distribution and show that it is essentially a straight line with slope approximately equal to -2.

8. It was found in a study of 1102 papers given before the American Mathematical Society that these were the production of 278 authors. The distribution observed was the following:

No. of Papers (x)	No. Giving x or More Papers (y)	No. of Papers (x)	No. Giving x or More Papers (y)
1	278	27	6
2	145	39	3
4	78	42	2
11	23	70	1
17	10		

Graph $\log y$ as a function of $\log x$ and determine the slope of the line thus obtained. On the basis of similar observations for other sciences, one sometimes speaks of the "inverse-square law of scientific production." Explain why.

3. *The Concentration Ratio*

In order to characterize the difference between the observed distribution of income and other statistical distributions, a quantity called the concentration ratio has been proposed as a measure of the difference.*

This ratio which we shall designate by the letter ρ is defined as the area between the line OA and the curve OCA (see Figure 45), divided by the area of the triangle OBA; that is

$$\rho = \frac{\text{Area ACOD}}{\text{Area AOB}} = 2 \text{ Area ACOD}.$$

By methods not available to us in this book it can be shown that the area ACOB = $1/(1 + \delta)$. Hence we get

$$\rho = 2[\frac{1}{2} - \frac{1}{1+\delta}] = \frac{\delta - 1}{\delta + 1}.$$

If we replace δ by its value in terms of a, namely by $\delta = a/(a-1)$, we obtain

$$\rho = \frac{1}{2a - 1}.$$

This function is observed to vary from 0 to 1 as a varies from ∞ to 1, or as δ varies from 1 to ∞.

For the Pareto value, $a = 1.5$ or $\delta = 3$, we get $\rho = \frac{1}{2}$. Thus if we regard the Pareto concentration as that of normal society, we can say that this mid-value, $\rho = \frac{1}{2}$, defines the observed concentration midway between a completely communistic state, $\rho = 0, a = \infty$ and a completely oligarchical state, $\rho = 1, a = 1$.

In order to establish his surprising discovery Pareto made an extensive investigation into the distributions of incomes in various states and cities where sufficient data could be found to measure it. He conjectured that a distribution of income differing in no essential way from those observed in modern European countries prevailed also in ancient Rome. Data sufficiently accurate to permit a testing of Pareto's conjecture have been assembled recently and the result of the computation amply confirms his thesis since the value of a at the time of Augustus Caesar was 1.5. These various results are summarized in the following table.

*Proposed by C. Gini: "Intorno alle curve di concentrazione," *Metron*, Vol. 9, 1932, Nos. 3-4, pp. 3-76.

POLITICAL SCIENCE AND THE DISTRIBUTION OF INCOME

Country	Value of a	Concentration Ratio (ρ)	Country	Value of a	Concentration Ratio (ρ)
Rome c. 28 B.C.	1.50	0.50	Anconia, Arezzo, Parma, Pisa	1.32	0.61
England (1086)	1.58	0.48	Italian cities	1.45	0.53
Peru (at the end of 18th century)	1.79	0.39	Basel	1.24	0.67
			Augsburg (1471)	1.43	0.54
England (1843)	1.50	0.50	(1498)	1.47	0.51
(1880)	1.35	0.59	(1512)	1.26	0.66
(1894)	1.50	0.50	(1526)	1.13	0.79
Prussia (1852)	1.89	0.38	United States (1914)	1.54	0.48
(1876)	1.72	0.41	(1920)	1.82	0.38
(1881)	1.73	0.41	(1925)	1.54	0.48
(1886)	1.68	0.42	(1929)	1.67	0.54
(1890)	1.60	0.45	(1930)	1.62	0.45
(1894)	1.60	0.45	(1932)	1.76	0.40
Saxony (1880)	1.58	0.46	(1935)	1.81	0.38
(1886)	1.51	0.50	(1940)	1.85	0.37
Florence	1.41	0.55	(1942)	1.93	0.35
Perugia (City)	1.37	0.57	(1948)	2.00	0.33
Perugia (County)	1.45	0.53	Japan (1938)	1.56	0.41

We see from this table that there has been considerable fluctuation in the ratio of concentration. The lowest value appears to be 0.33, the concentration of income observed in the United States in 1948 following a long series of actions on the part of the government to equalize income. The highest concentration is 0.79 observed for Augsburg in 1526. It is possible that this large value may be partly the result of faulty data, but during the period covered by the table this city was a very prosperous manufacturing and trade center rivaling Nuremburg as the center of commerce between Italy and Northern Europe. Its merchant princes rivaled the Medici of Florence. About this situation we shall have more to say later.

PROBLEMS

1. Graph the function: $\rho = \dfrac{\delta - 1}{\delta + 1}$, for values of δ from 1 to 10.

2. Graph the function
$$\rho = \frac{1}{2a - 1}$$
as a function of a. In selecting the range for a observe that by definition ρ can vary only between 0 and 1.

3. The rate of change of ρ with respect to a is given by the formula
$$\text{Rate of change of } \rho = - \frac{1}{(2a - 1)^2}.$$
Graph this formula and show that the rate of change in the concentration ratio decreases as a increases.

4. The Curve of Income Distribution.

Numerous attempts have been made since the announcement of Pareto's law to construct the curve of income distribution from the lowest level of income to the highest. Since the frequency distribution is abnormally skewed, as we have seen, this problem has been difficult to solve, and there is no curve which has yet been universally agreed upon as the proper one to represent the data.

But the general characteristics of the curve are readily stated. If we denote by y_x the number of people who have incomes x or greater, then there must exist a value c of x for which y equals the total number of income earners. If we denote this total number by N, we thus have $y_c = N$. The quantity c has been called the *wolf-point*, or the *poverty point*, a threshold income just large enough for the maintenance of life. Below this point the wolf, which lurks so close to the doors of the very poor, actually enters the house.

Moreover, when x is sufficiently large, then y_x must have the form $y_x = a/x^a$, where a, as we have seen, is close to 1.5 in conformity with Pareto's law.

A function containing only three statistical parameters has been constructed which satisfies the criteria set forth above. If we introduce a new variable $z = x - c$, so that $z = 0$ when $x = c$, then y_z is the frequency accumulated from the distribution function,

$$\Phi(z) = \frac{A}{z^{a+2}} \frac{1}{e^{b/z} - 1}.$$

Since an adequate mathematical discussion of this function is beyond the scope of this book, we shall consider only the case where $a = 1.5$ and reduce the description of y_z to tabular form. If I is the total income of the economy considered and if N is the total number of income earners, then it can be shown that A and b of the distribution function $\Phi(z)$ have the following values:

$$A = 0.29 \, I \left(\frac{I}{N}\right)^{1.5}, \quad b = 0.77 \frac{I}{N}.$$

It is then possible to show that the accumulated distribution, namely y_z, in an economy for which $a = 1.5$ is given by the function*

$$y_z = N \, G(z),$$

---

*The mathematical details of this derivation will be found in the author's work: *The Analysis of Economic Time Series*, 1941, Chapter 9.

POLITICAL SCIENCE AND THE DISTRIBUTION OF INCOME

where $G(z)$ is defined by the following table:

z/b	$G(z)$	z/b	$G(z)$	z/b	$G(z)$
0	1.00000	0.20	0.94375	5	0.03148
0.10	0.99907	0.25	0.88262	10	0.01147
0.111	0.99780	0.33	0.76700	15	0.00631
0.125	0.99490	0.5	0.56801	100	0.00037
0.143	0.98836	1.0	0.27490	1000	0.00001
0.167	0.97404	2.0	0.11353	5000	0.000001

It was this table which was used to compute the income distribution shown in Figures 4 and 5 of Chapter 1, the first of which pertained to the incomes in Rome at the time of Augustus Caesar and the second to the incomes in the United States in 1929.

Thus, in the case of the Roman figures, the wolf-point was found to be about 78 denarii and $b = 437$. Hence, to find the number of income earners in the class of the Knights, namely, with incomes not less than 6,000 denarii, we first compute $z = (6000 - 78)/437 = 13.5$. From the census figures of 28 B. C. we have $N = 4,063,000$. Therefore, estimating the value of $G(z)$ for $z = 13.5$ to be around 0.78, we get 31,690, which we know to be equal approximately to the number of Knights in the Roman Ager.

It is convenient sometimes to know what income might be used as the dividing line between the wealthy class and that of those who, while in comfortable circumstances, are not rich. This income, called the *midas-point*, can be defined as the income which one per cent of the income receivers have. In other words, it is the value of z for which $G(z) = 0.01$. From the above table this point can be estimated and will be found to be almost exactly given by

$$z = 11b.$$

Hence, in the Roman state, those who had an income in excess of $11 \times 437 = 4809$ denarii were rich. In the United States, where b approximated $1,000 before 1940, the midas-point was in the neighborhood of an income of $11,000.

Recently a very interesting study was carried out by Charles C. Slater to determine the distribution of income which prevailed in England at the time of the Norman Conquest. This analysis was based upon the record of the *Domesday Book*, an account of the great survey of England carried out by William the Conqueror (1027-1087) in 1086. An analysis of the data in this comprehensive census throws more light upon the state of feudal society, the relative position of its social classes, and the standards of living in the Middle Ages, than can be obtained, perhaps, from the volumes of words which have been written about its laws and functions.

Since England was at that time primarily an agricultural economy, Slater found it convenient to express income in terms of acres. Since the average yield per acre was approximately 7½ bushels of wheat, this value has been used as the primary *numéraire*, or unit of income. The lowest classes in the economy were the serfs or slaves and the cottagers. The serf class contained two types, the first of which were the domestic servants eating in the kitchens of their lords. This group was small and the number uncertain. Their annual income has been estimated to be equivalent to some value between 36 and 42 bushels of wheat, which, expressed in acre-income, is equal to the wheat produced by 5 or 6 acres of land. The second type of slave was the demesne serf, who tilled the soil of the lord of the manor. His annual income has been estimated to be equivalent to the wheat produced on an average of 14 acres of land. The cottagers formed a class of settled laborers long in straightened circumstances on small crafts and homesteads. Their income was probably between 10 and 12 acres, and the average of 11, equivalent to 82.5 bushels of wheat, has been assumed for the value of c in estimating the distribution of income, although the actual *wolf-point* was probably that of the lowest slave class as given above.

The distribution of income as finally determined for the recognizable classes in the England of 1086 is given in the following table:

Group	Population	Aver. Income in Acres	Total Wealth in Acres	Total Acres of Income
Cottagers or cotters	88,952	11[1]	6,523,147	978,472
Serfs	26,362	14	2,460,453	369,068
Villeins	108,456	30	21,691,200	3,253,680
Sokemen	23,090	40	6,157,333	923,600
Freemen	12,423	70	5,797,400	869,610
Tenants	7,871	100	5,247,333	787,100
Lords and nobles	1,367	502	4,574,893	686,234
Abbots	16	5,825	621,333	93,200
Bishops	14	7,856	733,227	109,984
Bishop of Bayeux	1	29,760	198,400	29,760
Count of Mortain	1	44,856	299,040	44,856
King William	1	174,348	1,162,320	174,348
Totals	268,554		55,466,079[2]	8,319,912

[1] Assumed value of c in computing distribution. [2] If half the wealth is assumed to be land, this is equivalent to 27,733,040 acres, which is slightly more than the area (27,079,074 acres) surveyed by the *Domesday Book*.

POLITICAL SCIENCE AND THE DISTRIBUTION OF INCOME 199

From these figures we compute $b = 24$, which shows that the midas-point is 264 acres of income, a value between the class of the tenants and the class of the lords and nobles. Making use of the table of values of $G(z)$ and observing that $c = 11$, we are now able to construct the accumulated distribution of income as shown in Figure 46, since the value of a is 1.58, very close to that of the Pareto distribution.

The only unusual departure of the actual distribution from the theoretical distribution is found in the last point. King William's wealth was greater than it should have been for the stability of the economy. That trouble developed later over this matter is found in the history of England. Thus, it is a matter of record that political strife developed between the barons and the king, not between the people and the barons, and this resulted years later in the famous struggle between the nobility and King John, which culminated in the signing of the *Magna Carta* in the year 1215.

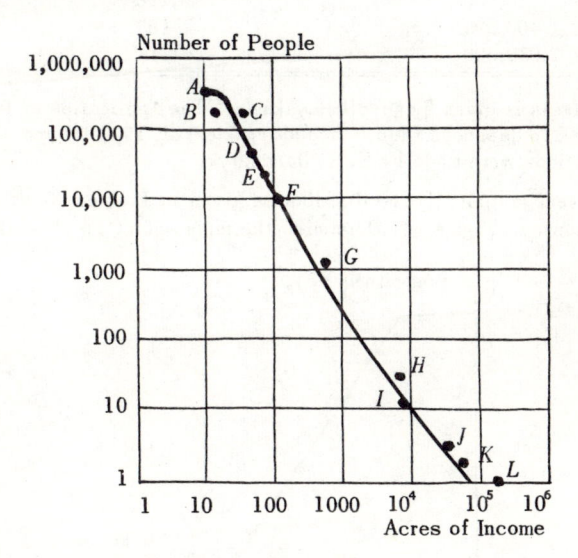

Figure 46.

Distribution of Income in England as Estimated from the Data given in the *Domesday Book* (1086). Lowest class included: A - Cotters; B - Serfs; C - Villeins; D - Sokemen; E - Freemen; F - Tenants; G - Lords and nobles; H - Abbots; I - Bishops; J - Bishop of Bayeux; K - Count of Mortain; L - King William.

PROBLEMS

1. Given $z = x - 1,000$, $b = 1,500$ and $N = 50,000,000$, compute y_x for the values of z/b = 0, 0.1, 0.5, 1, 2, 5, 10, 100, 1,000, and 5,000.

2. Represent graphically the computations of Problem 1 using x as the independent variable.

3. From the income data for Japan in 1938, one finds that $a = 1.56$, $b = 407$ yen, and $c = 100$ yen. If $N = 13,941,085$, obtain the following graduated distribution:

Income (x) in yen		Frequency values, y_x, for people having income x or greater
$0.1b + c =$	141	13,928,097
$0.5b + c =$	304	7,918,714
$1b + c =$	507	3,832,410
$2b + c =$	914	1,582,642
$5b + c =$	2,135	438,849
$10b + c =$	4,170	159,924
$100b =$	40,700	5,196
$1000b =$	407,000	165
$5000b =$	2,035,000	15

This analysis is given by Miyoji Hayakawa: "The Application of Pareto's Law of Income to Japanese Data," *Econometrica*, Vol. 19, 1951, pp. 174-183. The computations were made by E. W. Hanczaryk.

4. Represent graphically the distribution given in Problem 3 and obtain the curve shown in Figure 47. Determine the midas-point for the Japanese distribution.

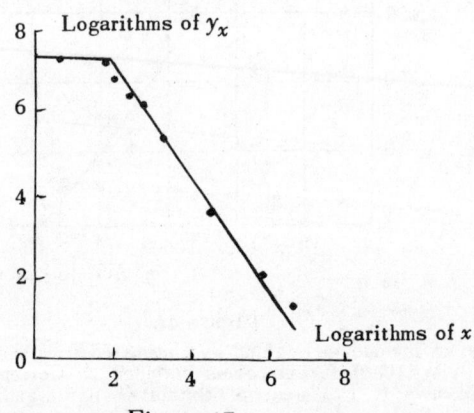

Figure 47.

5. The Concentration Ratio and Production.

Since the distribution of wealth and income appears to lie close to the fundamental problem of society, namely, that of preserving stable government, it will be of interest to examine the fluctuations in the concentration ratio, regarded as a function of time, and see what economic interpretation can be given to these variations.

It is interesting to examine the table of values given in Section 3. The largest of these concentrations is found in Augsburg in 1529 when ρ had the abnormal value of 0.79. Has this figure any significance? If we refer to the history of this interesting city we find that it was one of the wealthiest in Europe during the years recorded in our table. This is attested by the fact that the church of St. Ulrich and St. Afra, one of the most imposing of the late Gothic cathedrals, was built there between the years 1474 and 1500. The city was dominated by a group of merchant princes, the most famous of which were the members of the houses of the Fuggers and the Welsers. Jacob Fugger, the founder of the main branch of the first family, died in 1469, but was succeeded by his sons who carried on and extended the business well into the sixteenth century. Jacob II, who died in 1525, was called "the Rich," and was the builder of the famous Fuggerii, a settlement of low-rent buildings near Augsburg. No less successful was the family of the Welsers, whose principal member, Bartholomäus (1488-1561), was head of a banking and commercial firm which lent large sums to Charles V. We thus see that the concentration ratio of 0.79 was associated with mercantile and trade interests of large proportion.

If we turn to the United States we find a considerable variation in the concentration ratio over the spectacular period of three decades since 1914. While particular values of the ratio are given in the table in Section 3, it will be of interest to examine the fluctuations in more detail. We thus have the following values:

Year	ρ	Year	ρ	Year	ρ	Year	ρ	Year	ρ	Year	ρ
1914	0.481	1920	0.379	1926	0.476	1932	0.397	1938	0.400	1944	0.321
1915	0.556	1921	0.357	1927	0.490	1933	0.417	1939	0.369	1945	0.318
1916	0.595	1922	0.413	1928	0.543	1934	0.427	1940	0.370	1946	0.318
1917	0.505	1923	0.407	1929	0.543	1935	0.436	1941	0.370	1947	0.325
1918	0.435	1924	0.427	1930	0.446	1936	0.442	1942	0.350	1948	0.333
1919	0.413	1925	0.481	1931	0.413	1937	0.420	1943	0.317		

Ratio of Concentration of Income

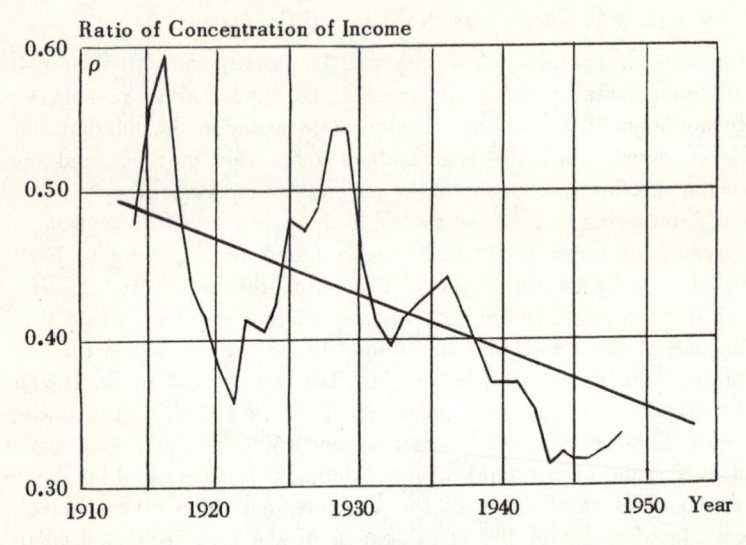

Figure 48.

These values of ρ are graphically represented in Figure 48 which includes a linear trend line to indicate the tendency toward socialism that has been a predominant consequence of recent governmental policies.

In order to apprehend in more detail the significance of the concentration ratio, let us consider Figure 49 which shows the Pareto curves for the observed incomes in each year from 1914 to 1948. The points at the lower end of each line represent the number of those who reported an income of $1,000,000 or over. The dotted line connecting these points shows how the number of high incomes has fluctuated with the business cycle observed over the same years. But since the recovery from the depression of 1932, a strange uniformity is observed in the number of high incomes. The points make a line which varies but little, when compared with the fluctuations observed in the years prior to 1932. A new element has entered the pattern of business and this, as one may readily understand, is government itself which since 1932 began a systematic program of deficit spending. The injection of new private capital into business, represented by the floating of long-term bond issues, showed a steady decline. For example, the long-term corporate debt which was 51.1 billion in 1930 was only 38.3 billion in 1945 and had only increased to 54.4 by 1949.

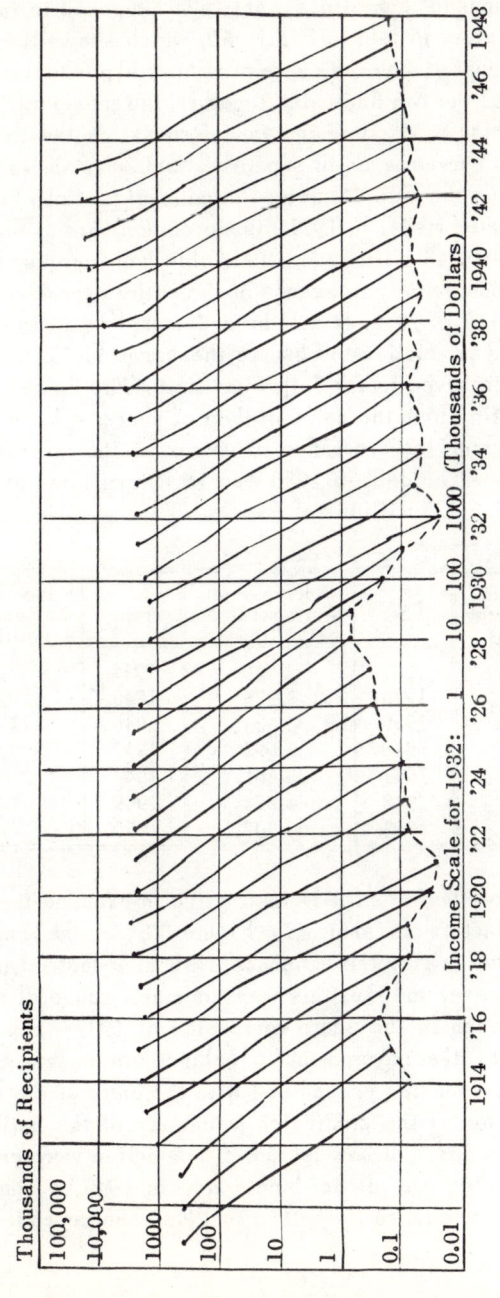

POLITICAL SCIENCE AND THE DISTRIBUTION OF INCOME 203

Figure 49. Comparison of Income Distributions in the United States, 1914-1948.

Cumulated frequencies, both scales logarithmic. The vertical lines are one cycle apart, as are the horizontal ones, the scale shifting one-half cycle to the right for each successive year. The point nearest the date in each case measures the number of incomes in excess of $1,000,000 in that year.

Under these unusual conditions what then happened to industrial production? The story is told in Figure 50, which shows the ratio of concentration compared with the curve of industrial production. In the years prior to 1932 the two fluctuated together, the concentration ratio preceding industrial production and thus forecasting the trend. But after 1932 the two curves began to separate. Each year showed a substantial increase in the national debt, a significant part of which went into production enterprises. In 1941, as we entered World War II, the debt stood at nearly 43 billions; by 1946 this had increased to 269 billions, a sum considerably in excess of the entire appraised wealth of the United States in 1932. It will be of interest in appraising the curve of industrial production to observe the magnitude of the deficit spending, which is given in the following table. The figures are obtained by subtracting from the national debt of year $x + 1$ the debt of year x, and assigning the difference to year x as the increase over that period of time. The debt in 1930 was 16,186 millions of dollars and in 1951 was 255,223 millions of dollars.

Year	Increase in National Debt (Millions)	Year	Increase in National Debt (Millions)	Year	Increase in National Debt (Millions)
1930	616	1937	739	1944	57,679
1931	2,686	1938	3,276	1945	10,740
1932	3,052	1939	2,528	1946	-11,136
1933	4,514	1940	5,992	1947	- 5,994
1934	1,648	1941	23,461	1948	478
1935	5,078	1942	64,274	1949	4,587
1936	2,646	1943	64,307	1950	- 2,134

With these figures before us it is instructive to examine the index of industrial production as shown in Figure 50. As the impact of deficit spending was felt by the economic system, industrial production began to increase, and that this was the major cause of the advance is clearly seen in the sharp regression of 1937 when an attempt was made by the government to balance its budget. An increased program of spending ensued and with the entry of the United States into World War II the production machinery of the nation not only ran at full capacity, but new factors of production were created. When excess spending was again decelerated in 1945, a sharp decline resulted, which reached its bottom in 1946. The dependence of

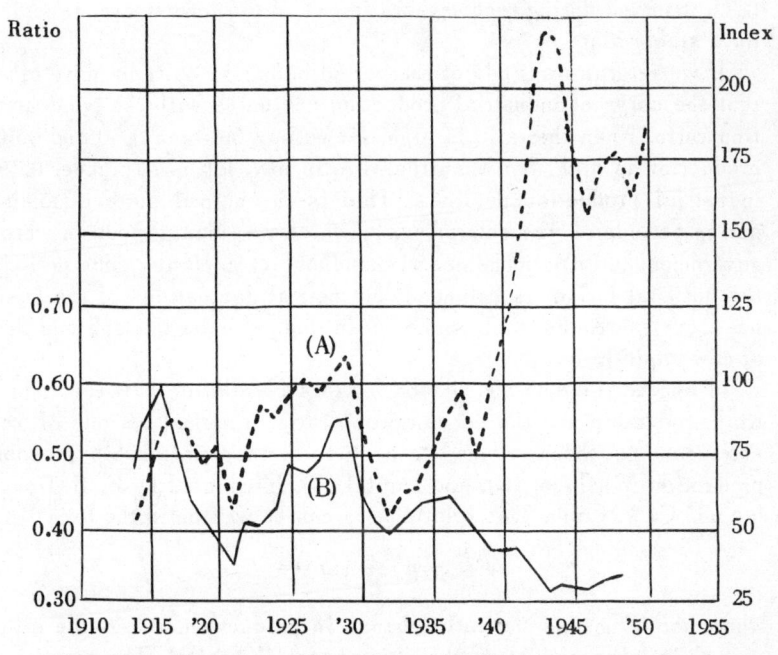

Figure 50. (A) Industrial Production. (B) Concentration Ratio.

industry upon the national budget is clearly shown in the fluctuations of the curve of production in recent years.

If one is not alarmed at a perpetually increasing government debt with its inevitable impact upon prices and taxes, then the picture of the economic system after 1932 is reassuring and presents a new principle of finance by means of which the flow of material goods can be maintained over long periods of time. The ultimate results of the program, however, are also clearly shown by the figures which have been presented. The concentration of wealth from which new capital is derived inevitably declines. The country progresses toward a form of state socialism in which government agencies with their control of new capital replace the entrepreneurs of the older system. The real questions involved here are two. Which capitalism in the long run produces the most efficient production? And can this production be maintained at a sufficiently high level so that the instability witnessed in all socialistic states up to the present time will not ultimately destroy the system? The current concentration ratio of about

0.32 observed during recent years is one of the lowest ever recorded for a stable state.

If we return to a study of the period before 1932, it is quite clear that the curve of industrial production fluctuates with the concentration ratio. When the ratio is high, let us say between 0.50 and 0.60, production is high, but when the ratio is low, let us say under 0.45, industrial production declines. This is the normal state of affairs during periods of *free enterprise*, by which we mean periods in which government activity in business is a minor factor. During such periods the national budget is balanced, but normal fluctuations of the business cycle are observed, since these depend upon the ebb and flow of new capital.

In another place,* the reason for this correlation between industrial production and the concentration ratio in normal periods of free enterprise has been reduced to a study of the relationship between production (P), labor (L), and capital (C), formulated by P. H. Douglas and C. W. Cobb. This relationship can be written in the form

$$\frac{\Delta P}{P} = p \frac{\Delta L}{L} + q \frac{\Delta C}{C}$$

where $\Delta P/P$ means the ratio change in production, $\Delta L/L$ the ratio change in labor, and $\Delta C/C$ the ratio change in capital. The quantities p and q are constants, the values of which were shown by Douglas and Cobb to be approximately equal to 0.75 and 0.25 respectively.

The rate of change of capital is assumed to be a function of the concentration ratio and, by arguments which cannot be developed here, may be written

$$\frac{\Delta C}{C} = \Delta(\rho)$$

where $\Delta(\rho)$ has the following values:

ρ	$\Delta(\rho)$	ρ	$\Delta(\rho)$
0.30	-0.54	0.55	0.23
0.35	-0.44	0.60	0.47
0.40	-0.31	0.65	0.81
0.45	-0.17	0.70	1.26
0.50	0.00	0.75	2.00

---

*See H. T. Davis: *The Analysis of Economic Time Series*, 1941, pp. 438-440.

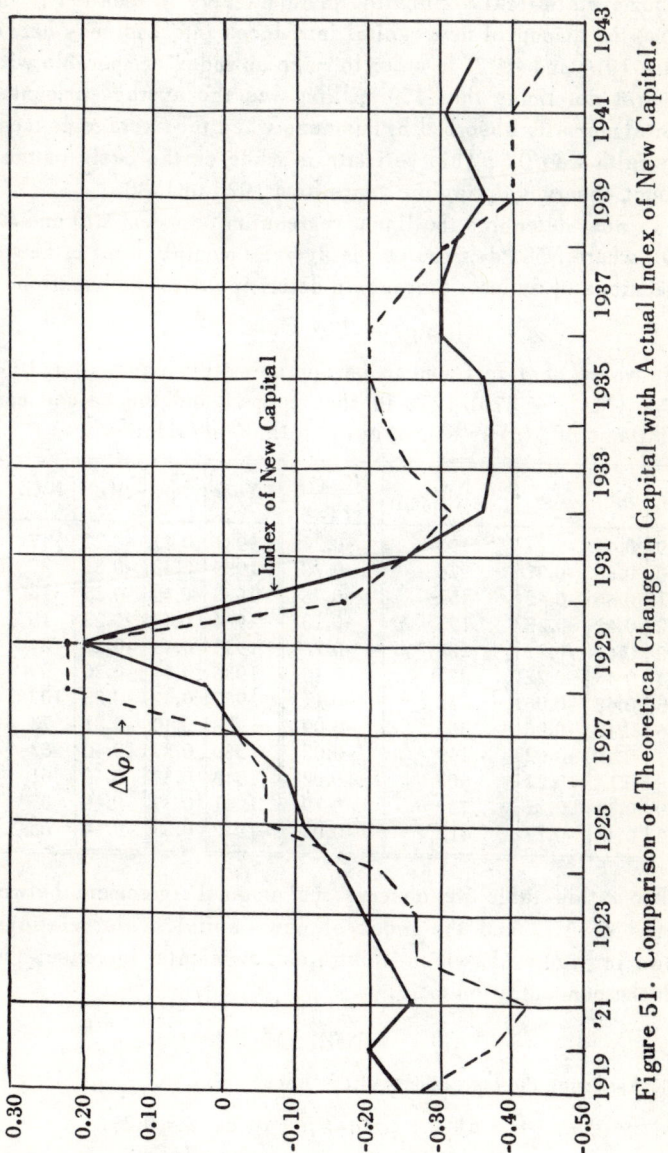

Figure 51. Comparison of Theoretical Change in Capital with Actual Index of New Capital.

Some statistical verification of this theory is afforded if one considers the amount of new capital introduced into business between the years 1919 and 1942. In order to make an index comparable with $\Delta(\rho)$ we first determine that 479 million was the average amount of new capital normally absorbed by business when the average concentration of wealth was 0.5. This estimate is made on the basis of the actual amount observed during the years from 1926 to 1930.

We next determine the linear regression between $\Delta(\rho)$ and (N.C. − 479), where N.C. designates the average monthly total of new capital in millions of dollars, that is, we determine A in the equation,

$$\Delta(\rho) = A \,(\text{N.C.} - 479).$$

This value of A is found to be approximately equal to 1/1253. The index (N.C. − 479)/1253 is then formed and the values compared with those of $\Delta(\rho)$ as shown in the following table:

Year	ρ	$\Delta(\rho)$	N.C. (New Capital)	$\dfrac{\text{NC}-479}{1253}$	Year	ρ	$\Delta(\rho)$	N.C.	$\dfrac{\text{NC}-479}{1253}$
1919	0.41	-0.27	192	-0.24	1931	0.41	-0.27	147	-0.27
1920	0.38	-0.37	226	-0.20	1932	0.40	-0.31	27	-0.36
1921	0.36	-0.42	152	-0.26	1933	0.42	-0.25	13	-0.37
1922	0.41	-0.27	195	-0.23	1934	0.43	-0.22	15	-0.37
1923	0.41	-0.27	225	-0.20	1935	0.44	-0.20	34	-0.36
1924	0.43	-0.22	277	-0.16	1936	0.44	-0.20	99	-0.30
1925	0.48	-0.06	342	-0.11	1937	0.42	-0.25	102	-0.30
1926	0.48	-0.06	363	-0.09	1938	0.40	-0.31	73	-0.32
1927	0.49	-0.02	449	-0.02	1939	0.37	-0.40	32	-0.36
1928	0.54	0.22	507	0.02	1940	0.37	-0.40	61	-0.33
1929	0.54	0.22	720	0.19	1941	0.37	-0.40	89	-0.31
1930	0.45	-0.17	412	-0.05	1942	0.35	-0.44	53	-0.34

From this table we observe the unusual agreement between the values of $\Delta(\rho)$ and the index of new capital. This relationship is shown in Figure 51, which illustrates how capital increases fluctuate with the concentration ratio.

PROBLEMS

1. Assuming the correctness of the law

$$\frac{\Delta P}{P} = p\frac{\Delta L}{L} + q\Delta(\rho), \quad p = 0.75, \quad q = 0.25,$$

compute what change in the labor ratio would be required to maintain normal production when $\rho = 0.40$; when $\rho = 0.35$.

2. How much above normal would production be if the labor ratio remained constant while $\rho = 0.70$?

6. *The Concentration Ratio and Political Disturbances.*

It is an interesting speculation to inquire into the possible political effects of an extensive deviation of the Pareto index from its assumed normal value of 1.5, or, perhaps, of the more descriptive ratio of concentration from its norm of 0.5. Thus, we observe in the critical years 1920 and 1921, when one of the most spectacular price declines in recent history occurred, that the concentration ratio was far below normal. Again, in the abnormal inflationary years 1928 and 1929, the concentration ratio was substantially above normal. The depression decade since the collapse of the great bull market in 1929 has witnessed a persistent decline in the concentration ratio. From the great sensitivity of the incomes of the upper Pareto classes to fluctuations in the business cycle, as described in the preceding section, it is not unreasonable to suppose that disturbances in the concentration ratio may be accompanied by economic and political disturbances. Whether the variation in these values is the cause or the effect of the observed events is a question for debate, although some indication of the causal relationships may be learned from the events in the decade between 1930 and 1940. Thus we may observe that the main effect of the legislation of that period was to lower the concentration ratio by transferring funds by taxation from the upper income classes to the lower. As this transfer took place, business failed to recover to the levels established around 1926, when the concentration ratio was approximately 0.5. Interest rates fell rapidly in this period, and there was a decline of approximately 15% in the capital structure of business despite a growing population and increasing demand.*

We shall tentatively assume, therefore, *that critical values of the Pareto index and of the concentration ratio exist for which we may expect major economic and political disturbances.*

In advancing this thesis we have distinguished authority in the theory of civil disturbance suggested to Aristotle by his observation of such events in the Greek states. Thus he says in his *Politics* (Book V, Chapter 1): "Everywhere inequality is a cause of revolution...," (Chapter 2) "The universal and chief cause of this revolu-

---
*This is based on the observation that long-term corporate debt fell from 51.1 billion dollars in 1930 to 43.7 billion dollars in 1940.

tionary feeling has already been mentioned; namely, the desire of equality, when men think they are equal to others who have more than themselves; or again, the desire of inequality and superiority, when conceiving themselves to be superior they think that they have not more but the same or less than their inferiors; pretensions which may or may not be just. Inferiors revolt in order that they may be equal, and equals that they may be superior. Such is the state of mind which creates revolutions." (Chapter 3) "Now, in oligarchies the masses make revolution under the idea that they are unjustly treated, because as I said before, they are equals, and have not an equal share, and in democracies the notables revolt, because they are not equals, and yet have only an equal share." (Chapter 4) "Revolutions also break out when opposite parties, namely the rich and the people, are equally balanced, and there is little or no middle class; for, if either party were manifestly superior, the other would not risk an attack upon them."

A very interesting exploration of the implications of Aristotle's theory has been given recently by Fred Kort in which the relationship between the earlier statement of the problem and the modern one has been carefully examined.* Thus he says: "Aristotle himself succeeded in obtaining verifying instances for his qualitatively conceived theory. The difficulty of dealing with qualitative relationships is to determine the pertinence of a particular situation to the general content of the hypothesis under investigation. For example, in order to appraise the adequacy of the American Civil War as a possible verifying instance of Aristotle's theory, it would be necessary to compare the degree of separation of political and economic power in that particular instance with the degree of separation envisaged by the theory. A comparison in qualitative terms would entail decisive handicaps. If, however, the degree of separation of political and economic power can be expressed in quantitative terms, the pertinence of the particular situation to the general content of the theory can be readily determined."

Unfortunately for the statistical verification of the thesis stated above, data are lacking from those national economies which have been disrupted by revolution and civil war. However, it is quite plausible to infer from historical sources that the French Revolution, the

---

*"The Quantification of Aristotle's Theory of Revolution," *The American Political Science Review*, Vol. 46, 1952, pp. 486-493.

POLITICAL SCIENCE AND THE DISTRIBUTION OF INCOME

Russian Revolution against the czars, and the more recent Spanish Revolution, the details of which we sketched in the first section, were aggravated, if not actually caused, by an undue concentration of wealth and income. Similarly, the socialistic trends of the Spanish Government after the overthrow of the monarchy must certainly have lowered greatly the ratio of concentration below its Pareto norm. The civil war may be considered, perhaps, as a direct consequence of this disruption. The relationship of the concentration ratio to the American Civil War will be discussed in the next section, but our conclusion that an anticipated disturbance in it was one of the primary causes of the struggle may be recorded here.

We shall advance, therefore, the tentative hypothesis that revolution is likely in any economy where the concentration ratio exceeds a certain critical value, $\rho_1 > 0.5$, and that a civil war is likely in any economy where the concentration ratio falls below a certain critical value, $\rho_2 < 0.5$. Since the mass of the people is affected adversely in the first instance, the revolution will be rapid and overwhelming. In the second instance, the upper economic classes, numerically small, but powerful in resources, are affected. Hence the civil war is slow to start and must be long in duration, since it must be waged to a considerable extent by mercenary means.

What these critical values are we have at present no way of estimating. In the United States the concentration ratio has varied from approximately 0.32 to approximately 0.60 without an undue amount of political unrest. One may observe, however, that the two major political reversals in the period covered by the data occurred at the two minimum points reached by the concentration ratio, namely in 1920, when the Republicans won the presidential election by a landslide after a long Democratic tenure, and in 1932, when the Democrats were swept into office by a similar decisive reversal of the opinion of the electorate.

Considerable unrest was observed in France prior to World War II, so that it becomes a matter of some interest to inquire into the income distribution of that republic. Unfortunately such data are not available, but figures on the French declaration of estates in the year 1935 throw some light on the matter. These figures are given in the accompanying table.

An examination of these data, using the last items, indicates that the Pareto index, a, is about 1.85, which corresponds to a concentra-

Range of Values in Francs	Number	Accumulated Frequency
1 to 500	26,382	370,150
501 to 2,000	46,103	343,768
2,001 to 10,000	121,581	297,665
10,001 to 50,000	127,694	176,084
50,001 to 100,000	25,529	48,390
100,001 to 250,000	14,789	22,861
250,001 to 500,000	4,637	8,072
500,001 to 1,000,000	2,004	3,435
1 to 2 millions	891	1,431
2 to 5 millions	418	540
5 to 10 millions	83	122
10 to 50 millions	37	39
Over 50 millions	2	2

tion ratio of 0.37. The obvious socialistic tendency of the French economy is thus apparent and there are reasons to believe that it progressed in this direction during the years between 1935 and the outbreak of World War II. Thus we find that the Chamber of Deputies had 100 socialists in 1928, 131 in 1932, and 149 in 1936. In these years the left wing representatives in the Chamber were respectively 56, 62, and 64 per cent of the total membership. It is now a matter of history that the industrial activity of France prior to the war was at a low ebb. The war machine of the Germans had little difficulty in piercing the Maginot line and the sudden collapse of the French government which followed indicated the essential weakness of the French economy. Was this forecasted by the low value of the concentration ratio, which appears to accompany a sluggishness in the industrial system?

7. *The American Civil War.*

Pursuing the thesis that civil wars are generally associated in some manner with the distribution of income, we shall find it instructive to examine the American Civil War from this point of view. Although the final issue which precipitated the struggle was the question of the right of the Southern States to secede from the Union, the fundamental dispute was over the problem of slavery.

In the years prior to the outbreak of the war there had been evolving throughout the world a movement against slavery, although the institution was as old as history itself. In the early eighteenth century many English writers such as Alexander Pope (1688-1744),

William Cowper (1731-1800), Laurence Sterne (1713-1868), John Wesley (1703-1791), Samuel Johnson (1709-1784) and numerous others had inveighed against the slave trade. But that the problem had an economic as well as a moral aspect was pointed out by Adam Smith (1723-1790) in his *Wealth of Nations*, in which he compared the return from slave labor with that from free labor to the disadvantage of the former.

The first abolition of slave trade was made by Denmark, which issued a royal order in 1792 that the traffic should cease in Danish possessions by 1802. The British Parliament in 1833 outlawed slavery in the Empire as of August 1, 1834 and by this act about 700,000 slaves were freed. To compensate the planters a sum of twenty million pounds was voted, which freed each slave at a cost just under 30 pounds per head. This action by Great Britain was followed by other European countries, notably by France in 1848, by Portugal in 1858, and by the Dutch Empire in 1863.

In the United States the movement toward abolition was marked by increasing tension between the Northern States, which had a small negro population with few slaves, and the Southern States, which required large numbers on their plantations. Thus New York had abolished slavery in 1827 and by 1850 there were 16 free states with a total population of 13,434,922 and a negro population of 196,116, or less than 1.5% of the total. In the same year there were 15 slave states with a total population of 9,612,979 of which 3,200,364, or 33.3% were slaves and 228,138, or 2.4%, were free negroes. Beginning with the acquisition of Louisiana in 1803, the debate progressed with ever growing rancor through the Missouri Compromise (1820), the annexation of Texas (1845), the Fugitive Slave Law (1850), the Kansas-Nebraska bill (1854), the Dred Scott decision (1857), and the hanging of John Brown in 1859.

In order that we may have some appreciation of the economic issue involved in the controversy between the states we shall examine a few of the significant data. The value of the slaves themselves was certainly one of the important matters. Although there was much philosophical argument at the time over the question of whether slaves were actually property, the existence of active markets in the South is sufficient to dispose of this proposition. Figure 52 shows the average price of prime field hands in the four markets of Virginia, Charleston, Georgia, and New Orleans from 1795 to the outbreak of the Civil War. The upward trend of prices, approximately $11.18 per

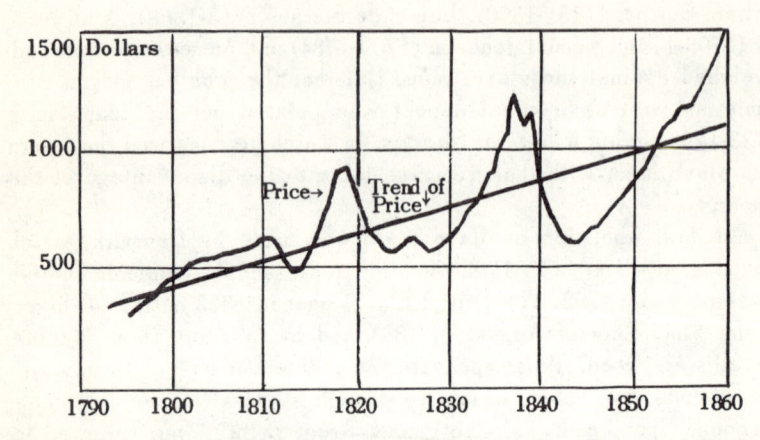

Figure 52. Average Price of American Slaves in Four Principal Markets.

year, when compared with the general index of prices that prevailed in this period* (see Figure 6, Chapter 1), is clear evidence of the growing demand in the South for slave labor. This became increasingly acute as one approached the period of the War, as is evident from the fact that the average price more than doubled between 1845 and 1860.

In a book entitled *The Impending Crisis of the South,* published in 1857 by H. R. Helper (1829-1909), there is set forth an abundance of statistical data concerning the economic strength of the Northern and the Southern States. This is an unusual treatise in many respects, but principally because it adopts the statistical approach to the problem, which was almost unknown in that period.

Helper estimated that the total wealth of the Northern States in 1850 was of the order of $4,102,172,000 and that of the Southern States of the order of $2,936,091,000. But a great difference is found in the nature of this wealth since the South owned 3,200,365 slaves, which Helper appraised at approximately $1,600,000,000. This seems like a reasonable enough figure for it implies an average price of $500 per slave, which compares favorably with the price of a male field hand somewhat in excess of $800 in 1850.

It is thus clear that more than half the wealth of the South (approximately 54%) was in slave property and this was threatened by

---

*These figures are taken from U. B. Phillips: *American Negro Slavery,* New York, 1918, xi + 529 p. In particular, Chap. 19.

POLITICAL SCIENCE AND THE DISTRIBUTION OF INCOME

the activities of the Northern abolitionists. One can readily understand the intense bitterness of the South as they saw so large a portion of their property in jeopardy of destruction.

It is instructive next to turn to the question of the distribution of wealth that then prevailed in the South. Since the percentage return on wealth is observed to fluctuate very little from one period to another, we may assume that the distribution of wealth and the distribution of income are highly correlated curves. To know one is to know the other. Also it is fair to assume that a large part of the income of the South depended directly upon the slaves since the maintenance and operation of plantations relied entirely upon slave labor. Hence to know the distribution of the slaves would be approximately to know the distribution of wealth and income as well.

Helper, in his useful book, has provided us with the distribution of the ownership of slaves. These data are given in the following table:

Number of Slaves Held	Number of Slave Holders	Number of Slaves Held (x)	Number Who Held x or Over (y)
1 slave	68,820	1	347,525
2 and under 5	105,683	2	278,705
5 and under 10	80,765	5	173,022
10 and under 20	54,595	10	92,257
20 and under 50	29,733	20	37,662
50 and under 100	6,196	50	7,929
100 and under 200	1,479	100	1,733
200 and under 300	187	200	254
300 and under 500	56	300	67
500 and under 1000	9	500	11
1000 and over	2	1000	2
Total	347,525		

The accumulated frequency distribution given by the last two columns of the table is graphically represented in Figure 53. That the distribution is not normal in the sense of Pareto is readily seen from the dotted line in the figure, which is computed from the function: $y = 347,525\ G(z)$, where $G(z)$ is the function defined in Section 4. We have assumed the relationship: $z = x - 1$, since $z = 0$, when $x = 1$ slave, and have computed b by means of formula (1), Section 4, where $I = 3,200,364$, and $N = 347,525$. We thus obtain the value $b = 7.09$.

It is instructive to determine next the concentration of wealth indicated by the curve. For this purpose we determine the slope from

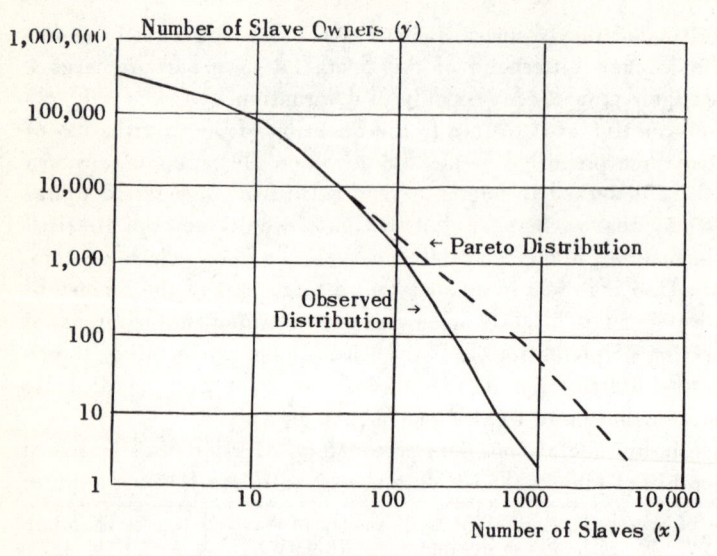

Figure 53.
Distribution of Slave Ownership in the South before the Civil War.

the last four points, and thus obtain $a = 3.00$. This leads to a concentration of 0.20, which is far below any of those observed in the stable economies studied by Pareto.

Is there any real significance to be attached to this unusual fact, that in an economy about to be torn by Civil War the fundamental distribution of wealth shows so low a concentration? It is obvious that no answer can be given to this question. But the fact itself is noticeable and one can argue that if a higher concentration had prevailed it is possible that the dispute might have been settled on terms other than war. Thus, let us suppose that the Pareto pattern had prevailed. A simple computation shows that instead of only two people having slave holdings in excess of 1,000, three persons would have had slave holdings in excess of 7,100. Appraising these holdings at $500 per head, we see that in the one case two people had wealth of the order of $500,000, while in the second three people had wealth in excess of $3,550,000. Now it is possible that the existence of such wealthy citizens in the state might have exerted a stabilizing influence in the debate. Their influence would certainly have been great in Congress and it is possible that a solution similar to that of England, namely, the purchase of the slaves by the government itself, might have been achieved.

If we look at the economic facts of the Civil War, we see that the peaceful solution of the problem would have been a distinct economic gain. For the estimated cost of the war was of the order of 10 billion dollars, and the cost in lives was around 600,000. In 1863, at the time when Lincoln issued his Emancipation Proclamation, the slave population had increased to 3,950,000. If these had been freed at the rate of $500 per head the total cost would have been less than two billion dollars, or a net gain of eight billion dollars in direct saving over the cost of the war itself.

But these are speculations about which no answer can be given. The only significant fact that emerges from the discussion is the existence of a concentration ratio of 0.20 in a state about to be torn by the ravages of civil war. About this there can be no debate, however one wishes to interpret its significance.

PROBLEMS

1. Represent graphically the French declaration of estates. Use logarithmic values for both the range of values and the accumulated frequencies. Hence verify the value of a from the slope of the tail of the distribution.

2. Compute what the distribution of slaves would have been if the distribution had been a normal Paretian one. Namely, compute the values of the function $N\,G(z)$, where $N = 347{,}525$, $z = x - 1$, $b = 7.09$.

8. *Conclusion.*

In the preceding pages of this chapter we have considered the problem of socialism from the point of view of the distribution of income. If we are to define in any measurable way the political theories which have developed around the general term of socialism one promising way seems to be in terms of the distribution of income, which is involved in all of these theories.

Such studies as we have made begin necessarily with the law of Pareto, which describes in simple form the pattern which appears to have prevailed in all stable economies from the time of the Roman Republic to the present day. Few social-economic laws seem to have such universal validity.

In order to put the Pareto law into a more tractable form for exhibiting the variations which occur in the general pattern of income distribution, the coefficient of concentration has been defined. This concentration is observed to vary between limits of 0.32 to 0.79. We have also given evidence to show that general economic and political well-being appears to prevail when the coefficient is of the order of 0.50 or higher. Industrial disturbance, with concomitant political troubles, seems to increase as the coefficient falls below 0.50.

One of the causes of industrial trouble as interpreted by the coefficient of concentration is found in the decline of new capital for business when the coefficient is reduced. In the American economy during the past few years this decline in new capital has been counteracted by deficit spending by the government itself, an experiment which maintains industrial production under conditions of low income concentration. But difficulties are apparent in this method, since it has led to the creation of a huge public debt and to price inflation. The move toward socialism under the experiment of governmental spending is indicated by the fact that the concentration ratio has declined to 0.32, one of the lowest observed in any large stable economic system.

Another significance of the coefficient of concentration has been indicated by its possible connection with the large political disturbances which finally terminate in revolutions and civil war. The danger of too high a concentration of wealth is seen in the revolutions which have destroyed certain governments in the past and the danger of too low a concentration is found in the civil wars which have also been observed. The only measured coefficient in a disruptive period of this kind was shown to have had the value of 0.20, which described the type of distribution of wealth and income that prevailed in the Southern States at the time of the Civil War. This theory, however, rests upon very tenuous statistical evidence and must be regarded at this time as nothing more than an engaging hypothesis.

CHAPTER 9
POLITICAL SCIENCE AND ECONOMICS
1. *The Mechanistic Theory of History*

SINCE POLITICAL science in one of its most important aspects studies the causes which underlie the rise and fall of governments, it will be of more than casual interest to us to examine certain theories of history. More precisely stated, these theories attempt to account for great historical movements in terms of economic, climatic, and other materialistic factors. Hence they become amenable to the methods of statistics.

To many the mechanistic theory of human behavior appears as a modern proposition, enunciated in the nineteenth century approximately contemporaneously by Karl Marx (1818-1883) and his followers on the one hand and by Henry Thomas Buckle (1821-1862) on the other. This is not the case for the theory has roots of great antiquity.

Thus we find that the ancient historian Polybius (c. 205-c. 125 B. C.) saw as clearly as any of our modern contemporaries that history is not a mere record of particular events, but is a kind of unfolding pattern into which a great complex of interconnected factors are woven. Thus in his *History*, which deals principally with the affairs of the Achaean League and the Punic Wars, and which was written some time between 146 B. C. and 122 B. C., Polybius says: "For we can get some idea of a whole from a part, but never knowledge or an exact opinion. Special histories, therefore, contribute very little to the knowledge of the whole and conviction of its truth. It is only indeed by study of the interconnection of all the particulars, their resemblances and differences, that we are enabled at least to make a general survey, and thus derive both benefit and pleasure from history."

It was not until the sixteenth century, however, that we again find anything comparable to the reflections of Polybius. Under the impact of the new forces unleashed in European thought by the Renaissance, a number of men turned to the problem of the philosophy of history. For the most part the writings of these men are vague and unsatisfactory gropings after a thread upon which the historical events might be hung.

Essentially different from that of most of his contemporaries was the writing of Jean Bodin (1530-1596), who published in 1566 a work entitled: *Methodus ad facilem historiarum cognitionem* (A method for the easy understanding of history), parts of which were amplified in his chief work, the *Six livres de la République*, published in Paris in 1576.

Bodin's contribution to the philosophy of history consisted in directing attention to the possibility of interpreting human action from a study of the impact of natural forces upon society. Although Bodin saw only the climatic factor as the dominating external influence, whence his theory is often called the *theory of climate*, he must be regarded as the first writer who apprehended the possibility of interpreting human history from a study of material factors.

The hope of establishing a deterministic basis for history, that is to say, of shifting the interpretation of events from conjecture to scientific precision, is clearly expressed by Bodin. The influence of this hope is to be found in the writings of Montesquieu (1689-1755), who nearly two centuries later in his treatise: *L'esprit des lois* (The spirit of the law) published in Geneva in 1748 devoted six books out of the original thirty-one to manners and customs and their dependence on climatic conditions. Although as Buckle pointed out many years later, "in this vast enterprise he almost entirely failed, Montesquieu performed a service to history by turning attention to the significance of external facts as the foundation for the interpretation of the vagaries of mankind."

Contemporary with Montesquieu we find the writings of G. B. Vico (1688-1774), who set forth an almost completely deterministic theory of history in his *Principii d'une scienza nuova* (Principles of a new science). This work evolved through two editions, one published in 1725 and the other five years later. Vico held to the belief that the laws of history are immutable and that a knowledge of them can be found only in human events and the human mind. But the immutability is placed in a profound metaphysics, since God is the ruler of the world and the unfolding patterns of history are an evolution from a period of primitive "poetical wisdom" to a period of civilized "occult wisdom." Vico sees in this divine development a periodic movement or law of cycles, which is "invariably followed by all nations."

Beginning with an aristocratic society, a nation evolves through the revolt of the populace into a democracy. But this in its turn gives way to empire, which finally breaks up under corrupt excesses and the nation disappears into barbarism. From this it again arises and the cycle is thus endlessly repeated.

The natural successor of Vico was G. W. F. Hegel (1770-1831), whose *Lectures on the Philosophy of History*, collected and published in 1837 by Edward Gans, have much in common with the Italian philosopher. Hegel divided the methods of treating history into three categories: I. Original History; II. Reflective History; III. Philosophical History. The first category consists of descriptions made by witnesses of the events themselves, such as the writings of Herodotus or Thucydides, which relate contemporaneous events over short periods of time. The second category, illustrated by the works of Livy and Diodorus, describes the history of a people, of a country, or of the world, not what has been seen by the author himself, but from the evidence of documents. The story thus told admits both abridgments and abstraction, since the spirit of the author and his reflections are incorporated in the history. A second part of this category (pragmatic history) admits more profound reflections and the introduction of generalizations, which seek to interpret the meaning of the events. Hegel cites Montesquieu as an example. A third part is critical history, or the history of history, which seeks to appraise the truth and the veracity of accounts.

But in spite of the great influence which both Vico and Hegel exerted upon the philosophy of history, their ideas were derived from an unrealistic metaphysics. A sort of rigid determinism is implied in their concepts of a plan for the world, which is revealed in the unfolding pattern of history, but no method is suggested by which the plan can be understood. Their reflections are philosophical rather than scientific.

We turn, therefore, from the metaphysics of history to a more realistic period in which the impact of the growing awareness of the scientific method began to make itself felt in theories about human society. This is found in the work of Karl Marx, Friedrich Engels, Henry Thomas Buckle, and their successors.

Although Karl Marx (1818-1883) and his collaborator Friedrich Engels (1820-1895) are generally credited with the modern enunciation of the materialistic theory of history, one will search in vain through their writings for any really satisfactory statement of the theory. Certainly no attempt was made by either of them to prove the proposition through the use of statistical data. *Das Kapital,* the first volume of which appeared in 1867 and the last three posthumously under the editorship of Engels, is the culmination of the ideas of Marx. But this work contains rather by inference than by scientific formulation the economic theory of history.

It was most unfortunate for the development of their general thesis, excellent in itself, that Marx and Engels associated their scientific and objective purpose with an inflammatory political idea. The war of the classes, the poor against the rich, the laborer against the capitalist, is envisaged as the connecting thread between the dramatic events of history. The war of the classes is founded upon the difficulties of production and the distribution of that which has been produced.

But this materialistic concept of the origin of historical conflict was fused with a revolutionary manifesto which made politically dynamic a theory that should have been tested scientifically first against the facts. It was this assumption of truth in what had merely been asserted, and the immediate attempt to put the theory into action, that removed the entire subject from the realm of scientific inquiry. As the revolutionary character of the theory became apparent, all interest seemed to vanish in the proposition of formulating it in terms palatable to science and of subjecting the postulates to careful statistical test.

If one turns from Marx and Engels to the work of Henry Thomas Buckle (1821-1862) on the *History of Civilization in England*, which appeared in 1857, he will find a much more careful statement of the materialistic influence upon historical events. The author begins his discussion with remarks which are highly suggestive of those which we have quoted earlier from Polybius. Thus he says: "... The unfortunate peculiarity of the history of man is, that although its separate parts have been examined with considerable ability, hardly any one has attempted to combine them into a whole, and ascertain the way in which they are connected with each other. In all the other great fields of inquiry the necessity of generalization is universally admitted, and noble efforts are being made to rise from particular facts in order to discover the laws by which these facts are governed. So far, however, is this from being the universal course of historians, that among them a strange idea prevails that their business is merely to relate events, which they may occasionally enliven by such moral and political reflections as seem likely to be useful."

Buckle examined and accepted the proposition that the cause of human action is to be found in the aspects of nature. In this he did not return to the climatic theory of Bodin and Montesquieu, but invoked rather the economic argument that wealth is derived from natural resources and productive scientific progress is derived from the capital reserves of wealth. Pursuing this thesis Buckle envisages the historical struggle as one of man against nature. Where nature becomes dominant, man yields to fear and superstition; but where man controls nature, then science and the human mind resume their importance.

Although Buckle's work abounds in special reference and copious illustrations taken from historical records, it necessarily lacks an adequate statistical basis, since the science of statistics had not advanced sufficiently far in his time to make this possible, nor were requisite data available for this purpose. That Buckle was aware of the importance of statistics in the problem is seen from his comment: "It becomes, therefore, in the highest degree important to ascertain whether or not there exists a regularity in the entire moral conduct of a given society; and this is precisely one of those questions for the decision of which statistics supply us with materials of immense value."

After Marx and Buckle we find a number of adherents to the mechanistic theory of history. Leo Tolstoy (1828-1910) in his *War and Peace*, which appeared between 1864 and 1869, proposed that history should be interpreted as a continuous unfolding of "the homogeneous tendencies of men." Thus he says: "For, studying the laws of history, we must absolutely change the objects of our observation, leave kings, ministers, and generals out of the account, and select for study the homogeneous, infinitesimal elements that regulate the masses. No one can say how far it is given to man to attain by this path an understanding of the laws of history."

Among other contributors to the subject should be mentioned A. A. Cournot (1801-1877), J. E. Thorold Rogers (1823-1890), and E. R. A. Seligman (1861-1939). Cournot's analysis is found in two works on the general subject of the *Connection of Fundamental Ideas in Science and History*, which appeared in 1861 and 1872 respectively. He considered the probability aspects of the subject. Roger's ideas are given in his work entitled: *The Economic Interpretation of History*, which appeared posthumously in 1909, nearly twenty years after the author's death. Rogers cited certain examples to show the impact of economic trends upon historical events, but he lacked adequate data to support his general thesis. Seligman's contribution was principally a defense of the economic theory of history and is contained in a series of articles which appeared near the beginning of the present century.

2. *The Growth of Population.*

In order that we may have a sufficiently broad view of the political events of the past we shall begin with a study of the trends of population. For we shall find that there are apparently cycles of civilization, if the term cycles can be applied to the irregular patterns with which history provides us. Even a casual inspection of the records of history shows that human culture and political institutions are not static phenomena. There are periods when the tide of progress appears to be running strongly, when achievements in philosophy, art, literature, and science are in the ascendant. These rare periods are subsequently known as Golden Ages, and one turns to them for inspiration and instruction in less fortunate times. Thus one finds the Golden Ages of Pericles, of Augustus, of Queen Elizabeth, the *siglo de oro* of Philip II, and a few others, for they are rare events in history. And there are other periods when the course of human effort seems to fail, when the tide of progress ebbs. Then it is that art and literature disappear; philosophy yields to mysticism, and science vanishes in the fog of superstition. To these dreary periods we give the name of Dark Ages.

W. M. Flinders Petrie (1853-1942), famous for his studies of ancient Egypt, in a suggestive volume entitled: *The Revolutions of Civilisation*, which appeared in 1922, advanced the theory of cycles in human institutions and defined eight of them. Only six may be regarded as belonging to historic times, and only the last two, the ancient Graeco-Roman and our own modern period, provide us with sufficient data to test hypotheses.

But a statistical measure of the rise and fall of civilizations is wholly lacking in Petrie's theory. Such a measure, applicable alike to ancient and modern cultures, would be difficult to define and probably impossible to reduce to satisfactory statistical series were an adequate definition achieved. For is civilization to be measured in terms of great literary achievement? or in terms of a standard of living? or by the environment which it provides for the growth of populations? We find high literary attainments in slave economies and low artistic development in periods of great material prosperity.

Recognizing thus the inadequacy of any index that may be devised, we can scan the historical civilizations, however, by observing how populations flourished or declined over long periods of time. These population estimates will serve at least the purpose of indicating how the underlying culture tended to ameliorate the struggle for existence, or how it aided the forces of dissolution which are ever present even in the best of human societies.

The estimated growth of population in Europe is given in Figure 54 from the year 400 B. C. down to the present time. This curve has been constructed from several sources, the most important of which are the extensive researches of K. J. Beloch (1854-1929), who surveyed the statistical evidence both for the ancient world and for the Middle Ages. We cannot attempt here to appraise this evidence, and the errors in the population estimates are admittedly large. Extrapolations to the European total have been made too often from knowledge about the growth of population in single countries, such as Rome in ancient times and England and France during the Mediaeval period.

Crude though much of the evidence may be for the population curve as it is here presented, there can be little doubt that it represents at least schematically the general pattern of the fluctuating fortunes of human society for more than twenty-two centuries. The data from which part of the curve is drawn are given in the following table. The rest is constructed from the estimated devastation of populations during known periods of great plague.

Population Growth in Europe in Millions

Countries	400 B.C.	1 A.D.	200	700	1000	1328	1400	1600	1900	1930	1940
European Russia	1	1	1	1	2	3	2.5	10	113	167	170
Scandinavia	2	2	3	1	1	2	1.5	2	10	13	14
Germany & Netherlands	3	3	7	3	9	9	7	12	61	74	88
British Isles	1	1	2	1	2	4	3	6.5	41	49	49
Spain & Portugal	2	6	12	4	5	6	4	10	24	30	33
Danube Basin	1	3	5	3	4	6	4	9	46	50	52
France, Belgium, and Switzerland	3	6.5	14	6	8	14	10	17	53	54	55
Italy	4	6	7	4	6	11	8	13	33	42	45
Southern Europe	1	3.5	6	1	0.5	1	1	3.5	17	20	22
Greece	4	5	6	3	3	3	3	4	4	6	7
Total Europe	22	37	63	27	40.5	59	44	87	402	505	535

226   POLITICAL STATISTICS

European Population (Unit = 1,000,000)

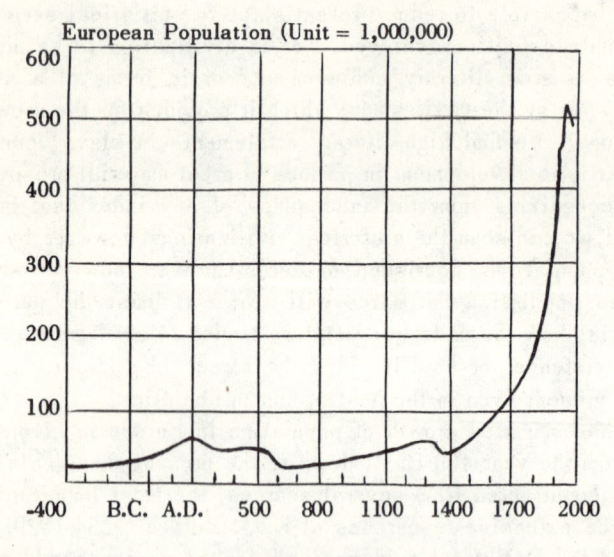

Figure 54.

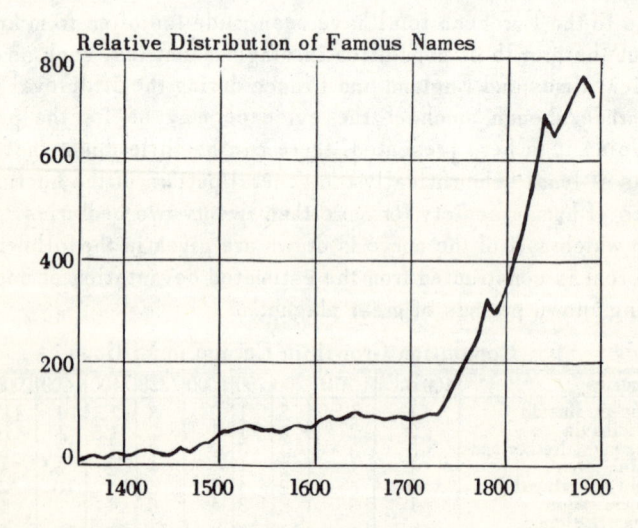

Relative Distribution of Famous Names

Figure 55.

If any one should doubt too seriously the general picture presented by the graph of the vicissitudes of population growth in Europe, he has a simple test in his own library. Let such a skeptic chart century by century the number of historical characters listed in the back of his dictionary. Let him then assume that the number of great names which emerge from history is roughly proportional to the number in the population which produces them. And lo! he will find that he has produced in miniature an approximation to the curve of population that has been given. Such a representation has been made in Figure 55. It is interesting in this connection to observe that statisticians are often forced to the necessity of constructing one set of data, which is inaccessible, from another set that can be obtained. The only requirement is that the two be highly correlated as in the present case. Thus, industrial production can be estimated from the production of pig iron, the number of automobiles from the amount of rubber used in tires, etc. We are thus able to confirm in a general way our population estimates from the number of great names.

Because of the great span of time covered by the data in Figure 54 and the lack of detail, only general trends can be observed. However, there are several special points to be observed. Thus we see that the high point of the population curve in classical times came near 200 A. D. The Roman Empire reached its fullest flower in the period of the Antonines (130-180) and it is reasonable to believe that the curve of population attained a maximum at that time.

Thereafter in the span of two centuries came the decline and fall of the Empire, induced by causes which we do not see too clearly. But there is no doubt that economic factors and wide-spread plagues were among the most important of these. The Roman Empire of the West disappeared in the confusion of one of the most savage monetary inflations ever suffered by any state. Coincident with this unhappy event we find the evidence of devastating plague. Thus in the reign of Gallienus (260-268 A.D.) more than half of the entire population of Alexandria was carried off, and this was only one city within which raged this violent pestilence that afflicted the Roman empire from 250 to 265 A. D.

Another and sharper dip is observed in the curve in the sixth century. The great plague which swept the Roman empire during the reign of Justinian (527-565) began at Pelusium, a city in the marshes of the most easterly mouth of the Nile, in 542 and spread over Europe.

It soon appeared in Constantinople, where it destroyed as many as 10,000 people in a single day. This plague continued with periods of great intensity for more than half a century, specially noteworthy epidemics being reported in Gaul in 546, in Italy in 565, in Liguria in 571, and in Rome in 590. The total population of Europe was unquestionably reduced in a significant ratio by this wide-spread calamity.

The next great cycle of the plague is found in the fourteenth century where it is generally referred to as the Black Death. Its origin was probably in the orient, but it reached Europe in 1347 by way of Sicily. The disease spread rapidly throughout Europe and did not abate its fury until after 1368. In England the plague was especially virulent during the reign of Edward III (ruled 1327-1377). It has been estimated that one-fourth of the population of Europe perished during this period. This disaster is reflected in Figure 54.

The last European pandemic began in 1663 and lasted for five years. It was especially severe in London which it reached in 1664. Following this violent event the plague mysteriously abated and has never returned to Europe in pandemic form.

That war, even in its most savage aspect, is second by a wide margin to the plague as a destroyer, is evident from Figure 54. Thus the effect of World War I is shown as a very minor dip in the curve between 1914 and 1918; it must be remembered also that considerable casualty in the last year of the war was occasioned by a pandemic attack of influenza. World War II is estimated to have been the direct cause of the death of something of the order of 35 million people in Europe. But in a population totalling approximately 535 million, this great destruction of human life was only 6.5% of the total, a far cry from the 25% of the Black Death. Only a small recession in the curve is observed as the result of this vast and sanguinary struggle.

From the standpoint of political science the remarkable increase in European population is a matter of first importance. The Renaissance was ushered in by a sudden and unexplained increase of population. By 1700 the rate of growth had become a noteworthy matter, and in the subsequent years developed into a phenomenon such as the world had never seen before. From a population estimated at around 87 millions in 1600 the nations of Europe had increased to the astounding total of 535 millions in 1940, a six-fold growth in the space of 340 years. No history can portray more vividly the causes of the incessant tumults of Europe than this simple fact. For the people of each nation press with ever increasing force against the boundaries of their neighbors and seek to escape the fate described by the Malthian theory that populations will ultimately outgrow their food supply. No league of nations and no court of international law can alter in the slightest degree the brutal facts presented by this picture of population growth.

PROBLEMS

1. Compute the average yearly rate of change of population between 1600 and 1900, namely, estimate on an annual basis the ratio $\Delta P/P$. Compare this with the rate of change between 1900 and 1930; between 1930 and 1940. What conclusions can be drawn from these values?

2. The following table gives estimates of the production of wheat in the world in terms of millions of bushels. (Figures for 1935 and 1939 exclude Russia and China.)

Year	Bushels of Wheat	Year	Bushels of Wheat
1925	4,102	1940	6,050
1930	4,867	1941	5,700
1935	3,582	1942	5,800
1939	6,216		

What political inferences can be made from these data in their relationship to the observed curve of population growth in Europe?

3. In spite of very grave difficulties connected with such an enumeration W. F. Willcox in his *Studies in American Demography* (1940) gives the following estimates of Chinese population since 1650 in terms of millions of people:

Year	Population	Year	Population
1650	113	1850	350
1750	199	1940	325
1800	264		

Compare this growth with that of European population. What conclusions can be drawn from these estimates?

4. From any handy collection of great names select 100 names at random. Using the date of birth plus 30 years to indicate the century in which the person flourished, find the numbers who belonged to the 18th and 19th centuries. Hence determine the respective probabilities of a great name chosen at random belonging to either of these two centuries. Are these probabilities

consistent with the proposition that the number of famous men produced in any century is proportional to the population of that century?

5. With respect to the great Alexandrian plague in the reign of Gallienus, Eusebius (c. 260 - c. 340) in his *Ecclesiastical History*, vii, 21, says that the number of people who survived between the ages of 14 and 80 years of age was about equal to those between the ages of 40 and 70 years in normal times. This statement has been interpreted to show that more than half the people died in this great plague. Actuarial figures for the ancient world are not available, but we can get some information from the following table of the Bureau of the Census pertaining to the year 1940 which shows the percentage distribution of the white population in the United States with respect to age groups:

Age Group	Per Cent of Population	Age Group	Per Cent of Population	Age Group	Per Cent of Population
Under 5	7.8	30 to 34	7.8	60 to 64	3.7
5 to 9	7.9	35 to 39	7.2	65 to 69	3.0
10 to 14	8.8	40 to 44	6.7	70 to 74	2.0
15 to 19	9.3	45 to 49	6.4	75 and over	2.0
20 to 24	8.7	50 to 54	5.7	Total	100.0
25 to 29	8.4	55 to 59	4.6		

Show that the statement of Eusebius, if applied to an American city, would have indicated a mortality considerably higher than 50 per cent. What added information would be necessary to get an exact picture of the Alexandrian plague? Has this anything to do with the average life expectation at different ages, which has changed from slightly over 30 (at age 5) in Roman Egypt to over 60 in the United States?

6. Petrie has advanced a theory of cycles of civilization which assumes that the emergence from a Dark Age follows a definite pattern. First comes a period of sculpture, then a period of painting, succeeded by eras of literature, mechanics, science, and wealth in that order. For the Graeco-Roman and the Modern civilizations he gives the following time table:

Civilization Beginning 450 B.C.				Civilization Beginning 1240 A.D.			
Years after the zero date when the phases begin				Years after the zero date when the phases begin			
Sculpture	0	Mechanics	450	Sculpture	0	Mechanics	550
Painting	100	Science	600	Painting	160	Science	650+
Literature	200	Wealth	650	Literature	360	Wealth	650+

From your general knowledge of history discuss the plausibility of this theory. Would you say that the theory can be proved statistically?

3. *The Relationship of Prices to Political Events.*

Throughout history governments, because of their control of the issuing of money, have had also some concern about prices and their movements. Hence, any adequate interpretation of great political events would be severely hampered unless some knowledge were available about the behavior of prices and their relationship to the wages of labor during the periods concerned.

But it is a matter of great difficulty to reconstruct the levels of prices which have prevailed in the past. In the first place we must determine the nominal weights of metal between various monetary units such as the drachma and the denarius in classical times, the florin, the peso, the shilling, and similar units in more recent history. But even when these relationships can be discovered the problem remains of determining the gold, silver, and copper contents of the coins themselves. A silver drachma at the time of the first Ptolemy had degenerated into a copper drachma at the time of the last Ptolemy; the silver denarius of Augustus Caesar had become a miserable bit of copper at the time of the successors of Diocletian three centuries later. When one combines with these difficulties the even more perplexing one of comparing weights and measures, an Alexandrian artaba with a Roman modius, for example, then the problem becomes even more puzzling.

However, there is one way to cut the Gordian knot and that is to refer all prices to what we might call the wheat *numéraire*, that is to say, to express prices in terms of bushels of wheat, or if a smaller unit is desired, in terms of pounds of wheat on the assumption that 60 pounds make a bushel. Since the ratios of ounces of gold to silver to wheat remained relatively fixed over long intervals of time, we are in possession of a fairly stable unit for the comparison of price levels at different periods if we use the wheat *numéraire*.

Until very recent times the value-ratio of gold to silver remained unusually stable. During classical times the ratio was about 12 to 1, that is to say, 12 units of silver by weight were equivalent to one unit of gold, or, as we might say otherwise, the price of an ounce of gold was 12 ounces of silver. The ratio remained at or near this figure until the beginning of the seventeenth century, when its more common value became approximately 15 to 1. During the greater part of the nineteenth century the ratio remained slightly under 16, but after 1875

232 POLITICAL STATISTICS

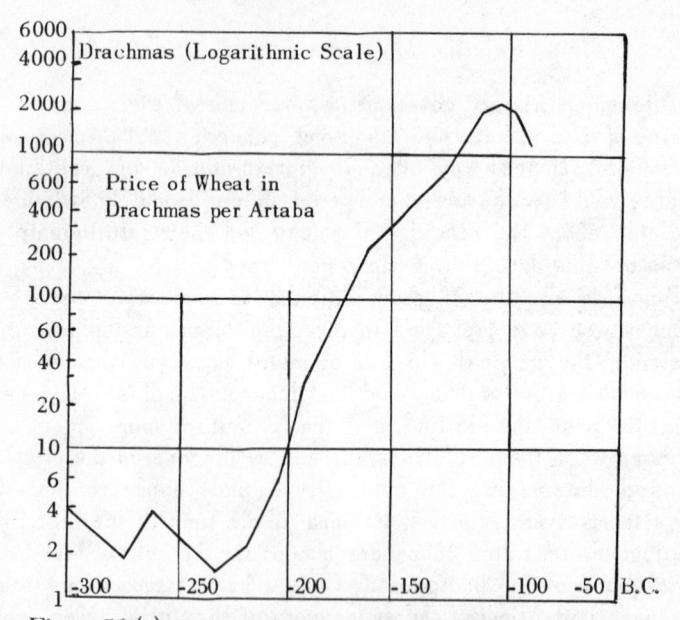

Figure 56 (a). Ptolemaic Inflation Shown in Price of Wheat.

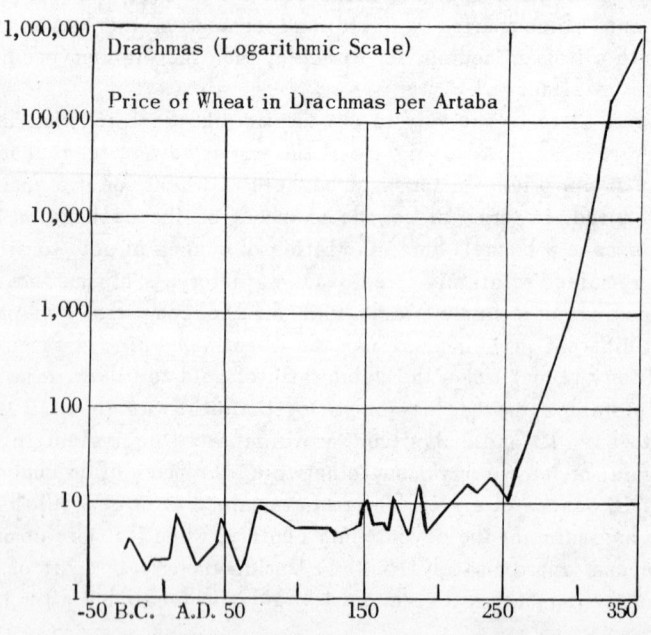

Figure 56 (b). Roman Inflation Shown in Price of Wheat.

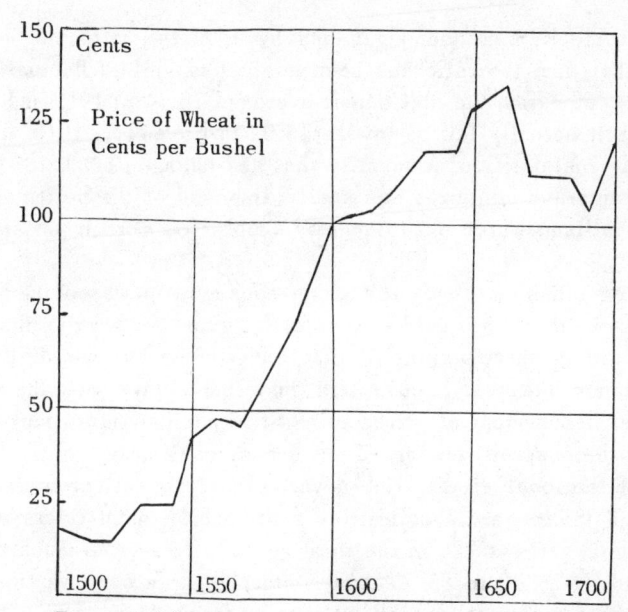

Figure 56 (c). English Inflation Shown in Price of Wheat.

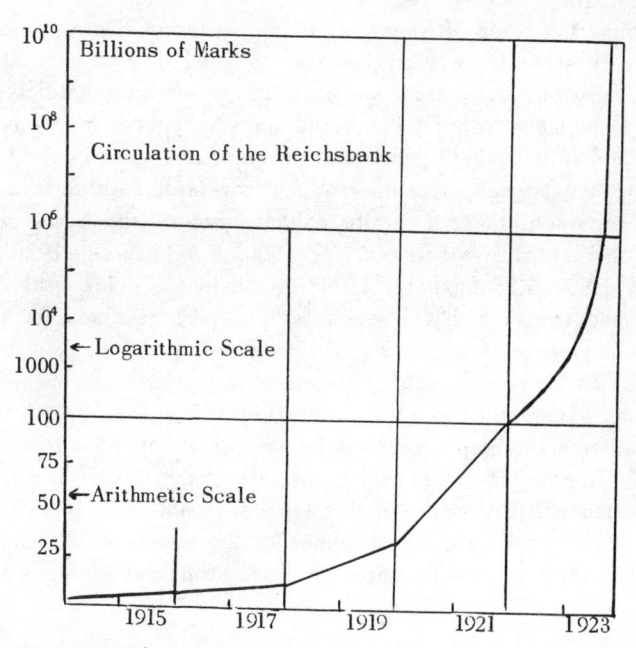

Figure 56 (d). German Inflation Shown in Terms of Circulation of Marks.

an appreciable increase began and by 1900 the ratio had doubled. Since that time the ratio has been subject to violent fluctuations as one may infer from the fact that it averaged 18.44 in 1919 and 100.55 in 1940. It actually fell as low as 15.02 in November, 1919. This remarkable instability of a quantity that had changed but little in more than twenty-five centuries has finally disposed of the political issue of bimetallism, which too frequently supplanted more important problems.

During classical times the silver-copper ratio was of much more importance than the gold-silver ratio, since this ratio fluctuated widely during short periods of time and caused extreme disturbance to economic patterns. Inflations in those early days took the form of a copper debasement of silver coins. The ancient rulers had not yet learned the possibilities of a fiat currency floating buoyantly upon an insecure national credit. But nevertheless, the silver-copper ratio furnished inflationary possibilities sufficient for most rulers since it varied from perhaps 120 in the third century B.C. to as much as 240, 375, and even 500 in the second century B.C. In our own times this ratio has shown great instability, ranging from 141 in 1885 to as low as 34 in 1916.

Although the price of wheat, measured in terms of a national currency, will show some variation due to good or bad harvests, its widest variations come from the fluctuations of the general level of prices. Over many years the demand for wheat as a food has been about equal to 8 bushels per capita per year and even in the United States in recent times, with the rich and varied diet which this country has provided, the per capita consumption is shown by the following characteristic averages: for 1900, 7.9 bushels; 1920, 6.11 bushels; 1925, 5.26 bushels; 1935, 5.02 bushels. This stability of demand and the fact that wheat prices can be obtained for almost every country over long periods of time make wheat the best *numéraire* for scanning price levels in centuries remote from our own.

Without examining too closely the details of their construction, let us consider the graphs given in Figure 56, which show four of the greatest price inflations known to history. Such events always accompany unusual movements of this kind. It is not to be inferred from this that rising prices are the causes of the events that ensue, but rather that they are symptomatic of great structural changes in the body politic. Prices are thus a kind of barometer of political weather, or, to the medically minded, form a temperature-chart telling the progress of a fever in the commonwealth.

The first of the graphs in Figure 56, namely (a), shows such details as we have of the wheat inflation in Alexandria during the rule of the Ptolemies. The history of prices after 200 B.C. is largely drawn from the studies of A. Segré,* but the evidence of its magnitude is well attested from other sources. Thus we find the following comments by M. Rostovtzeff in his monumental work on *The Social and Economic History of the Hellenistic World* (1940): "It is, however, certain that the relative value of silver coins was increasing and that these were gradually disappearing from circulation, being treated as mere bullion: 500 and more copper drachmas to the silver drachma became the common ratio of exchange. Simultaneously the tendency of the prices of foodstuffs, manufactured goods, and labor was consistently upward, though the rise was somewhat spasmodic. The government profited from the inflation by discharging its obligations to those in its employ (including the military) in debasing currency at a rate of exchange which did not correspond with the real value of copper money."

If one surveys the history of the period he will find that the Ptolemies who ruled during the century of inflation have a low rating as rulers, and there was much political strife between them and their subjects. One of the worst of these was Ptolemy IX, called by himself *Euergetes* II, or the *Benefactor*, but by his subjects, *Kakergetes*, or the *Malefactor*. History calls him *Physkon*, that is to say, the *Sausage*, "because of his excessive obesity and his dark and spotted complexion." Physkon ruled from 170 to 116. The final dissolution of the Ptolemaic kingdom came from the excesses of Ptolemy XIII, known to history as *Auletes*, or the *Flute-player*. He ruled from 80 to 51 B.C. and is known to history as the worst of the Ptolemies. He left his country with a completely debased currency, heavily in debt, and partly pledged to Rome, whose citizens held the notes. The dramatic events that ensued from this situation are found in the life of his daughter Cleopatra, who finally succeeded him to power. Although the story of Cleopatra is one of the most romantic tales in history, the political significance was much more profound. For at Cleopatra's

---

*See, for example, "The Ptolemaic Copper Inflation C.A. 230-140 B.C.," *American Journal of Philology*, Vol. 63, 1942, pp. 174-197.

death Alexandria came under the complete domination of the Romans; Egypt becamd a vassal state and thereafter its existence as an independent kingdom completely disappeared. It was not an historical accident that Pompey fled to Alexandria and that he was pursued there by Caesar. For both of these Roman citizens held the unpaid notes of Aulests. Hence, one was there in the expectation of assistance from a state so heavily endebted to him, and the other was on the scene in order to collect his own bills by force of arms.

PROBLEMS

1. The following table shows the ratio of silver to gold since 1870 formulated as the ounces of silver required to buy one ounce of gold. Ratios are computed by D. H. Leavens from prices taken from *Engineering and Mining Journal*, Vol. 153, 1952, p. 87.

Year	Ratio	Year	Ratio	Year	Ratio	Year	Ratio	Year	Ratio	Year	Ratio
1870	15.57	1884	18.61	1898	35.03	1912	33.62	1926	33.11	1940	100.55
1871	15.57	1885	19.41	1899	34.36	1913	34.19	1927	36.47	1941	100.52
1872	15.63	1886	20.78	1900	33.33	1914	37.37	1928	35.34	1942	91.21
1873	15.93	1887	21.10	1901	34.68	1915	40.48	1929	38.78	1943	78.13
1874	16.16	1888	22.00	1902	39.15	1916	30.78	1930	53.74	1944	78.13
1875	16.64	1889	22.10	1903	38.10	1917	24.61	1931	71.25	1945	67.35
1876	17.75	1890	19.75	1904	35.70	1918	21.00	1932	73.29	1946	43.62
1877	17.20	1891	20.92	1905	33.87	1919	18.44	1933	75.98	1947	48.68
1878	17.92	1892	23.72	1906	30.54	1920	20.28	1934	72.88	1948	47.02
1879	18.39	1893	26.49	1907	31.24	1921	32.76	1935	54.40	1949	48.61
1880	18.05	1894	32.56	1908	38.64	1922	30.43	1936	77.55	1950	47.14
1881	18.25	1895	31.60	1909	39.74	1923	31.69	1937	77.90	1951	39.12
1882	18.20	1896	30.59	1910	38.22	1924	30.80	1938	80.90		
1883	18.64	1897	34.20	1911	38.33	1925	29.78	1939	84.47		

Make a graph of these data. Explain the sudden change in the ratio in 1931. Did this jump in the ratio affect other prices? Answer this by observing the course of prices between 1930 and 1940. William Jennings Bryan (1860-1925) ran for president in 1896 on the free-silver platform, advocating a ratio of 16 to 1 in the issuing of money. Had he been elected what effects might have been anticipated?

2. The following table gives the index numbers of wholesale prices in Germany (1913 = 100) from 1918 to 1922 inclusive. Chart these data (using a logarithmic scale) and compare with the increase in the circulation of the Reichsbank as shown in Figure 56(d). What conclusions can you draw from this comparison?

Year	Jan.	Feb.	Mar.	Apr.	May	June	July	Aug.	Sept.	Oct.	Nov.	Dec.
1918	204	198	198	204	203	209	208	235	230	234	234	245
1919	262	270	274	286	297	308	339	422	493	562	678	803
1920	1260	1680	1710	1570	1510	1380	1370	1450	1500	1470	1510	1440
1921	1440	1380	1340	1330	1310	1370	1430	1920	2070	2460	3420	3490
1922	3670	4100	5430	6350	6460	7030	10060	19200	28700	56600	115400	147500

4. *The Diocletian Inflation and its Political Significance.*

If we examine the second of the graphs in Figure 56, namely (b), we see that the waning power of the Roman Empire was associated with an inflationary movement of gigantic proportions. It is very fortunate for our credence in what is portrayed that the Emperor Diocletian, who ruled from 284 to 305, issued a celebrated edict on prices in 301. This document we shall examine in some detail presently.

The graph in Figure 56 gives the price of wheat in terms of drachmas per artaba, but can be translated readily into Roman money. For the drachma was equal to the Roman denarius; and the artaba, essentially equal to an American bushel, was the equivalent of four Roman modii. The use of Alexandrian rather than Roman units was adopted since the data for Alexandria are more readily interpreted than those for Rome, where the monetary units were constantly changing at the whims of each succeeding emperor. But the Alexandrian economy was tied by commerce and dominion status to that of Rome so that the fluctuations in one are highly correlated with those in the other.

We first observe from the figure that there was a steady trend of debasement in the coinage from the time of Augustus Caesar (ruled 27 B.C. to 14 A.D.), when from two to five silver drachmas would buy a bushel of wheat, to the accession of Decius (249), when from 15 to 20 of the bronze coins would be required for the same purchase.

But after the brief reign of Decius, the turmoil of his succession and the obvious instability of the empire, which had ten emperors in a span of less than four decades, led to rapid deterioration of the currency. By the beginning of the fourth century the inflation had reached alarming proportions. Thereupon in 301 the Emperor Diocletian issued his famous edict, which established for that time and place an official ceiling to the prices of most of the goods and services useful to the Roman world.

There is a kind of modern tone to the following passages taken from the celebrated document of the old Roman emperor: "For who is so insensitive and so devoid of human feeling that he cannot know, or rather, has not perceived, that in the commerce carried on in the markets or involved in the daily life of cities, immoderate prices are so widespread that the uncurbed passion for gain is lessened neither by abundant supplies nor by fruitful years... Who does not know, therefore, that insolence, covertly attacking the public welfare... comes to the mind of the profiteer to extort prices for merchandise, not four-fold or eight-fold, but such that human speech is incapable of describing either the price or the act; finally that sometimes in a single purchase a soldier is deprived of his bonus and his salary, and that the contribution of the whole world to support the armies falls to the abominable profits of thieves...

"Since, therefore, it is agreed that even in the time of our ancestors it was customary in passing laws to restrain insolence by attaching a prescribed penalty..., it is our pleasure that anyone who shall have resisted the form of this statute shall for his daring be subject to a capital penalty..."

To this edict is then attached a list of prices which could not be exceeded without endangering the life of the seller. These prices are in terms of denarii, but they are readily interpreted if one remembers the equivalences: one denarius = one drachma, and four modii = one artaba = one bushel. Thus, employing the wheat *numéraire*, we see that 400 denarii will purchase one bushel of wheat. A few of these prices, the first general experiment by a government in the control of prices, are recorded in the table on the next page.

This astonishing document, as an interpreter of subsequent events in the declining empire, has not received from historians the attention which it probably deserves. It was unknown to Gibbon, whose *Decline and Fall of the Roman Empire* was published between 1776 and 1788, although a fragmentary copy of the edict had been found as early as 1709. The document shows the desperate state of the currency at the beginning of the fourth century. The ineffectiveness of Diocletian's efforts to make a currency reform are shown graphically in Figure 56 by the continued progress of the inflation. By 350 wheat had reached the dizzy height of something under a million denarii per bushel. Thereafter all was confusion and one cannot be surprised to read in history that the western Empire was at last in ruin.

Article	Price in Denarii	Article	Price in Denarii
Wheat (per modius)	100	Teacher of Greek or Latin literature and of geometry, per pupil, (monthly)	200
Barley (per modius)	60		
Rye (per modius)	60		
Wine, ordinary (per pint)	8	Teacher of rhetoric or public speaking, per pupil, (monthly)	250
Oil, ordinary (per pint)	12		
Beef, per pound	8		
Pork, per pound	12	Advocate for pleading a case	1,000
Lamb, per pound	12	Ox hides, tanned, each	750
Lentils, per modius	100	Bear skins, tanned, each	100
Farm labor, with maintenance, (daily)	25	Boots for soldiers	100
		Boots for women	60
Stone mason, with maintenance, (daily)	50	Shoes, patrician	150
		Travelling bag, best quality	1,500
Scribe, for 100 lines of best writing	25	Freight wagon	6,000
		White silk, per pound	12,000
Teacher, for each pupil, (monthly)	50	Silk, dyed purple, per pound	150,000
		Washed wool, per pound	175
Teacher of arithmetic, for each pupil, (monthly)	75	Saffron, from Arabia, per pound	2,000
Teacher of manuscript writing, each pupil, (monthly)	50	Gold, in bars or in coins, per pound	50,000

At this point it is worth our while to indicate the mathematical nature of price inflations. Diocletian in his edict blamed the speculators of the realm, but never once mentioned the real cause, namely, the debasement of the currency itself.

According to the quantity theory of money, the relationship between the quantity of money in circulation, designated by M, the velocity of its circulation, designated by V, that is to say, the number of times a quantity of money is exchanged in a year, the price, denoted by P, and the volume of trade, represented by T, is given by the equation:

$$MV = PT. \qquad (1)$$

Perhaps a better formulation is in the form of the following equivalence of ratio changes:

$$\frac{\Delta M}{M} + \frac{\Delta V}{V} = \frac{\Delta P}{P} + \frac{\Delta T}{T}, \qquad (2)$$

where ΔM, ΔV, ΔP and ΔT mean the changes respectively in the four variables from their initial values M, V, P and T.

Now it has been found by a study of modern data, that in a country like the United States, MV is approximately twelve times total income, that is to say,

$$MV = kI,$$

where k is approximately 12. This quantity k will vary from time to time and is greater in periods of speculation or inflation, since V has a tendency to increase as the value of money depreciates. Thus in 1929 at the top of the American speculation in stocks, k had a value of 21, and at the bottom of the subsequent depression k fell to as low as 9.2 in 1934.

The determination of the interrelationship between the four variables in equation (2) is a statistical problem of considerable difficulty and cannot be examined here. For our purpose it is sufficient to observe that in times when the velocity of money remains constant and trade does not change, then changes in the volume of money will be reflected in corresponding changes in price. In ancient economies which lacked the mobility of modern banking facilities, it is probable that the velocity of money remained fairly constant, although hoarding was at times an important factor. In great inflationary movements, such as that observed in Germany between 1920 and 1923, it is probable that velocity increases, while trade remains constant or declines. Thus, as the ratio $\Delta M/M$ increases, there is no compensatory change in the trade ratio, and prices consequently receive a strong upward thrust. This is why we always observe great price inflations in periods when the value of money is depreciated.

This is well illustrated in the disastrous German inflation which took place between 1914 and the end of 1923. The picture of the inflation is shown in Figure 56(d), which gives the number of marks issued by the Reichsbank within the ten year period. During this violent spiral of inflation, the index of prices increased in a compensatory manner. Thus, the index number of wholesale prices, which was around 1.00 in 1914 and 2.45 at the end of the war in 1918, rose rapidly to 8.02 in December, 1919, to 14.4 a year later, to 34.9 in December, 1921, to 1,475 in December, 1922 and to the fantastic level of 1,262 billion at the end of the deflation in 1923. There was also an increase in the velocity of the depreciating marks, but this could not possibly attain the same order of magnitude as the changes observed in both the money and the price ratios.

POLITICAL SCIENCE AND ECONOMICS

From the standpoint of history and political events, the German inflation was a world disaster. Out of the financial turmoil the Nazi regime gained adherence and political strength. The outcome of this movement needs no recounting here since it belongs to current history.

PROBLEMS

1. How much of a decline in an initial velocity of money equal to 30, that is, $V = 30$, would be required to balance an increase of 5% in the supply of circulating money so that neither price nor trade would change?

2. In a closed economic system, if a 10% increase is observed in prices, a 15% increase is noted in trade, and if $\Delta V = 0$, how large was the initial supply of money if $\Delta M = 100{,}000{,}000$?

3. In the following table is given the value of MV, where M is circulating deposits, and the national income, both expressed in billions of dollars, over the period 1920 to 1931 inclusive:

Year	MV	Income	Year	MV	Income
1920	782	74.3	1926	918	78.5
1921	623	52.6	1927	1234	77.2
1922	639	61.7	1928	1369	80.5
1923	751	69.8	1929	1678	79.1
1924	752	69.6	1930	1101	72.2
1925	871	77.1	1931	744	60.1

From these data compute the values of k from the equation: $k = MV/I$. How can one account for the variation in this value over the period studied? What happened to the velocity of money?

5. *The Price Inflation of the Sixteenth Century.*

While all great price inflations observed in the past have had associated with them historical and political events of great importance, these events are not always disastrous to the body politic. As evidence of this we may indicate the great rise in prices which took place in the fifteenth century. This is shown for English wheat prices in Figure 56(c) and for Spanish prices in Figure 57.

From both series of prices, and from similar series from other countries in the same period, we observe an inflation of the order of 500 per cent in the price level which took place between 1500 and 1650. But this inflation was an entirely different phenomenon from those observed in the other three pictured in Figure 56. Like those

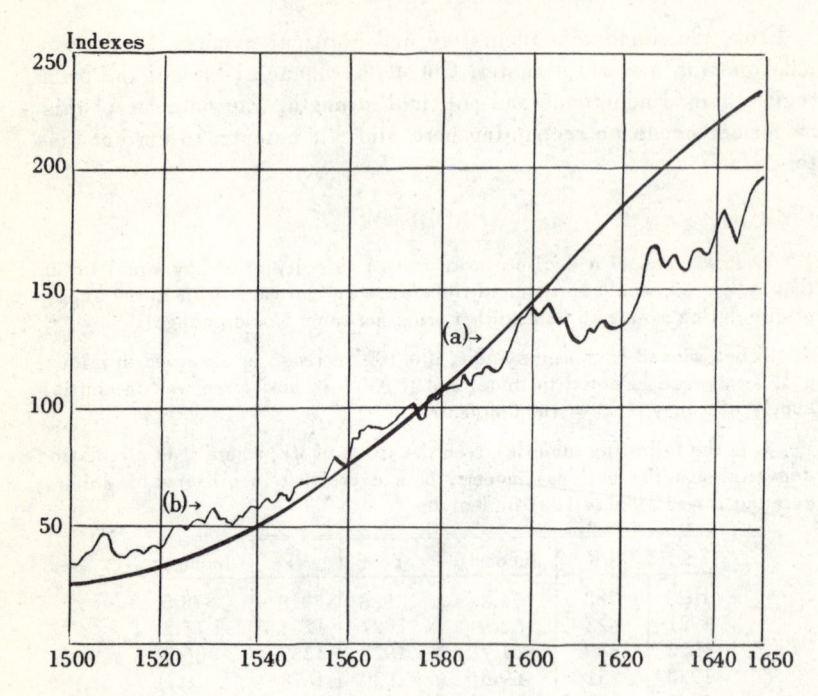

Figure 57. Indexes (a) Total Treasure (Soetbeer) and (b) Spanish Prices (Hamilton).

it was a monetary depreciation, for the importation of vast quantities of treasure from the Indies had cheapened the price of gold and silver and hence the value of money, but unlike the other inflations it was accompanied by a large and compensating increase in trade and commerce. Thus, in the equation of exchange, formula (2) of Section 4, while $\Delta M/M$ increased proportionally to the index of treasure as shown in Figure 57, there was a concomitant increase in the ratio $\Delta T/T$, which, while it was not sufficient to offset the change in the money factor and thus to hold prices constant, created prosperity and wealth throughout Europe.

This increase in trade is shown in Figure 1 of Chapter 1. The trade index was constructed entirely by means of the equation of exchange from the data shown in Figure 57, on the assumption that the velocity factor remained relatively constant during the period under observation.

POLITICAL SCIENCE AND ECONOMICS

Although one feels considerable confidence in such a statistical deduction, it is always reassuring to have some independent check on the conclusions derived from the computations. Several years after the construction of Figure 1, Chapter 1, some remarkable data became available which amply confirm the estimates obtained from the equation of exchange.

These data are obtained from the records of shipping which passed into the North Sea by way of the Sound. They are contained in a six-volume work by Nina Bang (d. 1928) published in Denmark with an introduction in both Danish and French. This work bears the title: *Tables de la Navigation et du Transport des Marchandises Passant par le Sunde 1497-1660* and (with Knud Korst) *Tables de la Navigation et du Transport des Marchandises Passant par le Sunde 1661-1783 et par le Grand-Belt 1701-1748*.

In these remarkable volumes we find the record of the number of ships passing into the North Sea by way of the Sound, together with their tonnage, cargoes, destination, and other facts. Details are given for nearly every year in the almost three centuries covered by the record between 1497 and 1783. As far as the writer knows, this is the longest continuous series of uniform economic data in existence.

Since the sixteenth, seventeenth, and eighteenth centuries were dominated by maritime trade, the general economic pattern of European countries is reflected in the statistics of shipping. Hence the data in the work just described, obtained as it was from the records of tolls kept at Elsinore, Denmark, between the years 1497 and 1783, affords a unique picture of European commerce. Elsinore stands upon the eastern shore of the Sound between the Cattegat, entrance to the North Sea, and the Baltic Sea; hence, a count of shipping from this vantage point would certainly correlate highly with a general index of maritime trade.

The data referring to the number of ships passing the Sound are represented in Figure 58.* A general trend line has also been given which is obtained by smoothing the yearly totals with a five-year moving average. This average removes the details of the short business cycle observed in many parts of the series, but otherwise preserves the major structure of the trends of trade.

---

*This general curve, expressed as yearly averages in each decennium, was published by L. R. Nienstaedt: *Economic Equilibrium, Employment and Natural Resources*, 1942, p. 87.

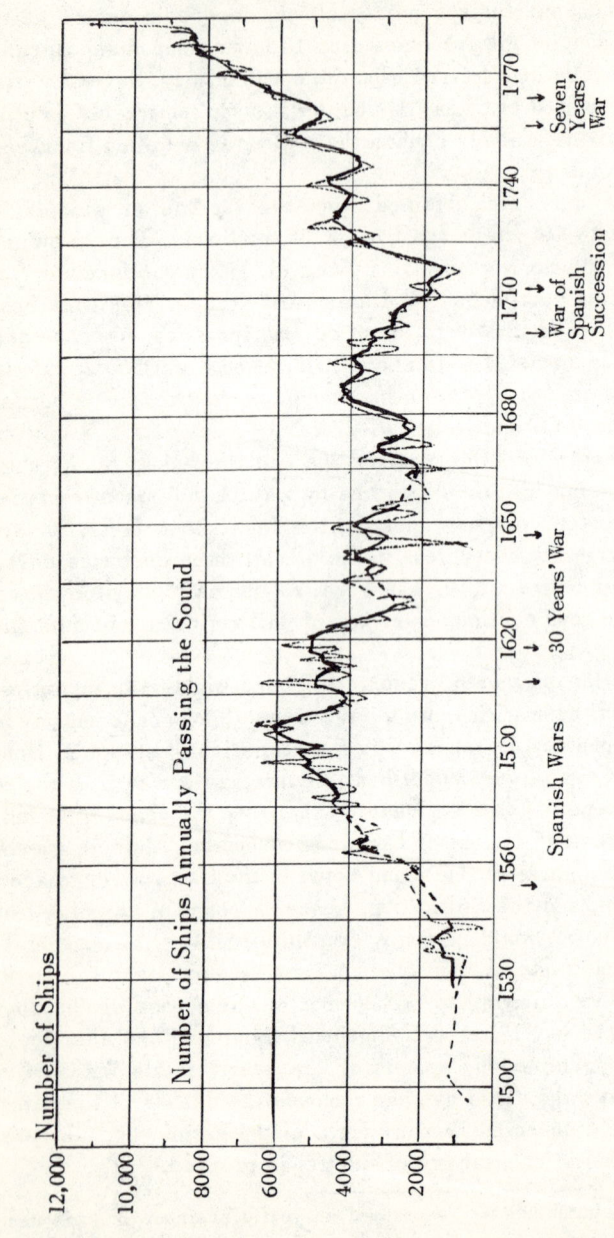

Figure 58. Total Number of Ships Passing Annually at Elsinore, Denmark.

A great deal of history can be read from Figure 1 of Chapter 1 and from Figure 58. In the first chart, which gives more detail in the advance of trade during the sixteenth century, we observe the effect of the Spanish armada, which set forth in the year 1588 for the conquest of England. But dramatic as that event is portrayed in history, and disastrous as it turned out to be to the hopes of Spain to become mistress of the seas, it is clearly a relatively minor incident in the history of that country. The sweep of trade, after a temporary recession, continued to increase until shortly after the beginning of the Thirty Years' War (1618-1648). The disastrous effect of this great struggle is shown in the decline of shipping, which was nearly fifty per cent. In Spain itself we see evidence of a great depression which developed between 1620 and 1630. It is interesting in interpreting the chart to observe that Philip IV, who succeeded to the Spanish throne at the death of his father in 1621, had a reign full of misfortunes. Both internally and externally affairs went badly and by 1640 the administration was so inert that Portugal was able to secede from the empire without striking a blow. To Philip IV is attributed by history the fall of Spain, but we can see from the details of Figure 58 that he had the misfortune to rule in a period of sharply declining trade. No man, however able, could have stemmed that disastrous tide.

Before turning to other considerations, let us observe from the index of trade and from the data on shipping that the sixteenth century, especially the latter half, was a period of unusual prosperity when compared with any other preceding period of time. Such sudden acquisition of great wealth on the part of many persons, as the trend indicates, should have considerable bearing upon the development of the arts. There was a residue of capital beyond the needs of living which was available for patronage and support of learning. And such, indeed, was the case.

As is well known, the golden age of Spanish literature belongs to the sixteenth and seventeenth centuries, extending approximately from 1550 to 1650. This was also a period of great literary, artistic, and scientific achievement throughout Europe. For this was the century of Shakespeare (1564-1616), Ben Jonson (1573?-1637), and Marlow (1564-1593) in England; Cervantes (1547-1616), and Lope de Vega (1562-1635) in Spain; Corneille (1606-1684), Molière (1622-1673), and Racine (1639-1699) in France. Modern science began almost contemporaneously with the renaissance in literature, for Galileo (1564-

Figure 59.

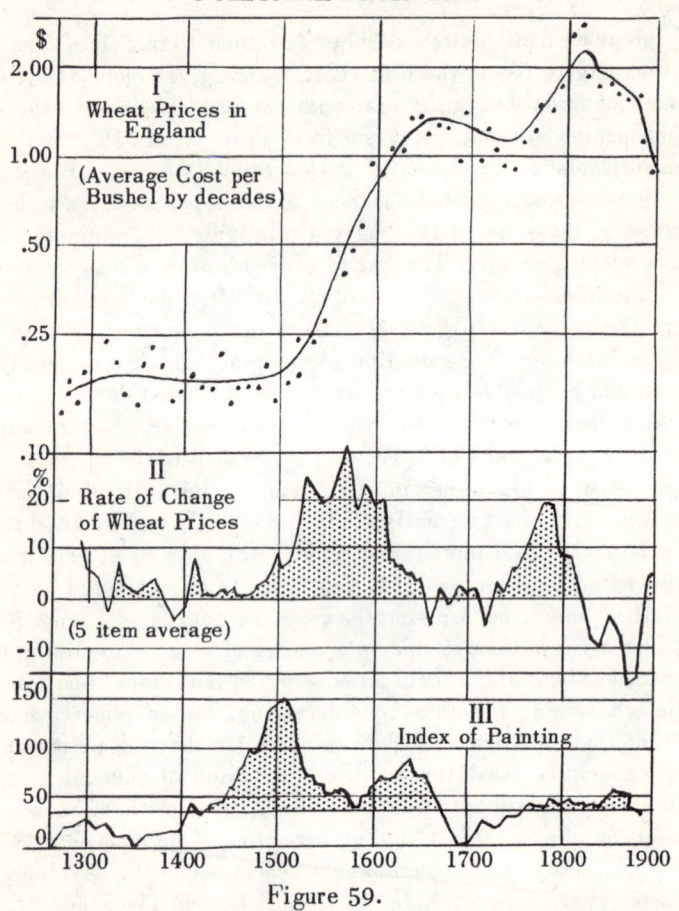

1642), Tycho Brahe (1546-1601), and Kepler (1571-1630) appeared as simultaneous stars in the scientific sky. Their work formed the basis for the great discoveries of Newton (1642-1727), Leibniz (1646-1716), and their illustrious colleagues of the eighteenth century.

The story of the development of art is shown in Figure 59, based upon a study by W. F. C. Nelson, which is designed to show the relationship between periods of great painting and the rate of change in the price of wheat. This hypothesis, without restrictions, is scarcely tenable, else art would have flourished vigorously at the end of both the Ptolemaic dynasty and the Roman Empire. Nevertheless, when the rise of price is accompanied by a rise in trade also, then we can expect to find development of the arts accompanying these movements. The index of painting was constructed by a weighting of great artists who flourished during the period shown in the figure. The change in price is based essentially upon the ratio $\Delta P/P$, where P is the observed price of wheat.

PROBLEMS

1. What events in Spain led to the trade declines of 1625, 1641, and 1646 which appear in Figure 1 of Chapter 1?

2. The following table shows the number of registered vessels sailing to and from the Indies from the ports of Spain from 1506 to 1555 inclusive:*

Year	No. of Vessels	Year	No. of Vessels	Year	No. of Vessels	Year	No. of Vessels	Year	No. of Vessels
1506	34	1516	52	1526	96	1536	151	1546	144
1507	51	1517	94	1527	109	1537	70	1547	158
1508	67	1518	98	1528	72	1538	104	1548	162
1509	47	1519	92	1529	104	1539	116	1549	174
1510	27	1520	108	1530	112	1540	126	1550	157
1511	34	1521	64	1531	87	1541	139	1551	162
1512	54	1522	43	1532	84	1542	150	1552	125
1513	61	1523	54	1533	97	1543	128	1553	79
1514	76	1524	70	1534	121	1544	76	1554	27
1515	63	1525	110	1535	128	1545	135	1555	109

Represent these data graphically and compare with those shown in Figure 58. What would you infer about trade with the Indies after 1555?

6. *How England Became Mistress of the Seas.*

The thoughtful student of history may have asked himself the question: How did it come about that the population of the British Isles, small in numbers and in natural resources when compared with

---

*Data from Appendix 8 of C. H. Harding's *Trade and Navigation between Spain and the Indies in the Time of the Hapsburgs*, Cambridge, Mass., 1918, xxvii + 371 pp. The author says: "The figures in these tables were secured from a volume in the Archivo de Indias (30.2.1/3) entitled: 'Libro de registros de las naos que han ido y venido á las Indias desde el año de 1504 en adelante.' It seems to be a sort of index or calendar of the registers which passed through the Casa de Contratación. Whether the list is complete or not there is no means of knowing."

the rest of Europe, should have succeeded to the lofty position of Mistress of the Seas in the course of two centuries.

There is probably no better way to tell this story than by an analysis of the growth of maritime commerce as shown in Figure 58 of the preceding section. But now it is necessary to separate the shipping which enters into the composite picture into its component parts. This is possible from the admirable data of Nina Bang, and the results of this analysis which interest us are the charts showing separately the number of ships from the Netherlands which annually passed through the Sound (Figure 60) and those which showed the British flag (Figure 61).

Referring first to Figure 60, we see that shipping from the Netherlands until 1650 was highly correlated with the general trend of Spanish trade. This was natural, of course, since the Netherlands had been a province of Spain from the time of Emperor Charles V, who, in 1506, fourteen years before he became emperor of the Holy Roman Empire, had inherited their sovereignty. The history of the Netherlands between the accession of Philip II to the Spanish throne in 1556 until the Peace of Münster in 1648 was one of almost constant warfare, with occasional uneasy truces while the exhausted country regained some measure of strength to renew the struggle.

From Figure 60 we observe a great trade decline between 1595 and 1605, and another between 1619 and 1630. The first appears to have been a general recession in a sterile period following the defeat of the Spanish armada by the British. It was also a period of intensive fighting in the Netherlands with a signal lack of success on the side of Spain, but not enough success on the part of the Dutch to achieve the freedom for which they fought. There was considerable political activity at this time, which resulted in 1596 in a triple alliance between England, France, and the United Provinces. Philip II died in 1598, but this event had little effect on the course of the war which terminated in a truce in 1609.

A period of economic prosperity ensued, as is evident from the abrupt increase in maritime trade. But this good fortune was short lived, as we see from the graph, and a great recession set in with the opening of the Thirty Years' War in 1618. This wretched struggle ended in 1648 and the Dutch at last, after just short of a century of bitter warfare, found themselves once more a free nation. The rise of the Dutch Republic had been achieved.

POLITICAL SCIENCE AND ECONOMICS

Scrutiny of the shipping data in the period of the Thirty Years' War reveals one point of some interest and shows how historical events are connected with those of economics. In the year 1645 we observe an apparent drop in Dutch shipping into the North Sea. Where 2,009 vessels passed through the Sound in 1644 and 2,038 in 1646, the data for 1645 give a total of only 59. Since such a change could be occasioned only by an event of major consequence, some interesting political situation is indicated. A survey of the history of that period gives the answer to the problem. Sweden, long in conflict with Denmark over the tolls imposed for passage through the Sound, declared war against the Danes. Since the Dutch were also economically affected by the tolls, they agreed to aid Sweden in this campaign. The climax came in the year 1645 and the explanation of the aberration in the data mentioned above is clearly given by the following passage from P. J. Blok's *History of the People of the Netherlands*, which describes the campaign of the Dutch fleet under the command of Admiral Witte de With:

"At the head of the 'armada' the fight-loving De With sailed in the middle of June, 1645, towards the Sound, escorting 300 merchantmen and intending, in case of war, to unite with the Swedish fleet against the Danes. The weaker Danish naval force at Copenhagen did not prevent his entrance into the Baltic, and amid the salutes of the rejoicing Swedes the entire fleet of 350 vessels sailed majestically in order of battle through the Sound, while there was no thought of paying toll, and the Danes looked on from their forts, armed to the teeth and enraged at this unprecedented violation of Danish rights, but not daring to attack the powerful enemy. On reaching the Baltic De With allowed the merchantmen to go their way. He remained in the Sound and cruised threateningly before Copenhagen, possessing 'the keys' of the strait. Under his protection the Dutch ships sailed unmolested to and fro through the Sound during the whole season."

The dispute was finally settled in August of that year by the treaty of Brömsebro, so the toll-count was resumed in 1646. And thus we see how the economic data have directed our attention to an interesting footnote in political history.

Other aberrations in the data are capable of similar explanation. Thus, in Figure 61, which gives the information about British shipping, we find that the number of ships passing the Sound dropped from 250 in 1664 to 4 in 1666 and did not return to normal until 1668.

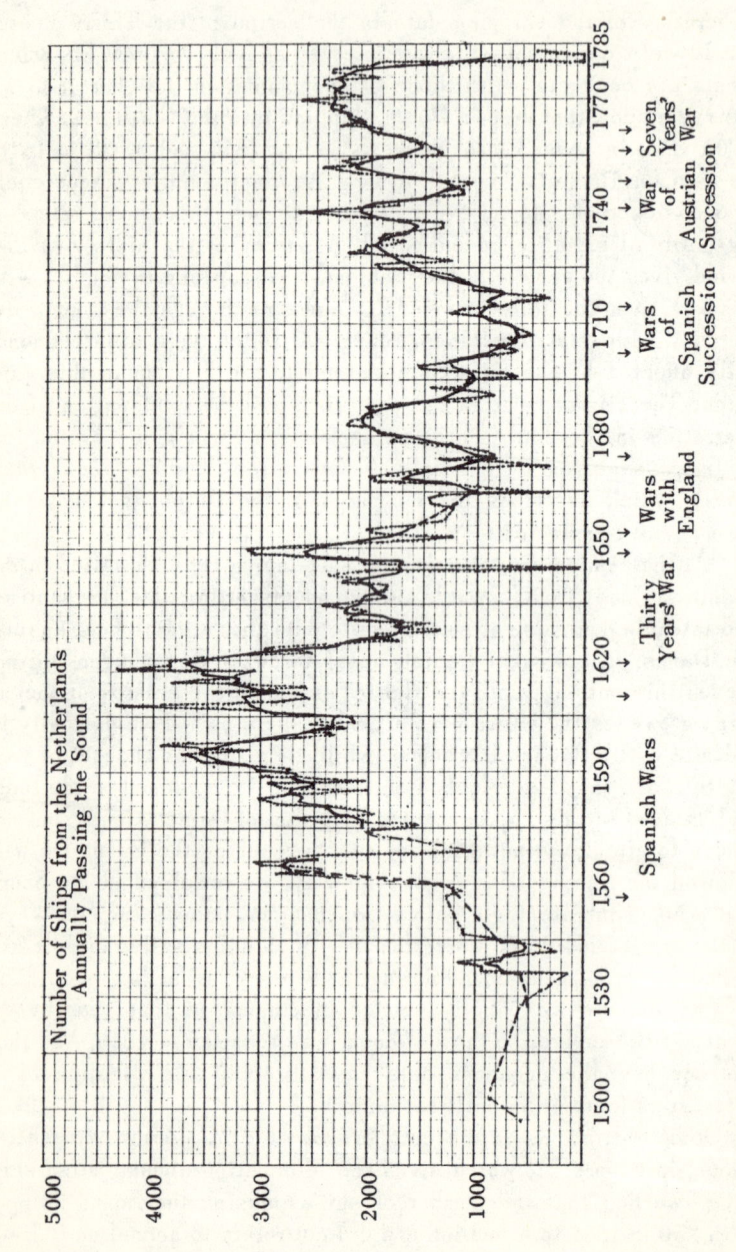

Figure 60. Total Number of Ships from the Netherlands Passing Annually at Elsinore, Denmark.

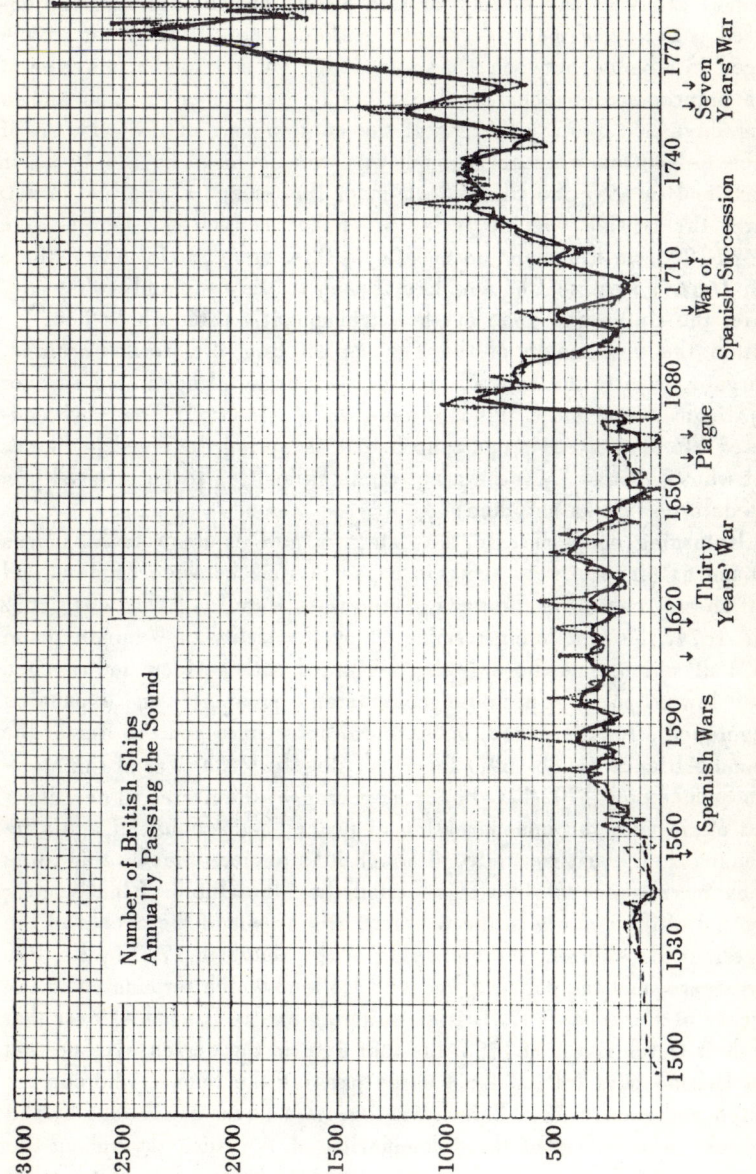

Figure 61. Total Number of British Ships Passing Annually at Elsinore, Denmark.

Casual study of the history of this period shows that England endured a series of major disasters in these years. The great plague raged in London between 1664 and 1666. To add to the miseries of the unfortunate citizens fire broke out on September 2, 1666 and in four days had destroyed most of the eastern part of the city. As if such calamities were not enough war was declared by the Dutch in 1665 and in 1667 the Dutch fleet under Ruyter and Cornelius de Witt burnt the British fleet as it lay at anchor at Chatam. John Evelyn (1620-1706) in his diary comments on this event as follows: "June 18, 1667, I went to Chatam, and thence to view not only what mischief the Dutch had done but how triumphantly their whole fleet lay within the very mouth of the Thames all from the North Foreland, Margate, even to the buoy of the Nore — a dreadful spectacle as ever Englishman saw and a dishonor never to be wiped off! Those who advised his Majesty to prepare no fleet this spring deserved — I know not what — but — ." And are not these calamities to be inferred from the data on British shipping?

Returning once more to the data, we now examine both Figures 60 and 61 since a great struggle began in 1652 between England and Holland for control of the seas. Three wars were fought between 1652 and 1674, the last being terminated by the treaty of Westminster in 1674 at which time the shipping series of both nations had reached their lowest point. A period of considerable prosperity and expansion developed after the peace, but this did not endure and the War of the Grand Alliance (1688-1697) followed closely by the War of the Spanish Succession (1702-1714) once more brought the series to new lows. But again with the consummation of peace, both countries again increased their maritime trade, although it is obvious that England was much more successful in this period than the Dutch. Finally, near the end of the century in the conflicts arising out of the events of the American Revolution, the harassing of the Dutch in 1780 by English privateers, and the ensuing war with Holland which terminated in the Treaty of Paris in 1787, British shipping finally triumphed over that of their Dutch rival. In 1783, the last date in the series, we find that the British paid toll on 2853 ships passing the Sound, whereas the Dutch had a mere 487. This advantage was never again lost by the British, who extended their domination of the seas throughout the next century. This is the dramatic story told by the data graphically represented in Figures 60 and 61.

7. *The Relationship of Wages to Change in Price.*

It is a common observation that healthy political states do not exist when the scale of labor is too low. At the present time the most important political question confronted by most governments is the relationship of labor to capital, or the return to the worker of the fruits of the factors of production which he operates. Hence no picture of the relationship of economic events to political history would be complete without some discussion of this subject.

It is somewhat shocking in a world of plenty to observe the low standards of living which prevailed in the classical world and even in modern countries, a century or more after the beginning of the Renaissance. To orient ourselves in the problem we shall consider the budget of Cato's slave which has come down to us from about 200 B. C. and provides a clear picture of the standards of living that prevailed in earlier times. With wheat quoted at 2½ denarii per bushel, the food and clothing of this slave, as given in detail by Cato, cost annually 78 denarii, or the equivalent of 31 bushels of wheat.

To some these figures may seem fantastic and even lack the aspect of truth. Let such skeptics consider the wages which have prevailed in recent years in the Orient. According to a detailed budget study made in 1928 the standards of living which prevailed in modern Shanghai are still those which were found in ancient Rome and in England at the beginning of the 17th century. The mill-workers and their families in this once thriving doorway to China lived on a per capita annual budget equal to 32 bushels of wheat (or rice), almost exactly that given by Cato to his slave. The daily wage of the mill-workers was equal to 9.5 pounds of wheat per day and that of the more skilled workmen slightly more than twice this amount, or an equivalent of 20.5 pounds of wheat per day. Assuming 300 working days in the year, these wages were the equivalent of 48 and 103 bushels of wheat annually.

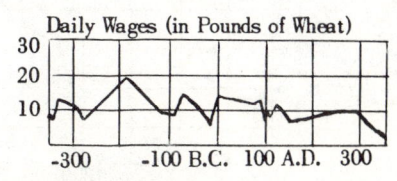

Figure 62. Graeco-Roman Wages in Pounds of Wheat per Day.

254   POLITICAL STATISTICS

If we now re-examine the edict of Diocletian, which was discussed in Section 4, we observe that the price of common labor was 25 denarii per day plus maintenance, and that of skilled labor was twice this figure. With wheat at 400 denarii per bushel, which we assume to have a weight of 60 pounds, then these wages become equivalent respectively to 7.5 and 15 pounds of wheat per day plus maintenance. Computing maintenance at from 2.5 to 5 pounds of wheat per day, we see that the daily wage prevailing in the empire of Diocletian's time was somewhere between 10 and 20 pounds, almost exactly that of the mill-workers of Shanghai. Thus we see that the twenty centuries intervening between the two budgets have not brought amelioration to the poor of those economic states that have failed to make use of scientific methods to increase their use of power.

It is also instructive to examine the wages of the school teacher in the Roman empire. From Diocletian's edict we see that the elementary teacher who was fortunate enough to have a class of 30 pupils received an equivalent of 45 bushels of wheat per year, or 9 pounds per working day, while even the highly paid professor of literature and geometry received only four times this amount, or 36 pounds for each day that he taught.

The wages which were paid to labor in the Graeco-Roman world during classical times are shown in Figure 62 and the corresponding wages paid in England in modern times appear in Figure 63. In the first case the wages of labor remained essentially at a level not far

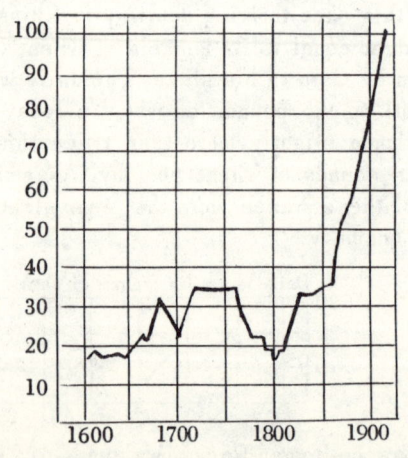

Figure 63. English Wages in Pounds of Wheat per Day.

removed from a scale of 10 pounds of wheat per day. In 1600 the daily wages of the laboring man in England would purchase 16 pounds of wheat per day, a figure little better than that which prevailed throughout Roman times. During the first quarter of the nineteenth century this purchasing power of labor had doubled. By 1882 it had doubled again, and in 1914, at the beginning of World War I, the price of a day's work had attained the level of 100 pounds of wheat. These estimates are graphically portrayed in Figure 63. But the end had not yet been reached, for during the quarter of a century that spans the two world wars the price of labor increased at least 150 per cent and stood in 1940 at 250 pounds of wheat per day.

But there is no significant relationship observable in these two figures between changes in the wage scale and changes in the level of prices. The great inflation of Diocletian did nothing to ameliorate the conditions of the poor, and there is even evidence to show in Figure 62 that the trend in the scale of wages was downward in the centuries during which prices steadily increased.

That this conclusion is justified, in spite of the admitted crudeness of the data from which it is drawn, is evident from a study of prices during the application of John Law's theory of money in France from its beginning in 1716 to its collapse in 1720. This study was made by E. J. Hamilton and his conclusions appear graphically portrayed in Figure 64.*

The name of John Law (1671-1729), a Scotch financier, is associated with what is called in history the Mississippi Bubble. Back of this remarkable inflation was the assumption of Law that scarcity of money restricts commerce and that this scarcity can be remedied by the issue of paper currency against physical properties. These physical properties were represented in his project by the unlimited wealth presumed to exist in the undeveloped lands along the Mississippi, then held by France. Since these lands were pictured as being of untold value it seemed logical that an almost unlimited currency could be issued against them.

The persuasive tongue of Law succeeded in interesting the French government. On May 20, 1716 Law was authorized to establish a *Banque général,* later converted into the *Banque royale* with a capitalization of 6,000,000 livres, divided into 1200 shares. We shall

---

*"Prices and Wages at Paris under John Law's System," *The Quarterly Journal of Economics,* Vol. 51, 1936, pp. 42-70.

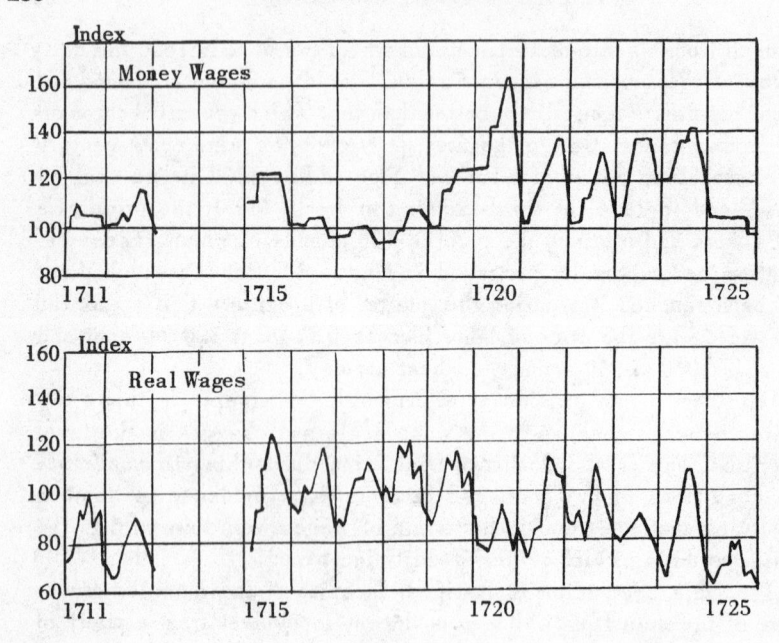

Figure 64. Comparison of Money Wages and Real Wages
at Paris under John Law's System. (Hamilton)

not trace the history of the inflation which followed this grand scheme. It is sufficient for our purpose to observe that an upward thrust was given to general prices, and that the bubble burst in a wave of financial ruin in May, 1720.

Our main interest in this historical speculation is to observe what happened to the level of wages. These naturally increased with the rising index of prices until the climax was reached in the latter part of 1720 as is shown in Figure 64. But in the same figure we also observe that as the inflation reached its peak, the index of real wages declined, and in the cyclical backwash of the financial catastrophe which ensued, real wages continued to drop substantially for the next five years.

PROBLEMS

1. Referring to Figure 63, how can one account for the rise in wages after 1800? Why do wages increase so sharply after 1860? Study the curve of the production of pig iron, Figure 41 of Chapter 7, and discuss the apparent

correlation between increase of wages and increase in tons of pig iron. What conclusions can be derived from such a comparison?

2. The following table gives the average weekly wages paid by manufacturers to production workers (Bureau of Labor Statistics) and the average price of wheat on the Chicago Exchange from 1939 to 1950 inclusive:

Year	Wages	Price of Wheat	Year	Wages	Price of Wheat
1939	$23.86	$0.76	1945	$44.39	$1.68
1940	$25.20	$0.86	1946	$43.82	$2.09
1941	$29.58	$1.12	1947	$49.97	$2.46
1942	$36.65	$1.36	1948	$54.14	$2.27
1943	$43.14	$1.67	1949	$54.92	$1.98
1944	$46.08	$1.58	1950	$59.33	$2.06

Assuming a working week of six days and the average weight of a bushel of wheat to be 60 pounds, reduce these figures to "pounds of wheat per day." Are wages in 1945 higher or lower than wages in 1939 and 1940?

3. The following table gives the increase in circulating money and in total bank deposits (both in billions of dollars) between 1939 and 1950:

Year	Money in Circulation	Total Bank Deposits	Year	Money in Circulation	Total Bank Deposits
1939	7.6	64.2	1945	28.5	151.0
1940	8.7	70.8	1946	29.0	159.2
1941	11.2	78.1	1947	28.9	153.2
1942	15.4	82.7	1948	28.2	156.4
1943	20.4	107.2	1949	27.6	156.5
1944	25.3	128.6	1950	27.7	170.7

Using 1939 = 100 reduce these figures to index numbers as well as the wages given in Problem 2. Now graph your three series on the same chart. What conclusions can one draw from this comparison?

4. The following table gives the index numbers (base = 1716-17) of commodity prices in Paris during the John Law expansion. (Data from Hamilton: *loc. cit.*) Graph these data and compare the French expansion with our own in the period around 1929.

Year	Jan.	Feb.	Mar.	April	May	June	July	Aug.	Sept.	Oct.	Nov.	Dec.
1711	123.2	114.4	115.1	108.7	111.1	105.8	104.0	115.6	113.3	111.9	112.0	124.6
1712	134.9	133.5	126.5	131.1	124.3	125.5	126.1	118.7	128.6	127.5	142.6	141.3
1713	146.9	147.4	138.6	142.2	137.7	137.7	138.4	144.1	139.7	139.1	154.6	159.7
1714	163.7	165.2	168.1	154.7	149.3	141.5	145.8	146.8	155.3	149.0	150.6	148.4
1715	139.6	128.4	123.3	118.9	113.4	115.5	106.3	106.2	108.7	108.9	104.2	104.5
1716	102.7	102.9	100.1	101.6	100.7	99.4	98.1	94.6	99.7	107.5	107.6	105.5
1717	105.8	104.4	100.3	100.9	98.0	98.6	96.0	95.5	93.7	93.4	94.7	95.9
1718	96.0	97.6	93.8	90.6	92.7	92.3	96.8	102.9	100.6	107.5	109.4	112.1
1719	111.6	114.3	107.5	109.0	106.9	111.7	116.1	119.7	124.9	120.1	129.3	136.3
1720	171.1	171.1	180.4	191.2	189.7	183.8	190.6	190.5	203.7	199.6	198.8	164.2
1721	162.8	149.4	142.6	137.6	130.1	132.3	124.9	133.4	136.0	134.5	133.0	137.2
1722	140.7	136.6	139.2	149.1	139.7	136.6	134.4	138.7	143.8	151.8	153.5	160.0
1723	161.7	156.8	151.4	156.7	163.9	156.3	156.6	159.5	163.0	174.8	175.2	180.4
1724	181.8	178.9	166.9	171.9	162.9	149.5	142.8	144.5	152.0	159.4	163.3	169.0
1725	169.7	161.4	163.7	151.1	146.6	144.1	147.0	144.6	164.2	159.4	155.7	158.0

8. Economic Variation and Politics.

It is clear from the evidence presented in earlier sections that the problem of price-change is intimately connected with the course of political events. But we should emphasize again that the variation in price is not the cause of the correlated political change; *it is an indicator of some deep-seated movement which is occurring in the economic structure.* It is this change that affects both the level of prices and the behavior of the political state.

In view of the importance of the economic factor in political events it has occurred to several investigators that this fact might be used to advantage in studying the changes that have taken place in the party control of various governments. A serious investigation of this problem was undertaken in 1944 by J. Åkerman in Sweden with respect to political changes in the United States and in certain countries in Europe.* This study was extended by S. Grönhagen in 1951 who investigated the shifting patterns of political control in the British government during the century from 1850 to 1950.[†] L. H. Bean in works published in 1940 and in 1948 considered the effects of the business index upon both presidential and congressional elections.[‡] H. F. Gosnell, whose extensive analysis of voting behavior in city and state elections has never been superseded, compared the influence of foreign crises with the effect of the business cycle in national elections, and reached the conclusion: "It is therefore difficult to evaluate the relative pulling power of these two influences — internal economic conditions and international relations — upon the voters."[§] The author of the present work examined the problem in 1941[||] and S. S. Nilson in 1950 made an extensive survey of the materialistic factor upon historical trends with special reference to voting behavior.**

---

* *Ekonomisk teorie*, Vol. 2, Lund, 1944, pp. 123-124; *Ekonomiskt skeende och politiska förändringar*, Lund, 1946; "Political Economic Cycles," *Kuklos*, Vol. 1, 1947, pp. 107-117.

[†] *Ekonomiskt Förlopp och allmänna val i Storbritannian 1850-1950*. Lund, 1951, 104 pp.

[‡] *Ballot Behavior and How to Predict Elections*. Washington, D. C., 1940; *How to Predict Elections*. New York, 1948, x + 196 pp.

[§] *Grass Roots Politics*. Washington, D. C., 1942. See pages 9-10.

[||] *The Analysis of Economic Time Series*. Bloomington, Ind., 1941.

** *Histoire et sciences politiques*. Bergen, 1950, 162 pp.

POLITICAL SCIENCE AND ECONOMICS

In order to appraise the influence of the economic factor in political trends we shall examine the changes that have occurred in the party control of government in the United States. These shifts of power we shall compare with the changes in certain basic economic series and thus explore the proposition that as business goes so goes political opinion.

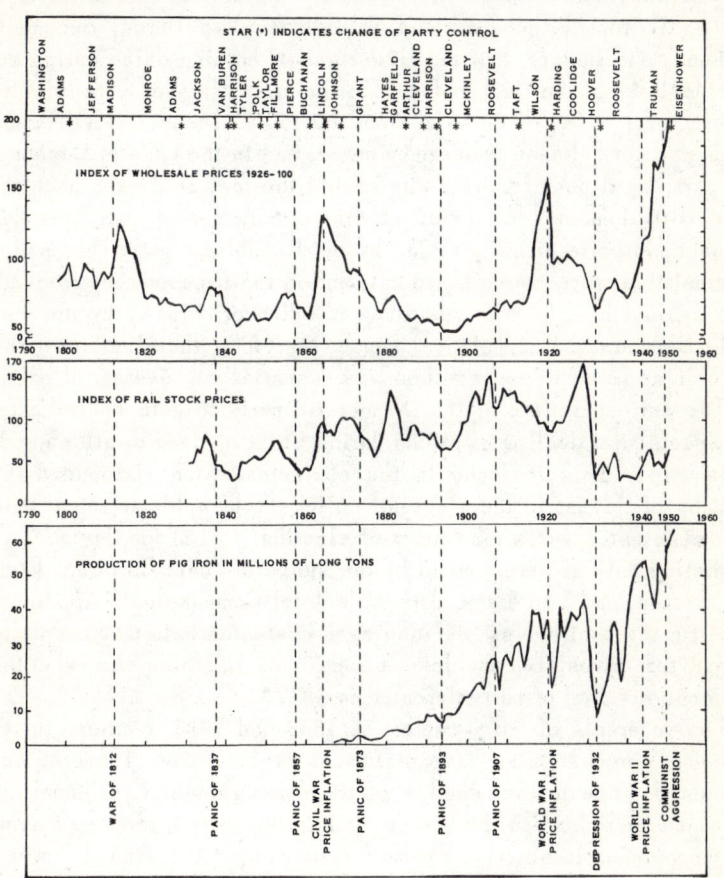

Figure 65. Interaction between Political Events and Economic Variations.

The general truth of this thesis is illustrated by Figure 65 which shows the changes in party control that have occurred between 1790 and 1950 together with three basic economic series. The first of these is wholesale prices, the second rail stock prices, and the third the production of pig iron. From this figure we observe that changes in political parties have occurred for the most part at the bottom of a severe drop in prices or during a protracted decline. Of the 15 such changes, excluding the changes occasioned by the deaths of William Henry Harrison and Lincoln, ten occurred during or at the bottom of such depression periods. It will be observed also that four of the most thoroughly repudiated American presidents, Van Buren, Buchanan, Johnson, and Hoover, had the misfortune of holding office during severe declines of the price index. Van Buren and Hoover were rejected by electoral votes of 60 to 234 and 59 to 472 respectively. Neither Buchanan nor Johnson was renominated, and in the case of Buchanan his party went out of power. Why should this not also have been the case with Johnson? A survey of this stormy period indicates that Johnson, in spite of his election by the Republican party, had had a long political career as a Democrat, and in the impeachment proceedings against him, he was sustained in office principally by the vote of 12 Democrats. In a political sense, therefore, the election of the Republican Grant to succeed him was essentially a reversal of party.

The curious failure of the Democratic party to gain control after the spectacular decline of prices during Grant's administration needs explanation. This is found in the confusion which surrounded the election of Hayes. In the electoral college Tilden, his opponent, had 184 uncontested votes, one short of election, to 163 for Hayes. Two conflicting ballots were sent in by the states of South Carolina, Florida, Oregon, and Louisiana. The "Electoral Commission," appointed to settle the controversy, decided each contested ballot by a vote of 7 to 8 for Hayes. By so close a margin as this was the expected economic reversal of party defeated in 1877!

The reversals of party control in 1853 and 1913, contrary to the economic forecast, also have historical explanations. The first was undoubtedly due to the shadow of the coming conflict, economic in large measure, between the slavery and anti-slavery interests. Favoring compromise in slavery, Fillmore failed to get the nomination and Pierce was chosen by an electoral vote of 254 to 42. In 1913 the split in the Republican pary, occasioned by the feud between Theodore Roosevelt and Taft, allowed the minority party to win. The popular vote for Roosevelt and Taft was 7,610,000; that for Wilson was 6,286,000. The electoral vote was 435 for Wilson, 88 for Roosevelt, and 8 for Taft.

The re-election of Monroe in 1821, during a period of price deflation, is a curious incident since it was nearly unanimous, one electoral vote only being cast against him. His second term was called "the era of good feeling." But the curve of industrial production for that period shows that the country was emerging rapidly from the effects of the deflation in prices. Trade was expanding and not unlikely the financial difficulties occasioned by the price decline were offset by the rapidly enlarging economic invasion of western territory.

There was a spectacular vindication in 1948 of the general thesis that an administration is not turned out, except under unusual circumstances, when the economic indexes are high. As we have shown earlier in Chapter 4, all polls prior to the election of that date were unanimous in agreeing that the Democratic party would be defeated. Estimates of the percentage of the total vote ranged from 37.5 to 45. Newspapers throughout the country regarded the actual counting of votes a formality necessary to confirm the general opinion. But there was one great factor which was not taken into account by these forecasters. The price index in 1948 was higher than in any year in recent history; industrial production and the production of pig iron had reached levels only slightly lower than those which had prevailed during the war; the great building boom was on. Since the international complications that were to be so important in the next election had not yet developed, there appeared to be no issue which transcended that presented by the picture of the great economic machine working at maximum capacity. When the votes were finally counted this factor had again prevailed and the percentage of the total vote cast by the Democratic party was 49.6 and that by the Republican party was 45.2.

That factors other than the economic can influence, and even decide, elections is a proposition that has been demonstrated on numerous occasions. One of these was the election of 1952. Business was again at a high level, but part of this activity was occasioned by an unpopular war. The "police action" in Korea, initiated in 1950, had developed into a protracted war by 1952 with no signs of a successful termination in sight. There is no way to separate from one another the factors which influenced voting behavior on this occasion, but it is clear that one not present in the election of 1948 was dominant in the election of 1952. The most obvious difference was the international situation. The Soviet threat, which had only begun to appear by 1948, was in full bloom by 1952. The electorate was shocked by the evidence of communist infiltration in the government. The abrupt dismissal of General McArthur, whose principal fault seemed to be that he advocated a policy which he believed would end the Korean War, was a matter of bitter controversy. Since none of these issues can be put to statistical test, one can merely observe that one or more factors other than the economic must have prevailed since the high business level was not sufficient to win the election for the party in power.

Another factor, one that is measurable, should be considered in connection with this election. As we have shown in Chapter 8, the distribution of income has had at times a very great influence in political affairs. One should observe that the ratio which measures the concentration of income had steadily declined from a value of 0.45 in 1930 to a value of 0.33 in 1948. Such a decline cannot be achieved without violent opposition from the classes most affected and the nature of this opposition has been frequently voiced in the public press. Since the classes most concerned have control of great wealth, it is natural that this influence should continue to grow as the concentration declined and should ultimately reach a point where it will exert great political pressure. Whether a concentration ratio of 0.33 is sufficiently low to cause a political revolution is of course debatable, but that it worked against the administration is easy to believe.

When the votes were finally counted the magnitude of the Republican victory was measured by the fact that the Republican candidate had received 55.1 per cent of the total vote and the Democratic candidate 44.3 per cent. That party lines were crossed by many voters, thus indicating the existence of factors other than the economic, is shown by the concurrent vote in the contests for governors in 29 states in which Republican candidates were opposed by Democratic candidates. This excluded the gubernatorial elections in Louisiana, where one Democrat ran against another, and in Texas, where there was a coalition ticket. In the 29 contests a total vote of 31,242,315 was cast, approximately one half of the total vote polled in the presidential race. It is a matter of much interest in the interpretation of this election that, of the gubernatorial vote, the Republicans secured only 49.7 per cent and the Democrats 50.3 per cent. In these same states the presidential vote was 56.4 per cent for Eisenhower and 43.6 per cent for Stevenson. Could the primarily party vote of the gubernatorial contests be attributed mainly to the economic factor?

From the evidence which we have given above, superficial as our analysis has been, it is clear that the economic factor plays an important role in the changing patterns of politics. In a study of congressional elections, L. H. Bean has reached much the same conclusion, which he summarizes as follows:

"If business activity remains unchanged between a presidential and an off-year election, normal political apathy causes the party in power to lose about 8 per cent of the two-party membership in the lower house, or 35 seats... In a mid-term election, the losses of the dominant party might be checked and cut in half if business activity has advanced 20 points since the previous election, or the losses might be doubled if business has declined 20 points. If the business index remains unchanged between presidential elections, the party in power neither gains or loses, but an advance of 20 points tends to give that party 35 to 40 additional seats. A similar decline in business tends to shift that many seats to the opposition."

A similar confirmation of the general thesis is found by J. Åkerman, who studied the economic effects upon both American and European elections. His conclusions are contained in the following statement:

"While studying French economic development in the period between the great depression around 1930 and the second World War, the author was struck by the close correlation between cycles of prosperity and depression on the one hand and the duration of different cabinets on the other. Each cabinet term seemed to be closely connected with an economic cycle, the cabinet being formed when an economic depression had deposed a worn-out prime minister and his colleagues and — after a brief period of recovery, followed by crisis and renewed depression — having to resign in the face of difficulties arising out of unemployment and business disorganization.

"This type of political economic cycle has apparently its causation in the domain of economics; the political events are primarily a function of the economic pattern though the government tries to stabilize financial and economic conditions, and for a brief period may suceed in doing so.

"In order to ascertain whether this connection is also to be found in other countries, an investigation was carried out concerning England (1855-1945), the United States (1865-1945), Germany (1871-1945), and Sweden (1866-1945). The result of this analysis, conducted on statistical and historical lines, may be summarized as follows: All general economic depressions in England — with the exception of the short period of unemployment after the crisis of 1907 — lead to cabinet crises and a change of the party in power. Only the cabinet crisis of 1859 occurs during a period of undeniable prosperity. — In the United States the presidential elections as a rule involve a change in party control when the votes are cast during a depression and maintenance of the party in office when the votes are cast during periods of prosperity... — In Germany there is a much less pronounced, yet a noticeable connection between business cycles and the tenure of chancellorship 1871-1914. — In Sweden only one third of the cabinet crises caused by majority changes can be accounted for in this way."

In conclusion it should be observed that while changes in political control appear to be sensitive to economic conditions, there is little evidence to show that the converse is also true, namely, that business cycles are correlated with changes in political power.

PROBLEMS

1. Black Friday, according to the Dictionary, is "any of various Fridays in which disastrous events occurred in the United States, as September 24, 1869, and September 19, 1873." Are these dates in evidence in Figure 65? What happened on each of these dates?

2. Referring to Figure 65, explain the defeat of Van Buren. What was the event that precipitated the price decline?

3. Explain the defeat of Buchanan by referring to Figure 65. What were the circumstances of the price decline?

9. *Concluding Summary.*

In the preceding sections of this chapter certain evidence has been presented in favor of the thesis that political events of major historical importance are closely associated with economic movements. It was also argued that for this reason an important segment of history is subject to description by numerical data and can thus be investigated by mathematical methods. The mechanistic theory of history, therefore, which has been properly distrusted because of its relationship to the inflammatory ideas of Marx and through lack of scientific scrutiny of its postulates, may now well become a proper subject for the attention of the scientist.

Since the cycles of history are long cycles and since some trends may endure for several centuries, it has been shown that there is great need for data over long periods of time. Short business cycles of three or four years are of minor importance in the interpretation of great historical movements. But the past is very jealous of its records and the labor of many men has been required in the construction of such time series as we now possess.

Most fundamental of all series is that of the growth of population, for this series shows more clearly than any other what has happened to nations and to groups of nations in the course of known history. The basic importance of man's conquest of disease is illustrated by the curve of population far more clearly than by any other way. Moreover, the political difficulties which have been brought about by this conquest are also apparent. Although the matter was only touched upon briefly in the text, it is clear that such political institutions as the League of Nations, the United Nations, and other similar organizations that may arise in the future, are doomed to failure in their control of events unless some solution is found to stabilize populations and their food supplies.

Next to population growth in political importance are the indexes of price. For these series are apparently measures of the health, or lack of health, of the body politic. Sufficient evidence was adduced to show how history can be interpreted by the variations in these price movements, and how even political changes can be foretold when the changes in the series are of sufficient magnitude. More evidence of their importance will be given in the next chapter.

From the brief resume of the subject given in this chapter it is clear that much remains to be done. Great intervals of time are without adequate data. Perhaps these can never be recovered. But such antiquities as the Doomsday Book, prepared under the direction of William the Conqueror (1027-1087), which has been discussed in the last chapter, can form a corner stone for the Middle Ages much as the edict of Diocletian has served the period of the Roman Empire. If political history is studied in this manner it is possible that some day one will be able to scan the fundamental statistical series of history and relate in a scientific manner the unfolding events of the past.

CHAPTER 10
THE PROBLEM OF CONFLICT

1. *The Problem*

UNFORTUNATELY the phenomenon of war, despite numerous schemes to eliminate it as a method for settling both internal and international disputes, is still the most important pattern in human relationships. In the past, if not in the recent present, the general attitude has not been far removed from the one set forth by Sir Francis Bacon (1561-1626), in his essay: "On the True Greatness of Kingdoms and Estates," wherein he says:

"But above all, for empire and greatness, it importeth most that a nation do profess arms as their principal honor, study, and occupation. For the things which we formerly have spoken of are but habilitations towards arms; and what is habilitation without intention and act?...

"No body can be healthful without exercise, neither natural body nor politic; and certainly to a kingdom or estate, a just and honorable war is the true exercise. A civil war is like the heat of a fever; but a foreign war is like the heat of exercise, and serveth to keep the body in health; for in a slothful peace, both courages will effeminate and manners corrupt. But howsoever it be for happiness, without all question, for greatness it maketh, to be still for the most part in arms; and the strength of a veteran army (though it be a chargeable business) always on foot is that which commonly giveth the law, or at least the reputation, amongst all neighbor states."

Since wars are the most fruitful causes of profound changes both in forms of government and in the social well-being of people, no study of political science would be complete without some investigation of these events. Our problem is not to discuss the ethical or philosophical implications of conflict, but rather to find those elements which can be represented and studied by statistical means. We shall begin with an investigation of the effect of war upon the economic structure of belligerent nations.

2. *War and Price Inflation*

War is the great inflator and without any exceptions in history we find an advance in prices as the most obvious economic effect of the conflict. Often, although not always, large wars begin near the top of a long trend of advancing trade. The nations are thus in a prosperous phase of their economic life and can hazard the contest with some hope of success. Perhaps it is the very aggression of economic interests which precipitates the war. Thus, in 1914 there was never a more prosperous moment in the history of nations. All the economic indexes had advanced since the depression period of the early nineties. Currencies of the major powers were stable; trade between the nations was vigorous; and the peoples of the world were beginning to enjoy the fruits of the great scientific discoveries of the preceding fifty years. Never was there a period in history when a major war seemed to be more inauspicious for the good of nations; but, for the same reason, there was never a moment when the nations could hope more successfully to wage a war.

The economic course of war can be traced advantageously through the curve of prices. The reactions of a war upon the economic systems involved in it, and hence the intensity of the struggle itself, can be measured with some accuracy by this index. Therefore, we shall advance the thesis that the intensity of war upon a belligerent nation is measured by the following ratio:

$$W(t) = \frac{P(t) - P_0}{P_0},$$

where P_0 is the level of prices at the beginning of the war and $P(t)$ is the price which prevails at the top of the war inflation. This top is usually not attained for several years after the actual belligerency has ceased. This *war-index* gives the values contained in the table on the next page for certain conflicts where the curve of prices has been determined.

The intensity of a war depends upon a number of factors. The first of these is the ratio of the number of men actually engaged in the war to the total population. A second is the duration of the conflict. A third is the ratio of the area occupied by enemy troops to the total area of the country, and the time of this occupation. But all these factors are represented in the index of prices, and hence this becomes a measure of the intensity of the struggle. This index is

Conflict*	Period of Inflation	Country	Initial Price Index (P_0)	$P(t)$	$W(t)$
Second Punic War	218 B.C.-201 B.C.	Rome	100	400	3.00
Napoleonic Wars	1797-1810	West. Europe	80	380	3.75
War of 1812	1811-1814	U.S.	86	125	0.45
Civil War	1861-1865	U.S. (North)	93	225	1.43
Franco-Prussian	1870-1873	Germany	92	120	0.30
Franco-Prussian	1870-1873	England	96	111	0.16
Revolutionary War	1775-1780	U.S.	75	232	2.09
Mexican War	1846-1847	U.S.	83	95	0.14
Spanish-American War	1898-1899	U.S.	70	83	0.19
World War I	1914-1920	U.S.	100	244	1.44
World War I	1914-1920	England	85	251	1.95
World War I	1914-1926	France	100	703	6.03
World War I	1914-1924	Germany	100	∞	∞
World War II	1939-1947	U.S.	100	206	1.06

thus a kind of barometer which responds to the impact of the various economic factors upon the commonwealth itself.

In the victorious country material goods become scarce; the supply of money has been increased to support the armed forces; industry has been disrupted as the factors of production have been changed from those of peace-time activity to those essential in maintaining the war machine. All these factors are inflationary and can be measured, at least roughly, by the rise in the level of prices. In the defeated country these disruptive influences are multiplied and the increase in prices is generally greater than that observed in the victorious country. If the defeat is one of universal disaster, the price rise may actually attain such heights as to be essentially infinite. This was the case in Germany after World War I and has been observed in less conspicious examples, such as the Chinese inflation after World War II.

The general pattern of the war inflation is given in Figure 66. There is an initial phase in which the price shows a mild inflationary

---

* This table has been constructed from various price indexes. For the United States the monthly wholesale price index of Warren-Pearson and the Bureau of Labor Statistics has been used.

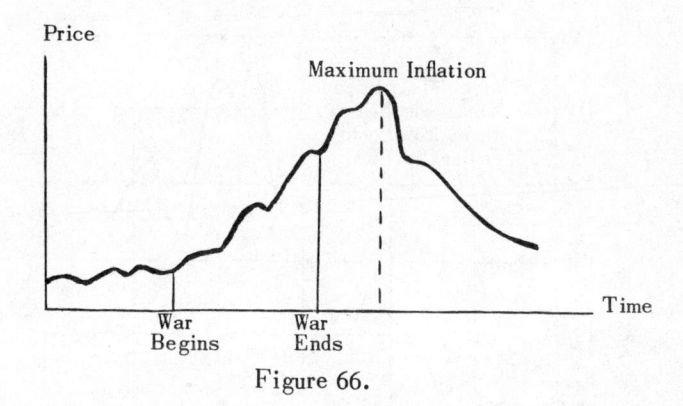

Price / Maximum Inflation / War Begins / War Ends / Time

Figure 66.

movement. The index then begins to move upward with increasing acceleration, although occasional brief recessions are often observed. The termination of the war does not end the inflationary movement, since the impact of new monetary issues has not expended itself. There is generally a sharp drop in prices after the maximum has been attained, and this may be of such magnitude and character that conditions approximating a major business panic may prevail for a short time. The price decline usually continues for a number of years after the conflict with short periods of business stability stopping its downward progress. The termination of the trend is usually a period of major business depression. No conspicuous economic decline was observed in the United States following World War II, but this was due in part to two factors: (a) the building cycle, which had been long retarded during the war, and (b) the Korean conflict, which tended to keep the economy on a war basis.

3. *Patterns of Prices in Modern Wars.*

In order that we may understand better the relationship between the intensity of war and the inflation in prices which it generates, we shall examine two patterns. The first of these is from the American Civil War and the second is from the first World War in its relationship to the United States.

In the first graph, Figure 67, we show the index of American wholesale prices from 1861 to 1866 by months. In Figure 6 of the first chapter one sees the inflation of this period in its relationship to the

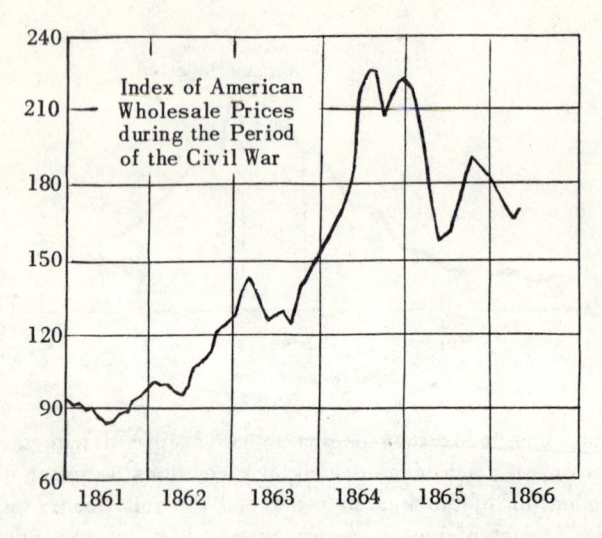

Figure 67.

prices that preceded and the prices that followed, but the actual details of the movement are lacking. These are revealed in the month by month chart of the inflationary progress.

If we examine the chart with attention, we see sudden recessions in the prices. Thus, such a recession began in March, 1863 and terminated in September of that same year. The cause of the decline is not clear, but such dramatic events had taken place as Lincoln's Emancipation Proclamation on January 1, Lee's defeat at Gettysburg, July 1 to July 3, and Grant's capture of Vicksburg on July 4. A similar decline appears between September and October of 1864, following the news of Sherman's march to Atlanta. Lee surrendered in April of the next year and the price decline had already anticipated the end of the war. The characteristic reaction to a long drop in prices is seen at the end of the graph.

In Figure 68 we see a similar pattern for the prices of World War I. The effect of the war upon prices in the United States was not felt until the end of 1915, but with increasing tension between this country and Germany in 1916, which resulted in a declaration of war in April, 1917, the general rise in prices began. With minor recessions this inflation continued until August, 1920, when a sudden collapse

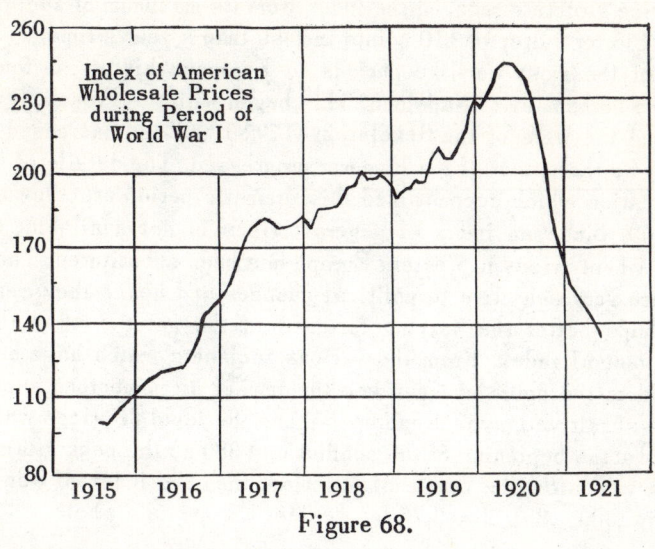

THE PROBLEM OF CONFLICT

Index of American Wholesale Prices during Period of World War I

Figure 68.

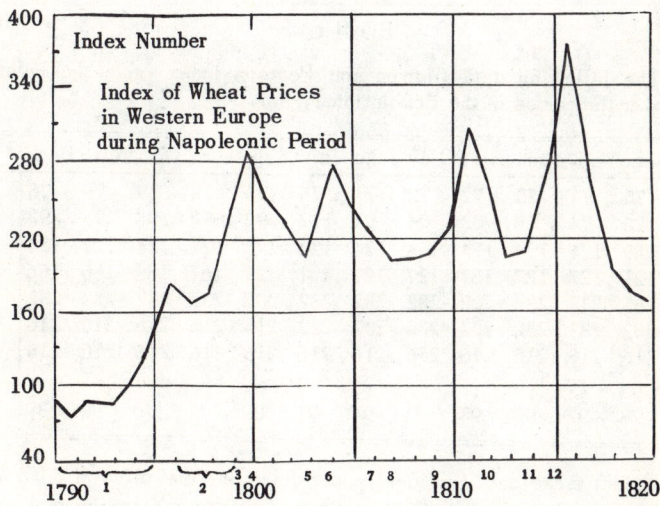

Index Number

Index of Wheat Prices in Western Europe during Napoleonic Period

1. Period of French Revolution; 2. Napoleon's Italian and Egyptian Campaigns; 3. Napoleon Made First Consul; 4. Marengo; 5. France Renews War with England; 6. Napoleon Crowned Emperor; 7. Austerlitz; 8. Jena; 9. Treaty of Vienna; 10. Retreat from Moscow; 11. Elba - Allies Enter Paris; 12. Waterloo.

Figure 69.

of the price structure reduced the index from its maximum of 245 to a level of 135, or a drop of 110 points in less than a year's time.

One of the most war-like periods in European history is found during the supremacy of Napoleon. This began with the French Revolution and the Wars of the Revolution (1792-1800) and increased in intensity as the career of the Emperor progressed. The details of the price inflation which accompanied this dramatic period are shown in Figure 69. Since an index of general prices is not available, the index of wheat prices in Western Europe has been substituted. These prices are very sensitive to political changes and hence they measure perhaps better the varying fortunes of the great conflict than a more general index. From the various incidents which have been appended to the figure one can see the impact of momentous events upon the sensitive curve. If one uses 80 as the level of prices which prevailed at the beginning of the conflict and 380 as the peak attained nearly a year after the Battle of Waterloo, then the index of war intensity is $(380 - 80)/80 = 3.75$ for Western Europe as a whole.

PROBLEMS

1. The following data (Warren and Pearson index) give the index of prices over the period of the Revolutionary War:

Year	Jan.	Feb.	Mar.	Apr.	May	June	July	Aug.	Sept.	Oct.	Nov.	Dec.	Avrg.
1775	75	74	72	72	72	71	74	75	78	79	79	76	75
1776	75	74	78	82	84	91	92	92	93	93	93	93	86
1777	109	124	124	124	124	124	124	124	124	124	124	124	123
1778	121	127	127	127	127	127	127	127	167	166	166	166	140
1779	165	232	232	232	232	232	232	232	232	232	232	232	226
1780	232	232	232	232	232	232	232	216	216	216	216	216	225
1781	216	216	216	216	216	216	216	216	216	216	216	216	216
...	...	...	...	...	...	...	...	...	...	...	...	...	...
1785	97	97	95	93	93	94	91	89	90	90	90	89	92

Represent these data graphically and determine the value of $W(t)$. What significance has the phrase "not worth a continental" in the problem of prices during this period? What additional facts might one want to know about the currency used at this time?

2. The price inflation observed during the period of the War of 1812 is shown by the following index of wholesale prices (Warren and Pearson) index:

Year	Jan.	Feb.	Mar.	Apr.	May	June	July	Aug.	Sept.	Oct.	Nov.	Dec.	Avrg.
1812	127	129	128	126	122	125	128	133	135	137	142	144	131
1813	150	152	153	157	160	158	159	161	164	171	178	186	162
1814	186	184	182	182	179	179	178	177	177	183	187	193	182
1815	193	185	176	166	164	165	163	165	166	166	168	163	170
1816	160	160	158	151	150	150	150	149	148	144	145	149	151

Represent these indexes graphically and determine the value of the war intensity. How does the price inflation of this war compare with that of the Revolution? with that of the Civil War?

3. The index numbers used in Problems 1 and 2 are from the table of values which uses as a base 1910-1914 = 100. What inference can be made about the stability of the level of American prices from this fact?

4. The Bureau of Labor Statistics publishes an index of wholesale prices which has 1926 = 100 as its base. In terms of this base the average index of prices for the five-year period 1910-1914 is 68.46. By what factor must the indexes given in Problems 1 and 2 be multiplied in order to conform to the base 1926 = 100? Show that this change in level would not change the value of $W(t)$. Prove in general that $W(t)$ is independent of the base used.

4. *The Frequency of War*

As we have seen in the first chapter, Thomas Hobbes regarded government as a protective device established by man to preserve himself in a world the natural tendency of which was toward war. This thesis, man's propensity to war, was naturally subject to bitter attack. But the statistical facts, both before and since the time of Hobbes, give overwhelming evidence of the correctness of his position. However repugnant the idea of conflict may be to the higher aspirations of man, there is no doubt that the tendency of society has been to persist toward a state of war. Periods of peace are uneasy interludes between the periods of conflicts which have ended and those which are soon to begin.

In the following table we have listed some of the major wars which have involved the pattern of European civilization and its closely related American development over the past twenty-five centuries. From this abbreviated list it is clear that in the nearly twenty-five centuries covered by the table there has been a succession of great wars. With the development of European culture, the expansion

POLITICAL STATISTICS

Years	Conflict	Years	Conflict
B. C.		1337-1453	Hundred Years' War
		1521-1544	Wars between Emperor Charles and Francis I of France
512-478	Persian Conquests of Greece	1524-1525	Peasants' War
431-404	Peloponnesian War	1556-1609	Spanish Wars
334-323	Conquests of Alexander the Great	1618-1648	Thirty Years' War
		1648-1659	Spanish-French War
264-241	First Punic War	1655-1660	First Northern War
218-201	Second Punic War	1667-1678	Dutch Wars
149-146	Third Punic War	1672-1679	First Coalition against Louis XIV
133- 82	Period of Civil War in Roman Republic	1688-1697	War of Palatinate — Second Coalition against Louis XIV
58- 52	Period of Wars of Julius Caesar	1700-1721	Second Northern War
49- 45		1701-1714	War of Spanish Succession
A. D.		1718-1720	Quadruple Alliance against Spain
180- 280	Period of Empirial Conflicts in Rome	1733-1738	War of Polish Succession
		1740-1748	War of Austrian Succession
447- 451	Conquests of Attila	1756-1763	Seven Years' War
624- 646	Period of the Conquests of the Saracens	1775-1783	American Revolution
673- 677		1792-1802	Wars of French Revolution
711- 732		1805-1815	Napoleonic Wars
1066-1070	Norman Conquest of England	1854-1856	Crimean War
		1861-1865	American Civil War
1096-1099	Crusade I	1866-1866	Austro-Prussian War
1147-1149	Crusade II	1870-1871	Franco-Prussian War
1189-1192	Crusade III	1904-1905	Russo-Japanese War
1202-1204	Crusade IV	1914-1918	World War I
1216-1220	Crusade V	1936-1939	Spanish Civil War
1227-1229	Crusade VI	1937-1945	Sino-Japanese War
1248-1254	Crusade VII	1939-1945	World War II
1270-1272	Crusade VIII	1950-	Korean War

of the arts, and sciences, the number and the size of wars have increased rather than diminished. A table of the wars of modern civilization between 1480 and 1941 has been prepared by Quincy Wright in his *Study of War* (1942). To this he has appended a statistical summary of the number of battles participated in by the contending forces. The grand total is 278 wars and 2,759 battles in the 461 years covered by the study, or an average of six wars per decade and 60 battles.* Since the average durations of the major wars in the four successive centuries beginning with the seventeenth were respectively 14, 8, 6, and 4 years,† it is evident that there could have been scarcely a significant period of time during which a state of belligerency did not prevail in the world.

The tendency to war which we have observed in modern civilization prevailed also in the less enlightened period of the ancients. This is attested by the fact that the doors of the Temple of Janus, which were opened during war and shut during times of peace, (*Livy* i, 19), were closed only four times before the beginning of the Christian era. More specifically, P. A. Sorokin (see Section 5) counted 71 Roman wars between 390 B. C. and 476 A. D.

The following table (abridged from Wright) summarizes the modern conflicts by comparable periods:

Period	1480-1550	1550-1600	1600-1650	1650-1700	1700-1750	1750-1800	1800-1850	1850-1900	1900-1941	Total
No. of wars										
Mainly in Europe	28	31	31	26	18	13	15	14	11	187
Outside Europe	4	0	3	4	0	7	26	34	13	91
Total	32	31	34	30	18	20	41	48	24	278
No. of battles										
Fought in Europe	39	48	116	119	276	496	432	130	744	2,400
Outside Europe	9	0	0	0	0	13	11	78	248	359
Total	48	48	116	119	276	509	443	208	992	2,759

* The sources from which these summaries were made include the following: Gaston-Bodart: *Militar-historisches Kriegslexicon* (1618-1905), Wien and Leipzig, 1908; Thomas B. Harbottle: *Dictionary of Battles from the Earliest Date to the Present Time*, London, 1904; Charles Oman: *A History of the Art of War in the Sixteenth Century*, New York, 1937. The most comprehensive work yet prepared on all phases of conflict is without doubt Quincy Wright's *A Study of War*, Vols. 1 and 2, Chicago, 1942, 1552 + xxiii + xvii pp.

† Wright: *op. cit.*, p. 650.

Period	1480-1550	1550-1600	1600-1650	1650-1700	1700-1750	1750-1800	1800-1850	1850-1900	1900-1941	Total
Aver. Duration of wars Mainly in										
Europe	3.5	4.9	8.2	4.9	4.9	3.6	3.7	1.1	3.7	---
Outside Europe	1.0	0.0	1.0	7.2	0.0	3.0	4.1	2.8	3.6	---
All Wars	3.8	4.9	7.6	5.2	4.9	3.4	4.2	2.7	3.6	---

In his classification of wars Wright found that conflicts fall natrally into four broad categories which he designated by the letters B, C, D, and I and defined as follows: "B = Balance-of-power war, in sense of a war among state members of the modern family of nations; C = Civil war, in sense of war within a state member of the modern family of nations; D = Defensive war, in sense of a war to defend modern civilization against an alien culture; I = Imperial war, in sense of a war to expand modern civilization at the expense of an alien culture." The Thirty Years' War and World Wars I and II are examples of the first category; the Peasants' War, the American Civil War, the Italian Revolution of 1860-61 belong to category C; the Saracen conquest of Europe, the ancient Greek wars against the Persians, the various Ottoman wars of modern times belong to class D; the Crusades, the conquests of Alexander the Great, the conquest of Peru in 1531, the Zulu war of 1879, the Boxer Expedition of 1900 and the more recent Italo-Ethiopian War are examples of category I. The wars since 1480 have been characterized by Wright as follows:

Type of War	1480-1550	1550-1600	1600-1650	1650-1700	1700-1750	1750-1800	1800-1850	1850-1900	1900-1941	Totals
B	18	12	13	14	13	10	17	23	15	135
C	4	14	14	8	5	5	11	12	5	78
D	6	5	4	4	0	0	2	0	0	21
I	4	0	3	4	0	5	11	13	4	44
Totals	32	31	34	30	18	20	41	48	24	278

It is instructive to observe from this table that contests over the balance of power between nations are the causes of nearly half the wars (48.6%) and that internal instability in nations accounts for more than one-fourth (28%) of the conflicts. Defensive wars against alien cultures are only 7.6% of the total and imperial conquests are approximately twice as frequent (15.8%).

Arguments for the creation of a super-state among the nations of the earth should take account of these interesting figures. For in such a super-state the balance-of-power wars would then assume the status of civil conflicts. But few states, ancient or modern, have been able to avoid the dangers of internal wars.

PROBLEMS

1. Determine the average length of major wars from the data on major conflicts given above. Compute the same average by centuries and compare with the figures quoted above from Wright.

2. Determine from the list of major wars given in the text the average length of time between them. Compute the same average by centuries and compare with the following estimates of Wright: 6, 8, 33, and 20.

3. In the literature of conflict there is frequent mention of the "fifty-year war cycle." Do American wars conform to such a pattern? What is the evidence obtained from the period of the Punic wars? What measure of belief can one put in the existence of such a cycle?

4. Wright gives the number of wars and the total number of years in each century, beginning with the 12th, during which one or more of the following countries were involved in conflict: France, Austria, Great Britain, Russia, Prussia, Spain, the Netherlands, Sweden, Denmark, Turkey, and Poland. These figures are contained in the following table:

Century	12th	13th	14th	15th	16th	17th	18th	19th	20th*	Total
Total Duration	90.5	85.0	108.0	320.5	609.0	661.5	400.0	297.0	297.0	2868.5
No. of Wars	26	46.5	42.5	134	211.5	239.5	149	215	74	1138

* The 20th century includes wars only to 1930.

Compute the average duration of wars in each of these centuries and determine whether there has been a conspicuous change in their length. Find the standard deviation of the average duration. Can any conclusions be drawn from this figure?

5. *The Size of Wars.*

It will be clear from the evidence presented on preceding pages of this chapter that war is the most conspicuous phenomenon in political science. It is found with varying intensities in almost every decade and among all people. The vistas of history supply nearly an unbroken sequence of declarations of war, endless campaigns, and treaties of peace designed to end the sequence, but never succeeding in their purpose. Yet in spite of this continuous stream of high political adventure, the data which we have on the size and cost of wars are among the most inaccurate and unsatisfactory that we possess. Generals have left only meager estimates of the size of their armies; and governments have tended to conceal the magnitude of their war budgets.

It is possible, however, to estimate the gross effects of war and several attempts have been made to determine the size of armies and the numbers of men under arms during periods of major conflict. The most comprehensive studies of this problem are those made by Pitirim A. Sorokin, published in Volume 3 of his *Social and Cultural Dynamics* (1937), and by J. C. King, which appears in Volume 1 of Wright's *Study of War* (1941). That the figures of these authorities differ significantly from one another even for wars of comparably recent times is an indication of the difficulty of estimating from available records. But in spite of these discrepancies and the obvious errors of the data they are valuable to us in their indication of the trend of war both in ancient and in modern times.

Therefore, with full recognition of the errors of estimate, we shall present the accompanying data taken mainly from Sorokin, but with some modification and addition, since his figures cover the longer span of time and are presumably consistent with one another. Their graphical representation is given in Figures 70, 71, and 72.

Estimate of the Number of Men Under Arms and the Number of Casualties for Each Quarter of a Century

I. Estimates for Ancient Greece.

Period	No. of Men	Casualties	Period	No. of Men	Casualties
B. C.			325-301	536,000	26,800
500-476	500,000	25,000	300-276	360,000	14,400
475-451	752,000	42,600	275-251	250,000	10,000
450-426	64,000	3,200	250-226	120,000	6,000
425-401	378,000	17,860	225-201	495,000	24,000
400-376	489,000	47,850	200-176	115,000	5,600
375-351	720,000	36,000	175-151	60,000	3,000
350-326	698,000	34,900	150-126	30,000	1,500

II. Estimates for Ancient Rome.

Period	No. of Men	Casualties	Period	No. of Men	Casualties
B. C.			26- 50	20,000	600
400-376	40,000	2,000	51- 75	280,000	14,000
375-351	220,000	11,000	76-100	160,000	8,000
350-326	140,000	7,000	101-125	360,000	18,000
325-301	460,000	23,000	126-150	200,000	10,000
300-276	581,000	41,100	151-175	320,000	16,000
275-251	732,000	45,200	176-200	240,000	12,000
250-226	440,000	22,000	201-225	20,000	600
225-201	1,564,000	141,200	226-250	440,000	22,000
200-176	240,000	12,000	251-275	1,040,000	52,000
175-151	80,000	4,000	276-300	120,000	6,000
150-126	560,000	28,000	301-325	320,000	16,000
125-101	780,000	39,000	326-350	30,000	1,200
100- 76	1,200,000	60,000	351-375	680,000	34,000
75- 51	1,734,000	86,700	376-400	205,000	10,250
50- 26	620,000	29,500	401-425	400,000	20,000
25- 1	120,000	6,000	425-450	120,000	6,000
A. D			451-476	880,000	44,000
1- 25	324,000	16,200			

III. Estimates for France.

Period	No. of Men	Casualties	Period	No. of Men	Casualties
976-1000	10,000	200	1451-1475	212,000	9,580
1001-1025	---	---	1476-1500	252,000	11,400
1026-1050	10,000	200	1501-1525	681,000	34,050
1051-1075	5,000	100	1526-1550	590,000	28,900
1076-1100	25,000	500	1551-1575	845,000	29,650
1101-1125	65,000	1,300	1576-1600	715,000	15,050
1126-1150	40,000	800	1601-1625	105,000	2,850
1151-1175	10,000	200	1626-1650	1,724,000	163,800
1176-1200	60,000	1,200	1651-1675	1,205,000	159,550
1201-1225	259,000	5,180	1676-1700	2,020,000	312,080
1226-1250	165,000	3,300	1701-1725	2,470,000	250,100
1251-1275	60,000	1,200	1726-1750	1,800,000	208,800
1276-1300	70,000	1,400	1751-1775	1,050,000	168,000
1301-1325	76,000	1,520	1776-1800	3,085,000	428,300
1326-1350	330,000	16,050	1801-1825	4,512,000	1,273,450
1351-1375	483,000	23,250	1826-1850	386,600	12,229
1376-1400	375,500	18,475	1851-1875	2,620,400	472,404
1401-1425	331,000	14,390	1876-1900	307,000	11,100
1426-1450	525,000	26,250	1901-1925	8,410,000	6,160,800

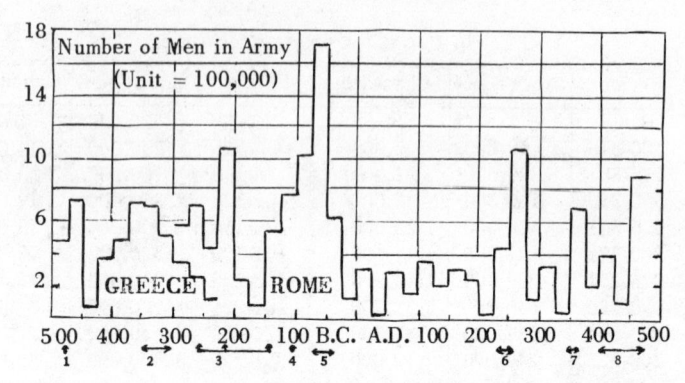

Figure 70. Intensity of Greek and Roman Wars Measured in terms of the Number of Men under Arms for each Quarter of a Century. Legend for Wars: 1. Persian Wars; 2. Period of Alexander; 3. Punic Wars I, II, III; 4. Civil War; 5. Period of Caesar and Pompey; 6. Persian Wars; 7. Wars of Julianus; 8. Gothic Wars.

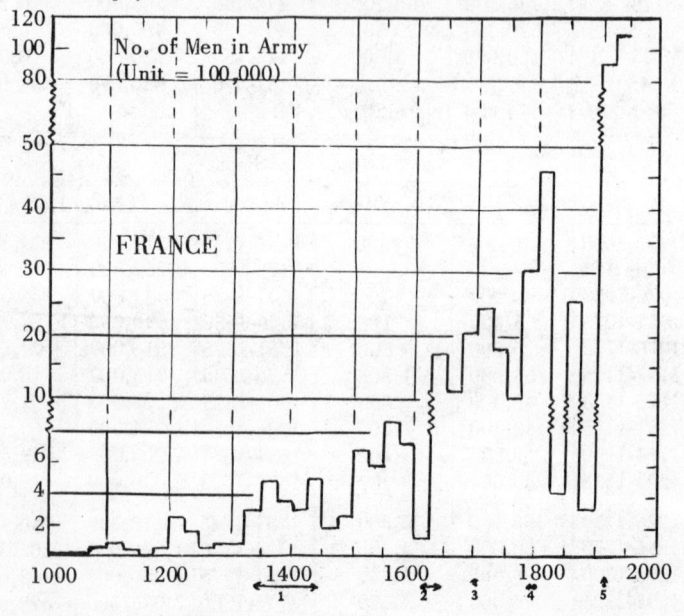

Figure 71. Intensity of French Wars Measured in Terms of the Number of Men under Arms for each Quarter of a Century.

Legend for Wars: 1. Hundred Years' War; 2. Thirty Years' War; 3. Spanish Succession; 4. Period of Napoleon; 5. World Wars.

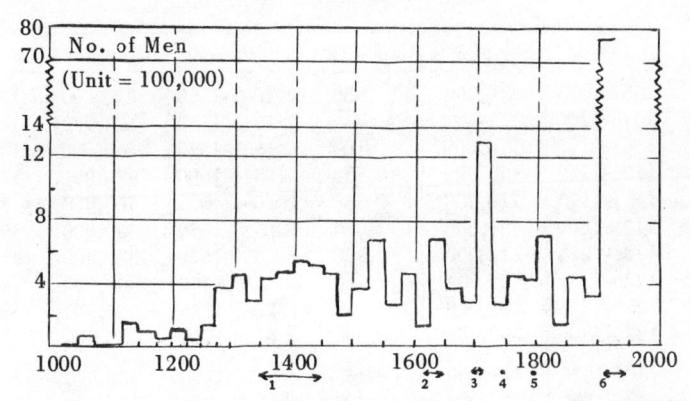

Figure 72. Intensity of English Wars Measured in Terms of the Number of Men under Arms in each Quarter of a Century.
Legend for Wars: 1. 100 Years' War; 2. 30 Years' War; 3. Spanish Succession; 4. 7 Years' War; 5. Napoleonic Wars; 6. World Wars.

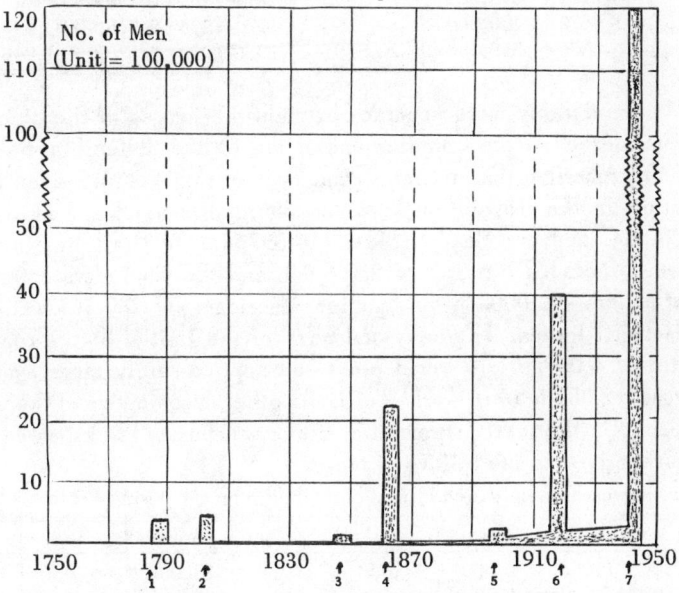

Figure 73. Intensity of the Wars of the United States Measured in Terms of the Number of Men under Arms.
Legend for Wars: 1. Period of Revolutionary War; 2. War of 1812; 3. Mexican War; 4. Civil War; 5. Spanish-American War; 6. World War I; 7. World War II.

IV. Estimates for England.

Period	No. of Men	Casualties	Period	No. of Men	Casualties
1051-1075	6,000	550	1501-1525	390,000	19,500
1076-1100	---	---	1526-1550	695,000	34,750
1101-1125	10,000	100	1551-1575	269,000	13,650
1126-1150	175,000	3,500	1576-1600	470,000	22,700
1151-1175	117,000	2,340	1601-1625	160,000	8,000
1176-1200	54,000	1,080	1626-1650	680,000	58,600
1201-1225	110,000	2,550	1651-1675	379,000	39,540
1226-1250	79,000	1,580	1676-1700	300,000	54,000
1251-1275	156,000	5,130	1701-1725	1,320,000	226,000
1276-1300	380,000	8,000	1726-1750	290,000	28,900
1301-1325	443,000	8,860	1751-1775	462,000	24,100
1326-1350	297,000	13,050	1776-1800	446,000	32,580
1351-1375	420,000	21,000	1801-1825	720,000	78,590
1376-1400	470,000	21,100	1826-1850	174,000	6,720
1401-1425	555,000	25,350	1851-1875	437,400	37,248
1426-1450	525,000	26,250	1876-1900	339,400	17,790
1451-1475	480,000	24,000	1901-1925	7,815,000	3,094,550
1476-1500	210,000	10,500	1926-1950	5,120,000	1,246,000

Considerably more accuracy attends the figures of the size of the armed forces of the Colonies and of the United States since the time of the American Revolution. Thus we find that the American participation in the Revolution involved 395,858 men, the War of 1812, 528,274, and the Mexican War, 116,597. In the Civil War the Union forces included a roster of 2,128,948 and the Confederate forces an estimated 900,000. In the Spanish-American war 280,564 were in the American forces. The army and navy of the United States reached a total of 4,057,101 in World War I and approximately three times this figure (12,300,000) in World War II. At other dates between the periods of conflict the total personnel of the armed forces is estimated at the figures given in the following table:

Total Personnel in the Armed Forces of the United States during Periods of Peace

Year	Army	Navy	Total	Year	Army	Navy	Total
1820	9,000	2,000	11,000	1910	81,000	60,000	141,000
1850	11,000	8,000	19,000	1914	98,000	66,000	164,000
1870	37,000	10,000	47,000	1921	190,000	131,000	321,000
1880	25,000	9,000	34,000	1930	137,000	93,000	230,000
1890	27,000	12,000	39,000	1935	138,000	93,000	231,000
1900	68,000	28,000	96,000	1940	264,000	151,000	415,000

THE PROBLEM OF CONFLICT

The armed strength of the United States since the Revolutionary War is graphically portrayed in Figure 73. The enormous growth of armies and navies is readily seen from the chart, but this growth is largely a function of the increase in the population itself. Thus, at the time of the Revolution, the population of the Colonies, estimated at 2,205,000, supported an armed force of 395,858, that is to say, 18% of the total population participated in the conflict. This was just twice the ratio observed in World War II, where a population in excess of 134 million provided an armed force of approximately twelve million men.

PROBLEMS

1. Using the following estimates of population size, compute the percentage of the population which was involved in actual military duty in the American wars:

War	Population	War	Population
Revolution	2,205,000	Spanish-American War	75,995,000
War of 1812	7,240,000	World War I	105,711,000
Mexican War	23,192,000	World War II	134,000,000
Civil War	35,000,000		

2. According to modern actuarial figures the per cent of the male population between the ages of 20 and 50 years is 28% (see the table, Problem 5, Section 2, Chapter 9). Assuming this figure as a constant, compute the percentage of the male population involved in each of the American wars. Compare this with the per cent of men involved in the second Punic war, using Sorokin's figures for the armed strength and the census quoted by Pliny of 214,000 free male citizens in the Roman state in 204 B. C. for the population.

3. Sorokin estimates that the Roman army during the Second Punic war varied from 34,000 to a maximum of 86,000 in 216, B. C. He then states that between 3.4 and 8.6 of the total free population of Rome was in the army at any time. Can these estimates be justified?

4. Using the data given in the text, estimate the per cent of casualties expected during major wars. How do these estimates compare with the casualties reported by the American forces in both World Wars?

5. The population of England in 1600 has been estimated at about 6.5 million. Can the estimates of the size of English armies in the seventeenth century be justified on the basis of a population of this size?

6. *The Cost of Ancient Wars.*

When one contemplates the long and almost unbroken sequence of European wars one is much intrigued to know the costs of these expensive adventures and how these costs have been met by the governments engaged in them.

In a very few instances it is possible to answer the first of these questions, although time has effaced most of the records. But in spite of these difficulties assiduous scholarship has been able occasionally to reconstruct the budget and describe the methods employed to balance it. As an example of this scholarship and as an illustration of how statistical inference from meager data can reach sound conclusions, let us consider the cost of the second Punic war.*

This great struggle, waged between Rome and Carthage between 218 B. C. and 201 B. C., involved military operations in Italy, Africa, and Spain. The military genius of Hannibal enabled a Carthaginian army of 20,000 foot soldiers and 6,000 horses to cross the Alps and occupy extensive areas of the Italian peninsula for fifteen years. The size of the army is probably more accurately known than that of more recent ones since Polybius in his *History* (3, 56) quotes the figures given above and then says: "as Hannibal himself distinctly states on the column erected on the promontory of Lacinium to record the numbers."

Some idea of the magnitude of the Roman forces can be obtained from the census of adult males for the Roman ager which Pliny gives, for the period which includes the war, as follows: Population for 233 B. C., 270,713; Population for 204 B. C., 214,000. The effect upon the male population in the great struggle is shown in the disappearance between the two dates of nearly 57,000 Roman citizens.

The cost of maintaining the army can be estimated from the following statement of Polybius (6, 39): "The pay of the foot soldier is $5\frac{1}{3}$ asses a day; of the centurion $10\frac{2}{3}$; of the cavalry 16. The infantry receive a ration of wheat equal to about $\frac{2}{3}$ of an Attic medimnus a month, and the cavalry 7 medimni of barley, and 2 of wheat; of the allies the infantry receive the same, the cavalry $1\frac{1}{3}$ medimnus of wheat and 5 of barley. This is a free gift to the allies; but in the case of the Romans, the Quaestor stops out of their pay the price of

---

* This is one of the few wars of ancient times for which a careful statistical estimate of costs has been made.

their corn and clothes, or any additional arms they may require at a fixed rate."

The following equivalents give a ready interpretation of these figures: Thus we have 16 asses = 1 denarius and 1 medimnus = 6 modii; the modius was approximately the equivalent of a modern peck. Reduced to a wheat *numéraire*, on the assumption that 4 modii of wheat could be purchased for 3 denarii, the pay of a foot soldier per year was 360 × 5⅓ asses = 1920 asses = 40 bushels of wheat.

Tenny Frank (1876-1939), who devoted a life-time of study to these problems, used the statement of Polybius to reconstruct the cost of a Roman legion as follows:[*]

Infantry, per legion: 4,140 men at 120 denarii per year = 496,800 denarii
Centurions, per legion: 60 men at 240 denarii per year = 14,400 denarii
Cavalry, per legion: 300 men at 360 denarii per year = 108,000 denarii

Total cost: 619,200 denarii

During the eighteen years of the war the number of legions varied from six to 25. An estimate by G. De Sanctis[†] indicates that the armed strength of the Romans throughout the war was equivalent to 353 legions for a single year of service.[‡] To err on the conservative side, Frank estimated 353 legions at an annual expense of 500,000 denarii per legion since "at times some of the troops were dismissed in winter to save expense." This gives a total expenditure of approximately 180,000,000 denarii.

In addition to this expense there should be added that of supplying four modii of wheat per man each month for about nine months of the year to allied troops, estimated at 5,000 men to each legion. Since some of this wheat was obtained by foraging, Frank estimated the cost at 2¼ denarii per 4 modii = one bushel. Again, making a conservative estimate, we see that the total cost from this source could not have been less than 36,000,000 denarii.

---

[*]See *An Economic Survey of Ancient Rome*, in six volumes, Baltimore, 1933-1940; in particular, Vol. I, from which our analysis is taken.

[†]*Storia dei Romani*, III, 2, p. 317 et seq. and p. 632 et seq.

[‡]This figure gives a total of 4500 × 353 = 1,587,500 men under arms for the 18 years of conflict. Sorokin's estimate (*op. cit.*, Vol. 3, p. 545) for the same period was 1,260,000, based on the size of the Roman army at the battle of Cannae in 216 B. C., namely 70,000 men. Considering the errors of estimate, the figures are reasonably consistent.

To this must be added the cost of army transportation, which may be estimated at 15,000,000 denarii, and the cost of metals and materials, which was not less than 20,000,000 denarii.

Although naval engagements were not a conspicuous part of the second Punic war, the Romans had about 250 vessels in continuous operation. To replace those lost or discarded probably 300 ships were constructed, which were assisted by an additional 600 transports. Frank, assuming a cost of 15,000 denarii per warship and 4,000 denarii per transport, found the cost of new naval construction to be about 7,000,000 denarii. Assuming further, 250 rowers for each of 200 warships and 60 for each of 500 transports, Frank estimated that 80,000 men were fed for six months of the year for about ten years of the war. This gives a cost of $80,000 \times 18$ ($= 24$ modii at $\frac{3}{4}$ denarii) $\times 10 = 14,400,000$ denarii. To this must be added 12,000,000 denarii as stipends to about 20,000 marines for something over ten years, and perhaps another 9,600,000 denarii for repairs and other incidental expenses. This would make an estimated total of 35,000,000 denarii for the naval expenditure of the war.

These figures can be summarized as follows:

Items of Expenditure	Cost in denarii
Cost of 353 legions	180,000,000
Wheat for allied troops	36,000,000
Land transportation	15,000,000
Metals and army equipment	20,000,000
Cost of navy	35,000,000
Total expenditure	286,000,000

This expenditure meant a total annual cost for each of the 18 years of the conflict of nearly 16 million denarii. The magnitude of these figures may be better appreciated perhaps by considering the total in comparison with the income of the citizens. Using Pliny's figures for the census of 204 B. C. and an argument based upon the distribution of income, it is possible to estimate the total income of the Roman commonwealth to have been of the order of 93,300,000 denarii at this time. Comparing this figure with the average expenditure for the war, we see that the annual cost of the conflict was approximately 17 per cent of the total income. Frank, using a statement of Livy, estimated the taxable property of all citizens to be of the order of 900 million denarii. Noting the reduction in manpower, a ten per cent return on capital, instead of the usual 16 per cent, does not seem to be an unreasonable assumption.

To appreciate the magnitude of the second Punic war let us compare its costs with the expenditure of the United States government for World War I during the four years from 1917 to 1920 inclusive. This expenditure totaled $39,680,540,000, or approximately ten billion dollars per year. Since the average annual income of the people based on these years was 64 billion dollars, we reach the conclusion that the annual government expenditure was 16 per cent of the average annual income. The devastating character of the second Punic war may be seen from the fact that it lasted for 18 years, as contrasted with the short duration of World War I.

We can compare the second Punic war more readily with the devastation of World War II. During this conflict, for the five years from 1941 to 1945 inclusive, the total expenditure of the United States government was 317.6 billions of dollars, or an average of 63.62 billions per year. During this period the average annual income of the citizens was not in excess of 150 billion dollars. Hence, the total cost of World War II to the American people was somewhat in excess of twice their total annual income. On the other hand, the Roman people, with an annual income of around 93.3 million denarii, spent 286 million denarii, which is a sum in excess of three times their annual income.

7. *The Cost of Modern Wars.*

The estimation of the cost of modern wars is a more complicated matter, since, as one commentator says, "so much depends upon book-keeping."Also, the cost of war does not end with belligerency, as is seen from the fact that the United States treasury gave a continually increasing estimate of the cost of World War I until 1934, when it reached a total of 41,765 millions of dollars.

However, there is one fairly accurate way to make these estimates and that is by observing the maximum increase in the national debts of the belligerents over the war period. This figure is considerably below the actual cost of the war, since taxation and the issuance of paper currency are used also in the process of financing. However, it is a matter of observation that the total cost of a modern war does not appear to be as great as twice the increase in the debt. Thus, for the United States, if we assume the actual cost of World War I to be of the order of 40 billions, and the increase in the national debt to be of the order of 24 billions, the ratio between these figures is 1.67. For World War II, if we estimate the cost at 318 billions and the increase in debt at 226 billions, the ratio is 1.41. The cost of the Boer War (1899-1902) has been estimated by F. W. Hirst* to be about 250 million pounds and the increase in the English debt 160 million pounds, or a ratio of 1.56. Similarly, the increase in the debt of England was of the order of 42 million pounds as the result of the Crimean War (1854-1856) and the cost was less than twice this figure, according to Hirst.

To this problem of the cost of war F. W. Hirst has devoted a careful study based upon the increase in national debts. The following figures to and through the Mexican War are taken from his work:

War	Country	Debt increase in Thousands of Pounds	War	Country	Debt increase in Millions of Dollars
2nd Coalition against Louis XIV (1689-97)	England	20,851	Revolution (1775-1783)	Colonies	75
War of Spanish Succession (1702-1713)	England	35,750	War of 1812 (1812-1814)	U. S.	82
War of Austrian Succession (1739-1748)	England	31,339	Mexican War (1846-1848)	U. S.	49
Seven Years' War (1756-1763)	England	64,533	Civil War (1861-1865)	U. S.	2,665
American Revolution (1775-1783)	England	121,267	Spanish-American War (1898)	U. S.	204
Napoleonic Period (1792-1815)	England	613,000	World War I (1917-1918)	U. S.	24,294
Crimean War (1854-1856)	England	42,000	World War II (1941-1945)	U. S.	226,504
Boer War	England	160,000			

If these figures are all multiplied by a factor of two we shall have an estimate which probably exceeds in every case the actual cost.

* F. W. Hirst: *The Political Economy of War*, London, 1915, xii + 327 pp

Thus, in the case of the American Civil War, which has been estimated to have had a total cost for both the Union and the Confederate sides of 10 billion dollars, we should have an estimate under 5.3 billion for the North and probably a similar figure for the South. Since the South was actually subject to military devastation, it is probable that the real costs were greater there than in the North, and the estimate of 10 billion can thus be justified.

8. *How Wars are Financed.*

In view of the great expense of protracted wars, which exact so large a toll from the current income of the people who engage in them, it is instructive to inquire into the methods by means of which they have been financed. Since no wars, except those of very recent date, have been studied by competent statisticians from this point of view, it will be enlightening to examine the various means adopted by the Roman government to finance the second Punic war, the cost of which we discussed in Section 6.

One of the first sources of income used by the Romans was a citizens' tax. In normal times the rate was about one mill, which on an assessed valuation of 900 million denarii, produced approximately 900,000 denarii annually. Tenny Frank assumed that this tax was advanced to an average of four mills for the period of the war, which produced a total revenue of 65 million denarii in 18 years.

It is also interesting to observe in this connection that the income tax is not a modern device, but has its origin in the remote past. Thus we find in Livy* the following statement: "But as there was a deficiency of sailors, the consuls, in conformity with a decree of the senate, published an order that those persons who themselves or whose fathers had been rated in the censorship of Lucius Aemilius and Caius Flaminius [219 and 217 B. C.], at from fifty to one hundred thousand asses [3,125 to 6,250 denarii], or whose property had since reached that amount, should furnish one sailor and six months' pay [100 den.]; from one to three hundred thousand [6,250 to 18,750 den.], three sailors with a year's pay [600 den.]; from three hundred thousand to a million, [18,750 to 62,500 den.], five sailors [1,000 den.]; above one million [62,500 den.], seven sailors [1,400 den.]; that senators should furnish eight sailors with a year's pay [1,600 den.]."

---

*History of Rome, 24, 11.

Making use of our previous estimate of Roman income (Section 6) and the theory of income distribution given in Section 4 of Chapter 8, it is possible to estimate the number of citizens within the brackets of the four classes, exclusive of the senatorial class, defined by Livy. To do this we first convert assessed valuation into income on the assumption that earning on such evaluation was of the order of 15 per cent. We thus obtain as the limits of income for the four classes, exclusive of the senatorial class, the following figures:

(1) First income class; 500 to 1,000 denarii; (2) Second income class: 1,000 to 3,000 denarii; (3) Third income class: 3,000 to 10,000 denarii; (4) Fourth income class: 10,000 denarii and over.

We now make use of the theory of income distribution given in Section 4 of Chapter 8 to compute the number of adult males, out of the total number of adult males, namely 214,000, who were in these four income classes. We thus obtain the following estimates:

(1) 43,000; (2) 19,500; (3) 3,500; (4) 742.

From the tax imposed upon the members of the four income classes it is apparent that the rate varied from 10 to 16 per cent of the actual income and that a substantial contribution to the war, somewhere between six and seven million denarii, resulted from this source if the full mandate of the consuls was actually carried out.

Those who inveigh in modern times against the wide-spread use of a sales tax may be surprised to find that such a tax functioned in the Roman ager. Thus, part of the expense of the war, estimated at about 10,000,000 denarii, was met by a sales tax of five per cent on the value of manumitted slaves, by import and export duties from 2½ to 5 per cent, and from a state salt monopoly and public lands.

There were also other sources of income. A tithe, levied upon Sicily and Sardinia, perhaps half a million bushels of wheat annually for 16 years, contributed another 24 million. The sacred treasure from the tax of manumitted slaves, a sum estimated by Frank at 5 million denarii, was used in 209 B. C. Booty from Capua, New Carthage, Tarentum, Africa, and elsewhere amounted to about 65 million denarii. We thus obtain the total given in the table on the next page.

This left a balance of 117 million denarii to be raised by other means. The first of these, one of the easiest political devices to execute, was a debasement of the coinage. Thus the bronze *as* was reduced from two ounces to one and the silver denarius from 72 to the pound to 84. The *as* was then equated to the denarius as 16 to 1

Source of Income	Amount in denarii
Citizens' tribute:	65,000,000
Sales tax, post duties, rentals:	10,000,000
Tithes:	24,000,000
Sacred treasure:	5,000,000
Booty:	65,000,000
Total Income	169,000,000

instead of 10 to 1 as it had been in the original ratio, since the word *denarius* means ten *asses*. In modern times this debasement is achieved by the issue of paper currency.

The second fiscal device was the acquiring of temporary loans both abroad and from the citizens themselves. In this we find actually the counterpart of the sale of government bonds. Voluntary contributions of jewelry, plate, and precious metals were requested by the state in return for a promise to repay them later.

The sale of public land was also authorized. The final indemnity from Carthage was only 10,000 talents, a sum equal to 60 million denarii, which was to be paid in fifty annual installments. If we assume an effective rate of interest of six per cent, the capitalized value of this sum would be worth less than four million denarii.

From the financial picture which these facts portray, we can assume that an inflation of considerable magnitude resulted. One item from Polybius [9, 44] confirms this conclusion for we read that "the scarcity at Rome [in 210 B. C.] has come to such a pitch, that a Sicilian medimnus has sold for fifteen drachmas." This would be equivalent to 2½ denarii per modius, or something around four times the normal price. The war index, defined in Section 2, was thus of the order of 3.00.

The wars of modern times have been financed much in the same way the Punic wars were financed with one very important exception. This is the creation of national debt, a device foreshadowed by the government borrowing mentioned in the balance sheet of the second Punic war. The history of government debt belongs to modern times, that of France having had its inception in 1522 during the reign of Francis I and that of England in 1689 in the reign of William and Mary.

Adequate data on national debts over long periods of time have not been available until recently when part of the obscurity was removed by E. J. Hamilton in a survey of the national debts of France and England from their beginnings.* Since the growth of national debts has an important bearing upon the problem of the cost of war, we give these data of Hamilton in the following table:

Growth of the Public Debt of France
(In Millions of Francs)

Year	Size of Debt	Year	Size of Debt	Year	Size of Debt	Year	Size of Debt
1522	0.2	1678	157	1783	3,302	1913	33,640
1536	0.5	1684	217	1799	926	1918	154,393
1543	0.725	1697	417	1814	1,266	1924	315,896
1560	42	1713	2,800	1830	4,426	1930	267,092
1576	100	1715	1,700	1848	5,954	1934	319,383
1595	300	1722	1,700	1873	21,700	1938	412,575
1642	600	1763	2,360	1883	27,400	1944	1,800,000
1643	250	1768	2,475	1903	30,800		

Growth of the Public Debt of England
(In Thousands of Pounds)

Year	Size of Debt	Year	Size of Debt	Year	Size of Debt	Year	Size of Debt
1697	21,516	1764	139,562	1852	779,000	1933	7,645,000
1701	16,395	1775	129,147	1857	808,000	1939	8,163,000
1714	53,681	1783	238,000	1886	742,000	1946	23,774,000
1722	55,283	1792	217,750	1900	628,000	1948	25,621,000
1739	46,955	1815	860,856	1903	745,000	1949	25,168,000
1748	78,293	1827	780,000	1914	661,000	1950	25,802,000
1755	72,290	1841	792,000	1921	7,623,000	1951	25,922,000

In order that one may appreciate better the significance of the figures given in the above tables, they have been graphically represented in Figures 74 and 75. Certain details of these interesting curves deserve special comment.

---

*"Origin and Growth of the National Debt in Western Europe," *American Economic Review, Proceedings*, Vol. 37, 1947, pp. 118-130.

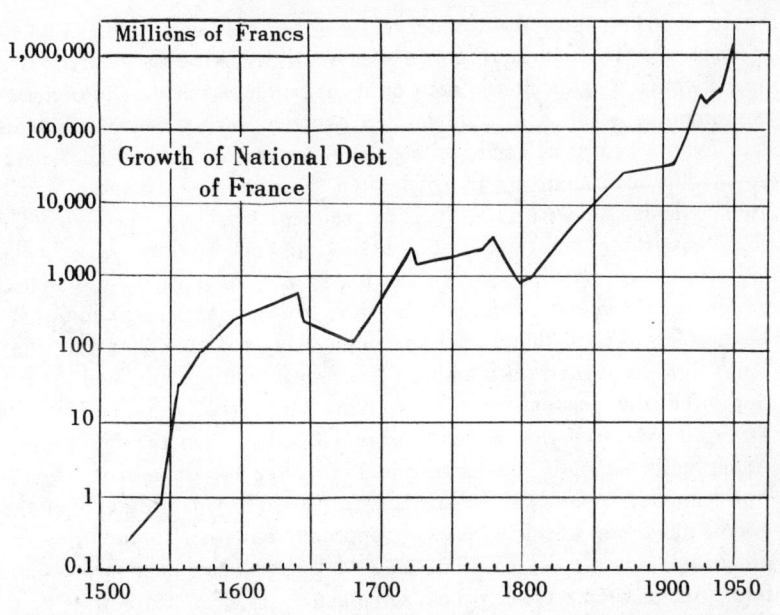

Figure 74. Growth of National Debt of France on Logarithmic Scale.
(Data from Hamilton)

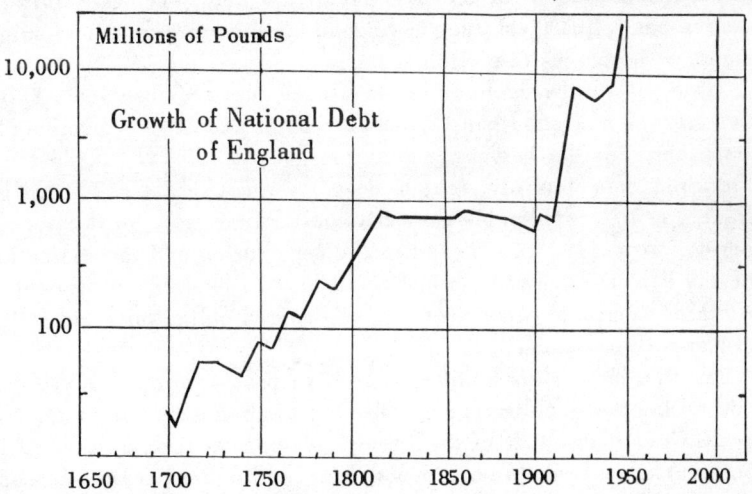

Figure 75. Growth of National Debt of England on Logarithmic Scale.
(Data from Hamilton)

In the first place we observe that the national debts of both France and England have grown exponentially, since a straight line trend would roughly fit the data on a logarithmic scale. The ultimate significance of such a trend for the economics of the two countries has been a matter of much debate for many years. Thomas B. Macaulay (1800-1859), writing in 1855 when the debt was around 800 million pounds, viewed it without apprehension. Thus he says:* "A long experience justifies us in believing that England may in the twentieth century be better able to pay a debt of sixteen hundred millions than she is at the present time to bear her present load. But be this as it may, those who so confidently predicted that she must sink... were beyond all doubt under a two-fold mistake. They greatly overrated the pressure of the burden: they greatly underrated the strength by which the burden was to be borne." On the other hand, Adam Smith (1723-1790), writing in 1776 when the debt was 129 million pounds, makes the following statement:†"The progress of the enormous debts which at present oppress, and will in the long run probably ruin, all the great nations of Europe, has been pretty uniform. Nations, like private men, have generally begun to borrow upon what may be called personal credit, without assigning or mortgaging any particular fund for the payment of the debt; and when this resource has failed them, they have gone on to borrow upon the assignments or mortgages of particular funds."

Two noteworthy declines in the French debt are observed: (1) between 1642 and 1643 and (2) between 1783 and 1799. According to Hamilton, "at the beginning of the reign of Louis XIV (1643-1715) the debt was forcibly scaled down to approximately 250 million francs, or by considerably more than half." Similarly, for the second period, we read: "In 1799, when the repudiation and the extinction of the debt through redemption in confiscated land and repayment in worthless currency were over, the recognized obligations had fallen to 926 million francs."

Another interesting feature of the French debt is found in the fact that during the Napoleonic era, while the English debt was increasing by 295 per cent, that of the French government rose by a mere 37 per cent. Napoleon, the aggressor, financed his campaigns by means of tribute levied upon the conquered countries and by high taxes im-

---
*History of England, (1855), Vol. 4, Chap. 19.
†The Wealth of Nations, (1776), Book 5, Chap. 3.

posed upon his own subjects. The final failure of French arms, however, and the indemnities imposed, together with an unfunded debt of nearly 800 million francs, rapidly raised the debt to a figure considerably in excess of that which had prevailed before the Revolution.

The principal difference between the British and the French debts appears to be in the attempts made by the English in time of peace to reduce their obligations. Commenting on this aspect of the figures, Hamilton says: "The reductions in peacetime [of the British debt], which have seemed ridiculously small to most contemporary economists, have accentuated the postwar crises... Is it not possible that the well-known immunity of France to depressions in the last seven decades of the nineteenth century was partially due to the continuous growth of the national debt?"

We turn next to a consideration of the debt of the United States, which, for all practical purposes, may be regarded as having started in 1861. In that year it was slightly in excess of 90 million dollars, but by 1866 it had reached the substantial figure of 2,756 millions as the result of the financial burden of the Civil War. The progress of the debt is shown in the following table:

Growth of the Public Debt of the United States*
(In Millions of Dollars)

Year	Size of Debt	Year	Size of Debt	Year	Size of Debt	Year	Size of Debt
1861	91	1880	2,091	1918	12,244	1940	42,968
1862	524	1885	1,579	1919	25,482	1942	72,422
1863	1,120	1890	1,122	1920	24,298	1943	136,696
1864	1,816	1893	961	1921	23,976	1944	201,003
1865	2,678	1895	1,097	1922	22,964	1945	258,682
1866	2,756	1900	1,263	1923	23,350	1946	269,422
1867	2,650	1905	1,132	1924	21,251	1947	258,286
1868	2,583	1910	1,147	1925	20,516	1948	252,292
1869	2,545	1915	1,191	1930	16,185	1949	252,770
1870	2,436	1916	1,225	1935	28,701	1950	257,357
1875	2,156	1917	2,976	1937	36,425	1951	255,222

*The term "public debt" is misleading, since various interpretations can be given to it depending upon the details of the accountancy. Public debt in recent years includes not only the debt of the national government, but of state governments as well. There is a gross public debt and a net public debt. Since our interest here is not in an accountancy examination of the debt, but in a general picture of the growth of the gross funded debt of

296   POLITICAL STATISTICS

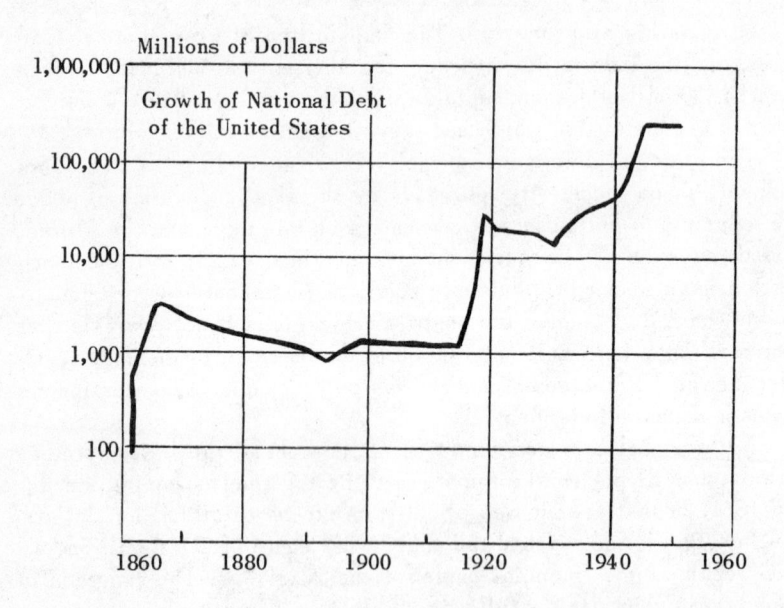

Figure 76. Growth of the National Debt of the United States on Logarithmic Scale. (Data from Treasury Statements).

The details of the debt can be grasped readily from the data shown in Figure 76. After the precipitous rise caused by the Civil War, the debt declined rapidly until it reached a low of 961 million dollars in the depression year of 1893. In the subsequent two decades only minor fluctuations are observed and the debt stood at 1,225 million dollars in 1916. The history of the participation of the United States in World War I is shown in the increase of the debt to a maximum of 25,482 millions in 1919. Again a decline is observed which reached a minimum of 16,185 millions in 1930, a year of crisis in the financial affairs of the nation. A program of deficit spending then ensued and the debt rapidly increased to approximately 40 billions in 1940. World War II then lifted the national obligations to the staggering total of 269 billions in 1946.

---

the national government, we have presented these figures obtained from Treasury Statements.

PROBLEMS

1. From the details of the French debt estimate the cost to France of the Crimean and the Franco-Prussian Wars.

2. Fit a linear trend to the logarithms of the items in the French debt. From this does one conclude that the French debt has increased exponentially? Can such an increase be continued indefinitely?

3. Fit a trend to the logarithms of the English debt. Has this debt increased exponentially? In view of the statistical analysis, toward which opinion does one tend, that of Macaulay or that of Adam Smith? Are there additional monetary considerations that might modify one's judgment?

4. The per capita debt of the United States is given in the following table:

Year	Debt	Year	Debt	Year	Debt	Year	Debt
1861	$ 2.83	1893	$14.49	1925	$177.82	1946	$1,905.42
1865	77.07	1895	15.91	1930	131.49	1947	1,792.05
1870	63.19	1900	16.56	1935	225.07	1948	1,720.71
1875	49.06	1905	13.60	1940	325.23	1949	1,694.75
1880	41.69	1910	12.69	1942	537.13	1950	1,696.61
1885	28.11	1915	11.83	1944	1,452.44	1951	1,655.37
1890	17.92	1920	228.33	1945	1,848.60		

Represent these data graphically and compare their growth with the growth of population as shown in Figure 40 of Chapter 7. If no additions were made to the debt for fifty years, what would the per capita debt then be, assuming the correctness of the population growth shown in Figure 40?

5. The present value of an annuity of P dollars for n years at a rate of interest i is given by the formula:

$$Present\ value = P\ \frac{1 - (1 + i)^{-n}}{i}.$$

Referring to the table of Problem 4, determine what per capita payment as of today would pay the present debt in 50 years if the debt were financed at 1%? at 2%? What would this per capita payment be in 1990?

6. Using the Roman figures given in Section 4 of Chapter 8, and noting that N (the total number of income earners) was approximately 214,000 at the time of the second Punic war, justify the estimates of the number of people in the four classes given in the text.

7. Compare the fluctuations of the English debt between 1700 and 1800 with the fluctuations in British shipping during the same period as shown in Figure 61 of Chapter 9. Estimate the correlation between the two curves.

9. The Theory of War Tensions.

In spite of the universal character of war and the extensive studies which have been devoted to the phenomenon, no satisfactory theory has yet been developed to account for the origin of war. Some authorities view the problem as one of psychological differences between nations and attempts have been made to express the tensions which lead to war in terms of social and cultural conflicts. Others see the problem as one based on economic factors which deveop out of the competition for international trade. Tensions arise from the covetousness of one nation for the territory of another or for the markets which have been developed in a competitive trade. These conflicting interests are intensified by growing populations and unsatisfactory internal conditions.

Quincy Wright has given an engaging theory based on the first premise, which assumes a system of "distances" between nations.* The greater these distances become the higher is the probability of conflict. Since this theory has some statistical aspects, it will be instructive to consider its salient features. Eight distances between nations are recognized as follows:

(1) *Technological* (T), which is measured by the cultural diffusion between countries. An approximate estimate of its magnitude can be made by observing the number of available channels of communication which exist between several states.

(2) *Strategic* (St), a distance, the magnitude of which is determined by the vulnerability to attack, the obstacles which must be overcome, etc.

(3) *Legal* (L), which is measured by "the degree of jural equality mutually recognized by two states."

(4) *Intellectual* (I), a distance dependent upon the intellectual resemblance or difference between two or more countries.

(5) *Social* (S), a magnitude estimated from the similarity or dissimilarity of the political, religious, economic, and social institutions between two or more states.

(6) *Political* (P), which depends upon the closeness of political institutions and forms of government. This distance is one phase of the social measure, but has been given a separate category because of its importance in the phenomenon of war.

---

* See *A Study of War, op. cit.*, Vol. 2, Appendixes XL and XLIII.

(7) *Psychic* (*Ps*), a distance which is measured by the degree of friendliness or suspicion observed between political entities. It is determined from the tenor of the utterances of public officials, opinions of the press, the results of public opinion polls, etc.

(8) *Expectancy of war* (*E*), which is measured by the representative view of the citizens with respect to the probability of peace or war.

Since the distance from country (*a*) to country (*b*) may not always be the same as from country (*b*) to country (*a*), subscripts are introduced to indicate this. Thus E_{ab} means the expectancy of country *a* going to war with country *b*, while E_{ba} signifies the expectancy of country *b* going to war with country *a*. For example, the strategic distances between England and France are very different, since it has always been much easier for England to cross the Channel into France, than for France to cross the Channel into England.

Lacking objective measures of these eight differences, Wright has used integers to express them, the greater distance being expressed by the greater integer. As an example, we shall use Wright's estimates for the distances between the United States, Great Britain, France, and Germany, which prevailed in 1939. These are recorded in the following table:

Power	T	St	L	I	S	P	Ps	E	Totals
United States									
Great Britain	1	1	1	1	1	1	1	1	8
France	2	2	2	2	2	2	2	2	16
Germany	3	6	5	3	3	3	6	5	34
Great Britain									
United States	1	2	1	1	1	2	1	1	10
France	2	1	2	2	2	1	2	2	14
Germany	3	4	3	3	4	6	5	6	34
France									
United States	4	4	2	2	3	3	1	1	20
Great Britain	1	3	1	1	1	2	2	2	13
Germany	2	2	4	4	5	5	6	5	33
Germany									
United States	4	5	5	5	5	5	4	3	36
Great Britain	3	3	2	3	3	3	3	4	24
France	2	1	4	2	4	4	5	5	27

If the totals for each pair of countries are added, then the relative distances between the countries, arranged from those which are closest to those which are the furthest apart, are given in the following table:*

Pairs of Countries	Total Distance	Pairs of Countries	Total Distance
United-States-Great Britain	18	Great Britain-Germany	58
Great Britain-France	27	France-Germany	60
United States-France	36	United States-Germany	70

In order to get a measure representing the probability of war between any pair of countries, Wright defined a quantity x which he assumed to be proportional to this probability. This quantity is expressed in terms of the distances as follows:

$$x = k[E + (2\ Ps - T) + (S - I) + (E_{ab} - E_{ba}) + (St_{ba} - St_{ab})$$
$$+ (P_{ab} - P_{ba}) + (L_{ba} - L_{ab}) + c], \quad (1)$$

where k and c are constants. The terms without subscripts are assumed to be the sums of the distances between the two countries, that is, $E = E_{ab} + E_{ba}$, etc.

The constant c is chosen so that all values of x are positive and the constant k so that the maximum value of x will be approximately equal to 100. In his computation Wright set $c = 100$ and $k = 2$. With these values we obtain the following estimates for x for the six pairs of countries given above:

Pairs of Countries	Total Distance	Pairs of Countries	Total Distance
France-Germany	82	Great Britain-France	38
Great Britain-Germany	68	United States-France	32
United States-Germany	60	United States-Great Britain	28

*This table and the one on the preceding page are abbreviated from longer ones which included Italy, Japan, and Russia. Since a rank scheme is used, the designation of distances is by means of the integers from 1 to 6.

THE PROBLEM OF CONFLICT 301

These estimates can be converted into relative probabilities by division by 100, or they can be used as index numbers of war potentialities between the powers.

It is obvious that a scheme of this kind is highly subjective, but nevertheless it appears to give an approximate measure of the relative stresses which exist between different pairs of countries. It has an inherent weakness in the fact that the relationship between one country and another is not independent of the relationships of the two nations with other countries. This is manifest from the fact that a declaration of war between two European powers usually explodes into a war between several.

PROBLEMS

1. Wright gives the following table of differences between France, Germany, Italy, and Russia as of 1939:

Power	T	St	L	I	S	P	Ps	E	Totals
France									
Germany	2	2	4	4	5	5	6	5	33
Italy	3	1	3	3	4	4	5	6	29
Russia	5	5	5	5	2	1	3	3	29
Germany									
France	2	1	4	2	4	4	5	5	27
Italy	1	2	1	1	1	1	1	1	9
Russia	5	4	6	4	6	6	6	6	43
Italy									
France	2	1	4	1	3	4	5	6	26
Germany	1	2	1	2	1	1	1	1	10
Russia	5	5	6	5	6	6	6	4	43
Russia									
France	3	4	2	4	1	1	1	1	17
Germany	1	2	4	1	5	5	6	5	29
Italy	6	5	5	3	4	6	4	4	37

Determine the total distance between these countries by pairs and arrange them in a table of increasing distances.

2. Using the table of Problem 1, compute the value of x as defined by equation (1) above for all the pairs of countries and arrange them in a decreasing sequence of values of x.

3. From the events which happened after 1939, how accurately did the theory of distances represent the alignments observed in World War II?

4. Make an estimate, based on present conditions, of the values of the factors T, St, P, and E for the following countries: United States, Great Britain, France, and Italy.

5. Answer Problem 4 for the countries: United States, Russia, and Japan.

10. *The Problem of International Trade.*

There is little doubt that the friction between states is intensified by international trade. Rivalry for world markets and the conflict of interests in external territories are fruitful breeders of conflict. Thus in the ancient world the Punic wars were precipitated by the rival interests of Rome and Carthage in the cities of Sicily. In more modern times the great wars of the seventeenth century owe much of their fury to the struggle between the European countries for the conquest of the rich lands of the New World. Trade with India and the development of interests in Canada were important issues which set England and France on opposite sides in the Seven Years' War fought near the middle of the eighteenth century.

Although it will not be possible to develop here the statistical implications of the extensive subject of international trade, we should not give a proper prospective to the problem of conflict if its importance were not urged in contrast to the psychological theory developed in the preceding section. The mechanistic theory of history requires a material basis for the interpretation of conflict and this can be found at least in part in the conflict of international trade.

One statistical measure of the intensity of trade wars is discovered in the variation which takes place between rival currencies on the world market. This variation is itself measured in a satisfactory manner by exchange ratios, that is to say, the parities of exchange between the unit of one currency and that of another. Thus we have the dollar-pound ratio, the franc-pound ratio, the mark-dollar ratio, etc. In 1914 the parities in terms of the dollar were for the pound, the franc, and the mark respectively $4.8665, $0.1929, and $0.2382. In 1940 these had become officially: $4.035, $0.020827, and $0.40021. The first figure reflects the attempt of the British and American governments to stabilize the pound-dollar ratio, the second shows the effect of the collapse of French finance at the end of World War I, and the third the stabilization achieved by the reichsmark as the result of keeping it on a gold basis, even though the German gold reserve was almost non-existent. The history of these three exchange ratios is graphically shown in Figure 77.

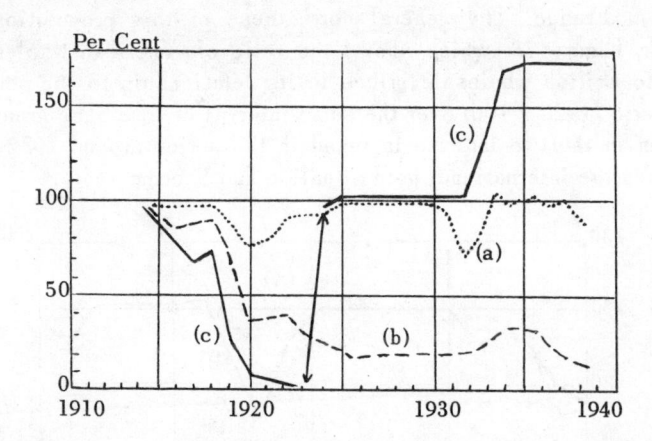

Figure 77. Values of the Ratios of Exchange in Terms of Dollars, Reduced to Per Cent of 1914 Values: (a) the Pound; (b) the Franc, (c) the Mark.

The devastating effect of war upon international currencies is clearly exhibited in the graphical representation of the ratios. From a world of trade-stability which prevailed in the years prior to 1914, the countries were precipitated by the war into a world where instability ruled. Under the impact of an inflation which carried the War index, $W(t)$, to a level of 6.03, the dollar-franc parity declined from 100 in 1914 to 17 in 1926 and has made no essential recovery since that time. The franc was not tied to a gold standard and hence it benefited but temporarily from the gold revaluation of 1934. Thus from an index of 20 in 1932 the dollar-franc ratio rose to 34 in 1935 and was back to 13 by 1939. The general weakness of the French economy is clearly revealed by this behavior of the franc.

As a result of World War II the currencies again showed a decline and in 1952 the dollar values of the pound, the franc and the mark had reached respectively the following levels: $2.80, $0.002875, and $0.2383.

Upon casual reflection it is easy to see that the parities of currencies depend largely upon the relative internal prices which exist in the different countries. Thus, when the dollar-franc ratio is 20 (base parity at 100 = 20 francs to one dollar), then an article which costs $100 in the United States should cost approximately 2,000 francs in France. The general correctness of this proposition is found in Figure 78, which shows the ratio of American wholesale prices to British wholesale prices in its relationship to the pound-dollar ratio (1926 = 100) over the same interval of time. The greatest variation in the two indexes is found in the period around 1932 and 1933 when the international gold situation had become acute.

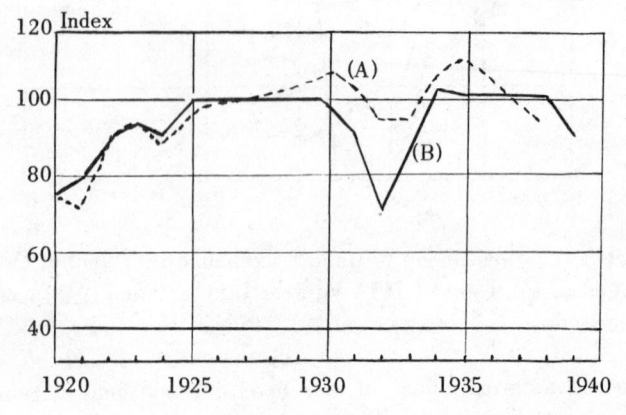

Figure 78. Relationship between Exchange Ratios of Internal Prices. (A) Ratio of American Wholesale Price Index to British Wholesale Price Index; (B) Pound-Dollar Exchange Ratio. (1926 = 100).

It is clear from the figure that all the variation in a ratio of currencies cannot be accounted for by the ratio of internal prices. The reason for this is not far to see, since the ratio between two currencies is not a function of the price levels of two countries alone, but it is related also to the economies of all other countries as well. This complicated relationship has never been satisfactorily formulated in mathematical and statistical terms.

In his classical work on the *Mathematical Principles of the Theory of Wealth* published in 1838, A. A. Cournot (1801-1877) attempted to account for the ratios of exchange in terms of an exchange of credits between financial centers in different countries over short periods of time. Although this theory exhibited clearly and satisfactorily the interrelationships which existed between the ratios of several countries, the modern development has shown that Cournot's theory is untenable. The *balance of trade*, which means the difference between the amount of goods exported and the amount imported by a country, has been enormously in favor of the United States since World War I. The accumulation of this favorable balance of trade between 1910 and 1933, when it reached its maximum value for the period prior to World War II, was in excess of 28 billion dollars. But the only result of this great balance of trade was to drain perhaps three-fourths of the world's supply of gold into the vaults of the United States and had little to do with the fluctuations of the various ratios of exchange. Hence it is clear that the ratios cannot be accounted for by Cournot's theory, but rather they are functions of the ratios of the internal prices of the various economies which trade in the markets of the world.

Our conclusion from this brief discussion of a complex and still somewhat mysterious situation is that no clear pattern of causal factors emerges to indicate why international frictions develop out of international trade. It is evident, nevertheless, that the ravages of war exert a profound change upon international moneys. But this change is very closely related to the one which we have used to measure the intensity of war, namely, the change in internal prices.

11. *Other Theories of Conflict.*

The theory of war tensions as developed in Section 9 is closely related to ideas which have been advanced in recent years by the Italian mathematician Vito Volterra (1860-1940) and by L. F. Richardson in England. The first theory was published in a treatise entitled: *Leçons sur la théorie mathématique de la lutte pour la vie*, Paris, 1931, the second in a monograph on "Generalized Foreign Policy," which appeared in 1939.*

The theory of Richardson attempts to develop measures to describe the effects upon two nations which menace one another by the size of their armaments. If x measures the armament of one country and y the armament of its rival, and if the derivatives of x and y with re-

---

*British Journal of Psychology, Monograph Supplements, Vol. 23, 1939.

spect to time (t) describe the rates of increase of these preparations for war, then, according to the theory advanced, the relationship between these variables can be represented by the following system of differential equations:

$$\frac{dx}{dt} = -ax + by + f, \qquad \frac{dy}{dt} = cx - dy + g, \qquad (1)$$

where a, b, f, and c, d, g are constants.

Since f and g can be removed by a linear transformation of variables, namely,

$$x = x' + h \text{ and } y = y' + k,$$

we can set f and g equal to zero without limiting the generality of the system.

If the first equation is differentiated with respect to t and if y and dy/dt are eliminated from the resulting system of three equations, it will be found that x satisfies the following equation:

$$\frac{d^2x}{dt^2} + (a+d)\frac{dx}{dt} + (ad - bc)x = 0. \qquad (2)$$

A similar elimination of x and dx/dt shows that y also satisfies the same equation.

If the parameters are all assumed to be positive, and if $(ad - bc)$ is also positive, then the characteristic solution of equation (2) is a damped harmonic function of the form:

$$x = A\,e^{-rt} \sin(kt + B), \qquad (3)$$

where $r = \frac{1}{2}(a + d)$, and A and B are arbitrary constants.

Since there appears to be little damping in the preparations for war over long periods of time, it is not unreasonable to assume that r is a quantity close to zero. This means that x and y vary in time in a sinusoidal manner, passing through periods of maximum armament and, after belligerency has passed usually by the termination of a war, passing through periods of minimum armament.

Since B in (3) is an arbitrary constant, it is clear that this description of the problem of the armament race between two powers takes account of the frequently observed fact that the preparations of one country may lag behind that of another, as in the case of Germany and Great Britain in the period before World War II.

The theory of Richardson is obviously an over-simplification of the problem, but it may serve as a first approximation to what is observed. Since most armament races involve more than one nation, it is probable that system (1) above should be augmented by other equations of the same form in which the armaments (u, v, w, etc.) of other nations are connected linearly with dx/dt, dy/dt, du/dt, etc. The solution of such a system, under proper assumptions with respect to the parameters, is expressed as the sum of harmonic terms.

The theory of Volterra was created to explain the "struggle for life" between two species, one of which preys on the other. Its application to the problem of war might be found in those conflicts which develop between nations over the question of territorial expansions. Such expansions are usually demanded by the pressure of populations, where one nation seeks room for its people at the expense of a neighboring nation. Such a conflict is found in the invasion of China by Japan in the period before World War II.

In order to reduce the problem to exact terms, let us consider two variables N_1 and N_2, which are assumed to work in opposition to one another. Thus N_1 might measure a population (A) which preys upon a second population (B) measured by N_2. If N_2 is large, then (A) in the presence of so much prey will flourish and N_1 will increase. But as N_1 increases, the prey will diminish, that is to say, N_2 will decrease, and there will ensue a period of starvation for population (A). Then, as N_1 decreases, the prey will again begin to flourish and the cycle passes into its second phase.

The situation which we have just described can be formulated in terms of the following system of equations:

$$\frac{dN_1}{dt} = a N_1 - b N_1 N_2, \qquad \frac{dN_2}{dt} = -c N_2 + d N_1 N_2, \qquad (4)$$

where a, b, c, and d are positive quantities.

If we change to the new variables: $x = N_1 d/c$ and $y = N_2 b/a$, then system (4) assumes the simpler form,

$$\frac{dx}{dt} = ax(1-y), \qquad \frac{dy}{dt} = -cy(1-x). \qquad (5)$$

The relationship between x and y is given by the equation,

$$cx + ay - c \log_e x - a \log_e y = K,$$

where K is an arbitrary constant.

By methods which are too complicated to be given here*, it is possible to determine x and y as functions of time. As in the theory of Richardson, these variables are roughly periodic, as is shown in Figure 79.

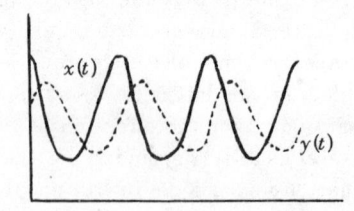

Figure 79. Components x and y as functions of time for Volterra's theory of the "struggle for life" corresponding to $a = 2$, $c = 1$.

The application of this theory to biological data has been made by G. F. Gause with encouraging results.† It would be interesting and doubtless instructive as well to see to what extent the theory might succeed in the description of wars of aggression between two contiguous powers, where the variables N_1 and N_2 are to be interpreted as measures of the territorial areas held at various times by the belligerents. The three struggles between Rome and Carthage, since they were not complicated by the activities of a third power, might furnish data for such an analysis.

The sinusoidal character of armament races can be illustrated in a rather crude manner by studying the war curve for Great Britain since the time of the Norman Conquest, correcting it for the factor of population. For this purpose we graph the ratio $y = x/P$, where x is the number of men under arms by quarter-century periods as given in Section 5 and P is the corresponding size of the population in millions of people. The resulting graph is shown in Figure 80, upon

---

*For this computation see either **Volterra** (*op. cit.*), or H. T. Davis: *The Analysis of Economic Time Series*, Bloomington, Ind., 1941, pp. 359-363.

†*The Struggle for Existence*, Baltimore, 1934.

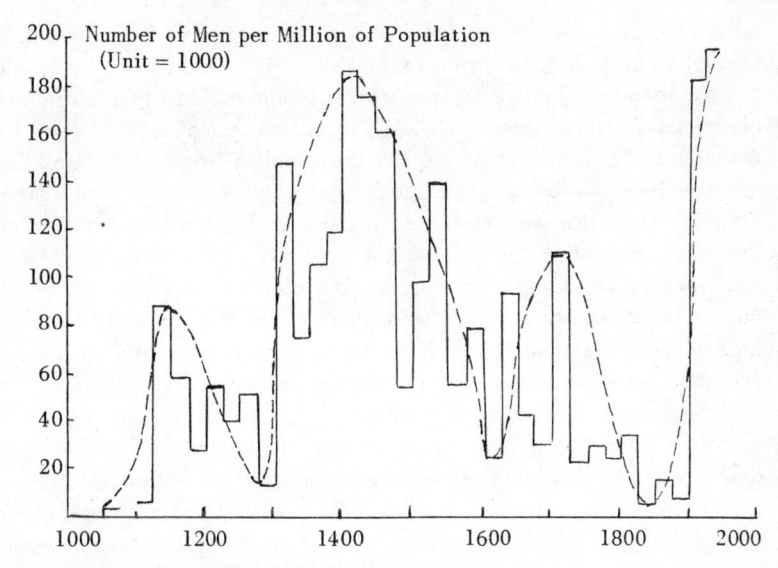

Figure 80. Men under arms in wars of Great Britain, corrected for Population.

which has been superimposed a sinusoidal trend crudely characteristic of the data. It is clear that neither the theory of Richardson nor that of Volterra will describe the pattern thus observed. But there is no reason to believe that they should do so, since the history of Great Britain has been complicated by constant involvement in the affairs of other European nations. The conflicts represented in Figure 80 have often been associated with the wars and the war-preparations of several powers at a time. It is clear that a description of these entanglements would require a more complicated system of equations than those given above in (1) and (5).

12. *History of Attempts to Solve the Problem of War.*

It is a belief, quite generally held, but never actually proved by an appeal to data, that the majority of mankind dislikes war and would go to great lengths to prevent it. Notable authorities do not agree entirely with this proposition. Students of the phenomenon have pointed out that, when a war fever seizes upon the population as a whole, only the smallest minority voices its disapproval. Bertrand Russell, an avowed pacifist, made the following comment in his work on *Why Men Fight* (1917): "War is accepted by men who are neither Germans nor diplomats with a readiness, which would not be possible if any deep repugnance to war were widespread in other nations or classes..." Hans Zinsser (1878-1940), a teacher of bacteriology and a thoughtful scientist, approached the problem from a contemplation of the effects of disease upon the fate of nations. His studied conclusion in the matter was stated as follows in his work on *Rats, Lice, and History* (1935): "If it were not for the fact that so many utterly uninterested people die of disease, or are killed in them, wars would not be taken so seriously. It is of course true that rapacity for territory, commercial rivalry, and all other expressions of that avarice which is as instinctive to the human species as the sexual and intestinal functions, have always been present as the underlying causes of war. But it is doubtful whether these more or less realistic reasons would fulminate to the actual point of explosion as often as they do if mankind did not, in spite of repeated demonstration, obstinately harbor a totally erroneous conception of what actually constitutes a war in terms of experience."

But it is true that men, from earliest times, have banded together for protection against the dangers of their external enemies, not in the sense of nations, but in the sense of groups of nations. One of the first adventures of this kind that had any degree of permanence was the famous Achaen league, which maintained something of an effective organization from about 368 B. C. to about 150 B. C. This federation bound together the ancient towns of Achaea, lying in the unprotected plain along the southern coast of the Corinthean Gulf. The success of the league, and its permanence when compared with other such organizations, was undoubtedly due to the close economic and political interests of the member cities.

Another organization, noteworthy because of its cohesion and long duration, was the Hanseatic league, an effective federation of towns lying for the most part in the great Baltic basin in northern Germany. The origin of the league is somewhat obscure, but can be traced back to the thirteenth century. Its zenith of power came in the period between 1356 and 1377, but it continued to exert great influence into the sixteenth century. Its decline was marked by its wars with the Scandinavian countries in the sixteenth century. In the period when the Thirty Years' War (1618-1648) was devastating Europe, its influence was negligible.

It is a matter of considerable interest to observe that the formation of the Hanseatic league was initiated by the same forces which brought into existence the earlier Achean league. In both cases a group of coastal towns, beset by the depredations of pirates, and faced with the same interests in trade and politics, were forced by their mutual desires and their common need for protection to create a federation. It is also significant, perhaps, to observe the relative stability of the two organizations. Both survived as efficient and influential forces for a period which exceeded two centuries.

The idea of a federation of states is as old as history itself. The countless treaties which have been made in attempts to preserve peace between nations are indications of this tendency toward federation. In the troubled history of Europe the principle of the *balance of power* came into play, in which attempts were made by treaty agreements to make it impossible for one coalition of states to dominate another. But the instability of the balance-of-power principle has been made manifest in the eruptions of World War I and World War II.

Observing the complex and competitive world, with territories divided among a host of states both great and small, with constant frictions generated by trade and political factors, idealistic people have long sought for a formula by means of which these difficulties could be settled outside of war. The first attempt in recent times to approach the problem was the formation of a Court of International Arbitration in 1899 at the Hague, which is often referred to as The Hague Tribunal.

People everywhere hailed the creation of the court with enthusiasm, and it was endorsed by a significant number of nations. A second conference was held in 1907 and a number of international disputes were adjudicated by the new judicial body. But underlying the work of the court and the measure of approval accorded it by the signatory powers, existed the menacing restriction that there would be reservation in accepting the judgment of the court on all questions involving "the vital interest, the independence, or honor of the nation." The importance of this restriction was not long in appearing. In August, 1914, just one year after the completion of the magnificent Peace Palace at the Hague, "the vital interest, independence, and honor" of a significant number of the signatory powers required the arbitration of war rather than the arbitration of an international court.

At the end of World War I a new and more ambitious attempt was made to establish machinery for the adjudication of international disputes. The League of Nations was established at Geneva, Switzerland January 10, 1920. The old Hague Tribunal was replaced by what was called the Permanent Court of International Justice, which was established at The Hague. But the same troubles beset the League which had rendered futile the work of the Hague Tribunal. International disputes which involved vital national interests were not referred to the League. In 1935 Italy invaded Ethiopia and in 1936 Civil War broke out in Spain. On September 25, 1937 the magnificent Assembly Hall of the League was opened in Geneva attended by 2,800 people from all corners of the earth. But in that fateful year the Sino-Japanese war broke out in spite of all the pressure that could be brought to bear by the League, and this was the prelude to the most devastating conflict in the history of the world. The high hopes of those who sought to create a world of peace through arbitration were again shattered.

But the fate of the League of Nations did not prevent another trial of the judicial methods which so far had proved futile. Upon the ruins of the old League a new organization was founded almost before the guns of World War II had had time to cool. The creation of the new federation was effected in a conference held between April 25 and June 26, 1945 in San Francisco, and the charter was signed by fifty nations. The new league to preserve the peace of the world was given the name of the United Nations, a somewhat unfortunate designation as it turned out, since there immediately developed violent disunities, which have threatened the existence of the organization almost from the beginning.

The assets of the League of Nations were turned over to the new federation. Permanent headquarters were established on the east side of Manhattan. The judicial branch of the United Nations was established in an organ now called the International Court of Justice, which, like its predecessor, functions at The Hague.

The high hopes of the founders of the United Nations received a rude shock when a violent difference broke out between the block of western nations, headed by the United States, and the Soviet block, headed by the Union of Soviet Socialist Republics. The world was then accorded the remarkable spectacle of an organization designed to preserve the peace of the world, itself entering upon a war which became one of first magnitude. On June 25, 1950 the Republic of

Korea was invaded by the armed forces of communistic North Korea. The Security Council of the United Nations declared the invasion a breach of the peace and called for a withdrawal of the invading forces to the 38th parallel. By a vote, in which the representatives of the Soviet Union were absent, the members of the United Nations were called upon to enforce the resolution. The brunt of the ensuing war was borne by the troops of the United States and South Korea, with battle casualties through 1952 of approximately 300,000. The casualties of the invading forces, supplemented by troops from China, are estimated to be of the order of 1,659,000.

13. *Cohesion and its Significance in the Theory of Tensions.*

It is clear from the historical outline given in the preceding section that the success of international organizations designed to preserve peace in the world has been imperiled by the political tensions existing between member states. Although there does not appear to exist machinery readily available for reducing these tensions, a forward step would be achieved if it were possible to measure the magnitude of existing tensions.

Such a measure would necessarily depend upon a number of factors, and thus would present a problem of great complexity. However, one possibility of approximating such a measure has been suggested. This is found in an application of a theory of *cohesion* defined a number of years ago by Stuart A. Rice in his classical work on *Quantitative Methods in Politics* (1928). Although currency was given to this theory by Rice, including examples of its application, the idea appears to have been advanced independently at the same time by W. F. Ogburn and D. A. Peterson.*

The cohesion within some political body is measured by the voting behavior of its members on one or more problems. Let us assume that some question at issue has been reduced to a yea/nay vote, and that x is the percentage of the group which has voted in the affirmative. *Cohesion* is then measured by the departure of x from the neutral position where the group divides evenly between the affirmative and the negative positions.

---

*"Political Thought of Social Classes," *Political Science Quarterly*, Vol. 31, pp. 300-317.

Reduced to mathematical terms, the *index of cohesion* (*C*), defined by Rice, is given by the following formula:

$$C = 2\,|50 - x|.$$

For example, if the members of a group cast an affirmative vote of either 30% or 70%, the cohesion is measured by an index of 40. If the group divides evenly, that is to say, 50% vote in the affirmative (or negative), then the cohesion is zero; but if all the members vote in the affirmative (or in the negative), then the index of cohesion is 100. In the case of a number of roll calls, the *average cohesion* is determined by taking an unweighted arithmetical mean of the individual cohesions.

Rice extended this idea to include a comparison between two groups. He introduced a coefficient of *likeness* (*L*), which in mathematical terms, may be written,

$$L = 100 - |x - y|,$$

where x and y are the respective percentages cast in the affirmative by each group. Thus, if $x = 30$, and $y = 70$, then the *likeness* is measured by the quantity $L = 100 - 40 = 60$. The index varies from 0, when x (or y) = 100 and y (or x) = 0, to 100 when $x = y$.

Rice applied his measures of cohesion and likeness both to the voting of seven groups of the New York Assembly of 1921 and to the Assembly as a whole. It will serve our purpose, as an illustration of what might be expected in such voting, to consider the values obtained for three groups: (1) the entire Assembly; (2) the Republican members; (3) the Democratic members. Basing his computations upon 169 roll calls which contained six or more opposing votes, Rice obtained the following values for *C* and *L*:

Groups	Cohesion (*C*)	Comparison Groups	Likeness (*L*)
(1) Entire Assembly	51.4	(1) and (2)	87.3
(2) Republicans	74.8	(1) and (3)	49.5
(3) Democrats	77.4	(2) and (3)	37.1

One can readily observe from the values of *C* and *L* that the Assembly in the year 1921 was predominantly Republican.

We turn next to an application of the concept of cohesion to voting in the United Nations, where a lack of unity has been quite conspicuous. The problem, however, is complicated by the fact that three modes of voting have been used by the members of both the General Assembly and of the Security Council, namely, (a) an affirmative vote; (b) a negative vote; (c) an abstaining vote. The latter is not an absent vote, but a vote which declares that the nation does not care either to support or to oppose the question at issue.

In order to take account of this trichotomy in voting, a new measure of cohesion was required. This was formulated by Edris P. Smith.* Observing that the definition of Rice is a measure of the departure of the vote from the neutral position of half positive and half negative, Mrs. Smith assumed as neutral, or zero cohesion, a vote evenly divided between the three alternatives. Thus, if V is the total vote, then zero cohesion would correspond to a vote of $V/3$ for each case. Cohesion would be increased by any vote which departed from this neutral position. To obtain such a measure, let U be the most cohesive vote, that is to say, the maximum number among the votes for the three alternatives. It is clear that the quantity $U - V/3$ can not be negative, and that its maximum value is attained when $U = V$. If, now, we divide $U - V/3$ by $V - V/3 = \tfrac{2}{3}V$, and multiply by 100, we shall have a measure which varies from 0, when $U = V/3$, to 100, when $U = V$.

This ratio was introduced by Mrs. Smith as an index of cohesion, that is, the quantity:

$$I = 100 \, \frac{U - V/3}{V - V/3} = 50 \, [3(U/V) - 1].$$

For example, if 9 states vote, with 3 affirmative, 2 negative, and 4 abstaining, then $V = 9$, $U = 4$, and $I = 50 \, [3(\tfrac{4}{9}) - 1] = 16.7$. In measuring the cohesion based upon a number of votes, the arithmetic mean of the individual cohesions is used.

By means of this index Mrs. Smith measured the cohesion exhibited by the voting behavior of a number of special blocs among the member nations. The measure was applied to voting both in the General Assembly and in the Security Council. The unity within the

---

*In her Doctor's Dissertation: *Regionalism Within the United Nations*, 422 pp., Northwestern University, written under the direction of Dr. Kenneth Colegrove.

blocs and the comparative disunity of the general group is shown by the following table:

Groups	No. in Blocs	First* Session	Second** Session	Third Session	Fourth Session
(1) Arab	6	90.4	90.2	77.0	85.0
(2) Soviet	6	89.4	93.6	95.6	93.3
(3) British Commonwealth	6-7	75.5	56.2	55.0	58.9
(4) Western Europe	10	70.5	74.6	81.7	66.3
(5) North Atlantic	7-8	69.9	74.3	79.8	60.5
(6) Western Democracies	10-12	71.1	70.2	81.5	66.2
(7) General Assembly	51-59	50.4	41.0	47.1	51.3

*Includes votes of First Special Session; **Includes votes of Second Special Session.

From this table it is easily seen that the element of tension existed between the various blocs to such an extent that the cohesion of the General Assembly ranged around a mean value of 50%. This lack of cohesion is sharply in contrast with the high cohesion of the Soviet and Arab blocs, which often voted in opposition to the majority of the membership.

14. Conclusion.

We have seen from the foregoing sections of this chapter that the problem of conflict, while it is one of the most important ones faced both by the governments of the world and by the people subject to their rules, is yet in an unsatisfactory statistical form. The most vital data are lacking for most of the great wars of the past. We have been forced to use crude estimates of the number of participating forces; and the total costs are almost wholly lacking for most of the conflicts. The only data of reasonable accuracy are found in the price increases which accompany all wars and measure their intensities, and in the growth of national debts during periods of national struggle.

We have not been able to achieve a satisfactory theory of the general origin of wars, although the concept of "distances" between nations is a suggestive thesis which has provided a realistic measure of the tensions between the powers. The difficulty with this theory obviously resides in its subjective character, although the possibility exists that objective measures might be achieved ultimately through the definition by statistical means of the different distances that have been described. Measures of cohesion have been introduced as evidence of the existence of these international tensions and as a means of estimating their magnitudes.

Another promising approach appears to be through the channel of international trade. Friction between nations from this cause has long been known. Thus Adam Smith in his *Wealth of Nations* (1776), while arguing the advantages of free trade between England and France, admitted that "the very circumstances which would have rendered an open and free commerce between the two countries so advantageous to both, have occasioned the principal obstructions to that commerce. Being neighbors, they are necessarily enemies, and the wealth and power of each becomes, upon that account, more formidable to the other; and what would increase the advantage of national friendship serves only to inflame the violence of national animosity. They are both rich and industrious nations; and the merchants and manufacturers of each dread the competition of the skill and activity of those of the other. Mercantile jealousy is excited, and both inflames, and is itself inflamed, by the violence of national animosity."

Unfortunately no adequate measures have been devised to measure the national tensions engendered by international trade. The effects of war can be observed in the fluctuations of the various ratios of exchange, but when these are traced back to their causes we find that they are the results of fluctuations in the structure of internal prices. Since we have already used these very price variations in our index of war intensity, we find that we have discovered nothing essentially new by this approach to the problem of conflict.

Our conclusion from these investigations seems to be that the essential causal thread of conflict is still elusive. But in spite of this lack of success, there has been no evidence adduced which would show that the statistical approach to the problem of conflict will not ultimately provide some rational theory for the cause of international ruptures and at the same time create a measurable basis for the tensions which exist between the nations of the world.

APPENDIX

APPENDIX

1. *The Laws of Exponents*

In arithmetic one learns that $2 \times 2 \times 2$ when multiplied by 2×2 equals $2^3 \times 2^2 = 2^5$. The theory of exponents is a generalization of this simple arithmetical fact. Thus, if a is a positive number, and if m and n are any numbers whatsoever, we can assume the general truthfulness of the following relationship:

$$a^m \cdot a^n = a^{m+n}, \quad a \neq 0. \tag{1}$$

This identity is called the *index law*. The number a is the *base* and m and n are *exponents*.

If m and n are positive integers, then the law is self-evident. But when m and n are not positive integers, the meaning of the law is not immediately clear. The extention of the law to include exponents other than positive integers is achieved through the following equations, which are derived as consequences of the index law. Proofs are given in textbooks on algebra.

I. $a^0 = 1,$

II. $a^{-n} = \dfrac{1}{a^n},$

III. $a^{p/q} = \sqrt[q]{a^p} = (\sqrt[q]{a})^p,$

where p and q are positive integers.

These relationships can be illustrated by examples.

Example 1. Show by means of the index law that $2^0 = 1$.

Solution. Referring to (1) we choose $a = 2$ and $m = 0$. We then have by this law that $2^0 \cdot 2^n = 2^{0+n} = 2^n$. Hence 2^0 must equal 1 since 1 is the only multiplier which leaves a number unchanged.

Example 2. Evaluate $2^{-2} + 8^{2/3}$.

Solution. From II we have $2^{-2} = 1/2^2 = 1/4$. From III we get $8^{2/3} = (\sqrt[3]{8})^2 = 2^2 = 4$. Hence the desired sum is $1/4 + 4 = 17/4$.

Example 3. Find the value of $(64/27)^{2/3} + (81/16)^{-3/4}$.

Solution. By II and III we get,

-321-

$$\left(\frac{64}{27}\right)^{2/3} + \left(\frac{81}{16}\right)^{-3/4} = \left(\frac{64}{27}\right)^{2/3} + \left(\frac{16}{81}\right)^{3/4} = \left(\sqrt[3]{\frac{64}{27}}\right)^2 + \left(\sqrt[4]{\frac{16}{81}}\right)^3$$

$$= \left(\frac{4}{3}\right)^2 + \left(\frac{2}{3}\right)^3 = \frac{16}{9} + \frac{8}{27} = \frac{56}{27}.$$

Other consequences follow from the index law. Thus if n is replaced by $-n$, and account taken of II, we get

$$a^m \cdot a^{-n} = \frac{a^m}{a^n}. \tag{2}$$

From successive applications of the index law, on the assumption that n is an integer, we obtain

$$a^m \cdot a^m \cdot a^m \cdots \text{(to } n \text{ factors)} = a^{m+m+m+\cdots} \text{ to } n \text{ terms} = a^{mn}.$$

This can be written in the form

$$(a^m)^n = a^{mn}. \tag{3}$$

Although this law has been derived for the case when n is an integer, it can be shown to hold generally for all values of m and n.

When more than one base is employed the following identities hold:

$$a^n \cdot b^n = (ab)^n, \tag{4}$$

$$\frac{a^n}{b^n} = \left(\frac{a}{b}\right)^n.$$

PROBLEMS

1. Express the following numbers in the form 10^n: 100; 10,000; 1; 0.01; 0.00001; one million; one billion; 1,000 trillions.

Evaluate the following:

2. $125 \cdot 5^{-5}$.
3. $x \cdot x^2 \cdot x^3 \cdot x^5$.
4. $(0.01)^{-2}$.
5. 10^{-5}.
6. $8^{-3/2} + (1/16)^{3/4}$.
7. $(25)^{-1/2} + (625)^{-1/4}$.
8. $2^{-1} + 2^{-2} + 2^{-3}$.
9. $\sqrt[3]{\sqrt{729}}$.
10. $(3^m \cdot 5^m)^2$.
11. $\sqrt{3} \cdot \sqrt[3]{3} \cdot \sqrt[4]{3}$.
12. $(0.01)^{-3} \cdot (0.001)^{-4}$.
13. $(2^{-2} \cdot 16^{-3/4})^3$.

14. Simplify the following: $(3^{-3} 27^{2/3})^2$; $(64 x^4 y^8)^{1/4}$.

15. Find the value of: $64^{-4/3} - 81^{-3/4}$.

16. Evaluate the product: $(2\sqrt{2} + 3\sqrt{3})(3\sqrt{2} - \sqrt{3})$.

17. If $x = 3$ and $y = 2$, evaluate the fraction $\dfrac{(x^2 - y^2)^2}{(x+y)^2}$.

APPENDIX

2. Logarithms

Logarithms were originally invented as an aid to numerical computation, but they have numerous applications in applied problems beyond the purpose for which they were first designed.

A logarithm is customarily defined in terms of the theory of exponents as follows: By a logarithm, to the base a, of the number m is meant a number x to which power the base must be raised in order to produce the number m. Expressed in symbols, this definition says:

$$\text{If } a^x = m, \text{ then } \log_a m = x.$$

From this definition and the laws of exponents we obtain the following theorems:

I. $\log_a 1 = 0$, since $a^0 = 1$.

II. $\log_a xy = \log_a x + \log_a y$.

Proof: Let $\log_a x = m$ and $\log_a y = n$. From the definition of a logarithm, we have: $a^m = x$ and $a^n = y$. Therefore, from the index law, we get the product: $a^m \cdot a^n = a^{m+n}$, and from the definition again we obtain the desired relationship: $\log_a xy = m+n = \log_a x + \log_a y$.

III. $\log_a \dfrac{x}{y} = \log_a x - \log_a y$.

Proof: Letting $\log_a x = m$ and $\log_a y = n$, we have from the definition: $a^m = x$ and $a^n = y$. Then making use of (2) in the theory of exponents (Section 1), we get: $x/y = a^m/a^n = a^{m-n}$. If we now reduce this statement to logarithms by making use of the definition, we have: $\log_a x/y = m - n = \log_a x - \log_a y$.

IV. $\log_a x^n = n \log_a x$.

Proof: If one lets $\log_a x = m$, it follows by definition that $a^m = x$. Therefore, raising both sides to the power n and referring to the theory of exponents, we get: $x^n = (a^m)^n = a^{mn}$. It follows from this that: $\log_a x^n = mn = n \log_a x$.

Sometimes it is necessary to transfer logarithms from one base a to a second base b. For example, *common* or *Briggsian** logarithms,

---

*Named after Henry Briggs (1561-1631), who was the first to calculate a table of logarithms to the base 10.

are computed to the base 10, and *natural* logarithms are computed to the base designated by the symbol e, where $e = 2.71828\ldots$. This number, often called *Napier's number*, is one of the most important in mathematics. Its use in statistics is illustrated by the discussions in Section 5, Chapter 4, and in Section 7, Chapter 7. The following formula allows one to change from one system of logarithms to another:

$$\text{V. } \log_a x = \frac{1}{\log_b a} \log_b x.$$

Proof: Let $\log_a x = m$; then, by the definition of a logarithm, $a^m = x$. Taking logarithms to the base b of both sides of this equation, we get

$$\log_b a^m = \log_b x.$$

Applying IV above, we obtain

$$m \log_b a = \log_b x;$$

whence, substituting $m = \log_a x$, we get

$$\log_a x \cdot \log_b a = \log_b x,$$

and hence

$$\log_a x = \frac{1}{\log_b a} \log_b x.$$

It is useful to specialize this theorem for the case of common and natural logarithms. Thus, to go from the common to the natural system, we use

$$\text{V(a). } \log_e x = 2.30259 \log_{10} x,$$

and from the natural to the common system,

$$\text{V(b). } \log_{10} x = 0.43429 \log_e x.$$

Example 1. Calculate the value of $\log_2(8^{3/2}/16^{1/3})$.

Solution. Making use of the properties III and IV given above we have

$$\log_2(8^{3/2}/16^{1/3}) = \log_2 8^{3/2} - \log_2 16^{1/3} = \tfrac{3}{2}\log_2 8 - \tfrac{1}{3}\log_2 16.$$

But since $8 = 2^3$ and $16 = 2^4$, we see that $\log_2 8 = 3$ and $\log_2 16 = 4$. Hence we get

APPENDIX 325

$$\log_2(8^{3/2}/16^{1/3}) = \tfrac{3}{2}(3) - \tfrac{1}{3}(4) = \tfrac{9}{2} - \tfrac{4}{3} = 3\tfrac{1}{6}.$$

Example 2. Given $\log_{10} 2 = 0.3010$, find $\log_{10} \sqrt[3]{25}$.

Solution. By proposition IV above we have

$$\log_{10}\sqrt[3]{25} = \log_{10}(5^2)^{1/3} = \log_{10} 5^{2/3} = \tfrac{2}{3}\log_{10} 5.$$

But since $5 = \tfrac{10}{2}$, we have $\log_{10} 5 = \log_{10} 10 - \log_{10} 2 = 1 - \log_{10} 2 = 0.6990$. Hence we get

$$\log_{10}\sqrt[3]{25} = \tfrac{2}{3}\log_{10} 5 = \tfrac{2}{3}(0.6990) = 0.4660.$$

Example 3. Given $\log_{10} 2 = 0.3010$ and $\log_{10} 6 = 0.7782$, calculate the value of $\log_2 6$.

Solution. Making use of V above, we have

$$\log_2 6 = \frac{1}{\log_{10} 2}\log_{10} 6 = \frac{0.7782}{0.3010} = 2.5854.$$

Example 4. Calculate $\log_e 1000$.

Solution. By means of V(a) above, we get

$$\log_e 1000 = 2.30259 \log_{10} 1000 = 2.30259 \times 3 = 6.90777.$$

PROBLEMS

Find the following logarithms:

1. $\log_7 49$.
2. $\log_3 27$.
3. $\log_2 64$.
4. $\log_5 125$.
5. $\log_3 1$.
6. $\log_n(n^{-1/2})$.
7. $\log_{10} 1000$.
8. $\log_{10} 0.001$.
9. $\log_x(x \cdot \sqrt{x})$.
10. $\log_{1/2} 8$.
11. $\log_4 32$.
12. $\log_9 \sqrt{729}$.

Find the values of x:

13. $\log_2 x = 8$.
14. $\log_5 x = -2$.
15. $\log_3 x = -1$.
16. $\log_{10} x = 5$.
17. $\log_{1/2} x = 4$.
18. $\log_x x = 1$.
19. $\log_a x = -2$.
20. $\log_7 x = 3$.
21. $\log_{25} x = \tfrac{1}{2}$.
22. $\log_{81} x = \tfrac{1}{4}$.
23. $\log_{10} x = -5$.
24. $\log_{10} x = -\tfrac{3}{2}$.

Using $\log 2 = 0.3010$ and $\log 3 = 0.4771$, evaluate the following:

25. $\log_{10}(\sqrt[3]{9}/\sqrt{125})$. Hint: $\log_{10} 5 = \log_{10} 10 - \log_{10} 2$.
26. $\log_{10}(\sqrt[3]{4} \cdot \sqrt[5]{125} \cdot \sqrt{27})$.
27. $\log_{10}(625 \cdot \sqrt{8} \sqrt{15})$.

3. *Determination of Logarithms*

Logarithms to the base 10 are adapted to numerical computation. Because of their frequent occurrence, the base need not be repeated in each symbol; thus $\log_{10} x$ may be written simply $\log x$. A table of common logarithms is easily constructed for special values of x. Thus one has:

$$10^0 = 1, \quad \log 1 = 0,$$
$$10^1 = 10, \quad \log 10 = 1,$$
$$10^2 = 100, \quad \log 100 = 2,$$
$$10^3 = 1000, \quad \log 1000 = 3;$$

and for negative exponents:

$$10^{-1} = 0.1, \quad \log 0.1 = -1,$$
$$10^{-2} = 0.01, \quad \log 0.01 = -2,$$
$$10^{-3} = 0.001, \quad \log 0.001 = -3.$$

It will be seen that the integral part of the logarithm of any number can be determined from the above table and its extension. Thus, $\log 753.4$ lies between 2 and 3, since 753.4 lies between 100 and 1000; similarly, $\log 0.07534$ lies between -1 and -2, since 0.07534 lies between 0.1 and 0.01. Hence we can write

$$\log 753.4 = 2 + a,$$
$$\text{and} \quad \log 0.07534 = -2 + a,$$

where a is a positive number less than one. The numbers 2 and -2 are called the *characteristics* of the logarithm and a the *mantissa*.

Definition: The integral part of a logarithm is called the *characteristic*, and the decimal part, when it is written as a positive number, is called the *mantissa*.

The characteristic of the logarithm of a number can be found from the following rules:

I. *The characteristic of the logarithm of a number greater than unity is one less than the number of digits to the left of the decimal point.*

II. *The characteristic of the logarithm of a positive number less than unity is negative and numerically equal to the place of the first digit to the right of the decimal place.*

APPENDIX

For example, the characteristic of 78.32 is 1; of 8756.4 is 3; of 667 is 2; of 0.245 is -1; of 0.00002355 is -5.

The mantissa of a number is found from a table of logarithms. Table II at the end of the book gives the mantissas of logarithms from 1 to 1,000, computed to four significant figures. This table will be sufficient for the purposes of this book, but it should be observed that tables to 5 and 7 places are used in the common application of logarithms.

The following examples sufficiently illustrate how the logarithm of a given number is found and, conversely, how a number is found which corresponds to a given logarithm.

To find the logarithm of a given number.

Example 1. Find log 684.

Solution. The characteristic is 2. To find the mantissa, enter the table with the first two digits 68. Then under the column headed 4 find the required mantissa, namely, 8351. Hence log 684 = 2.8351.

Example 2. Find log 0.0684.

Solution. The characteristic in this case is -2, and the mantissa, as in the first example, is 8351. We thus have log 0.0684 = -2 + 0.8351. The logarithm may be written in either of the following ways:

$$\log 0.0684 = \bar{2}.8351$$

or, $\log 0.0684 = 8.8351 - 10$.

In the first case the minus sign is written above the 2 to indicate that it pertains to that number alone. The advantage of the second case lies in the fact that the logarithm is written as the difference of two positive numbers.

Example 3. Find log 68.43.

Solution. Since the logarithm of a number of four figures cannot be looked up directly in the table, one must use what is called *interpolation*. The mantissa corresponding to 6843 lies between the mantissa of 684 and 685, namely, between 8351 and 8357. Since 68.43 is 0.3 of the interval between 684 and 685, the mantissa for 68.43 is assumed to be 0.3 of the interval between the mantissas for 684 and 685. The difference between 8351 and 8357, called the *tabular difference*, is 6. This computation can be shown as follows:

mantissa of log 685 = 8357
mantissa of log 684 = 8351
tabular difference = 6.

Therefore, the mantissa of log 68.43 = 8351 + 0.3×6 = 8353. From this we get, log 68.43 = 1.8353.

To find the number corresponding to a given logarithm.

Example 1. Find x, where log x = 1.6484.

Solution. Entering the table of mantissas with the number 6484, we see that this corresponds to the number 445. Since the characteristic is 1, x = 44.5.

Example 2. Find x, where log x = 8.6484 - 10.

Solution. Since the mantissa is the same as in the first example, the problem is merely that of placing the decimal point. Hence we get x = 0.0445.

Example 3. Find x, where log x = 0.5710.

Solution. Since the table of mantissas does not include the number 5710, we must interpolate to find x. The process is shown in the following computation:

mantissa of log 373 = 5717   mantissa of log x = 5710
mantissa of log 372 = 5705   mantissa of log 372 = 5705
tabular difference = 12   tabular difference = 5.

Hence the number corresponding to the mantissa 5710 is 372 + $5/12$ = 372.4. Since the characteristic of log x is 0, we get from this computation x = 3.724.

PROBLEMS

Find the logarithms of the following numbers:

1. 2.87.
2. 6.54.
3. 56.8.
4. 999.
5. 0.0837.
6. 0.5532.
7. 38.55.
8. 298.5.
9. 154300.
10. 0.003667.
11. π = 3.142.
12. e = 2.718.
13. $1/\pi$ = 0.3183.
14. $\log_e 10$ = 2.303.
15. $\log_{10} e$ = 0.4343.
16. 16.27.
17. 561.8.
18. 0.008123.
19. 0.1234.
20. 3443.

Find the values of x:

21. log x = 1.4914.   22. log x = 2.8779.   23. log x = 8.7427 - 10.

APPENDIX

24. $\log x = \overline{1}.4857$.   25. $\log x = 0.6325$.   26. $\log x = 0.4971$.
27. $\log x = 0.4343$.   28. $\log x = 2.3991$.   29. $\log x = 9.6378 - 10$.
30. $\log x = 0.1320$.   31. $\log x = 2.3125$.   32. $\log x = 7.5029 - 10$.
33. $\log x = \overline{2}.9033$.   34. $\log x = 6.6185$.   35. $\log x = 3.8132$.

4. Calculation by Logarithms

The use of logarithms as a calculation device depends upon the properties developed in Section 2. The methods of computation are most simply explained by means of typical examples.

Example 1. Find the value of x, where $x = 435 \cdot 87.6 \cdot 0.00432 \cdot 5.92$.

Solution. To make the calculation we use property II of Section 2, which states in effect that the logarithm of a product is equal to the sum of the logarithms of the factors of the product. Thus, taking the logarithm of x, we get

$$\log x = \log 435 + \log 87.6 + \log 0.00432 + \log 5.92.$$

Considerable simplification in actual computation is achieved by making an outline of the problem first and then filling in with the values of the logarithms. The finished work should appear as follows:

$$\begin{aligned}
\log 435 &= 2.6385 \\
\log 87.6 &= 1.9425 \\
\log 0.00432 &= 7.6355 - 10 \\
\log 5.92 &= 0.7723 \\
\hline
\log x &= 2.9888 \\
x &= 974.5.
\end{aligned}$$

Example 2. Find the value of x, where $x = (\sqrt[3]{34.67} \cdot \sqrt{596.3})/6.742$.

Solution. To make the calculation we use properties III and IV of Section 2. Thus we have,

$$\log x = \tfrac{1}{3} \log 34.67 + \tfrac{1}{2} \log 596.3 - \log 6.742.$$

The actual computation can be shown as follows:

$$\begin{aligned}
\tfrac{1}{3} \log 34.67 &= 0.5133 \\
\tfrac{1}{2} \log 596.3 &= 1.3877 \\
\text{sum} &= 1.9010 \\
\log 6.742 &= 0.8289 \\
\hline
\log x &= 1.0721 \\
x &= 11.81.
\end{aligned}$$

Example 3. Compute x, where $x = \sqrt[3]{0.0006329}$.

Solution. From IV, Section 2, we have

$$\log x = \tfrac{1}{3} \log 0.0006329,$$

where $\log 0.0006329 = \overline{4}.8013 = 6.8013 - 10$.

Since this logarithm must be divided by 3, it is obviously more convenient to write it in the equivalent form: $26.8013 - 30$. We thus get

$$\tfrac{1}{3} \log 0.0006329 = \tfrac{1}{3}(26.8013 - 30),$$

$$\log x = 8.9338 - 10,$$

$$x = 0.08586.$$

PROBLEMS

Find the values of the following:

1. $x = 764 \cdot 325 \cdot 45.8$.
2. $x = 372.5 \cdot 389.3$.
3. $x = 0.00219 \cdot 0.00631$.
4. $x = 1984 \cdot \sqrt{56.77}$.
5. $x = 4342 \cdot 7154 \cdot 0.00237$.

6. $x = 6.32 \cdot \sqrt[3]{45.22}$.
7. $x = 97.32 \cdot 0.000777 \cdot 3.104$.
8. $x = 9.978 \cdot 552.3 \cdot 0.0164$.
9. $x = \sqrt[3]{9.832} \cdot \sqrt{78.99}$.
10. $x = (1.078)^2 \cdot (3.261)^{-\frac{1}{2}}$.

Evaluate the following quotients:

11. $\dfrac{365}{924}$.

12. $\dfrac{6.294}{1.873}$.

13. $\dfrac{67.3 \cdot 45.6}{21.3 \cdot 60.4}$.

14. $\dfrac{0.003987 \cdot 0.6529}{0.01692 \cdot 0.00444}$.

15. $\dfrac{76.33 \cdot 0.00003456}{2.289 \cdot 0.5678 \cdot 23}$.

16. $\dfrac{\log 45.22}{\log 3.245}$.

17. $\dfrac{467000 \cdot 7852000}{32.44}$.

18. $\left(\dfrac{0.002876 \cdot 0.002483}{2.341 \cdot 67.5 \cdot 3.333}\right)^2$.

Compute the values of the following by means of logarithms:

19. $(2.37)^3$.
20. $(1950)^{\frac{1}{2}}$.
21. $\sqrt{0.03545}$.
22. $\sqrt[3]{0.0007865}$.
23. $(3.142)^{2.7}$.
24. $(5280)^{1.5}$.

25. The probable error of the mean is $0.6745\sigma/\sqrt{n}$. Evaluate this when $\sigma = 67.23$ and $n = 2037$.

26. Evaluate: $y = \dfrac{1}{\sqrt{2\pi}} e^{-\frac{1}{2}t^2}$, when $t = 0.135$. Use $e = 2.718$, and $\pi = 3.142$.

27. Find by logarithms the geometric average (Chap. 3, Section 8) of the numbers 2, 3, 4, 5.

28. Compute the coefficient of variability (Chap. 3, Section 5), if $\sigma = 2.13$ and $A = 6.29$.

APPENDIX

5. *Exponential Equations*

An *exponential equation* is an equation of the form

$$y = a^x, \qquad (1)$$

where a is a known constant, usually assumed to be a positive number.

The value of x in terms of y can be found by taking logarithms of both sides of the equation. Thus we have

$$\log y = \log a^x = x \log a.$$

From this equation we immediately compute:

$$x = \frac{\log y}{\log a}. \qquad (2)$$

Example 1. Given $y = 3^x$, find x when $y = 326$.

Solution. Employing formula (2), we have

$$x = \frac{\log 326}{\log 3} = \frac{2.5132}{0.4771} = 5.268.$$

Example 2. When will a population double itself if it increases at a rate of 2 per cent annually?

Solution. According to the compound interest law, if P is the initial population, then the population at the end of x years will be given by the formula:

$$y = P(1.02)^x.$$

Referring to the problem, we see that the value of x is required which corresponds to the value $y = 2P$. That is to say, we must solve the equation:

$$(1.02)^x = 2.$$

Making use of (2), we get,

$$x = \frac{\log 2}{\log 1.02} = \frac{0.3010}{0.0086} = 35.$$

PROBLEMS

1. Solve the equation: $2^x = 100$.

2. The law of legislative tenure for Iowa (see Section 5, Chapter 6) is $y = 730.1 \cdot (0.47)^x$. To what value of x corresponds the value $y = 35$?

3. The population of the United States was 5.3 millions in 1800 and 76.0 millions in 1900. What was the average annual rate of growth?

6. Semi-logarithmic and Double-logarithmic Scales

If one is required to represent graphically the equation,

$$y = K a^x, \qquad (1)$$

he will usually find it convenient first to take logarithms of both sides. The equation then reduces to

$$\log y = x \log a + \log K. \qquad (2)$$

By writing $z = \log y$, one sees that (2) represents a straight line if the logarithm of y is plotted on the vertical axis instead of y itself.

To facilitate such graphing *semi-logarithmic paper* has been devised. This is a coordinate paper in which the rulings on the y-axis are spaced according to the logarithms of the numbers, while those on the x-axis are spaced arithmetically.

In the accompanying figure the population growth of the United States is shown on semi-logarithmic paper. This chart can be compared with the arithmetic representation of the same data shown in Figure 40 of Chapter 7. The semi-logarithmic paper exhibits clearly the almost constant rate of growth of the United States over the first century since the initial census was taken in 1790.

In the figure we observe that two separate logarithmic scales are shown. These are called *cycles* or *phases*, and it is customary to refer to semi-logarithmic paper as consisting of two-cycles (or phases), etc., depending upon the number of scales used. It will be observed that the initial value of each cycle is ten times that of the one below it.

Various examples will be found earlier in the book to illustrate the use of semi-logarithmic paper. Thus in Figure 3 of Chapter 1 a three-cycle chart is given. In Figure 56 of Chapter 9, where great inflations of the order of 10^{10} were exhibited, it would have been impossible to show the behavior of prices without use of a logarithmic scale. In particular, Figure 56(d) uses both an arithmetic scale, for small variations, and a logarithmic scale, for the very great changes shown.

Of similar use is the *double-logarithmic paper*, which differs from semi-logarithmic paper in the fact that it uses logarithmic scales for both the abscissas and the ordinates. Its usefulness is found in representing a function of the form:

$$y = A x^k,$$

APPENDIX 333

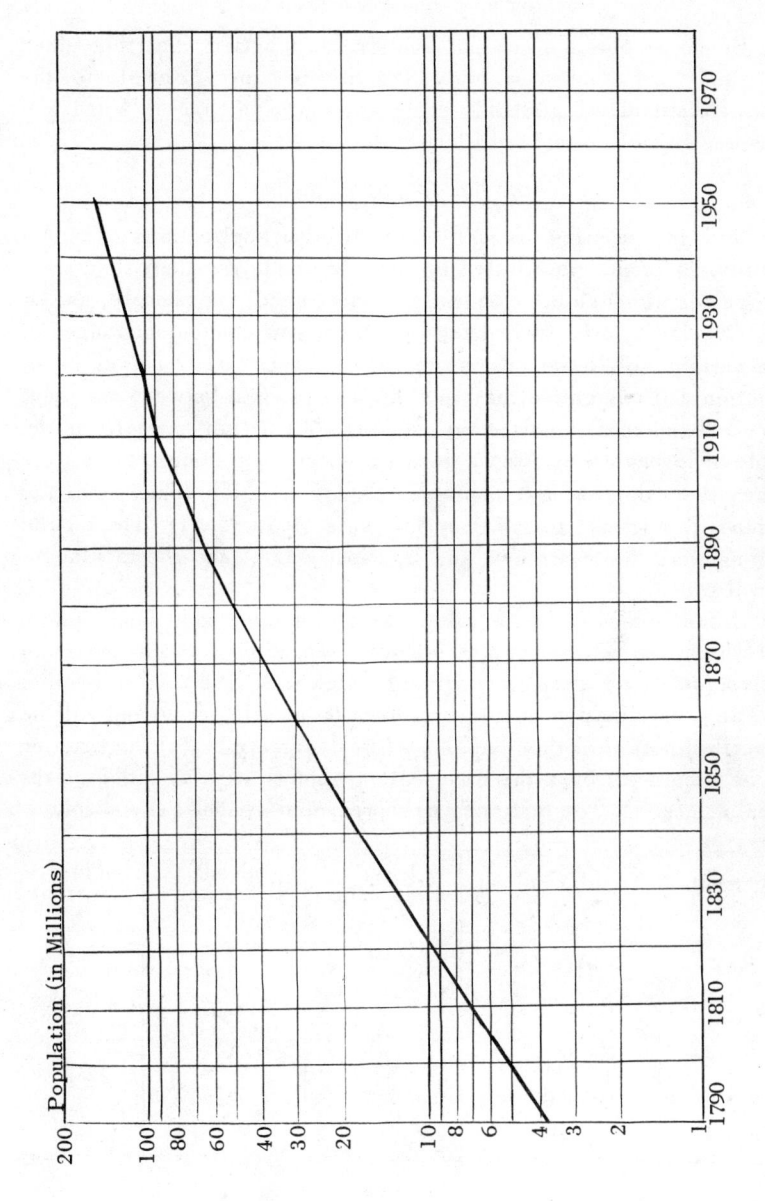

Figure 81. Population of the United States.

for if we take logarithms of both sides of this equation we get

$$\log y = \log A + k \log x.$$

Hence we obtain a straight line for this function when the values of x and y are graphed on double-logarithmic paper. Examples of the use of the double-logarithmic scale are shown in Figures 4 and 5 of Chapter 1 and Figure 44 of Chapter 8.

7. *The Use of Tables*

Work in statistics, as well as in all other applications of mathematics, is greatly facilitated by the use of tables. Many functions, the values of which are frequently needed, such, for example, as $\sqrt{x}$, x^2, $1/x$, $\log x$, etc., have been tabulated over convenient ranges of the variable x. These values are called the *tabular values* of the function and x is called the *argument*. The interval between one value of x and the next is called the *tabular interval*. For example, in the table of logarithms which we used in preceding sections, there were given the values of the mantissas of $\log x$ which corresponded to values of x from 1 to 1,000 by intervals of one unit. The tabular values were the mantissas, the argument was x, and the tabular interval was 1.

If one wishes to find a value which is not recorded in the table, but which lies between two recorded values, he does this by means of *interpolation*, an elementary form of which was described in Section 3. The generalization of this method is frequently useful and will be described here. For this purpose, let us designate by $f(x)$ the function to be tabulated, by x the argument, beginning with a, and by d the tabular interval. The table can be represented symbolically as follows:

Argument x	Tabular Value $f(x)$	First Difference Δ	Second Difference Δ^2	Third Difference Δ^3
a	$f(x)$			
$a + d$	$f(x + d)$	Δ_0	Δ_0^2	
$a + 2d$	$f(x + 2d)$	Δ_1	Δ_1^2	Δ_0^3
$a + 3d$	$f(x + 3d)$	Δ_2	Δ_2^2	Δ_1^3
$a + 4d$	$f(x + 4d)$	Δ_3		

APPENDIX

The differences in the table are defined as follows: $\Delta_0 = f(a+d) - f(a)$, $\Delta_1 = f(a+2d) - f(a+d)$, etc., and $\Delta_0^2 = \Delta_1 - \Delta_0$, $\Delta_0^3 = \Delta_1^2 - \Delta_0^2$, etc.

Now if a value of the function is desired for some value of the argument which is not explicitly given in the table, let us say, for $a + pd$, where p is not an integer, this value can be approximated by means of the following formula, which is generally known as *Newton's formula of interpolation:*

$$f(a+pd) = f(a) + p\Delta_0 + \frac{p(p-1)}{2!}\Delta_0^2 + \frac{p(p-1)(p-2)}{3!}\Delta_0^3 + \ldots \quad (1)$$

The following examples will illustrate the use of this formula:

Example 1. Compute the square of 4.2 from the following table:

x	$f(x) = x^2$	Δ	Δ^2
1	1		
		8	
3	9		8
		16	
5	25		8
		24	
7	49		8
		32	
9	81		

Solution. Since the square of 4.2 is required, we let $a = 3$ and hence use the differences: $\Delta_0 = 16$, $\Delta_0^2 = 8$. Since d (the tabular interval) equals 2, we compute p from the equation: $pd = 4.2 - 3 = 1.2$, that is, $p = 0.6$.

If only two terms of (1) are used we are employing *linear interpolation,* that is,

$$(4.2)^2 \approx 9 + 0.6 \times 16 = 9 + 9.6 = 18.6,$$

where the sign "$\approx$" means "is approximately equal to." In some cases, as in the use of logarithms previously described, linear interpolation gives a sufficiently close approximation. But in the present example, we must use three terms of (1). Hence we get:

$$(4.2)^2 = 9 + 0.6 \times 1.6 + \frac{0.6(1 - 0.6)}{2}8$$
$$= 9 + 9.6 - 0.96 = 17.64,$$

which is exact.

Example 2. Compute the reciprocal of 1.64 from the following table of reciprocal values.

x	$f(x) = 1/x$	Δ	Δ^2
1.4	0.7143		
		-0.0476	
1.5	0.6667		0.0059
		-0.0417	
1.6	0.6250		0.0049
		-0.0368	
1.7	0.5882		0.0042
		-0.0326	
1.8	0.5556		0.0033
		-0.0293	
1.9	0.5263		

Since we are required to find the reciprocal of 1.64, we let $a = 1.6$. Moreover, since $d = 0.1$, we have $p = 0.4$. Now observing that the first differences in this example are negative, we compute:

$$\frac{1}{1.64} = 0.6250 + 0.4 \times (-0.0368) + \frac{0.4(1-0.4)}{2} \times 0.0042$$

$$= 0.6250 - 0.0147 - 0.0005 = 0.6098,$$

which is correct to the four decimal places given.

It is sometimes important to be able to reverse the process explained above and find the value of the argument corresponding to a given value of the function. That is to say, we are given a value $f(a + pd)$, to calculate p. Thus, in Section 3 we were required to find the number which corresponds to a given logarithm. This process is called *inverse interpolation*.

It is at once seen that an approximate answer can be obtained by computing p from the formula,

$$f(a + pd) = f(a) + p\Delta_0, \qquad (2)$$

which is merely (1) with all terms except the first two omitted.

Denoting the value of p obtained from this equation by p_1, we solve for p and thus obtain:

$$p_1 = \frac{f(a + pd) - f(a)}{\Delta_0}. \qquad (3)$$

This value is called a *first approximation*.

To obtain a second approximation, we can use the following formula, which is obtained from (1) by replacing all of the p's except the first in each term by the approximate value p_1:

APPENDIX 337

$$p_2 = \frac{f(a+pd) - f(a)}{\Delta_0 + \frac{(p_1-1)}{2!}\Delta_0^2 + \frac{(p_1-1)(p_1-2)}{3!}\Delta_0^3} \quad . \tag{4}$$

This approximation, p_2, can be substituted in turn in (4) in place of p_1 to obtain a third approximation, and the process thus continued to any desired accuracy.

The following example will illustrate the process of inverse interpolation as it has been described above:

Example 3. From the table of Example 1 compute the square-root of 30.

Solution. Referring to the table, we see that 30 lies between 25 and 49 and hence the desired value of x is equal to $5 + 2p$, since 2 is the tabular interval. We thus have $f(a) = 25$, $f(a + pd) = 30$, $\Delta_0 = 24$, and consequently obtain from equation (3) the approximation:

$$p_1 = \frac{30-25}{24} = 0.2083,$$

which gives the value: $5 + 2p_1 = 5.4166$.

Substituting p_2 in equation (4) and noting that $\Delta_0^2 = 8$, $\Delta_0^3 = 0$, we obtain:

$$p_2 = \frac{30-25}{24 + \frac{1}{2}(0.2083 - 1)\times 8} = 0.2400.$$

From this we obtain the approximation: $5 + 2p_2 = 5.4800$.

Repeating the computation with p_2 instead of p_1 in (4), we get as a third approximation: $p_3 = 0.23854$, and hence as the desired square-root: $5 + 2p_3 = 5.4771$, which is in error by only one unit in the last place.

PROBLEMS

1. From the table of Example 1, compute $(5.4)^2$ and $(5.42)^2$.

2. From the table of Example 2, find the values of $1/1.73$ and $1/1.735$.

3. Using the table of the first example, find by inverse interpolation the values: $\sqrt{10}$ and $\sqrt{40}$.

4. Given $1/x = 0.56$, use inverse interpolation to obtain the value of x from the table of Example 2.

5. Given the function $f(x) = x^3 - 5x + 1$, observe that $f(2) = 8 - 10 + 1 = -1$ and $f(3) = 27 - 15 + 1 = 13$. Make a brief table of the values of $f(x)$ between $f(2)$ and $f(3)$ and determine by inverse interpolation the value of x for which $f(x) = 0$.

8. *The Validity and Analysis of Data.*

One of the most important problems in statistics is the collection of the data themselves, for the validity of any conclusion derived from them depends entirely upon their accuracy. But this problem is one for which no formal rules can be set down, since the methods for obtaining facts about any field of knowledge depend upon the problem that is studied. Astronomers with their telescopes, physicists with their galvanometers, and chemists with their test-tubes are just as truly statisticians in search of data as the economist gathering facts about prices and the political scientist investigating the political composition of a legislative body. In fact, it is probable that the first discovery ever made by statistical analysis was in the field of astronomy when Hipparchus about 150 B. C. discovered the precession of the equinoxes from observations on the position of certain stars reported more than a century earlier.

Before statistical study can proceed it is necessary to begin with a definition of the objects to be investigated. This is a fundamental matter and not one to be regarded lightly. Sometimes a long period of investigation precedes the final formulation of definitions, as is shown by the fact that at least half a century was required by the physicists to make precise their definitions of quantities in the field of electrical transmission. How much more difficult the matter may be in the field of social studies. Thus, in census enumeration, while it is an easy enough matter to define what is meant by the member of a community, the problem of counting the number of persons who are "unemployed" is one of considerable difficulty. It is obviously a matter requiring great ingenuity to formulate a satisfactory definition of an "unemployed" person. Similarly, the term "index of prices" is difficult to define. For there are many prices, namely, wholesale prices, retail prices, agricultural prices, the cost of living, the general level of prices, etc. Even the definition of a single commodity, such as wheat, is hard to formulate, since there are different grades of wheat to be considered, the prices in different markets such as Kansas City and Chicago, and the prices of Spring wheat, May wheat, December wheat, etc. Even in what might at first appear to be a simple matter, namely, the enumeration of major crimes as given in the table on page 27 of Chapter 1, a problem of some difficulty is presented. What is meant by larceny? Each state has its own penal code and these codes often differ significantly from one another. The data in question are from *Uniform Crime Reports*, a publication of the Federal Bureau of Investigation.

One of our primary sources of data is the decennial publication of the United States Census Bureau. The highest order of enumeration is employed here backed by years of experience. But even in a matter as simple apparently as the differentiation of urban and rural population the Census Bureau has changed its definition several times. At present this definition states that "the urban area is made up for the most part of cities and other incorporated places having 2,500 inhabitants or more, places of this type contributing about 96 per cent of the urban places in the U. S." But the remaining four per cent requires two exceptions since certain states, principally in New England, do not grant incorporation to places under 10,000 people and introduce population divisions called townships. Even with the vast machinery of the Bureau some of its reports have been suspected by statisticians, as, for example, the census figures for 1860 and 1870 when the country was disrupted by the events associated with the Civil War. These reports give population counts, namely, 31,443,000 for 1860 and 38,558,000 for 1870, which lie, one significantly above and the other significantly below, interpolation curves that fit the counts of other reports. This has been regarded as a suspicious circumstance by statisticians.

As we have just indicated, the collection of data presents numerous difficulties. It is easy enough for an individual to gather a hundred elm leaves and to measure their lengths, but it requires the resources of the government itself to estimate the size of crops at various times during the growing season, or to count the votes in a national election. Many agencies have been set up to gather statistics. Some of these are private institutions like the Brookings Institution, the Cleveland Trust Company, the Standard and Poor's Corporation, the U. S. Chamber of Commerce, some Life Insurance companies, and similar organizations. One of the largest sources of information is the government itself. We have already mentioned the Bureau of the Census. Other similar agencies are the Bureau of Labor Statistics, the Department of Agriculture, numerous bureaus in the Department of Commerce, etc. Most states also maintain statistical departments and issue yearbooks based upon the data collected. One should also not forget that all scientific laboratories are themselves primarily established to collect data on special problems and as a whole probably contribute more actual statistical information than other agencies especially designated as statistical organizations.

It is a matter of prime importance to know the source of statistical information and to form some judgment as to its validity. This is not an easy matter and usually requires a great deal of experience in the special field of investigation. Primary sources should always be used in any careful study. But where secondary sources are employed, as is sometimes unfortunately necessary, methods should be devised to check the reliability of the reporting agencies. Sometimes data on the same problem are published by independent investigators and the comparisons which such data provide will often furnish significant tests of their reliability.

From what has now been said it is clear that the collection of data and the appraisal of their validity present problems that cannot be readily solved. Each investigation has its own techniques, its own schedule of questions to be answered, its own apparatus for the collection of information.

We have listed below a few of the agencies which provide reliable sources of data, but many more could be added to the list, especially if we enlarged our inquiry to include the work of scientific laboratories:

1. U. S. Publications.
    (a) Decennial Census. A treasury of information about the people of the country and of the American possessions.
    (b) Five year Census of Manufacturers.
    (c) Special bulletins.
2. Agricultural Year Book, Dept. of Agriculture, Washington, D.C. An authoritative collection of data on crops and prices.
3. Statistical Abstract of the U. S. Issued annually by the Department of Commerce. A compendium of detailed information about population, production, prices, banking, etc.
4. Trade and Security Statistics. Issued currently by Standard Statistics and Poor's Corporation.
5. Commerce Year Book, I. United States, II. Foreign Countries. Issued annually by the Bureau of Foreign and Domestic Commerce.

APPENDIX 341

6. Balance of International Payments of the United States. Issued annually by the Bureau of Foreign and Domestic Commerce.
7. Publications of the U. S. Bureau of Labor Statistics. These include bulletins on wholesale and retail prices, changes in the cost of living, data on employment, unemployment, production of labor, wages and hours of labor, etc.
8. Commercial and Financial Chronicle.
9. Dun and Bradstreet Review.

9. *Sources of Data Used in the Body of the Text.*

The sources of the data from which the various charts in the text have been constructed are given below as follows:

Figure 1. Index of Spanish Trade. Based on Soetbeer's Treasure Series, 1501-1650.

Source: This index was constructed from data on treasure given by A. Soetbeer and Spanish prices by E. J. Hamilton using the equation of exchange. Soetbeer's estimates are given by J. D. Magee, "The World Production of Gold and Silver from 1493 to 1905," *Journal of Political Economy,* Vol. 18, 1910, pp. 50-58. For Hamilton's data see the source for Figure 57 below. For details of the calculation see H. T. Davis: *The Analysis of Economic Time Series,* 1941, pp. 489-495.

Figure 2. Growth of Population in Europe.

Source: See origin of data for Figure 54 below.

Figure 3. Law of Legislative Tenure.

Source: C. S. Hyneman: "Tenure and Turnover of the Indiana General Assembly,"*American Political Science Review,* Vol. 32, 1938, pp. 51-67, 311-331. For computation see Section 5, Chapter 6 of this book.

Figure 4. Distribution of Income in Rome at the Time of Augustus Caesar.

Source: Constructed on the basis of data from Tenny Frank: *Rome and Italy of the Republic,* Vol. 1 of *An Economic Survey of Ancient Rome,* Baltimore, 1933, xiv + 431 pp.

Figure 5. Distribution of Income in the United States in the Year 1929.

Source: V. vonSzeliski: *Econometrica,* Vol. 2, 1934, pp. 215-216.

Figure 6. Prices in America in Three Centuries.

Source: From *Prices* by G. F. Warren and F. A. Pearson, New York, 1933. Originally published by Warren, Pearson, and H. M. Stoker:

"Wholesale Prices for 213 Years, 1720 to 1932," Cornell Uni. Agri. Experimental Station, *Memoir* 142, Nov., 1932. From 1890 the index of the Bureau of Labor Statistics is used.

Figure 7. Bar Chart Showing the Number of Cities in Each Urban Class.

Source: United States Bureau of the Census.

Figure 12. Pound-Dollar Exchange Ratio.

Source: Board of Governors of the Federal Reserve System. Published in the *Federal Reserve Bulletin* and also in the *Statistical Abstract of the United States*.

Figure 33. Number of Traffic Accidents in Chicago.

Source: Annual Reports of the Chicago Police Department.

Figure 34. Prices of Railroad Stocks in the United States, 1830-1930.

Source: Data compiled by the Cleveland Trust Co.

Figure 35. Ratio of Population to Representatives in the House of Representatives.

Source: Ratio compiled from data of the Bureau of the Census.

Figure 36. Rate of Divorce in the United States.

Source: Federal Security Agency. Bureau of the Census and the *Statistical Abstract of the United States*.

Figure 37. Composite Index of Building Activity, 1830-1947.

Source: G. F. Warren and F. A. Pearson: *World Prices and the Building Industry*, New York, 1937, v + 240 pp. The index is based upon studies by J. R. Riggleman and Roy Wenzlick to 1936. Since 1936 the index is constructed from data on permit valuations of urban building from the U. S. Bureau of Labor Statistics adjusted to 1935-39 = 100.

Figure 40. Growth of Population of the United States, 1790-1920.

Source: The data are from the Bureau of the Census. The logistic trend is the one originally computed by Raymond Pearl and L. J. Reed: "On the Rate of Growth of the Population of the United States since 1790 and its Mathematical Representation," *Proc. Nat. Academy of Science*, Vol. 6, 1920, pp. 275-288. Reproduced in Pearl's *Studies in Human Biology*, Baltimore, 1924.

Figure 41. Production of Pig Iron.

Source: American Iron and Steel Institute.

Figure 42. Electrical Production.

Source: The Federal Power Commission.

APPENDIX

Figure 43. Production of Wheat; Production of Corn.

Source: U. S. Dept. of Agriculture.

Figure 44. Cumulative Frequency Distribution of Incomes in the United States, 1918, on Double Logarithmic Grid.

Source: Income in the United States, its Amount and Distribution, 1909-1919. National Bureau of Economic Research, Vol. 1, New York, 1921, 152 pp., Vol. 2, 1922, 420 pp. For data see Vol. 1, pp. 132-133.

Figure 46. Distribution of Income in England (1086).

Source: Data from the *Domesday Book* as analyzed by Charles C. Slater in an unpublished manuscript.

Figure 47. Income Distribution in Japan (1938).

Source: Moyoje Hayakawa: "The Application of Pareto's Law of Income to Japanese Data," *Econometrica*, Vol. 19, 1951, pp. 174-183.

Figure 49. Comparison of Income Distributions in the United States, 1914-1948.

Source: To 1933: N. O. Johnson: "The Pareto Law," *The Review of Economic Statistics*, Vol. 19, 1937, pp. 20-26. After 1933, continued from the *Statistical Abstract of the United States*.

Figure 51. Comparison of Theoretical Change in Capital with Actual Index of Capital.

Source: Commercial and Financial Chronicle. Reported in Standard-Poor's *Trade and Securities Statistics*.

Figure 52. Average Price of Slaves in Four Principal Markets.

Source: U. B. Phillips: *American Negro Slavery*. New York, 1918, xi + 529 pp. In particular, p. 370.

Figure 53. Distribution of Slave Ownership in the South Before the Civil War.

Source: H. R. Helper: *The Impending Crisis of the South*. New York, 1857, 420 pp. In particular, p. 146.

Figure 54. Population in Europe.

Source: The estimates are based upon the following: J. Beloch: (1)*Die Bevölkerung der Griechisch-Romeschen Welt*. Leipzig, 1886, xvi + 520 pp.; (2) "Die Bevölkerung im Altertum," *Zeitschrift für Socialwissenschaft*, Vol. 2, 1899, pp. 505-514, 600-621; (3) "Die Bevölkerung Europas zur Zeit der Renaissance," *Ibid.*, Vol. 3, 1900, pp.765-786. See also Quincy Wright: *A Study of War*, Chicago, 1942, Vol. 1, p. 467.

344 POLITICAL STATISTICS

Figure 55. Distribution of Famous Names, 1350-1900.

Source: Constructed from the names listed in Webster's *New International Dictionary,* 1936. Names were assigned to 10 year intervals by the date of the person's twenty-fifth birthday, if this were known.

Figure 56. Four Famous Inflations. (a) Ptolemaic; (b) Roman; (c) English; (d) German.

Source: (a) A. Segré: "The Ptolemaic Copper Inflation C. A. 230-140 B. C.," *American Journal of Philology,* Vol. 63, 1942, pp. 174-197. Also: Segré: *Circolozione monetaria e prezzi nel mondo antico ed in particolare in Egitto.* Rome, 1922, 175 pp.; *Metrologia e circolazione monetaria degli antichi.* Bologna, 1928, xiv + 546 pp. (b) To Diocletian's edict from data in Allan C. Johnson: *Roman Egypt to the Reign of Diocletian.* Baltimore, 1936, x + 732 pp., Vol. 2 of *An Economic Survey of Ancient Rome,* and from Tenny Frank: *Rome and Italy of the Empire.* Baltimore, 1940, xvi + 445 pp., Vol. 5 of *An Economic Survey of Ancient Rome.* After Diocletian's edict data taken from Segré's *Circolozione monetaria,* etc. (c) The data, reduced to cents per bushel based upon equivalent values of gold and silver, are from N. C. Murray: "Wheat Prices in England," Clement, Curtis, and Co., Chicago, 1931. Also available in U. S. Dept. of Agriculture Yearbook for 1922. The basic data are from J. E. T. Rogers: *A History of Agricultural Prices in England,* Oxford, 7 vols. (1866-1902). (d) C. Brescioni-Turroni: *The Economics of Inflation.* London, 1937, 464 pp. First issued in Italian in 1931.

Figure 57. Indexes (a) Total Treasure (Soetbeer) and (b) Spanish Prices (Hamilton).

Source: (a) Same as for Figure 1 above. (b) E. J. Hamilton: *Treasure and the Price Revolution in Spain, 1501-1650.* Cambridge, Mass., 1934, xxxv + 428 pp.

Figure 58. Total Number of Ships Passing at Elsinore, Denmark.

Source: Nina E. Bang: *Oeresundstolden. Tables de la Navigation et du Transport des Merchandises Passant par le Sunde 1497-1660* and (with Knud Korst) *Tables de la Navigation et du Transport des Marchandises Passant par le Sunde 1661-1783 et par le Grand-Belt 1701-1748.*

Figure 59. Relationship of Great Paintings to Rate of Change of Wheat Prices.

Source: From a manuscript prepared by W. F. C. Nelson for the Cowles Commission for Research in Economics, 1935. Wheat prices are the same as those used in Figure 56 (c). The index of painting was constructed through weighting famous painters by members of the staff of the Colorado Springs Fine Arts Center.

APPENDIX

Figure 60. Total Number of Ships from the Netherlands Passing Annually at Elsinore, Denmark.

Source: Same as for Figure 58.

Figure 61. Total Number of British Ships Passing Annually at Elsinore, Denmark.

Source: Same as for Figure 58.

Figure 62. Roman Wages in Pounds of Wheat per Day.

Source: Same as for Figure 4.

Figure 63. English Wages in Pounds of Wheat per Day.

Source: W. Hardy: "History of Wages, A Record of Seven Centuries," *London Times,* 42503, Aug. 31, 1920, p. 16. Reprinted in G. F. Warren and F. A. Pearson: *Gold and Prices.* 1935, p. 324. Also J. Schoenhof: *A History of Money and Prices.* New York and London, 1896, p. 313.

Figure 64. Comparison of Money Wages and Real Wages at Paris under John Law's System.

Source: E. J. Hamilton: "Prices and Wages at Paris under John Law's System," The *Quarterly Journal of Economics,* Vol. 51, 1936, pp. 42-70.

Figure 65. Interaction Between Political Events and Economic Variation.

Source: Constructed from the price series of Figure 6, the rail stock price series of Figure 34, and the production of pig iron of Figure 41.

Figure 67. Index of American Wholesale Prices During Period of the Civil War.

Source: Monthly figures from the sources used in Figure 6.

Figure 68. Index of American Wholesale Prices During Period of World War I.

Source: Monthly figures from the sources used in Figure 6.

Figure 69. Index of Wheat Prices in Western Europe During Napoleonic Period.

Source: Sir William H. Beveridge: "Weather and Harvest Cycles," *The Economic Journal,* Vol. 31, 1921, pp. 429-452. Fifty separate prices over long periods of time were combined. These prices were from England, Scotland, Holland, Flanders, France, Northern Germany, Southern Germany, Alsace, Bohemia, and Austria.

Figure 70. Intensity of Wars of Greece and Rome.

Source: P. A. Sorokin: *Social and Cultural Dynamics.* New York, Vol. 3, *Fluctuations of Social Relationships, War and Revolution.* 1937.

Figure 71. Intensity of Wars of France.

Source: Same as for Figure 70.

Figure 72. Intensity of Wars of England.

Source: Same as for Figure 70.

Figure 73. Intensity of Wars of the United States.

Source: Adjutant General's Office, U. S. Army.

Figure 74. Growth of National Debt of France, on Logarithmic Scale.

Source: E. J. Hamilton: "Origin and Growth of the National Debt in Western Europe," *American Economic Review,* Vol. 37, 1947, pp. 118-130.

Figure 75. Growth of National Debt of England, on Logarithmic Scale.

Source: Same as for Figure 74.

Figure 76. Growth of National Debt of the United States, on Logarithmic Scale.

Source: Treasury Department. Reported in *Statistical Abstract of the United States.*

Figure 77. Values of the Ratios of Exchange in Terms of Dollars Reduced to Per Cent of 1914 Values: (a) The Pound; (b) The Franc; (c) The Mark.

Source: Same as for Figure 12.

Figure 78. Relationship between Exchange Ratios and Ratios of Internal Prices. (A) Ratio of American Wholesale Price Index to British Wholesale Price Index; (B) Pound-Dollar Exchange Ratio. (1926 = 100).

Source: For (A) data from *Statistical Yearbook of the League of Nations;* (B) same as for Figure 12.

Figure 80. Men Under Arms in Wars of Great Britain Corrected for Population.

Source: Data for men under arms same as for Figure 72. For early period estimates of population are taken from the sources for Figure 54. From 1800 to date the population figures are from official reports. Between 1600 and 1800 the population is estimated by means of an exponential interpolation.

TABLES

TABLE I. POWERS AND ROOTS

No.	Sq.	Sq. Root	Cube	Cube Root	No.	Sq.	Sq. Root	Cube	Cube Root
1	1	1.000	1	1.000	51	2,601	7.141	132,651	3.708
2	4	1.414	8	1.260	52	2,704	7.211	140,608	3.733
3	9	1.732	27	1.442	53	2,809	7.280	148,877	3.756
4	16	2.000	64	1.587	54	2,916	7.348	157,464	3.780
5	25	2.236	125	1.710	55	3,025	7.416	166,375	3.803
6	36	2.449	216	1.817	56	3,136	7.483	175,616	3.826
7	49	2.646	343	1.913	57	3,249	7.550	185,193	3.849
8	64	2.828	512	2.000	58	3,364	7.616	195,112	3.871
9	81	3.000	729	2.080	59	3,481	7.681	205,379	3.893
10	100	3.162	1,000	2.154	60	3,600	7.746	216,000	3.915
11	121	3.317	1,331	2.224	61	3,721	7.810	226,981	3.936
12	144	3.464	1,728	2.289	62	3,844	7.874	238,328	3.958
13	169	3.606	2,197	2.351	63	3,969	7.937	250,047	3.979
14	196	3.742	2,744	2.410	64	4,096	8.000	262,144	4.000
15	225	3.873	3,375	2.466	65	4,225	8.062	274,625	4.021
16	256	4.000	4,096	2.520	66	4,356	8.124	287,496	4.041
17	289	4.123	4,913	2.571	67	4,489	8.185	300,763	4.062
18	324	4.243	5,832	2.621	68	4,624	8.246	314,432	4.082
19	361	4.359	6,859	2.668	69	4,761	8.307	328,509	4.102
20	400	4.472	8,000	2.714	70	4,900	8.367	343,000	4.121
21	441	4.583	9,261	2.759	71	5,041	8.426	357,911	4.141
22	484	4.690	10,648	2.802	72	5,184	8.485	373,248	4.160
23	529	4.796	12,167	2.844	73	5,329	8.544	389,017	4.179
24	576	4.899	13,824	2.884	74	5,476	8.602	405,224	4.198
25	625	5.000	15,625	2.924	75	5,625	8.660	421,875	4.217
26	676	5.099	17,576	2.962	76	5,776	8.718	438,976	4.236
27	729	5.196	19,683	3.000	77	5,929	8.775	456,533	4.254
28	784	5.292	21,952	3.037	78	6,084	8.832	474,552	4.273
29	841	5.385	24,389	3.072	79	6,241	8.888	493,039	4.291
30	900	5.477	27,000	3.107	80	6,400	8.944	512,000	4.309
31	961	5.568	29,791	3.141	81	6,561	9.000	531,441	4.327
32	1,024	5.657	32,768	3.175	82	6,724	9.055	551,368	4.344
33	1,089	5.745	35,937	3.208	83	6,889	9.110	571,787	4.362
34	1,156	5.831	39,304	3.240	84	7,056	9.165	592,704	4.380
35	1,225	5.916	42,875	3.271	85	7,225	9.220	614,125	4.397
36	1,296	6.000	46,656	3.302	86	7,396	9.274	636,056	4.414
37	1,369	6.083	50,653	3.332	87	7,569	9.327	658,503	4.431
38	1,444	6.164	54,872	3.362	88	7,744	9.381	681,472	4.448
39	1,521	6.245	59,319	3.391	89	7,921	9.434	704,969	4.465
40	1,600	6.325	64,000	3.420	90	8,100	9.487	729,000	4.481
41	1,681	6.403	68,921	3.448	91	8,281	9.539	753,571	4.498
42	1,764	6.481	74,088	3.476	92	8,464	9.592	778,688	4.514
43	1,849	6.557	79,507	3.503	93	8,649	9.644	804,357	4.531
44	1,936	6.633	85,184	3.530	94	8,836	9.695	830,584	4.547
45	2,025	6.708	91,125	3.557	95	9,025	9.747	857,375	4.563
46	2,116	6.782	97,336	3.583	96	9,216	9.798	884,736	4.579
47	2,209	6.856	103,823	3.609	97	9,409	9.849	912,673	4.595
48	2,304	6.928	110,592	3.634	98	9,604	9.899	941,192	4.610
49	2,401	7.000	117,649	3.659	99	9,801	9.950	970,299	4.626
50	2,500	7.071	125,000	3.684	100	10,000	10.000	1,000,000	4.642

TABLE II. FOUR PLACE TABLE OF LOGARITHMS

N	0	1	2	3	4	5	6	7	8	9
10	0000	0043	0086	0128	0170	0212	0253	0294	0334	0374
11	0414	0453	0492	0531	0569	0607	0645	0682	0719	0755
12	0792	0828	0864	0899	0934	0969	1004	1038	1072	1106
13	1139	1173	1206	1239	1271	1303	1335	1367	1399	1430
14	1461	1492	1523	1553	1584	1614	1644	1673	1703	1732
15	1761	1790	1818	1847	1875	1903	1931	1959	1987	2014
16	2041	2068	2095	2122	2148	2175	2201	2227	2253	2279
17	2304	2330	2355	2380	2405	2430	2455	2480	2504	2529
18	2553	2577	2601	2625	2648	2672	2695	2718	2742	2765
19	2788	2810	2833	2856	2878	2900	2923	2945	2967	2989
20	3010	3032	3054	3075	3096	3118	3139	3160	3181	3201
21	3222	3243	3263	3284	3304	3324	3345	3365	3385	3404
22	3424	3444	3464	3483	3502	3522	3541	3560	3579	3598
23	3617	3636	3655	3674	3692	3711	3729	3747	3766	3784
24	3802	3820	3838	3856	3874	3892	3909	3927	3945	3962
25	3979	3997	4014	4031	4048	4065	4082	4099	4116	4133
26	4150	4166	4183	4200	4216	4232	4249	4265	4281	4298
27	4314	4330	4346	4362	4378	4393	4409	4425	4440	4456
28	4472	4487	4502	4518	4533	4548	4564	4579	4594	4609
29	4624	4639	4654	4669	4683	4698	4713	4728	4742	4757
30	4771	4786	4800	4814	4829	4843	4857	4871	4886	4900
31	4914	4928	4942	4955	4969	4983	4997	5011	5024	5038
32	5051	5065	5079	5092	5105	5119	5132	5145	5159	5172
33	5185	5198	5211	5224	5237	5250	5263	5276	5289	5302
34	5315	5328	5340	5353	5366	5378	5391	5403	5416	5428
35	5441	5453	5465	5478	5490	5502	5514	5527	5539	5551
36	5563	5575	5587	5599	5611	5623	5635	5647	5658	5670
37	5682	5694	5705	5717	5729	5740	5752	5763	5775	5786
38	5798	5809	5821	5832	5843	5855	5866	5877	5888	5899
39	5911	5922	5933	5944	5955	5966	5977	5988	5999	6010
40	6021	6031	6042	6053	6064	6075	6085	6096	6107	6117
41	6128	6138	6149	6160	6170	6180	6191	6201	6212	6222
42	6232	6243	6253	6263	6274	6284	6294	6304	6314	6325
43	6335	6345	6355	6365	6375	6385	6395	6405	6415	6425
44	6435	6444	6454	6464	6474	6484	6493	6503	6513	6522
45	6532	6542	6551	6561	6571	6580	6590	6599	6609	6618
46	6628	6637	6646	6656	6665	6675	6684	6693	6702	6712
47	6721	6730	6739	6749	6758	6767	6776	6785	6794	6803
48	6812	6821	6830	6839	6848	6857	6866	6875	6884	6893
49	6902	6911	6920	6928	6937	6946	6955	6964	6972	6981
50	6990	6998	7007	7016	7024	7033	7042	7050	7059	7067
51	7076	7084	7093	7101	7110	7118	7126	7135	7143	7152
52	7160	7168	7177	7185	7193	7202	7210	7218	7226	7235
53	7243	7251	7259	7267	7275	7284	7292	7300	7308	7316
54	7324	7332	7340	7348	7356	7364	7372	7380	7388	7396

TABLE II. FOUR PLACE TABLE OF LOGARITHMS

N	0	1	2	3	4	5	6	7	8	9
55	7404	7412	7419	7427	7435	7443	7451	7459	7466	7474
56	7482	7490	7497	7505	7513	7520	7528	7536	7543	7551
57	7559	7566	7574	7582	7589	7597	7604	7612	7619	7627
58	7634	7642	7649	7657	7664	7672	7679	7686	7694	7701
59	7709	7716	7723	7731	7738	7745	7752	7760	7767	7774
60	7782	7789	7796	7803	7810	7818	7825	7832	7839	7846
61	7853	7860	7868	7875	7882	7889	7896	7903	7910	7917
62	7924	7931	7938	7945	7952	7959	7966	7973	7980	7987
63	7993	8000	8007	8014	8021	8028	8035	8041	8048	8055
64	8062	8069	8075	8082	8089	8096	8102	8109	8116	8122
65	8129	8136	8142	8149	8156	8162	8169	8176	8182	8189
66	8195	8202	8209	8215	8222	8228	8235	8241	8248	8254
67	8261	8267	8274	8280	8287	8293	8299	8306	8312	8319
68	8325	8331	8338	8344	8351	8357	8363	8370	8376	8382
69	8388	8395	8401	8407	8414	8420	8426	8432	8439	8445
70	8451	8457	8463	8470	8476	8482	8488	8494	8500	8506
71	8513	8519	8525	8531	8537	8543	8549	8555	8561	8567
72	8573	8579	8585	8591	8597	8603	8609	8615	8621	8627
73	8633	8639	8645	8651	8657	8663	8669	8675	8681	8686
74	8692	8698	8704	8710	8716	8722	8727	8733	8739	8745
75	8751	8756	8762	8768	8774	8779	8785	8791	8797	8802
76	8808	8814	8820	8825	8831	8837	8842	8848	8854	8859
77	8865	8871	8876	8882	8887	8893	8899	8904	8910	8915
78	8921	8927	8932	8938	8943	8949	8954	8960	8965	8971
79	8976	8982	8987	8993	8998	9004	9009	9015	9020	9025
80	9031	9036	9042	9047	9053	9058	9063	9069	9074	9079
81	9085	9090	9096	9101	9106	9112	9117	9122	9128	9133
82	9138	9143	9149	9154	9159	9165	9170	9175	9180	9186
83	9191	9196	9201	9206	9212	9217	9222	9227	9232	9238
84	9243	9248	9253	9258	9263	9269	9274	9279	9284	9289
85	9294	9299	9304	9309	9315	9320	9325	9330	9335	9340
86	9345	9350	9355	9360	9365	9370	9375	9380	9385	9390
87	9395	9400	9405	9410	9415	9420	9425	9430	9435	9440
88	9445	9450	9455	9460	9465	9469	9474	9479	9484	9489
89	9494	9499	9504	9509	9513	9518	9523	9528	9533	9538
90	9542	9547	9552	9557	9562	9566	9571	9576	9581	9586
91	9590	9595	9600	9605	9609	9614	9619	9624	9628	9633
92	9638	9643	9647	9652	9657	9661	9666	9671	9675	9680
93	9685	9689	9694	9699	9703	9708	9713	9717	9722	9727
94	9731	9736	9741	9745	9750	9754	9759	9763	9768	9773
95	9777	9782	9786	9791	9795	9800	9805	9809	9814	9818
96	9823	9827	9832	9836	9841	9845	9850	9854	9859	9863
97	9868	9872	9877	9881	9886	9890	9894	9899	9903	9908
98	9912	9917	9921	9926	9930	9934	9939	9943	9948	9952
99	9956	9961	9965	9969	9974	9978	9983	9987	9991	9996

TABLE III.

VALUES OF $I(t)$, AREA UNDER NORMAL PROBABILITY CURVE

t	0	1	2	3	4	5	6	7	8	9
0.0	0.00000	00399	00798	01197	01595	01994	02392	02790	03188	03586
0.1	0.03983	04380	04776	05172	05567	05962	06356	06749	07142	07535
0.2	0.07926	08317	08706	09095	09483	09871	10257	10642	11026	11409
0.3	0.11791	12172	12552	12930	13307	13683	14058	14431	14803	15173
0.4	0.15542	15910	16276	16640	17003	17364	17724	18082	18439	18793
0.5	0.19146	19497	19847	20194	20540	20884	21226	21566	21904	22240
0.6	0.22575	22907	23237	23565	23891	24215	24537	24857	25175	25490
0.7	0.25804	26115	26424	26730	27035	27337	27637	27935	28230	28524
0.8	0.28814	29103	29289	29673	29955	30234	30511	30785	31057	31327
0.9	0.31594	31859	32121	32381	32639	32894	33147	33398	33646	33891
1.0	0.34134	34375	34614	34850	35083	35314	35543	35769	35993	36214
1.1	0.36433	36650	36864	37076	37286	37493	37698	37900	38100	38298
1.2	0.38493	38686	38877	39065	39251	39435	39617	39796	39973	40147
1.3	0.40320	40490	40658	40824	40988	41149	41309	41466	41621	41774
1.4	0.41924	42073	42220	42364	42507	42647	42786	42922	43056	43189
1.5	0.43319	43448	43574	43699	43822	43943	44062	44179	44295	44408
1.6	0.44520	44630	44738	44845	44950	45053	45154	45254	45352	45449
1.7	0.45543	45637	45728	45818	45907	45994	46080	46164	46246	46327
1.8	0.46407	46485	46562	46638	46712	46784	46856	46926	46995	47062
1.9	0.47128	47193	47257	47320	47381	47441	47500	47558	47615	47670
2.0	0.47725	47778	47831	47882	47932	47982	48030	48077	48124	48169
2.1	0.48214	48257	48300	48341	48382	48422	48461	48500	48537	48574
2.2	0.48610	48645	48679	48713	48745	48778	48809	48840	48870	48899
2.3	0.48928	48956	48983	49010	49036	49061	49086	49111	49134	49158
2.4	0.49180	49202	49224	49245	49266	49286	49305	49324	49343	49361
2.5	0.49379	49396	49413	49430	49446	49461	49477	49492	49506	49520
2.6	0.49534	49547	49560	49573	49585	49598	49609	49621	49632	49643
2.7	0.49653	49664	49674	49683	49693	49702	49711	49720	49728	49736
2.8	0.49744	49752	49760	49767	49774	49781	49788	49795	49801	49807
2.9	0.49813	49819	49825	49831	49836	49841	49846	49851	49856	49861
3.0	0.49865	49869	49874	49878	49882	49886	49889	49893	49897	49900
3.1	0.49903	49906	49910	49913	49916	49918	49921	49924	49926	49929
3.2	0.49931	49934	49936	49938	49940	49942	49944	49946	49948	49950
3.3	0.49952	49953	49955	49957	49958	49960	49961	49962	49964	49965
3.4	0.49966	49968	49969	49970	49971	49972	49973	49974	49975	49976
3.5	0.49977	49978	49978	49979	49980	49981	49981	49982	49983	49983
3.6	0.49984	49985	49985	49986	49986	49987	49987	49988	49988	49989
3.7	0.49989	49990	49990	49990	49991	49991	49992	49992	49992	49992
3.8	0.49993	49993	49993	49994	49994	49994	49994	49995	49995	49995
3.9	0.49995	49995	49996	49996	49996	49996	49996	49996	49997	49997

INDEXES

INDEX OF NAMES

Aemilius, L., 289.
Akerman, J., 258, 263.
Alexander the Great, 185, 276.
Alfonso XIII, 186.
Antoinette, Marie, 185
Antoninus Pius, 144.
Apollonius of Tyanna, 187.
Aquinas, Saint Thomas, 2.
Aristotle, 1-2, 7, 210.
Augustus Caesar, 22, 25, 185, 194, 224, 231, 341.

Bacon, Sir Francis, 5, 266.
Bang, Nina E., 243, 248, 344.
Bean, L. H., 120, 258, 263.
Bellamy, Edward, 5, 187.
Beloch, J., 225, 343.
Bertrand, J., 155.
Beveridge, Sir William H., 345
Block, P. J., 249.
Bodart, G., 275.
Bodin, J., 6, 14, 220.
Brahe, Tycho, 246.
Brescioni-Turroni, C., 344.
Briggs, Henry, 323.
Brown, John, 213.
Bryan, William Jennings, 236.
Buchanan, James, 260, 264.
Buckle, Thomas, 6, 14, 219, 221-223.
Bukharin, N. I., 186.
Butler, Samuel, 5.

Cabet, Étienne, 5.
Caesar, Julius, 185, 236.
Campanella, Tommaso, 5.
Cato, 253.
Cervantes, 245.
Charles V, 210, 248.

Chatters, C. H., 49.
Cicero, 2, 21.
Cleopatra, 235.
Cobb, C. W., 206.
Condorcet, N. C. de, 154.
Corneille, P., 245.
Cournot, A. A., 223, 304-305.
Cowper, William, 213.
Crossley, A. M., 97-99.

Davis, H. T., 206, 308, 341.
Decius, 25, 237.
Deming, W. E., 97.
De Sanctis, G., 285.
Descartes, René, 33.
De Witt, Cornelius, 252.
Diocletian, 25, 231, 237-239, 254.
Diodorus, 221.
Douglas, P. H., 206.
Duns Scotus, 2.

Edward III, 228.
Eisenhower, Dwight D., 262.
Elizabeth, Queen, 224.
Engels, Friedrich, 221-222.
Euclid, 3, 11.
Eusebius of Caesarea, 230.
Evelyn, John, 252.

Fillmore, Millard, 260.
Fisher, Irving, 160, 162-164.
Flaminius, C., 289.
Fourier, F. M. C., 6, 187.
Francis I, 291.
Franco, Francisco, 186.
Frank, Tenny, 285-287, 290, 341, 344.
Fugger, Jacob, 201.

Galileo, 245.

-355-

Gallienus, 227, 230.
Gallup, G. H., 97-98.
Gans, E., 221.
Gause, G. F., 308.
Gauss, K. F., 10.
Gibbon, Edward, 144, 238.
Gini, C., 194.
Gosnell, H. F., 135, 258.
Gracchi, the, 16, 185.
Grant, U. S., 260, 270.
Grönhagen, S., 258.

Hamilton, E. J., 242, 255-257, 292, 294, 295, 341, 344-346.
Hanczaryk, E. W., 200.
Hankins, F. H., 12.
Hannibal, 284.
Harbottle, T. B., 275.
Harding, C. H., 247.
Hardy, W., 345.
Harrington, James, 5.
Harrison, William Henry, 260.
Hayakawa, M., 200, 343.
Hayes, Rutherford B., 260.
Hegel, G. W. F. G., 6, 14, 221.
Helper, H. R., 214, 343.
Herodotus, 221.
Hipparchus, 338.
Hirst, F. W., 288.
Hobbes, Thomas, 2-3, 7, 25, 273.
Hoover, Herbert, 14, 260.
Huntington, E. V., 138.
Hyneman, C. S., 144, 148, 341.

Jevons, W. S., 4.
John, King, 199.
Johnson, Allan C., 344.
Johnson, Andrew, 260.
Johnson, N. O., 343.
Johnson, Samuel, 213.
Jonson, Ben, 245.
Justinian, 227.

Kamenev, L. B., 186.
Kelvin, Lord, 9, 19.
Kepler, Johannas, 10, 246.
King, J. C., 278.
Korst, K., 243, 344.

Kort, F., 210.

Laplace, P. S. de, 155-157.
Laspeyres, E., 160, 164-165.
Law, John, 255-257, 345.
Leavens, D. H., 236.
Lee, Robert E., 270.
Leibnitz, G. W., 246.
Lexis, W., 93.
Lincoln, Abraham, 260, 270.
Livy, 221, 289, 290.
Locke, John, 3, 7.
Louis XIV, 294; XV, 185; XVI, 185.
Lytton, Bulwer, Edward, 5.

McArthur, Douglas, 262.
Macaulay, T. B., 294, 297.
MacDonald, A. F., 147.
Magee, J. D., 341.
Mahaffy, J. P., 185.
Malthus, Thomas R., 17, 19, 177.
Marcus Aurelius Antoninus, 144.
Marius, Gaius, 185.
Marlow, C., 245.
Marshall, Alfred, 4-5.
Marsilius of Padua, 2.
Marx, Karl, 6, 14, 187, 219, 221-223, 264.
Mill, John Stuart, 4.
Molière, 245.
Monroe, James, 261.
Montesquieu, Baron de, 6, 220-221.
More, Sir Thomas, 5.
Murray, N. C., 344.

Napier, John, 324.
Napoleon, 17, 186, 272, 294.
Nelson, W. F. C., 246, 344.
Nero, 25.
Newton, Sir Isaac, 3, 19, 246.
Nicholas II, 186.
Nienstaedt, L. R., 243.
Nilson, S. S., 258.

Ogburn, W. F., 313.
Oman, C., 275.
Owen, Robert, 6, 187.

INDEX OF NAMES

Paasche, H., 160, 164-165.
Pareto, Vilfredo, 5, 13, 189, 194, 211, 215-216.
Pearl, Raymond, 179, 342.
Pearson, Frank A., 268, 272, 341, 342-345.
Pericles, 224.
Perkins, J. A., 147.
Peterson, D. A., 313.
Petrie, W. M. Flinders, 224, 230.
Philip II, 224, 248; IV, 27, 245.
Phillips, U. B., 214, 343.
Philostratus, 187.
Pierce, Franklin, 260.
Pindar, 185.
Plato, 1-2, 7, 13, 144, 192.
Pliny, 283, 284, 286.
Plutarch, 188.
Poe, E. A., 74.
Poisson, S., 94, 155.
Polybius, 14, 219, 222, 284, 291.
Pompey, 236.
Pope, Alexander, 212.
Ptolemy I, or Soter, 231; IX, or Physkon, 235; XIII, or Auletes, 235-236.

Quetelet, Adolphe, 12.

Racine, J. B., 245.
Reed, L. J., 179, 347.
Ricardo, David, 4.
Rice, S. A., 313-315.
Richardson, L. F., 305, 307.
Ricketts, E. F., 144, 148.
Riggleman, J. R., 342.
Rogers, J. E. Thorold, 223-224, 344.
Roosevelt, F. D., 135-136.
Roosevelt, Theodore, 260.
Roper, E., 97-99.
Rostovtzeff, M., 235.
Rousseau, J. J., 4.
Russell, Bertrand, 309.
Ruyter, M. A. de, 252.
Rykov, A. I., 186.

Schoenhof, J., 345.
Segré, A., 235, 344.

Seligman, E. R. A., 223-224.
Shakespeare, William, 245.
Sherman, W. T., 270.
Slater, C. C., 197-198, 343.
Smith, Adam, 4, 213, 294, 297, 317.
Smith, Alfred, 135-136.
Smith, Edris P., 315.
Snyder, Carl, 179.
Socrates, 154.
Soetbeer, A., 17, 242, 341, 344.
Solomon, S. R., 147.
Solon, 188.
Sorokin, P. A., 275, 278, 283, 285, 345.
Stalin, Joseph, 186.
Sterne, Laurence, 213.
Stevenson, A., 262.
Stoker, H. M., 341.
Sulla, Lucius Cornelius, 185.

Taft, William H., 260.
Thucydides, 221.
Tilden, S. J., 260.
Tolstoy, L., 27, 223.
Trotsky, Leon, 186.

Van Buren, Martin, 14, 260, 264.
Vega, Lope de, 245.
Verhulst, P. F., 179.
Vico, G. B., 6, 220-221.
Volterra, V., 305, 309.
von Szeliski, V., 341.

Warren, G. F., 268, 272, 341-342, 345.
Wells, H. G., 5.
Welser, Bartholomäus, 201.
Wenzlick, R., 342.
Wesley, John, 213.
Willcox, W. F., 229.
William of Occum, 2.
William the Conqueror, 197-199, 265.
Wilson, Woodrow, 260.
With, Witte de, 249.
Wright, Quincy, 6, 274-278, 298-301, 343.

Zinoviev, G. E., 186.
Zinsser, Hans, 17, 310.

INDEX OF SUBJECTS

Abscissa, definition of, 33.
Absolute value, definition of, 60.
Achaen league, 310.
American Civil War, 212-217; price patterns in, 269-270.
Annuity, present value of, 297.
Antonines, the, 144, 227.
A posteriori probability, 71.
A priori probability, 71.
Argument, in tables, 324.
Aristotle's *Politics*, 1-2.
Arithmetic average, 50, 51-57; simplification in computation of, 54-57.
Armies, size of, for Ancient Greece, 278, 280; for Ancient Rome, 279, 280; for France, 279, 280; for England, 281, 282; for U.S., 281-283.
Averages, Chap. 3; arithmetic, 50, 51-57; simplification in computation of, 54-57; median, 50, 64-66; mode, 50, 66-68; quadratic, 50, 57-61; geometric, 50, 68-69; harmonic, 50, 57-61; root-mean-square (see Quadratic average); standard deviation, 58-61.

Balance of trade, 305.
Bank deposits, 257.
Bar charts, 31-32.
Bias in index numbers, 162.
Bimetalism, 234.
Bimodal distribution, 66.
Binomial coefficients, 42-43.
Binomial frequencies, 42-45, 47-48; and probability, 78-80.

Black Death, 17, 228.
Black Friday, 264.
Boer War, cost of, 288.
Bolshevism, 187.
Brook Farm Experiment, 6, 187.
Building activity, index of, 173.
Business cycles, 172.

Cato's slave, budget of, 253.
Central tendency of data, Chap. 3; 40.
Chance, (see Probability).
Characteristic of logarithm, 326.
Cicero's *De Republica*, 2.
Circular gap, 164.
Circular test for index numbers, 164-166.
Circulating money, 257.
Civil War, 25; theory of, 209-212; American, 212-217, 270; price patterns in American, 269-270.
Class interval, 30.
Class mark, 31.
Class range, 30.
Coefficient of correlation, 118; properties of, 121-123; interpretation of, 122; standard error of, 119; rank, 120.
Coefficient of variability, 61-64.
Communism, definition of, 187.
Concentration ratio, defined, 187; values of, 195, 201-202; production and, 201-208; political disturbance and, 209-217.
Conflict, the problem of, Chap. 10; theories of, 305-309.
Congressional district, the size of, 169-170.

-359-

Corn, production of, 182.
Correlation, theory of, Chap. 5; 117-definition of, 117; examples of, 127-132; standard error of forecast, 142; coefficient of, 118; properties of, 121-123; interpretation of, 122; standard error of, 123; rank, 120.
Crime, data on, 26-27, 120.
Crimean War, cost of, 288.
Critical point, in population growth, 178.
Cumulative frequencies, 45-49.
Cycles, problems of, 172-177; of civilization, 230; tables on, 230.

Data, definition of, 29; graphical representation of, 31-37; central tendency of, Chap. 3; validity and analysis of, 338-341; sources of, 341-346.
Debt, public, (see Public debt).
Deposits, bank, 257.
Determinism, postulate of, 7; variability in, 8.
Deviation, definition of, 58; standard, 58-61.
Diocletian edict, 237-239, 254-255.
Diocletian inflation, 237-241.
Dispersion, 61,
Divorce rate, 171.
Doomsday Book, 197, 265.
Double-logarithmic scale, 332-334.
Douglas-Cobb production function, 206.
Dynamics, 20, 28; political, 23-26.

e, 90, 324.
Economics and political science, 14-16; Chap. 9.
Edgeworth-Marshall aggregative index number, 164.
Edict of Diocletian (see Diocletian edict).
Elections, forecasting of, 99-106.
Electrical production, 181.

Enumeration, Chap. 2.
Era of good feeling, 261.
Erratic element in cycles, 173.
Error, normal curve of, 35, 80-81; table of ordinates of, 81; area under, 83-87, 352; probable, 87; standard, 88; examples of, 89-92; of forecast, 132.
Euclid's *Elements*, 3, 11.
Exchange ratio, pound-dollar, 36; general discussion of, 302-305.
Exponential, simple, 149; fitting to data of, 150-151; equations, 331.
Exponents, laws of, 321-322.

Fabianism, 187.
Factorial symbol, definition of, 43.
Factor reversal test for index numbers, 163-164.
Famous names, distribution of, 226.
Forecast, standard error of, 132.
Forecasts of election, 96-106; by price changes, 258-264.
French declaration of estates, 211-212, 217.
Frequency, total, 30.
Frequency distributions, Chaps. 2 and 4; 29, 38-42; binomial, 42-45, 47-48, 78-80; cumulative, 45-49; skewed, 40; rectangular, 47-48, 92-93; normal, 80-87; non-normal, 92-96; of Lexis type, 93-94, 101; of Poisson type, 94; hypernormal, 94-95; subnormal, 95.
Fuggerii, the, 201.
Function, definition of, 108; symbol, of, 109; graphical representation of, 34-36, 109-110; linear, 110-111.

Geometric average, 50, 68-69.
German inflation, 233, 236-237, 240-241.
Gerrymander, 21.
Golden ages, 224.

INDEX OF SUBJECTS

Gold-silver ratio, history of, 231; data on, 236.
Governing authority, tenure of, 62-63.
Governors, occupations of, 147-148.

Hanseatic league, 310-311.
Harmonic average, 50, 68-69.
Histogram, 40.
History, mechanistic theory of, Chap. 9; 6, 24, 219-224.
House of Representatives, 45, 50; political composition of, 38-39; ogive of, 48; representation in, 138-143; population ratio of, 170.
Hypernormal frequency distribution, 94-95.

"Ideal" index number, 160, 161, 163-164.
Income, distribution of, Chap. 8; 13, 188-194; in Roman Republic, 22; in U. S. (1929), 22; cumulative in U. S., 190; ogive of, 192; concentration ratio of, 194-195; curve of distribution of, 196-200; relationship to MV, 240.
Independent events, probability of, 74-75.
Index of cohesion, 314-316.
Index law, 331-332.
Index numbers, Chap. 7; 23, 158-167; definition of, 159; types of, 160-162; "ideal", 160, 161, 163-164; tests for, 162-166.
Inflations, 232-233; Diocletian, 27, 232, 237-241, 255; German, 233, 240-241; Ptolemaic, 25, 232-236; sixteenth century, 241-247; war and, 267-269.
Intercept, 106.
International trade, 302-305.
Interpolation, 327, 334-337; Newton's formula for, 335; linear, 335; inverse, 336-337.

Inverse interpolation, 336-337.
Inverse probability, 155.
Isomorphism, 11.

Judgment of tribunals, 154-157.
Jury systems, American-English, 156; Athenian, 154, 157.

Kelvin's postulate on measurement, 9.
Kinematics, 20.
Kinetics, 20.

League of Nations, 312.
Least squares, method of, 113.
Legislators, occupations of, 144-147.
Legislative tenure, law of, 20; problem of, 148-153; in Iowa, 149, 153; in Indiana, 152-153.
Legislatures, size of, 41-42, 126-132; ogive of, 49; limits to the length of sessions of, 53; tenure in, 20, 148-153.
Leviathan of Hobbes, 2-3.
Lexis frequency distribution, 93-94, 96, 101.
Lexis ratio, 93.
Likeness, coefficient of, 314.
Linear interpolation, 335.
Linear trend, 167.
Lines of regression, 123-126; angle between, 126.
Locke's *Treatises on Government*, 3.
Logarithmic scale, 332-337.
Logarithms, 323-330; definition of, 323; common or Briggsian, 323; natural, 324; determination of, 326-329; characteristic of, 326; mantissa of, 326; calculation by, 329-330; table of, 350-351.
Logistic curve, 179.
Lorenz curve, 47-48.

Magna Carta, 199.
Malthian theory, 17, 19, 229.
Mantissa, 326.
Maritime trade, (1500-1800), 243-

247; Spain with the Indies, 247; of England, 247-252.
Mathematics, role of, 11-13.
Means, Chap. 3; (see Averages).
Mechanistic theory of history, Chap. 9; 6, 24; development of, 219-224.
Median, 50, 64-66.
Meditations of Marcus Aurelius, 135.
Midas point, 27, 197.
Mississippi Bubble, 355-356.
Mode, 50, 66-68.
Money, quantity theory of, 239-242; gold, silver, and copper as, 231, 234; circulating, 257; John Law's theory of, 255-256; (see Numéraire).
Moving average, 173-174.
Mutually exclusive events, probability of, 74, 76.

Napier's number, 80, 324.
Napoleonic Wars, price patterns in, 271-272.
National debts, growth of, (see Public debt).
Natural logarithm, 324.
New Atlantis of Bacon, 5.
New capital, index of, 207-208.
New Harmony Experiment, 6, 187.
Non-normal frequency distributions, 92.
Normal curve, 35, 80-81; table of, 81; area under, 83-87; values of areas under, 352.
Normal equations, 112.
Normal frequency distribution, 80-83; table of, 81.
Numéraire, wheat as, 231-234.

Ogive, 45-49; of income distribution, 192.
Ordinate, definition of, 33.

Painting and wheat prices, 246-247.
Pareto's law, 189-200.

Pareto's constant, 194-195.
Patents, number of, 184.
Phalansteries, 6, 187.
Philosopher king, 1; problem of, 21, 144-148.
Pie charts, 31-32.
Pig iron, production of, 180.
Plague, political effects of, 17; data on, 227-228; Alexandrian, 227, 230. (See Black Death).
Plato's *Republic*, 1-2.
Poisson's frequency distribution, 94, 96.
Political dynamics, 23-26.
Political events and prices, 231-237, 258-264.
Political science, economics and, 14-16, Chap. 9; sociology and, 16-19; history of, 1-6; problems in, Chap. 6; problem of representation, 138-143; size of legislatures, 41-42, 126-132; problem of philosopher king, 21, 144-148; problem of legislative tenure, 148-153; problem of judgment of tribunals, 154-157.
Political statics, 20-23.
Politics as a science, 7-9.
Polls of public opinion, 96-99.
Population, growth of, 224-230; European, 18, 225-227; Chinese, 229; distribution by age groups, 230; urban in Kansas, 29-32; urban in Colorado, 37; trends of, 177-179; of U. S., 178, 333.
Postulates, role of, 9-11.
Pound-dollar exchange ratio, 36.
Powers and roots, table of, 349.
Presidents, occupation of, 147.
Prices, index of wholesale, in U. S., 24; in Spain (1500-1650), 242; in equation of exchange, 239; wholesale in Germany (1914-1923), 237; political events and, 231-237, 258-264; in Paris (1711-1725), 257; wages and,

INDEX OF SUBJECTS

253-257; of wheat in England, 233; of wheat in Western Europe, 271; patterns of, in modern wars, 269-273.
Priority list in problem of representation, 142-143.
Probability, theory of, Chap. 4; definition of, 70; *a priori*, 71; *a posteriori*, 71; multiplication of, 74-76; addition of, 74, 76-78; joint, 75.
Probable error, definition of, 87. examples of, 89-92.
Production function of Douglas and Cobb, 206.
Production trends, 179-183; of pig iron, 180; of electrical power, 181; of wheat and corn, 182.
Ptolemaic inflation, 25, 232-236.
Public debt, definition of, 295; of France, 292-293; of England, 292-293; of U. S., 295-296.
Public opinion polls, 96-99.
Punic War, cost of second, 284-287; financing of, 289-291.

Quadratic mean, 50, 57-61.
Quality control, 107.
Quantity theory of money, 239-242.

Rank correlation, 120.
Rectangular frequency distribution, 48-49.
Regression lines, 123-126; angle between, 126.
Representation, problem of, 138; measure of inequality of, 139-143.
Representatives, House of, number in, 45, 50; representation in, 138-143; composition of, 38-39; ogive of, 48; population-ratio of, 170.
Revolutionary War, price patterns in, 272.

Revolution, theory of, 211; French, 185-186; Spanish, 186; Bolshevik, 186.
Roman wages, 253.
Root-mean-square, 50, 57-61.
Saint-Simonianism, 187.
Salaries, distribution of, 193.
Sampling, 89-92.
Saturation level, 178.
Scatter diagram, 119; examples of, 130.
Secular trend, 167.
Semi-logarithmic scale, 332-334.
Shipping, into North Sea, 243-247; from ports of Spain, 247.
Siglo de oro, 224.
Sixteenth century price inflation, 241-247.
Skewed frequency distributions, 40.
Skewness, 67.
Slavery, history of abolition of, 212-214.
Slaves, price of, 214; ownership of, 215; distribution of, 216.
Socialism, Chap. 8; 21; definition of, 187.
Social services, sources of funds for, 49.
Social theories, history of, 185-188.
Sociology and political science, 16-19.
Solon's classes, 188.
Spanish trade, 15.
Standard deviation, 58-61.
Standard error, definition of, 88; examples of, 89-92; of forecast, 132; of correlation coefficient, 123.
State legislatures, size of, 41-42, 126-132.
Statics, 20.
Straight line, 110; fitting to data of, 111; general formulas for, 115-116; of regression, 123-126.
Stratification of samples, 97.
Struggle for life, 307-309.

Subnormal frequency distributions, 95.

Tables, 347-352; use of, 334.
Tabular difference, 327.
Tabular interval, 324.
Tabular values, 334.
Taxes, type and sources of, 49.
Tension, theory of war, 298-302.
Tenure of governing authority, 62-63.
Time reversal test of index numbers, 162-163.
Time series, statistics of, Chap. 7; definition of, 158.
Tolerance limits, 107.
Trade, volume of, 239.
Traffic problem, 132-135.
Trends, problem of, 167-172; production, 179-183; population, 177-179; secular, 167; linear, 167.
Tribunals, judgment of, 154-157.

Uni-modal distributions, 66.
United Nations, 312-313.
Urban concentration, in Kansas, 29-32; in U. S. by Years, 37.
Utilitarianism, 2-3, 7, 25.
Utopia of Sir Thomas More, 5.
Utopias, 5-6.

Validity of data, 338-341.
Variability, coefficient of, 61-64.
Variable, definition of, 108.
Variance, definition of, 58.
Velocity of money, 239.
Voting behavior, problem of, 135-137.

Wages, and prices, 253-257; of common labor, 257; English, 254; Roman, 253.
War of 1812, price patterns in, 273.
War-index, definition of, 267; values of, 268.
Wars, theory of, 26, Chap. 10; frequency of, 273-277; list of, 274; classification of, 275-276; size of, 277-283; cost of ancient, 284-287; cost of modern, 287-289; financing of, 289-297; military deaths in, 26, 278-279, 282; intensity of, 267-269; price patterns in, 269-273; theory of civil wars, 24, 211-217; American Civil War, 212-217, 270-271; World War I, 270-271, 287; cost of, 287; Napoleonic, 271-272; American Revolutionary, 272; of 1812, 273; Punic, 284-287; financing of Punic, 289-291; World War II, 287; Boer War, cost of, 288; Crimean War, cost of, 288.
War tensions, 298-302.
Wealth of Nations, of Adam Smith, 4, 213, 294, 317.
Wheat, growth of, 19; as a numéraire, 231-234; demand for, 234; painting and price of, 246; production of, in U. S., 182, in the world, 229; price of, 257; in England, 233; in Rome, 232; in Ptolemaic Egypt, 232; in Western Europe, 271.
Wolf point, 27, 196, 198.
World War I, 270-271, 287; cost of, 287.
World War II, cost of, 287.